Clashing Views in

Management

THIRD EDITION

Selected, Edited, and with Introductions by

Marc D. Street
Salisbury University

and

Vera L. Street
Salisbury University

 **Higher Education**

Boston   Burr Ridge, IL   Dubuque, IA   New York   San Francisco   St. Louis
Bangkok   Bogotá   Caracas   Kuala Lumpur   Lisbon   London   Madrid   Mexico City
Milan   Montreal   New Delhi   Santiago   Seoul   Singapore   Sydney   Taipei   Toronto

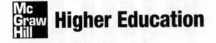

Higher Education

TAKING SIDES: CLASHING VIEWS IN MANAGEMENT, THIRD EDITION

Published by McGraw-Hill, a business unit of The McGraw-Hill Companies, Inc., 1221 Avenue of the Americas, New York, NY 10020. Copyright © 2010 by The McGraw-Hill Companies, Inc. All rights reserved. Previous edition(s) 2007, 2005. No part of this publication may be reproduced or distributed in any form or by any means, or stored in a database or retrieval system, without the prior written consent of The McGraw-Hill Companies, Inc., including, but not limited to, in any network or other electronic storage or transmission, or broadcast for distance learning.

Some ancillaries, including electronic and print components, may not be available to customers outside the United States.

Taking Sides® is a registered trademark of the McGraw-Hill Companies, Inc.
Taking Sides is published by the **Contemporary Learning Series** group within the McGraw-Hill Higher Education division.

1 2 3 4 5 6 7 8 9 0 DOC/DOC 0 9

MHID: 0-07-352732-7
ISBN: 978-0-07-352732-1
ISSN: 1552-4477

Managing Editor: *Larry Loeppke*
Senior Managing Editor: *Faye Schilling*
Senior Developmental Editor: *Jill Meloy*
Editorial Coordinator: *Mary Foust*
Production Service Assistant: *Rita Hingtgen*
Permissions Coordinator: *Shirley Lanners*
Editorial Assistant: *Cindy Hedley*
Senior Marketing Manager: *Julie Keck*
Marketing Communications Specialist: *Mary Klein*
Marketing Coordinator: *Alice Link*
Senior Project Manager: *Jane Mohr*
Design Specialist: *Tara McDermott*
Cover Graphics: *Rick D. Noel*

Compositor: Macmillan Publishing Solutions
Cover Image: (Montage beginning left) © The McGraw-Hill Companies, Inc./John Flournoy, photographer, © Getty/Images/RF, © Stockbyte/Punchstock/RF, US Fish and Wildlife Service, The McGraw-Hill Companies, Inc./Andrew Resek, photographer, and (background) © Getty Images/RF

Editors/Academic Advisory Board

Members of the Academic Advisory Board are instrumental in the final selection of articles for each edition of TAKING SIDES. Their review of articles for content, level, and appropriateness provides critical direction to the editors and staff. We think that you will find their careful consideration well reflected in this volume.

TAKING SIDES: Clashing Views in MANAGEMENT
Third Edition

EDITORS

Marc D. Street
Salisbury University

Vera L. Street
Salisbury University

ACADEMIC ADVISORY BOARD MEMBERS

Editors/Academic Advisory Board continued

Preface

He who knows only his side of the case knows little of that. His reasons may have been good, and no one may have been able to refute them. But if he is equally unable to refute the reasons on the opposite side he has no ground for preferring either opinion.

—John Stuart Mill[1]

The United States criminal system is adversarial in nature; two sides with incompatible goals meet in front of a judge and jury in order to determine the fate of an individual charged with a crime. Underlying this process is the presupposition that truth can be reached through the presentation of conflicting viewpoints. This book, the third edition of *Taking Sides: Clashing Views in Management,* is predicated on this very same presupposition. Each of the debates presented here mimics the courtroom: There are two opposing sides, each vigorously presenting its evidence and questioning their opponent's case; there is a judge, the reader, who considers the relative merits of each side, hopefully maintaining objectivity while searching for truth; and there is a verdict, signaling innocence for one side and conviction for the other.

This text consists of 18 debates on controversial issues in the field of business management. Each issue consists of opposing viewpoints presented in a pro and con format. It is your role as judge to give each side a fair and unbiased hearing. This will be a difficult task, for each of the authors of the 36 articles is an expert and defends his or her position with great vigor. To help in your task, we suggest that you ask difficult questions, make notes on troubling points, and interact with the material. Most importantly, if you have a preconceived opinion about an issue, force yourself to look critically at the side you support. This, too, is difficult to do; it's much easier to find the weaknesses in the opposing side than in your own. Nonetheless, doing so helps protect against self-deception and, frequently, strengthens your original belief. And, perhaps most importantly, it makes you think!

Organization of this book The text is divided into four sections, each addressing a different aspect of management. At the beginning of each section is a list of Internet site addresses (URLs) designed to encourage readers to explore the topics further. This is followed by a unit opener that briefly identifies the specific issues in the section. Next are the issues themselves, each of which starts with an introduction that sets the stage for the debate as it is argued in the YES and NO selections. The postscript follows the selections and provides some final observations and comments about the topic. The postscript also contains suggestions for further reading that should prove beneficial in

---

[1]M. Neil Browne and Stuart M. Keeley, *Asking the Right Questions,* 6th ed., Prentice Hall, 2001.

the event you are still undecided or want to learn more about the issue. Keep in mind that the selections represent only two possible viewpoints on a topic; there may well be other positions on these subjects beyond the two in the book. Finally, at the back of the book is a list of all the contributors to this volume. Biographical information on the philosophers, economists, social commentators, educators, political analysts, and other experts that contributed articles can be found here.

We'd like to make a few comments on this new edition. Those familiar with the second edition will notice that we have made several significant changes to this third version. First, we dropped six issues from the second edition that proved too inaccessible, not particularly controversial, somewhat outdated, or too similar to another topic. Second, of the twelve topics carried over from the second edition, eleven have been updated with newer articles by different authors. Finally, and perhaps most significantly, we have added six new, topical issues. Three of these—English-only, workplace monitoring, and protectionism—were test driven by the first author with resounding success. Both his undergraduate and graduate students found the topics to be very controversial, topical, and compelling.

Overall, of the 36 articles comprising the 18 topics, 29 are new to this edition, thus explaining why we feel that this 3rd edition is virtually a brand new text. And, of course, we hope that you find the topics to be not only controversial, but interesting and educational as well. We thank you for your interest in our work!

Acknowledgments We would like to thank our Salisbury University undergrad and graduate students for their comments, feedback, and topic and article suggestions. We would also like to extend our heartfelt thanks to our superb editor at McGraw-Hill, Jill Meloy. Once again, her calmness, professionalism, and flexibility made our task considerably easier and more enjoyable than we had the right to expect. So here's to you, Jill! Thanks! Once again, thank you Jill! Lastly, we'd like to once again thank our family and friends for their continued support and encouragement. Thanks to you all!

Contents In Brief

Contents

Robert Hay and Edmund Gray use stakeholder theory and a historical accounting of the evolution of managerial thinking to reach their conclusion that enlightened management is socially responsible management. In his classical defense of the profit motive, Nobel laureate Milton Friedman attacks social responsibility, arguing that spending shareholders' property against their wishes is immoral, illegal, and ultimately unproductive.

BusinessWeek argues that many U.S. corporations have been guilty of negligence in monitoring and controlling the quality of working conditions in their overseas sweatshop operations, resulting in continued abuse and exploitation of workers. In testimony to a U.S. Senate subcommittee, Daniel Griswold, an expert scholar in labor issues for the Cato Institute, argues that anti-sweatshop legislation is unwise and contrary to the interests of both U.S. corporations and the citizens of the host countries.

Arguing that US CEOs are substantially overpaid in a 2008 study conducted for the Institute for Policy Studies is compensation expert and IPS Fellow Sarah Anderson and her colleagues. Ira Kay is an expert in executive compensation and a consultant at Watson Wyatt Worldwide. He argues persuasively that market forces play an important role in executive compensation, which is, on the whole, fair and equitable.

Ian Meklinsky and Anne Ciesla Bancroft, experts in employment law, provide insightful analysis of this issue while explaining how, when, and why monitoring can and should be used in the workplace. The National Workrights Institute acknowledges that monitoring is legal for most employers most of the time but argues that more stringent laws should be enacted to provide more protection of employee rights.

Dr. Carl Cohen is a philosophy professor who believes that affirmative action is not only ineffective but also immoral. In addition to his charge of immorality, he presents three additional points against affirmative action. Garth Massey, Professor of Sociology and Director of the International Studies Program at the University of Wyoming, readily admits that traditional defenses of affirmative action are weak and counter-punches by presenting three unusual and "new" arguments in support of affirmative action.

Scholars Elaine Davis and Stacie Hueller provide an analysis on how and why businesses should address the growing use of methamphetamines in the workplace. Former talk radio host and social commentator Russ Belville cites results of several studies questioning the effectiveness of workplace drug testing. He further argues that given their expense, drug-testing policies are not sound strategic initiatives.

Stephen J. Rose and Heidi I. Hartmann, scholars at the Institute for Women's Policy Research, argue in their 2004 study that discrimination is still the main reason for the persistence in the gender gap. Frank Zepezaur strongly disagrees with the position taken by Rose and Hartmann. Zepezaur, an English graduate from the University of Chicago and a prominent influence in the men's rights movement, marshals considerable data in support of his view that there are many factors that contribute to the wage gap.

F. Vincent Vernuccio, a labor expert and scholar at the Competitive Enterprise Institute, argues that EFCA is unconstitutional because it does away with the secret ballot in the union creation process. He also shows that it is self-contradictory because other provisions of the bill actually allow for the use of secret ballot voting. Ross Eisenbrey and David Kusnet, scholars writing for the Economic Policy Institute, argue that much of the criticism of the EFCA is based on misunderstandings and incomplete analysis. In their defense of the bill, they address common complaints and questions about the EFCA.

K. C. McAlpin, the Executive Director of ProEnglish, a national organization that supports English-only rules for the workplace, defends his position primarily through his attack on the EEOC and its rationale and methods of prosecuting US firms that employ English-only rules. Legal scholar Amy Crowe provides a detailed analysis of the relationship between the US courts and the EEOC as it pertains to English-only policies and, in so doing, supports the EEOC and its rationale and methods for identifying and prosecuting discrimination in the workplace resulting from the implementation of English-only rules.

UNIT 3   STRATEGIC MANAGEMENT   193

Authors Andrew Simone and Brian Kleiner acknowledge that downsizing carries significant risks, but they believe that, if implemented correctly, downsizing can be an invaluable strategic program. They offer insightful suggestions to help ensure a successful downsizing initiative. East Stroudsburg University researchers Kenneth Levitt, Terry Wilson, and Edna Gilligan examine the effects of downsizing on those that "survive" the layoffs. Their results indicate that survivors are subject to several negative effects, thereby undermining the effectiveness of the downsizing intervention itself.

BusinessWeek writers argue that outsourcing is likely to become even more important to corporate America in the near future. Indeed, they suggest that it has the potential to transform whole industries. *InfoWorld* columnist Ephraim Schwartz explores the often-overlooked costs associated with failed outsourcing initiatives. His analysis consists of four brief case studies of outsourcing initiatives that turned out badly.

Marc Epstein feels that the negative attention that M&As receive is largely due to faulty analysis of M&A activity. He contends that M&A transactions should be considered when a firm's strategic managers are looking for vehicles for growth. Success, however, is contingent upon several factors outlined by the author. In the "No" side selection, Anand Sanwal examines 33 large M&A transactions from Europe, Canada, and the United States. The evidence is that a great deal of these M&A transactions have actually destroyed value. He also contends of the transactions that did fare well, luck was often a large factor.

Scholars William T. Robinson and Sungwook Min provide results of a study indicating that the advantages from being first outweigh the risks of implementing the strategy. William Boulding and Markus Christen take a contrary position and argue that first moving is not necessarily a wise strategy, presenting evidence from their own research that, in the long run, first-movers actually experience performance disadvantages.

Clayton M. Christensen and Michael E. Raynor argue that firms are subject to pressures to continually grow from sources both inside and outside of the organization. Business scholars Jim Mackey and Liisa Välikangas cite many interesting statistics to support the view that lasting growth is elusive and unrealistic and, thus, not necessary to define a firm as successful.

UNIT 4   ENVIRONMENTAL AND INTERNATIONAL MANAGEMENT ISSUES   293

The Sierra Club is a leading environmentalist organization and has consistently advocated for the implementation of CSR policies in the workplace. The selection presented here provides insight into their philosophy and expectations as they relate to corporate behavior and its impact on the natural environment. Paul Driessen, trained in environmental science and a major advocate for the world's poor, writes a blistering attack on CSR and its constituent policies. He argues that these policies bring misery and death to the world's poor and act as camouflage for the environmentalist's anti-capitalism, pro-statism agenda.

Columnist Steven Malanga believes the influx of unskilled immigrants results in job loss by native workers and lower investment in labor-saving technology. He also contends that illegal immigration taxes our already-strained welfare and social security systems. Diana Furchtgott-Roth, senior fellow at the Hudson Institute and a former chief economist at the US Department of Labor, points out that annual immigration represents a small portion of the US labor force, and, in any event, immigrant laborers complement, rather than replace, legal American citizens in the workplace.

Arguing that globalization is good for humankind are Paul Gigot and
Guy Sorman. They outline seven ways in which globalization has
positively impacted life and what needs to be done to further its
advancement. Branko Milanovic, an economist with both the Carnegie
Endowment for International Peace and the World Bank, is against
globalization. He addresses several reasons for his views while
emphasizing the incompatibility of globalization with the ages-old ethnic
and religious traditions and values that characterize much of the world.

Issue 18. Are Protectionist Policies Beneficial to Business? 345

In support of the idea that protectionist policies help business, Ha-Joon
Chang focuses attention on developing industries in poor countries.
Further, he describes and advocates historical protectionist policies from
around the world. In the "No" selection, Robert Krol describes the findings
of various economic studies of international trade. The areas that he
surveys include the effect of trade on employment and wages as well of
the costs of trade restrictions. He concludes that overall the benefits from
protectionist policies are overshadowed by their negative effects.

Correlation Guide

The *Taking Sides* series presents current issues in a debate-style format designed to stimulate student interest and develop critical thinking skills. Each issue is thoughtfully framed with an issue summary, an issue introduction, and a postscript. The pro and con essays—selected for their liveliness and substance—represent the arguments of leading scholars and commentators in their fields.

Taking Sides: Clashing Views in Management, 3/e is an easy-to-use reader that presents issues on important topics such as *ethical issues for managers, organizational behavior and human resource management, strategic management,* and *environmental and international management issues.* For more information on *Taking Sides* and other McGraw-Hill Contemporary Learning Series titles, visit http://www.mhcls.com.

This convenient guide matches the issues in *Taking Sides: Management, 3/e* with the corresponding chapters in three of our best-selling McGraw-Hill Management textbooks by Ghillyer, Bateman/Snell, and Jones/George.

Taking Sides: Management, 3/e	Management: A Real World Approach by Ghillyer	M: Management by Bateman/Snell	Contemporary Management, 6/e by Jones/George
Issue 1: Do Corporations Have a Responsibility to Society Beyond Maximizing Profit?	**Chapter 14:** Management in the 21st Century	**Chapter 3:** Ethics and Corporate Responsibility	**Chapter 4:** Ethics and Social Responsibility **Chapter 6:** Managing in the Global Environment
Issue 2: Is It Immoral for U.S. Corporations to Use Cheap Overseas Labor?	**Chapter 8:** Organizing Structure	**Chapter 8:** Managing the Diverse Workforce	**Chapter 1:** Managers and Managing **Chapter 12:** Human Resource Management
Issue 3: Are U.S. CEOs Paid More than They Deserve?	**Chapter 6:** Leadership and Culture	**Chapter 3:** Ethics and Corporate Responsibility **Chapter 7:** Managing Human Resources **Chapter 10:** Motivating People	**Chapter 12:** Human Resource Management
Issue 4: Does an Employer's Need to Monitor Workers Trump Employee Privacy Concerns?	**Chapter 10:** Motivating People **Chapter 11:** Management Control	**Chapter 1:** Managing **Chapter 7:** Managing Human Resources	**Chapter 1:** Managers and Managing **Chapter 4:** Ethics and Social Responsibility **Chapter 11:** Organizational Control and Change **Chapter 13:** Motivation and Performance
Issue 5: Has Affirmative Action Outlived Its Usefulness in the Workplace?	**Chapter 9:** Organizing People	**Chapter 8:** Managing the Diverse Workforce	
Issue 6: Is Workplace Drug Testing a Wise Corporate Policy?		**Chapter 7:** Managing Human Resources	

(Continued)

Taking Sides: Management, 3/e	Management: A Real World Approach by Ghillyer	M: Management by Bateman/Snell	Contemporary Management, 6/e by Jones/George
Issue 7: Is Gender Discrimination the Main Reason Women are Paid Less Than Men?	**Chapter 9:** Organizing People	**Chapter 7:** Managing Human Resources **Chapter 8:** Managing the Diverse Workforce	**Chapter 5:** Managing Diverse Employees in a Multicultural Environment
Issue 8: Should Employees be Allowed to Vote by Secret Ballot When Deciding Whether to Support Unionization in the Workplace?		**Chapter 7:** Managing Human Resources	**Chapter 12:** Human Resource Management
Issue 9: Should Corporations Be Allowed to Implement English-Only Rules in the Workplace?	**Chapter 13:** Contemporary Issues	**Chapter 8:** Managing the Diverse Workforce	**Chapter 5:** Managing Diverse Employees in a Multicultural Environment
Issue 10: Is Downsizing a Sound Strategic Initiative?	**Chapter 8:** Organizing Structure **Chapter 9:** Organizing People	**Chapter 6:** Organizing for Action **Chapter 7:** Managing Human Resources	
Issue 11: Is Outsourcing a Wise Corporate Strategy?	**Chapter 8:** Organizing Structure	**Chapter 8:** Managing the Diverse Workforce	**Chapter 1:** Managers and Managing **Chapter 12:** Human Resource Management
Issue 12: Does Expanding Via Mergers and Acquisitions Make for Sound Corporate Strategy?		**Chapter 2:** The Environment of Business	
Issue 13: Is First-To-Market a Successful Strategy?			
Issue 14: Is Growth Always an Inherent Corporate Value?	**Chapter 5:** Planning and Strategic Management		
Issue 15: Should Corporations Adopt Environmentally Friendly Policies of CSR and Sustainable Development?	**Chapter 14:** Management in the 21st Century	**Chapter 3:** Ethics and Corporate Responsibility	
Issue 16: Do Unskilled Immigrants Hurt the American Economy?	**Chapter 6:** Leadership and Culture **Chapter 9:** Organizing People	**Chapter 2:** The Environment of Business **Chapter 5:** Entrepreneurship **Chapter 8:** Managing the Diverse Workforce	**Chapter 5:** Managing Diverse Employees in a Multicultural Environment
Issue 17: Is Economic Globalization Good for Humankind?	**Chapter 13:** Contemporary Issues	**Chapter 1:** Managing **Chapter 8:** Managing the Diverse Workforce	**Chapter 6:** Managing in the Global Environment **Chapter 8:** The Manager as a Planner and Strategist
Issue 18: Are Protectionist Policies Beneficial to American Business?	**Chapter 13:** Contemporary Issues		**Chapter 6:** Managing in the Global Environment

Introduction

Controversial Issues in Management

This introduction consists of four sections, each of which briefly discusses a different area of business management. Each section provides important information about a specific management area and, in so doing, sets the stage for the debate topics that comprise the four parts of this book. This essay is organized in a manner paralleling the presentation of the debate topics in the text: business ethics is discussed in the first section, organizational behavior and human resource management in the second, strategic management in the third, and environmental and international management-related issues in the final section.

Business Ethics and Management

Many business ethics scholars analyze this complex management topic at two levels. The macro-level involves issues broad in nature and relevant for analysis at the organizational level. In this text, we limit our discussion to a specific macro-level issue, albeit a critically important issue. This topic concerns the degree of moral responsibility an organization has to the society in which it functions. At the micro-level of analysis, business ethics is concerned primarily with the ethical decision-making process of individuals in the workplace. Both of these levels of analysis are expanded on briefly below.

Macro-level Analysis: Corporate Social Responsibility vs. Profit Maximization

Twenty-five years ago, corporate America measured success by the creation of shareholder wealth. Companies that increased shareholders' wealth were successful, and those that didn't, were not. In the early years of the new century, determining corporate success is a much more complicated affair. The traditional *shareholder theory* of profit maximization has been replaced with a new method of defining corporate success known as *stakeholder theory.*

Stakeholder theory and social responsibility. This approach to defining corporate success differs dramatically from the traditional shareholder approach. In this view, a stakeholder is any entity that contributes resources to the firm and, therefore, has a "stake" in the firm's survival. A typical list of an organization's stakeholders includes customers, employees, management, suppliers, shareholders, partners, governments, and society at large. Each stakeholder determines organizational performance independent of the others and, since each stakeholder has contributed different resources, each is likely to use different criteria by which to evaluate performance. This can lead to situations where one set of stakeholders is pleased with firm performance while another feels the firm has performed very poorly.

An important implication of stakeholder theory is that managers have obligations that go beyond profit maximization since they are concerned with satisfying the needs of all of its stakeholders. Thus, those firms that do not place the interests of one set of stakeholders above the rest are acting in a *socially responsible* manner, whereas firms that stick to the traditional emphasis of maximizing profit with disregard of other stakeholder interests are irresponsible and immoral.

Shareholder theory and profit maximization. Standing in complete contrast to the current trend towards stakeholder-driven social responsibility is the traditional economic advocacy of shareholder theory. Advocates of free-market capitalism believe that the only responsibility an organization has is to maximize profits for its shareholders. They point out that shareholders own the companies in which they invest, not employees, customers, suppliers, or other stakeholders. Their investment subjects them to the risks and rewards associated with ownership and, therefore, entitles them to expect management to act in accordance with their wishes. If, for example, management acts against shareholder interests by spending profits for a social program rather than increasing dividends, they have, in effect, stolen from the owners of the firm. Thus, it is not surprising that most free-market advocates view stakeholder theory as promoting behaviors and outcomes that are both illegal and immoral.

Micro-level Analysis: Ethical Decision-Making

At the micro-level of analysis, business ethics is the study of the influences and processes involved in individual ethical decision-making (EDM). The primary focus is to identify those factors that affect an individual's decision to act morally (or not) at the workplace. Understanding these factors is of prime importance for managers, not only to understand their own ethical behavior, but that of their employees as well. Over the years, EDM scholars have developed many different models of ethical behavior but, despite these efforts, there is currently no dominant model accepted by all. However, scholars have managed to identify several factors that appear to be predictive of ethical behavior. We briefly discuss these next.

Personal characteristics. Research has shown that individuals who score high on *Machiavellianism* are more likely to act unethically than those who score low. Machiavellianism is a personality trait best described with the adage, "the ends justify the means". High Machs, as they are known, are more concerned with reaching their goals than in the manner in which they achieved them. *Locus of control* measures the extent to which an individual feels that luck, fate, or forces beyond his control are primarily responsible for what happens to him in life. Individuals that strongly believe this to be the case (known as externals) are much more likely to engage in unethical behavior than are individuals that strongly disagree with this view (known as internals). *Gender* has also been shown to predict ethical behavior. All things equal, females are much more likely to act ethically than are males.

Situational characteristics. EDM scholars have noted that several characteristics of the ethical decision situation play a role in whether an individual acts morally or not. One of the strongest predictors is the *likelihood of getting caught;* the greater it is, the lower the probability of unethical behavior. Peer behavior also plays a significant role in ethical behavior. An individual is more likely to act unethically if his/her peers are acting unethically. This is known as *differential association*—basically we tend to do what our peers do. Finally, the probability of unethical behavior increases if the *costs* of getting caught acting unethically are perceived as being less than the *benefits* from doing so.

Business Ethics and Taking Sides

The first portion of this book consists of four debates, two at the macro and two at the micro-levels of analysis. We have already looked at background information about the CSR vs. profit maximization controversy; Issue 1 frames this organizational-level topic in a debate format and presents articles supportive of each side.

Â Â Â The second issue in section 1 involves the contentious issue of overseas "sweatshops". Increasingly, U.S. firms (and, to be fair, large corporations from other developed countries) are adopting to increased global competition by reducing labor costs thorough the shifting of manufacturing functions to countries with an abundance of cheap labor. But what about the human element involved? Typically, overseas employees work in—by Western standards— primitive conditions and are paid a mere fraction of the pay of an American employee for doing comparable work. Once these "sweatshop" conditions are factored into the equation, doesn't the moral aspect of the decision to outsource become more obvious?

Â Â Â Issue 3 examines another highly controversial topic, the issue of executive pay. In recent years, the business and news media have portrayed numerous examples of U.S. CEOs receiving millions of dollars in salary and benefits while their organizations were posting losses, laying off workers and, in some instances, declaring bankruptcy. As a result of the public outrage generated by these stories, the question of top-level management compensation has taken on greater importance in the field of management. Here we are concerned with the specific question of whether or not CEO pay is unjust; put another way, do U.S. CEOs receive more pay than they deserve?

Â Â Â The final topic in this section is the first of six new issues in this edition and involves a battle of rights between management and employees. Specifically, the two articles comprising this debate examine whether a firm has the right to monitor its employee's behavior in the workplace or whether doing so violates employees' rights to privacy. As is the case with other issues in our text, it seems that the more you learn about this topic the more difficult it becomes to draw a conclusion!

Organizational Behavior and Human Resource Management

Organizational Behavior Basics

Most introductory textbooks on organizational behavior (OB) generally view OB as the study of individual human behavior in the context of the workplace. Some business scholars (including the lead author of this book) refer to OB as "psychology in the workplace"; an apt description given that much of what we know about human behavior at work is based on the application of knowledge generated by the psychological sciences. This is really not surprising considering that the main goal of OB is to generate knowledge about human behavior as a means to improving organizational effectiveness.

The value of OB to the practicing manager.   The field of organizational behavior has value for managers to the extent that it can positively affect important organizational outcomes. And although OB scholars study many different aspects of workplace behavior, a core group of four critically important outcomes has received the most research attention over the years.

U.S. corporations lose billions of dollars each year as a result of employees failing to report to work. Loss of labor hours is only part of the cost; *absenteeism* frequently upsets the flow of work and results in operational inefficiencies. Fortunately, OB scholars know quite a bit about what causes absenteeism and how it can be reduced. For example, research consistently shows that females tend to be absent more frequently than males, primarily because of family-related concerns (pregnancy, raising children, etc.). As a result of this finding, many managers reduce the impact of absenteeism by allowing female employees greater flexibility in their work schedules.

Turnover occurs when an employee, voluntarily or not, permanently leaves the organization. Like absenteeism, turnover is extremely costly to employers, affecting productivity and upsetting the flow of work. By some conservative accounts, turnover costs can run as high as $15,000–$20,000 per employee. Understanding why an employee leaves an organization is a terrifically complicated process; nevertheless, OB scholars have made inroads here as well. For example, research shows that the more an employee is committed to the organization and its goals, the less likely he/she is to leave.

A third important outcome is *job satisfaction*. This is one of the most studied variables in organizational behavior, a fact attesting to its importance in the workplace. OB scholars have established, for example, that organizations with highly satisfied workers have lower absenteeism and turnover rates and higher levels of productivity than do organizations whose employees are less satisfied with their jobs. So, what can managers do to increase job satisfaction? Research suggests four ways: provide mentally challenging work, fair and equitable rewards, supportive working conditions, and supportive colleagues.

The fourth important outcome is *productivity*. OB scholars have studied this variable from the perspective of the organization as well as the employee. We've already seen that at the organizational level, job satisfaction, absenteeism, and turnover have been shown to impact organizational productivity. At the individual level, the belief is that the more motivated an individual is, the more productive he or she is likely to be. The OB literature contains many different models of workplace motivation, each offering managers various suggestions as to how they can motivate their employees.

Other OB topics of interest to managers. Organizational behavior has much to say about other issues of interest to managers beyond those discussed above. *Personality* researchers are concerned with, among other things, identifying the various components of personality and exploring whether some personality traits are predictive of success on the job. Another important area of research involves *decision-making.* This multifaceted field offers many different theories about how humans make decisions and offers managers much insight into the factors that lead to poor decision-making and how to avoid them. Over the last 25 years, *work teams* have become an important work unit at most major corporations in America. As a result, many OB scholars study work group dynamics and processes and have learned much about what differentiates an effective work team from an ineffective one. One of the oldest areas of OB research concerns *leadership and the use of power and politics* in the workplace. Despite the large body of research on this topic, OB scholars have a less than impressive record of providing useful insights and suggestions to practicing managers about how to develop, identify, or create effective leaders in the workplace.

Human Resource Management Basics

Human resource management (HRM) is the design and implementation of formal systems that utilize human resources to accomplish organizational goals (Mathis and Jackson, *Human Resource Management,* 12th edition, South-Western Thompson, 2008). Although the fields of organizational behavior and human resource management are both conducted primarily at the individual level of analysis, HRM is a much more practical area of management than is OB. It is only a slight stretch to describe OB as a field characterized by theories and concepts while laws, regulations, and formal systems characterize HRM.

Typical HRM functions. Virtually every major U.S. corporation has a HR department that is in charge of managing several interlinked activities concerning the firms' employees. Although it varies from firm to firm, in general HR managers are responsible for at least seven different human resource functions: HR planning, equal employment opportunity compliance, staffing, human resource development, compensation, health and safety concerns, and employee/management relations.

    Human resource planning involves anticipating and responding to the forces that will affect the supply of and demand for employees. For example, firms that are growing usually have a need for more employees; HR managers are responsible for determining how many are needed, where they are needed, and when they are needed. *Equal employment opportunity (EEO)* compliance affects every aspect of HR management and has become the single most important area of HR management over the last two decades. It is absolutely imperative that managers are aware of the requirements of affirmative action and the necessity of developing a diverse workforce. Firms that are oblivious to—or worse, ignore—the dictates of EEO risk severe damage to their reputations and will likely face costly legal proceedings due to discrimination lawsuits.

Staffing consists of three HR functions: job analysis, recruiting, and selecting. Job analysis tells HR managers what workers do and provides the basis for recruiting qualified applicants to apply for open positions. Selecting is the process of choosing from among the group of qualified applicants. *Human resource development* is concerned with such activities as new employee orientation, skills training, career development, career planning, and evaluating employee performance. *Compensation* is another crucial HR function and, along with pay and incentives for good performance, includes the distribution of employee benefits. HR managers help develop wage and salary systems, incentive and bonus plans, and competitive benefits packages.

Complying with federal safety regulations, dealing with drug-related issues, and managing workplace security, particularly in a post-9/11 America, are a few of the challenges involved in the *Health and Safety* HR function. Last, but certainly not least, is the HR function that monitors the *relationship between employees and management.* There has been a dramatic increase in the number of lawsuits brought by disgruntled employees who believe their rights to privacy, for example, have been violated by inappropriate corporate policies. Courts have been very receptive to such accusations; consequently, it is critical that the HR department develops, updates, and communicates organizational policies so that all parties involved know what is expected.

OB, HRM, and Taking Sides

Three of the five debates in this section involve the topic of discrimination in one form or another. Issue 5 wonders if affirmative action has outlived its usefulness in the workplace, while Issue 7 asks if the persistent wage gap between men and women is due primarily to sexual discrimination or to some other factors such as individual career and/or educational choices. And new to this edition, our ninth debate involves the question of whether employers should be allowed to require that only English is spoken in the workplace, a particularly salient issue given the tremendous increase in the importance of the larger immigration issue over the last decade or so.

The second topic in this section, Issue 6, asks if workplace drug testing is a wise corporate strategy, particularly in light of the seemingly obvious concerns about privacy rights. Issue 8 is yet another new topic and is concerned with the Employee Free Choice Act (EFCA). An important aspect of this piece of legislation involves proposed changes to the voting methods used in unionization campaigns. Critics of the EFCA claim that it eliminates the secret ballot process that has characterized union campaigns for 70 years; proponents argue that it is necessary to correct the mountain of perceived injustices perpetrated by management and directed at workers since the end of World War II.

Strategic Management
Strategic Management Basics

While OB and HRM are primarily concerned with understanding, motivating, and managing individual employees in the workplace, the focus of strategic management is on the organization as a whole. As you might expect, the basic unit of strategic management is a *strategy*. At its most basic, a strategy is a plan designed to achieve a specific goal. In the business world, strategic management refers to the process of effectively developing and executing the collection of plans designed to achieve the organization's goals. Typically, the goals of the organization reflect the overall purpose of the company as spelled out in the firm's mission statement. In most large companies, top-level executives and managers are responsible for the development of the organization's strategies, while mid-level managers and supervisors are typically in charge of making sure the strategies are implemented successfully. Thus, the executives are involved in *strategy formulation*, while the managers and supervisors are concerned with *strategy implementation*.

SWOT Analysis as a source of strategy formulation.   So far so good, but where do the strategies come from in the first place? Perhaps the most frequent method used by executives to develop strategies is a SWOT analysis. In this procedure, the organization identifies its strengths, weaknesses, opportunities, and threats. Once this information has been gathered, top management develops plans of attack that a) capitalize on the firm's strengths, and b) allow the organization to take advantage of available opportunities. Management must also be careful, however, to a) try and counter potential threats from the external environment (such as competitors), b) while also avoiding spending excessive resources on weak areas. Thus, the most effective strategies are those that support the mission of the organization by taking advantage of the firm's strengths and opportunities and minimizing the effects of threats and weaknesses. In an ideal world, the firm can turn its strengths into a *sustained competitive advantage*. This occurs when an organization is able to consistently out-perform its competitors even though the competitors have tried to reduce its advantage by duplicating the firm's sources of strength.

Levels of strategies.   Many corporations in the United States and abroad conduct business in more than one industry and/or in more than one market. Consequently, they have a need for more than one level of strategy. When top management develops plans and sets goals for the overall corporation, it is engaging in *corporate-level strategy* development. When top management chooses a specific set of strategies for a particular business or market, it is engaging in *business-level strategy* development.

Types of strategies.   There are several different models for identifying the major strategic approaches available to organizations when conducting business-level strategy development. One of the most popular approaches is Michael Porter's three generic strategies framework. Firms that attempt to distinguish themselves from competitors by virtue of the quality of their products or services are using a *differentiation* strategy. Other firms try to achieve success by keeping costs of production lower than their competitors, thus employing a *cost leadership strategy*. Still other firms will concentrate their efforts on a specific geographic region or market, employing what Porter calls a *focus strategy* approach.

At the corporate-level of strategic development, perhaps the most important question concerns the extent and nature of *diversification*. Diversification refers to the number of distinct businesses an organization is involved in and the degree to which they are related to each other. Some companies, such as WD-40, make just one product and are not concerned with strategic issues of diversification; theirs is a single-product strategy. Others, like General Motors for example, are involved in literally hundreds of businesses. Firms such as GM need to make corporate-level strategic decisions about the nature and type of diversification they should employ. *Related diversification* occurs when the organization runs several different businesses that are linked to each other in some manner. RJR Nabisco, for example, has numerous different businesses that share the same distribution mechanism—your local grocery store. The main advantage of implementing a related diversification strategy is that it reduces the firm's dependence on a specific business, thereby lowering its economic risk. *Unrelated diversification* is a strategy in which the organization's multiple businesses do not share any obvious links. During the 1980s, this was a favored approach of many large non-financial corporations interested in establishing themselves in the securities industry. Sears, for example, adopted an unrelated diversification strategy when it bought Dean Witter, as did GE when it purchased Kidder Peabody. Interestingly, research strongly suggests that unrelated diversification is not a sure road to success, which probably accounts for why its popularity as a corporate-level strategy has waned in recent years.

Strategic Management and Taking Sides

Section Three of your text contains issues particularly relevant to the topic of strategic management. Increasingly, U.S. firms are adopting the view that reducing costs through labor force reductions—downsizing—should not be reserved only for desperate firms on the edge of bankruptcy. Indeed, many organizations now routinely reduce their workforce even when the firm is profitable and its future prospects appear positive. Closely related to downsizing is the corporate strategy of outsourcing. While moving domestically expensive operational functions to a country with lower wage rates may reduce costs, many have argued that it is an unpatriotic strategy and should not be condoned, particularly when the economy is in bad shape, as it is at the time of this writing. We'll let you decide for yourself when you read Issue 11.

The next issue in section three, another new topic, looks at mergers and acquisitions as corporate initiatives. Although M&A as a mode of corporate expansion has been around since at least the Industrial Revolution, it exploded in the 1980s during Ronald Reagan's term as president. And during the current downtrend, merger activity seems to be continuing unabated as firms seek strength and security in size. Here, we inquire as to whether or not expanding via mergers and/or acquisitions really is wise strategy.

Our next debate involves the often-employed corporate strategy of first-to-market leadership. Common financial wisdom tells us that firms will take extraordinary risks only if extraordinary gains from success are possible. Given that adopting a "first-mover" strategy is a common in corporate America, we would expect experience to show that doing so results in superior financial returns. But not so fast—interestingly, research on this topic is anything but unequivocal. In Issue 13, we present the question of whether a first-mover strategy is a successful strategy and invite you to decide for yourself.

The last issue in Part 3 presents an intriguing, though seldom discussed, question: must firms grow in order to be considered successful? As you interact with this debate, try to avoid adopting the seemingly obvious "of course!" perspective before you've read both sides of the argument; you might be surprised at your final answer.

Environmental and International Management Issues

Over the last quarter century, two managerial challenges have grown in importance so dramatically that executives in corporate America have no alternative but to take them into account when formulating organizational strategy. The first of these challenges originates in the conflict between an organization's need to be financially successful and society's expectations that it conduct its business in a socially responsible manner. In its broadest sense, this is the topic we tackle in Issue 1. More specifically, U.S. organizations now face the difficult challenge of maintaining financial success while recognizing obligations to protect and maintain the world's physical environment. The second major challenge also involves competitive pressures. U.S. firms need to develop successful responses to the threats and opportunities resulting from the tremendous increase in international competition and the expansion of global markets that has occurred over the last 25 years.

The Environmental Challenge

As noted in the Ethics section of this introduction, the corporate social responsibility (CSR) doctrine holds that organizations have obligations to society that extend beyond merely maximizing profit for their shareholders. For example, an important obligation of every firm, according to the CSR perspective, is to conduct business in a way that, at a minimum, is respectful of the natural environment. The history of business in America is full of stories of companies carelessly polluting rivers and streams, pumping tons of soot and chemicals into the air, cutting down and destroying millions of acres of forest and wetlands, and causing ecological disasters such as the Exxon *Valdez* oil spill. Not surprisingly, CSR advocates—primarily environmentalist groups—have applied tremendous public pressure on U.S. corporations to act responsibly towards the environment. The federal government has responded to the decades of environmental neglect by passing numerous laws forcing corporations to regulate their environmentally damaging behaviors. And although many major corporations have responded to the challenge, the constant stream of ominous reports on the decline of the earth's environment indicate that there is still much to be done.

For managers, the problem is that complying with all the laws and regulations, as well as conducting their business operations in a socially responsible manner, can be very costly. Firms often spend millions of dollars bringing their operations into compliance with federal laws and regulations, thus diverting funds that would normally go to profitable projects. Clearly, then, twenty-first century managers in corporate America face a difficult challenge: conducting their business operations in a manner respectful of the environment while successfully responding to the rapidly increasing levels of competition both domestically and abroad.

The International Challenge

In the early 1980s, the U.S. lighting industry was dominated by the General Electric corporation. GE's reign as the major player in the field came under serious attack, however, when Westinghouse, its major domestic competitor, sold its lamp operations to the huge Dutch conglomerate, Phillips Electronics. Virtually overnight, GE's competitive picture changed and they found themselves suddenly on the defensive. In response, GE went global; they bought a Hungarian electronics firm and entered into a joint venture with Hitachi in order to break into the Asian markets. In 1990, GE generated less than 20% of its lighting sales from abroad; today the number is closer to 50%. (This information taken from, Gary Dressler, *Management,* Prentice Hall, 2001).

GE's experiences are not uncommon, nor are they unique to American firms. In response to the tremendous growth of competition from international firms, corporations all over the world have embraced the idea of globalization by extending sales and/or production operations to markets abroad. Globalization offers firms many advantages: access to new sources of cheap labor; access to new sources of highly skilled labor; access to established markets; and access to emerging markets (China, Russia, and India, for example). These advantages come with a cost, however: globalization, by its very definition, means greater competition. Thus, a second critical challenge facing U.S. managers is responding successfully to the tremendous growth of competition from international firms, both here and abroad.

Environmental Management, International Management, and Taking Sides

An underlying assumption of the environmental movement in the United States and abroad is that the health of the planet is deteriorating and that business activity is primarily responsible. An important idea that emerged in the 1980s in response to this assumption is the concept of sustainable development. This idea, a conceptual child of CSR, holds that corporations should conduct their business activities and develop their plans and goals within a framework that recognizes that the earth's resources are limited and must be preserved. Consequently, corporations should take into account the needs of future generations when mapping out future growth strategies. Not surprisingly, however, this concept is controversial to many. So, in yet another new topic, we ask whether firms are wise to adopt and implement sustainable development in the workplace.

The next debate involves one of the most important and controversial social issues of our time and its impact on corporate America. Very few dispute that the growing number of illegal aliens poses a serious problem to the United States and is likely to be an important political, social, and economic issue for the foreseeable future. In Issue 16, we ask whether United States firms should be allowed to tap into this reservoir of labor legally or whether doing so hurts the American economy. Passions run high when this topic is raised, so it's no surprise that the two articles presented here come to completely different conclusions.

A growing number of countries around the world have embraced the idea of globalization as a means of raising the standard of living for their citizens. But despite the fact that much evidence attests to the economic benefits that accrue as a result of globalization, there are those that question whether globalization on the whole is a positive occurrence. Issue 17 provides two competing answers to the question, "Is economic globalization good for humankind?"

The final issue in this book is also our final new topic. There are a growing number of politicians, media pundits, and business experts who are calling for the Obama administration to help the United States economy by enacting a wide-range of protectionist economic policies. On the other hand, the vast majority of economists are skeptical of protectionism and have much empirical and historical evidence on their side to support their view. For our purposes, what this amounts to is an interesting final question: Are protectionist policies beneficial to business?

Internet References . . .

The W. Maurice Young Centre for Applied Ethics

The mission of the centre is to bring moral philosophy into the public domain by advancing research in applied ethics, supporting courses with a significant ethical component, and acting as a community resource.

http://www.ethics.ubc.ca/about.htm

The National Workrights Institute

The Institute's creation grew from the belief that the workplace is a critical front in the fight for human rights and the belief that this effort required the creation of a new organization dedicated to human rights in the workplace. The Institute's mission is to be the one human rights organization which commits its entire effort to workplace issues such as employee privacy concerns.

http://www.workrights.org/about.html

The Ludwig von Mises Institute

Named after famed economist Ludwig von Mises, the institute works to advance the Austrian School of Economics by defending the market economy, private property, sound money, and peaceful international relations, while opposing government intervention as economically and socially destructive. Check this Web site for insightful comments on corporate social responsibility, downsizing, and insider trading.

http://www.mises.org/

The Adam Smith Institute

The Adam Smith Institute is the U.K.'s leading innovator of market economic policies. Named after the great Scottish economist and author of *The Wealth of Nations,* its guiding principles are free markets and a free society. Many social issues, such as downsizing, are covered here.

http://www.adamsmith.org/about/

Ethical Issues for Managers

An old saying holds that business ethics is an oxymoron. For years, the generally accepted view on morality and business was that they don't mix, that business is a game played by a different set of rules. To act morally was to act weakly. And in the business arena, weak firms were dead firms.

Well, things certainly change. In today's business arena, firms are finding that immoral behavior can prove fatal. The recent experiences of the financial industry amid the financial meltdown in the fall of 2008 appear to lend credence to those who believe that ethical behavior is an afterthought in corporate boardrooms. Well, they are certainly not an afterthought in this, the opening section of your text. Indeed, Unit 1 examines several ethically laden issues of importance to many managers in corporate America.

- Do Corporations Have a Responsibility to Society Beyond Maximizing Profit?

- Is it Immoral for U.S. Corporations to Use Cheap Overseas Labor?

- Are U.S. CEOs Paid More Than They Deserve?

- Does an Employer's Need to Monitor Workers Trump Employee Privacy Concerns?

ISSUE 1

Do Corporations Have a Responsibility to Society Beyond Maximizing Profit?

YES: Robert D. Hay and Edmund R. Gray, from "Introduction to Social Responsibility," in David Keller, man. ed., *Ethics and Values: Basic Readings in Theory and Practice* (Pearson Custom Publishing, 2002)

NO: Milton Friedman, from "The Social Responsibility of Business Is to Increase Its Profits," in Laura P. Hartman, ed., *Perspectives in Business Ethics*, 3rd ed. (New York Times Magazine, 2005)

ISSUE SUMMARY

YES: Robert Hay and Edmund Gray use stakeholder theory and a historical accounting of the evolution of managerial thinking to reach their conclusion that enlightened management is socially responsible management.

NO: In his classical defense of the profit motive, Nobel laureate Milton Friedman attacks social responsibility, arguing that spending shareholders' property against their wishes is immoral, illegal, and ultimately unproductive.

Not surprisingly, in the wake of the subprime mortgage, housing-bubble meltdown, and the associated chaos in the financial services industry, attitudes toward US corporations have turned decidedly negative. A 2008 survey conducted by Gallup found that a third of those polled believe that big business represents the single largest threat to our country's future (http://www.gallup.com/poll/5248/Big-Business.aspx). And in a fall 2008 Pew Research Center poll, nearly 6 in 10 respondents (59%) indicated that business corporations make too much profit. The survey also reported that 62 percent believe that financial executives in America are "more greedy than they were in the past" (http://people-press.org/report/?pageid=1399). Indeed, during the latter months of 2008, social commentators and political analysts placing the blame for the debacle on the pursuit of profit were ubiquitous.

An interesting outcome of this attention on corporate behavior was a renewed interest in the question of what the purpose of business is, in general. This is not a new topic, but it is one that generates passionate debate. So, in the first issue of the current volume, we focus on this issue by asking the question, "Do corporations have a responsibility to society beyond maximizing profit?"

Those that answer in the affirmative usually provide a two-pronged response, the first based on stakeholder theory and the second on practical observations and assertions. Stakeholder theory argues that the manager's job is to balance interests among the various groups with a stake in the company's survival. Consequently, management's obligations have been expanded beyond focusing primarily on financial gain for shareholders to include satisfying the needs and concerns of all of its stakeholders. Organizations that recognize this expansion and act on it accordingly are said to be acting in a socially responsible manner, whereas firms that stick to the traditional emphasis of increasing share price as priority one are deemed irresponsible and immoral. The second prong in the "yes" response consists of more practical arguments. One point often raised is that because corporations are the source of many problems in society—pollution, corruption, discrimination, and so on—they should be required to resolve those problems. After all, the community in which the corporation resides is a legitimate stakeholder of the firm. Also, business organizations are members of society and, as such, should assume the responsibilities of membership. Another argument holds that organizations frequently have a lot of financial resources and, therefore, are in position to use the money for social good and not just for increasing the power and wealth of the firm and its shareholders.

On the other side of the debate, the strongest and most consistent defender of shareholder theory has been free-market economist and Nobel laureate Milton Friedman. In his anti-stakeholder approach, Friedman argues that shareholders—not employees, customers, or suppliers—own the companies in which they invest and, consequently, have the legal right to expect management to comply with their desires (which is usually to maximize the value of their investments). Consider the example of a corporation whose management, without shareholder consent, wants to use some of the company's profits on its local community by contributing to the creation of a park project. If management chooses to reduce profit distribution to its shareholders and spend it on the project, its members have acted both immorally and illegally because they have, in effect, stolen from the shareholders. If they choose to pay shareholders out of profit and instead finance the project by reducing labor costs, the employees will suffer. If they choose to avoid antagonizing shareholders and employees and contribute to the park by raising product prices, they will hurt their customers and possibly price themselves out of the market. Thus, according to Friedman, doing anything other than increasing shareholder wealth is tantamount to theft, is immoral, and is ultimately self-defeating for the organization.

The following two selections address the question of whether or not corporations have responsibilities to society that extend beyond profit maximization. The "pro" selection is by Robert D. Hay and Edmund R. Gray. Their argument uses stakeholder theory and is presented in the form of a historical account of the evolution of managerial thinking, concluding that enlightened management is socially responsible management. For the "con" side, we present Milton Friedman's classic anti-stakeholder article. Originally written in 1970, it is reprinted here and provides you with the second side of this fascinating and controversial management topic. A final word: Issue 15 in this volume looks at a closely related subject and is highly recommended, particularly if you found this issue to be of interest.

YES

Robert D. Hay and
Edmund R. Gray

Introduction to Social Responsibility

It was Jeremy Bentham, late eighteenth century English philosopher, who espoused the social, political, and economic goal of society to be "the greatest happiness for the greatest number." His cardinal principle was written into the Declaration of Independence as "the pursuit of happiness," which became a societal goal of the American colonists. Bentham's principle was also incorporated into the Constitution of the United States in the preamble where the goal was stated "to promote the general welfare."

The economic-political system through which we in America strive to achieve this societal goal emphasizes the economic and political freedom to pursue individual interests. Adam Smith, another English political economist of the late eighteenth century, stated that the best way to achieve social goals was as follows:

> Every individual is continually exerting himself to find out the most advantageous employment for whatever capital he can command. It is his own advantage, indeed, and not that of the society, which he has in view. But the study of his own advantage naturally, or rather necessarily, leads him to prefer that employment which is most advantageous to the society. . . .
>
> As every individual, therefore, endeavors as much as he can both to employ his capital in the support of domestic industry, and so to direct that industry that its produce may be of the greatest value, every individual necessarily labours to render the annual revenue of the society as great as he can. He generally, indeed, neither intends to promote the public interest, nor knows how much he is promoting it. By preferring the support of domestic to that of foreign industry, he intends only his own security; and by directing that industry in such a manner as its produce may be of the greatest value, he intends only his own gain, and he is in this, as in many other cases, led by an invisible hand to promote an end which was not part of his intention. Nor is it always the worse for the society that it was no part of it. By pursuing his own interest he frequently promotes that of the society more effectually than when he really intends to promote it. I have never known much good done by those who affected to trade for the public good. It is an affectation, indeed, not very common among merchants, and very few words need be employed in dissuading them from it.

Adam Smith's economic values have had an important influence on American business thinking. As a result, most business people for the first hundred and fifty years of our history embraced the theory that social goals could be achieved by pursuing individual interests.

By 1930 American values were beginning to change from that of the individual owner ethic to that of the group or social ethic. As part of this changing mood, it was felt that Smith's emphasis on owner's interests was too predominant at the expense of other contributors to a business organization. Consequently, a new philosophy of management took shape which stated that the social goals could be achieved by balancing the interests of several groups of people who had an interest in a business. It was stated by Charles H. Percy, then president of Bell and Howell, in the 1950s as follows:

> There are over 64 million gainfully employed people in the United States. One half of these work directly for American corporations, and the other half are vitally affected by business directly or indirectly. Our entire economy, therefore, is dependent upon the type of business management we have. Business management is therefore in many respects a public trust charged with the responsibility of keeping America economically sound. We at Bell & Howell can best do this by keeping our own company's program on a firm foundation and by having a growing group of management leaders to direct the activities of the company.
>
> Management's role in a free society is, among other things, to prove that the real principles of a free society can work within a business organization.
>
> Our basic objective is the development of individuals. In our own present program we are doing everything conceivable to encourage, guide, and assist, and provide an opportunity to everyone to improve their abilities and skills, thus becoming more valuable to the company and enabling the company to improve the rewards paid to the individual for such additional efforts.
>
> Our company has based its entire program for the future on the development of the individual and also upon the building of an outstanding management group. This is why we have emphasized so strongly the supervisory training program recently completed by all Bell & Howell supervisors, and why we are now offering this program to others in the organization training for future management responsibilities.
>
> But a company must also have a creed to which its management is dedicated. I hope that we can all agree to the following:
>
> We believe that our company must develop and produce outstanding products that will perform a great service or fill a need for our customers.
>
> We believe that our business must be run at an adequate profit and that the services and products that we offer must be better than those offered by competitors.
>
> We believe that management must serve employees, stockholders, and customers, but that we cannot serve the interests of any one group at the undue expense of the other two. A proper and fair balance must be preserved.

We believe that our business must provide stability of employment and job security for all those who depend on our company for their livelihood.

We believe that we are failing in our responsibility if our wages are not sufficiently high to not only meet the necessities of life but provide some of the luxuries as well. Wherever possible, we also believe that bonus earning should be paid for performance and output "beyond the call of duty."

We believe that every individual in the company should have an opportunity for advancement and growth with the organization. There should be no dead-end streets any place in an organization.

We believe in the necessity for constantly increasing productivity and output. Higher wages and greater benefits can never be "given" by management. Management can only see that they are paid out when "earned."

We believe in labor-saving machinery. We do not think human beings should perform operations that can be done by mechanical or electronic means. We believe in this because we believe in the human dignity and creative ability of the individual. We are more interested in the intellect, goodwill, initiative, enthusiasm, and cooperativeness of the individual than we are in his muscular energy.

We believe that every person in the company has a right to be treated with the respect and courtesy that is due a human being. It is for this reason that we have individual merit ratings, individual pay increases, job evaluation, and incentive pay; and it is why we keep every individual fully informed—through The Finder, through our annual report, through Family Night, and through individual letters—about the present program of the company and also about our future objectives.

We believe that our business must be conducted with the utmost integrity. We may fight the principle of confiscatory taxation, but we will pay our full share. We will observe every governmental law and regulation, local, state, and national. We will deal fairly with our customers, we will advertise our product truthfully, and we will make every attempt to maintain a friendly relationship with our competitors while at the same time waging the battle of free competition.

Some business leaders, on the one hand, preach the virtues of the free enterprise, democratic system and, on the other hand, run their own business in accordance with autocratic principles–all authority stemming from the top with little delegation of responsibility to individuals within the organization. We believe in democracy–in government and in our business.

We hope that every principle we believe in is right and is actually being practiced throughout the company as it affects every individual.

Then in the late 1960s American business leaders began to take another look at the problems of society in light of the goal of "the greatest happiness for the greatest number." How could people be happy if they have to breathe foul air, drink polluted water, live in crowded cities, use very unsafe products, be misled by untruthful advertising, be deprived of a job because of race, and face many other problems? Thus, another philosophy of management emerged. It was voiced by several American business leaders:

> Business must learn to look upon its social responsibilities as insepara-
> ble from its economic function. If it fails to do so, it leaves a void that
> will quickly be filled by others–usually by the government. (George
> Champion, Chase National Bank, 1966.)
>   I believe there is one basic principle that needs to be emphasized
> more than ever before. It is the recognition that business is successful in
> the long term only when it is directed toward the needs of the society.
> (Robert F. Hansberger, Boise Cascade, 1971.)
>   The actions of the great corporations have so profound an influ-
> ence that the public has come to judge them not only by their profit-
> making record, but by the contribution of their work to society as a
> whole. Under a political democracy such as ours, if the corporation fails
> to perceive itself and govern its action in essentially the same manner
> as the public at large, it may find itself in serious trouble. (Louis B.
> Lundborg, Bank of America, 1971.)

With these remarks we can see that there has been a shift in managerial emphasis from owners' interests to group interests, and finally, to society's interests. Managers of some American businesses have come to recognize that they have a social responsibility.

Historical Perspective of Social Responsibility

The concept of the social responsibility of business managers has in recent years become a popular subject of discussion and debate within both business and academic circles. Although the term itself is of relatively recent origin, the underlying concept has existed as long as there have been business organiza-tions. It rests on the logical assumption that because the firm is a creation of society it has a responsibility to aid in the accomplishment of society's goals. In the United States concepts of social responsibility have moved from three distinct phases which may be labeled Phases I, II, and III.

Phase I—Profit Maximizing Management

The Phase I concept was based on the belief that business managers have but one single objective—maximize profits. The only constraint on this pursuit was the legal framework within which the firm operated. The origin of this view may be found in Adam Smith's *Wealth of Nations*. As previously noted, Smith believed that individual business people acting in their own selfish interest would be guided by an "invisible hand" to promote the public good. In other words, the individual's drive for maximum profits and the regulation of the competitive marketplace would interact to create the greatest aggregate wealth for a nation and there-fore the maximum public good. In the United States this view was universally accepted throughout the nineteenth century and the early part of the twentieth century. Its acceptance rested not only on economic logic but also on the goals and values of society. America in the nineteenth and first half of the twentieth centuries was a society of economic scarcity; therefore, economic growth and the accumulation of aggregate wealth were primary goals. The business system with its emphasis on maximum profit was seen as a vehicle for eliminating economic scarcity. In the process employee abuses such as child labor, starvation wages, and unsafe working conditions could be tolerated. No questions were raised with regard to using up the natural resources and polluting streams and land. Nor was anyone really concerned about urban problems, unethical advertising, unsafe products, and poverty problems of minority groups.

The profit maximization view of social responsibility also complemented the Calvinistic philosophy which pervaded nineteenth and twentieth century American thinking. Calvinism stressed that the road to salvation was through hard work and the accumulation of wealth. It then logically followed that a business person could demonstrate diligence (and thus godliness) and accumulate a maximum amount of wealth by adhering to the discipline of profit maximization.

Phase II—Trusteeship Management

Phase II, which may be labeled the "trusteeship" concept, emerged in the 1920s and 30s. It resulted from structural changes in both business institutions and in society. According to this concept, corporate managers were responsible not simply for maximizing the stockholders' wealth but rather for maintaining an equitable balance among the competing claims of customers, employees, suppliers, creditors, and the community. In this view the manager was seen as "trustee" for the various contributor groups to the firm rather than simply an agent of the owners.

The two structural trends largely responsible for the emergence of this newer view of social responsibility were: (1) the increasing diffusion of ownership of the shares of American corporations, and (2) the development of a pluralistic society. The extent of the diffusion of stock ownership may be highlighted by the fact that by the early 1930s the largest stockholders in corporations such as American Telephone and Telegraph, United States Steel, and the Pennsylvania Railroad owned less than one percent of the total shares outstanding of these companies. Similar dispersion of stock ownership existed in most other large corporations. In such situations management typically was firmly in control of the corporation. Except in rare circumstances, the top executives were able to perpetuate themselves in office through the proxy mechanism. If an individual shareholder was not satisfied with the performance of the firm, there was little recourse other than to sell the stock. Hence, although the stockholder's legal position was that of an owner—and thus a principal-agent relationship existed between the stockholder and the managers—the stockholder's actual position was more akin to bondholders and other creditors of the firm. Given such a situation it was only natural to ask, "To whom is management responsible?" The "trusteeship" concept provided an answer. Management was responsible to all the contributors to the firm—that is, stockholders, workers, customers, suppliers, creditors, and the community.

The emergence of a largely pluralistic society reinforced the logic of the "trusteeship" concept. A pluralistic society has been defined as "one which has many semi-autonomous and autonomous groups through which power is diffused. No one group has overwhelming power over all others, and each has direct or indirect impact on all others. From the perspective of business firms this translated into the fact that exogenous groups had considerable impact upon and influence over them. In the 1930s the major groups exerting significant pressure on business were labor unions and the federal government. Today the list has grown to include numerous minority, environmental, and consumer groups among others. Clearly, one logical approach to such a situation is to consider that the firm has a responsibility to each interested group and that management's task is to reconcile and balance the claims of the various groups.

Phase III—Quality of Life Management

Phase III, which may be called the "quality of life" concept of social responsibility, has become popular in recent years. The primary reason for the emergence of this concept is the very significant metamorphosis in societal goals which this nation is experiencing. Up to the middle part of this century, society's principal goal was to raise the standard of living of the American people, which could be achieved by producing more goods and services. The fact that the U.S. had become the wealthiest nation in the world was testimony to the success of business in meeting this expectation.

In this process, however, the U.S. has become what John Kenneth Galbraith calls an "affluent society" in which the aggregate scarcity of basic goods and services is no longer the fundamental problem. Other social problems have developed as direct and indirect results of economic success. Thus, there are pockets of poverty in a nation of plenty, deteriorating cities, air and water pollution, defacement of the landscape, and a disregard for consumers to mention only a few of the prominent social problems. The mood of the country seems to be that things have gotten out of balance—the economic abundance in the midst of a declining social and physical environment does not make sense. As a result, a new set of national priorities which stress the "quality of life" appear to be emerging.

Concomitant with the new priorities, societal consensus seems to be demanding that business, with its technological and managerial skills and its financial resources, assume broader responsibilities—responsibilities that extend beyond the traditional economic realm of the Phase I concept or the mere balancing of the competing demands of the sundry contributors and pressure groups of the Phase II concept. The socially responsible firm under Phase III reasoning is one that becomes deeply involved in the solution of society's major problems.

Personal Values of the Three Styles of Managers

Values are the beliefs and attitudes which form one's frame of reference and help to determine the behavior which an individual displays. All managers have a set of values which affect their decisions, but the values are not the same for each manager; however, once values are ingrained in a manager, they do not change except over a period of time. It is possible to group these values into a general pattern of behavior which characterizes three styles of managers—the profit-maximizing style, the trusteeship style, and the "quality of life" style of management.

Phase I Managers

Phase I, profit-maximizing managers have a personal set of values which reflects their economic thinking. They believe that raw self-interest should prevail in society, and their values dictate that "What's good for me is good for my country." Therefore, Phase I managers rationalize that making as much profit as is possible would be good for society. They make every effort to become as efficient as possible and to make as much money as they can. To them money and wealth are the most important goals of their lives.

In the pursuit of maximum profit the actions of Phase I managers toward customers are reflected in a *caveat emptor* philosophy. "Let the buyer beware" characterizes decisions and actions in dealing with customers. They are not necessarily concerned with product quality or safety, or with sufficient and/or truthful information about products and services. A profit-maximizing manager's view toward employees can be stated as, "Labor is a commodity to be bought and sold in the marketplace." Thus, chief accountability lies with the owners of the business, and usually the Phase I manager is the owner or part owner of the organization.

To profit maximizers technology is very important. Machines and equipment rank high on their scale of values, therefore, materialism characterizes their philosophy.

Social values do not predominate the thinking of Phase I managers. In fact, they believe that employee problems should be left at home. Economics should be separate from societal or family concerns. A Phase I manager's leadership style is one of the rugged individualist—"I'm my own boss, and I'll manage my business as I please." Values about minority groups dictate that such groups are inferior, so they must be treated accordingly.

Political values are based on the doctrine of laissez faire. "That government is best which governs the least" characterizes the thinking of Phase I managers. As a result anything dealing with politicians and governments is foreign and distasteful to them.

Their beliefs about the environment can be stated, "The natural environment controls one's destiny; therefore, use it to protect your interests before it destroys you. Don't worry about the physical environment because there are plenty of natural resources which you can use."

Aesthetic values to the profit maximizer are minimal. In fact, Phase I managers would say, "Aesthetic values? What are they?" They have very little concern for the arts and cultural aspects of life. They hold musicians, artists, entertainers, and social scientists in low regard.

The values that a profit-maximizing manager holds were commonly accepted in the economic textbooks of the 1800s and early 1900s although they obviously did not apply to all managers of those times. It is easy to see how they conflict with the values of the other two styles of management.

Phase II Managers

Phase II, trusteeship managers have a somewhat different set of values. They recognize that self-interest plays a large role in their actions, but they also recognize the interests of those people who contribute to the organization—the customers, employees, suppliers, owners, creditors, government, and community. In other words, they operate with self-interest plus the interests of other groups. They believe that "What is good for my company is good for the country." They balance profits of the owners and the organization with wages for employees, taxes for the government, interest for the creditors, and so forth. Money is important to them but so are people, because their values tells them that satisfying people's needs is a better goal than just making money.

In balancing the needs of the various contributors to the organization, Phase II managers deal with customers as the chief providers of revenue to the firm. Their values tell them not to cheat the customers because cheating is not good for the firm.

They are concerned with providing sufficient quantities of goods as well as sufficient quality for customer satisfaction. They view employees as having certain rights which must be recognized and that employees are more than mere commodities to be traded in the marketplace. Their accountability as managers is to owners as well as to customers, employees, suppliers, creditors, government, and the community.

To the trusteeship-style manager, technology is important, but so are people. Innovation of technology is to be commended because new machines, equipment, and products are useful to people to create a high standard of living. Materialism is important, but so is humanism.

The social values held by trusteeship managers are more liberal than those held by profit maximizers. They recognize that employees have several needs beyond their economic needs. Employees have a desire for security and a sense of belonging as well as recognition. Phase II managers see themselves as individualists, but they also appreciate the value of group participation in managing the business. They view minority groups as having their place in society. But, a trusteeship manager would add: "Their place is usually inferior to mine; they are usually not qualified to hold their jobs but that's not my fault."

The political values of Phase II managers are reflected in recognizing that government and politics are important, but they view government and politics as necessary evils. They distrust both, recognizing that government serves as a threat to their existence if their firms do not live up to the laws passed since the 1930s.

The environmental beliefs of trusteeship managers are stated as follows: "People can control and manipulate their environment. Therefore, let them do it for their own benefit and incidentally for society's benefit."

Aesthetic values are all right to the trusteeship manager, but "they are not for our firm although someone has to support the arts and cultural values."

Phase III Managers

In contrast to profit maximizers and trustee managers, "quality of life" managers believe in enlightened self-interest. They agree that selfishness and group interests are important, but that society's interests are also important in making decisions. "What's good for society is good for our company" is their opinion. They agree that profit is essential for the firm, but that profit in and of itself is not the end objective of the firm. As far as money and wealth are concerned, their set of values tells them that money is important but people are more important than money.

In sharp contrast to *caveat emptor* in dealings with customers, the philosophy of Phase II managers is *caveat venditor*, that is, let the seller beware. The company should bear the responsibility for producing and distributing products and services in sufficient quantities at the right time and place with the necessary quality, information, and services necessary to satisfy customers' needs. Their views about employees are to recognize the dignity of each, not treating them as a commodity to be bought and sold. Their accountability as managers is to the owners, to the other contributors of the business, and to society in general.

Technological values are important but people are held in higher esteem than machines, equipment, computers, and esoteric products. A "quality of life" manager is a humanist rather than a materialist.

The social values of "quality of life" managers dictate that a person cannot be separated into an economic being or family being. Their philosophy is, "We hire the whole person including any problems that person might have." Phase III managers recognize that group participation rather than rugged individualism is a determining factor in an organization's success. Their values about minority groups are different from the other managers. Their view is that "A member of a minority group needs support and guidance like any other person."

The political values of "quality of life" managers dictate that government and politicians are necessary contributors to a quality of life. Rather than resisting government, they believe that business and government must cooperate to solve society's problems.

Their environmental beliefs are stated as, "A person must preserve the environment, not for the environment's sake alone, but for the benefit of people who want to lead a quality life."

As far as aesthetic values are concerned, Phase III managers recognize that the arts and cultural values reflect the lives of people whom they hold in high regard. Their actions support aesthetic values by committing resources to their preservation and presentation.

Milton Friedman   ➡ **NO**

The Social Responsibility of Business Is to Increase Its Profits

When I hear businessmen speak eloquently about the "social responsibilities of business in a free-enterprise system," I am reminded of the wonderful line about the Frenchman who discovered at the age of 70 that he had been speaking prose all his life. The businessmen believe that they are defending free enterprise when they declaim that business is not concerned "merely" with profit but also with promoting desirable "social ends; that business has a social conscience" and takes seriously its responsibilities for providing employment, eliminating discrimination, avoiding pollution and whatever else may be the catchwords of the contemporary crop of reformers. In fact they are— or would be if they or anyone else took them seriously—preaching pure and unadulterated socialism. Businessmen who talk this way are unwitting puppets of the intellectual forces that have been undermining the basis of a free society these past decades.

The discussions of the "social responsibilities of business" are notable for their analytical looseness and lack of rigor. What does it mean to say that "business" has responsibilities? Only people can have responsibilities. A corporation is an artificial person and in this sense may have artificial responsibilities, but "business" as a whole cannot be said to have responsibilities, even in this vague sense. The first step toward clarity in examining the doctrine of the social responsibility of business is to ask precisely what it implies for whom.

Presumably, the individuals who are to be responsible are businessmen, which means individual proprietors or corporate executives. Most of the discussion of social responsibility is directed at corporations, so in what follows I shall mostly neglect the individual proprietor and speak of corporate executives.

In a free-enterprise, private-property system, a corporate executive is an employee of the owners of the business. He has direct responsibility to his employers. That responsibility is to conduct the business in accordance with their desires, which generally will be to make as much money as possible while conforming to the basic rules of the society, both those embodied in law and those embodied in ethical custom. Of course, in some cases his employers may have a different objective. A group of persons might establish a corporation for an eleemosynary purpose—for example, a hospital or a school. The manager of such a corporation will not have money profit as his objective but the rendering of certain services.

In either case, the key point is that, in his capacity as a corporate executive, the manager is the agent of the individuals who own the corporation or establish the eleemosynary institution, and his primary responsibility is to them.

Needless to say, this does not mean that it is easy to judge how well he is performing his task. But at least the criterion of performance is straightforward, and the persons among whom a voluntary contractual arrangement exists are clearly defined.

Of course, the corporate executive is also a person in his own right. As a person, he may have many other responsibilities that he recognizes or assumes voluntarily—to his family, his conscience, his feelings of charity, his church, his clubs, his city, his country. He may feel impelled by these responsibilities to devote part of his income to causes he regards as worthy, to refuse to work for particular corporations, even to leave his job, for example, to join his country's armed forces. If we wish, we may refer to some of these responsibilities as "social responsibilities." But in these respects he is acting as a principal, not an agent; he is spending his own money or time or energy, not the money of his employers or the time or energy he has contracted to devote to their purposes. If these are "social responsibilities," they are the social responsibilities of individuals, not of business.

What does it mean to say that the corporate executive has a "social responsibility" in his capacity as businessman? If this statement is not pure rhetoric, it must mean that he is to act in some way that is not in the interest of his employers. For example, that he is to refrain from increasing the price of the product in order to contribute to the social objective of preventing inflation, even though a price increase would be in the best interests of the corporation. Or that he is to make expenditures on reducing pollution beyond the amount that is in the best interests of the corporation or that is required by law in order to contribute to the social objective of improving the environment. Or that, at the expense of corporate profits, he is to hire "hard-core" unemployed instead of better-qualified available workmen to contribute to the social objective of reducing poverty.

In each of these cases, the corporate executive would be spending someone else's money for a general social interest. Insofar as his actions in accord with his "social responsibility" reduce returns to stockholders, he is spending their money. Insofar as his actions raise the price to customers, he is spending the customers' money. Insofar as his actions lower the wages of some employees, he is spending their money.

The stockholders or the customers or the employees could separately spend their own money on the particular action if they wished to do so. The executive is exercising a distinct "social responsibility," rather than serving as an agent of the stockholders or the customers or the employees, only if he spends the money in a different way than they would have spent it.

But if he does this, he is in effect imposing taxes, on the one hand, and deciding how the tax proceeds shall be spent, on the other.

This process raises political questions on two levels: principle and consequences. On the level of political principle, the imposition of taxes and the expenditure of tax proceeds are governmental functions. We have established elaborate constitutional, parliamentary and judicial provisions to control these functions, to assure that taxes are imposed so far as possible in accordance with the preferences and desires of the public—after all, "taxation without representation" was one of the battle cries of the American Revolution. We have a system of checks and balances to separate the legislative function of imposing taxes and enacting expenditures from the executive function of collecting taxes and administering expenditure programs and from the judicial function of mediating disputes and interpreting the law.

Here the businessman—self-selected or appointed directly or indirectly by stockholders—is to be simultaneously legislator, executive and jurist. He is to decide whom to tax by how much and for what purpose, and he is to spend the proceeds—all this guided only by general exhortations from on high to restrain inflation, improve the environment, fight poverty and so on and on.

The whole justification for permitting the corporate executive to be selected by the stockholders is that the executive is an agent serving the interests of his principal. This justification disappears when the corporate executive imposes taxes and spends the proceeds for "social" purposes. He becomes in effect a public employee, a civil servant, even though he remains in name an employee of a private enterprise. On grounds of political principle, it is intolerable that such civil servants—insofar as their actions in the name of social responsibility are real and not just window-dressing—should be selected as they are now. If they are to be civil servants, then they must be selected through a political process. If they are to impose taxes and make expenditures to foster "social" objectives, then political machinery must be set up to guide the assessment of taxes and to determine through a political process the objectives to be served.

This is the basic reason why the doctrine of "social responsibility" involves the acceptance of the socialist view that political mechanisms, not market mechanisms, are the appropriate way to determine the allocation of scarce resources to alternative uses.

On the grounds of consequences, can the corporate executive in fact discharge his alleged "social responsibilities"? On the one hand, suppose he could get away with spending the stockholders' or customers' or employees' money. How is he to know how to spend it? He is told that he must contribute to fighting inflation. How is he to know what action of his will contribute to that end? He is presumably an expert in running his company—in producing a product or selling it or financing it. But nothing about his selection makes him an expert on inflation. Will his holding down the price of his product reduce inflationary pressure? Or, by leaving more spending power in the hands of his customers, simply divert it elsewhere? Or, by forcing him to produce less because of the lower price, will it simply contribute to shortages? Even if he could answer these questions, how much cost is he justified in imposing on his stockholders, customers and employees for this social purpose? What is the appropriate share and what is the appropriate share of others?

And, whether he wants to or not, can he get away with spending his stockholders', customers' or employees' money? Will not the stockholders fire him? (Either the present ones or those who take over when his actions in the name of social responsibility have reduced the corporation's profits and the price of its stock.) His customers and his employees can desert him for other producers and employers less scrupulous in exercising their social responsibilities.

This facet of "social responsibility" doctrine is brought into sharp relief when the doctrine is used to justify wage restraint by trade unions. The conflict of interest is naked and clear when union officials are asked to subordinate the interest of their members to some more general social purpose. If the union officials try to enforce wage restraint, the consequence is likely to be wildcat strikes, rank-and-file revolts and the emergence of strong competitors for their jobs. We thus have the ironic phenomenon that union leaders—at least in the U.S.—have objected to Government interference with the market far more consistently and courageously than have business leaders.

The difficulty of exercising "social responsibility" illustrates, of course, the great virtue of private competitive enterprise—it forces people to be responsible for their own actions and makes it difficult for them to "exploit" other people for either selfish or unselfish purposes. They can do good—but only at their own expense.

Many a reader who has followed the argument this far may be tempted to remonstrate that it is all well and good to speak of government's having the responsibility to impose taxes and determine expenditures for such "social" purposes as controlling pollution or training the hard-core unemployed, but that the problems are too urgent to wait on the slow course of political processes, that the exercise of social responsibility by businessmen is a quicker and surer way to solve pressing current problems.

Aside from the question of fact—I share Adam Smith's skepticism about the benefits that can be expected from "those who affected to trade for the public good"—this argument must be rejected on grounds of principle. What it amounts to is an assertion that those who favor the taxes and expenditures in question have failed to persuade a majority of their fellow citizens to be of like mind and that they are seeking to attain by undemocratic procedures what they cannot attain by democratic procedures. In a free society, it is hard for "good" people to do "good," but that is a small price to pay for making it hard for "evil" people to do "evil," especially since one man's good is another's evil.

I have, for simplicity, concentrated on the special case of the corporate executive, except only for the brief digression on trade unions. But precisely the same argument applies to the newer phenomenon of calling upon stockholders to require corporations to exercise social responsibility (the recent G.M. crusade, for example). In most of these cases, what is in effect involved is some stockholders trying to get other stockholders (or customers or employees) to contribute against their will to "social" causes favored by the activists. Insofar as they succeed, they are again imposing taxes and spending the proceeds.

The situation of the individual proprietor is somewhat different. If he acts to reduce the returns of his enterprise in order to exercise his "social responsibility," he is spending his own money, not someone else's. If he wishes to spend his money on such purposes, that is his right, and I cannot see that there is any objection to his doing so. In the process, he, too, may impose costs on employees and customers. However, because he is far less likely than a large corporation or union to have monopolistic power, any such side effects will tend to be minor.

Of course, in practice the doctrine of social responsibility is frequently a cloak for actions that are justified on other grounds rather than a reason for those actions.

To illustrate, it may well be in the long-run interest of a corporation that is a major employer in a small community to devote resources to providing amenities to that community or to improving its government. That may make it easier to attract desirable employees, it may reduce the wage bill or lessen losses from pilferage and sabotage or have other worthwhile effects. Or it may be that, given the laws about the deductibility of corporate charitable contributions, the stockholders can contribute more to charities they favor by having the corporation make the gift than by doing it themselves, since they can in that way contribute an amount that would otherwise have been paid as corporate taxes.

In each of these—and many similar—cases, there is a strong temptation to rationalize these actions as an exercise of "social responsibility." In the present climate of opinion, with its widespread aversion to "capitalism," "profits," the "soulless corporation" and so on, this is one way for a corporation to generate goodwill as a by-product of expenditures that are entirely justified in its own self-interest.

It would be inconsistent of me to call on corporate executives to refrain from this hypocritical window-dressing because it harms the foundations of a free society. That would be to call on them to exercise a "social responsibility"! If our institutions, and the attitudes of the public, make it in their self-interest to cloak their actions in this way, I cannot summon much indignation to denounce them. At the same time, I can express admiration for those individual proprietors or owners of closely held corporations or stockholders of more broadly held corporations who disdain such tactics as approaching fraud.

Whether blameworthy or not, the use of the cloak of social responsibility, and the nonsense spoken in its name by influential and prestigious businessmen, does clearly harm the foundations of a free society. I have been impressed time and again by the schizophrenic character of many businessmen. They are capable of being extremely far-sighted and clear-headed in matters that are internal to their businesses. They are incredibly short-sighted and muddleheaded in matters that are outside their businesses but affect the possible survival of business in general. This short-sightedness is strikingly exemplified in the calls from many businessmen for wage and price guidelines or controls or income policies. There is nothing that could do more in a brief period to destroy a market system and replace it by a centrally controlled system than effective governmental control of prices and wages.

The short-sightedness is also exemplified in speeches by businessmen on social responsibility. This may gain them kudos in the short run. But it helps to strengthen the already too prevalent view that the pursuit of profits is wicked and immoral and must be curbed and controlled by external forces. Once this view is adopted, the external forces that curb the market will not be the social consciences, however highly developed, of the pontificating executives; it will be the iron fist of Government bureaucrats. Here, as with price and wage controls, businessmen seem to me to reveal a suicidal impulse.

The political principle that underlies the market mechanism is unanimity. In an ideal free market resting on private property, no individual can coerce any other, all cooperation is voluntary, all parties to such cooperation benefit or they need not participate. There are no "social" values, no "social" responsibilities in any sense other than the shared values and responsibilities of individuals. Society is a collection of individuals and of the various groups they voluntarily form.

The political principle that underlies the political mechanism is conformity. The individual must serve a more general social interest—whether that be determined by a church or a dictator or a majority. The individual may have a vote and a say in what is to be done, but if he is overruled, he must conform. It is appropriate for some to require others to contribute to a general social purpose whether they wish to or not.

Unfortunately, unanimity is not always feasible. There are some respects in which conformity appears unavoidable, so I do not see how one can avoid the use of the political mechanism altogether.

But the doctrine of "social responsibility" taken seriously would extend the scope of the political mechanism to every human activity. It does not differ in philosophy from the most explicitly collectivist doctrine. It differs only by professing to believe that collectivist ends can be attained without collectivist means. That is why, in my book "Capitalism and Freedom," I have called it a "fundamentally subversive doctrine" in a free society, and have said that in such a society, "there is one and only one social responsibility of business—to use its resources and engage in activities designed to increase its profi ts so long as it stays within the rules of the game, which is to say, engages in open and free competition without deception or fraud."

POSTSCRIPT

Do Corporations Have a Responsibility to Society Beyond Maximizing Profit?

Advocates of the shareholder approach generally believe that free-market capitalism is the best mechanism for addressing social problems. They argue that the free market, guided by Adam Smith's invisible hand and based on the view that organizations exist to maximize shareholder wealth, will provide the necessary incentives for solving problems society considers important. Some organization somewhere, driven to maximize shareholder wealth, will provide a solution and reap its just rewards. In this view, all parties involved are better off when the company concerns itself with trying to make as much money as it can for its shareholders and does not distract itself with the claims of other groups with which it interacts. Critics point out that this scenario fails to take into account the issue of time. Consider a situation where a community has a pollution problem that, for whatever reason, cannot be solved by current pollution-control technology. Free-market advocates would argue that someone will invent the necessary technology because doing so will result in large financial gains. Maybe so, say the critics. But what if it takes 10 years for the technology to be developed? What happens to the community in the meantime? The point is that situations occur where the time lag between the onset of a problem and its free-market solution can be so long as to be problematic. And, when considered from the context of the growing concerns over global warming, this criticism seems particularly salient.

As you have just seen, Milton Friedman takes no prisoners in his direct attack on the stakeholder theory's justification for CSR. Regardless of whether you found his arguments convincing or not, the fact is that trouble can result if corporations become too involved in the concerns of their stakeholders. One obvious problem is the potential for conflicts of interest: Managers may see fit to play one group of stakeholders off against another. And, of course, such situations are ripe for unscrupulous behavior on the part of all parties involved. Another problem concerns the concentration of power that could result. Consider, for example, that many people already fear WalMart wields too much economic power in our society. Indeed, in the Pew survey noted in the introduction to this debate, almost four in five respondents (78%) indicated that "too much power [was in] the hands of large corporations" (http://people-press.org/report/?pageid=1400).

We conclude, then, that both sides of this debate have powerful arguments to draw on. Where do you stand on this issue? Should the only purpose of an organization be to maximize profit, or do other stakeholders have a legitimate claim to the fruits of the organizations' success?

Suggested Readings

Paul Driessen, The social responsibility of profit. http://www.eco-imperialism
.com/content/article.php3?id=242

David Henderson, The case against corporate social responsibility. *Policy,*
Winter 2001, Vol. 17, No. 2. The Center for Independent Studies.
http://www.cis.org.au/policy/winter01/polwin01-6.pdf

David Cavett-Goodwin, Making the case for social responsibility. *Cultural
Shifts,* December 2007. http://culturalshifts.com/archives/181

R. Edward Freeman, Fixing the ethics crisis in corporate America. *Miller
Center Report;* Fall 2002

Laura P. Hartman, *Perspectives in business ethics,* 3rd ed. (McGraw-Hill,
2007)

ISSUE 2

Is it Immoral for U.S. Corporations to Use Cheap Overseas Labor?

YES: *BusinessWeek,* from "Secrets, Lies, and Sweatshop" (November 27, 2006), http://www.businessweek.com/print/magazine/content/06_48/b4011001.htm?chan=gl

NO: Daniel Griswold, from "Overseas Sweatshop Abuses, Their Impact on U.S. Workers, and the Need for Anti-Sweatshop Legislation," Testimony before the Senate Commerce, Science, and Transportation Committee, Trade, Tourism, and Economic Development Subcommittee (February 14, 2007)

ISSUE SUMMARY

YES: *BusinessWeek* argues that many U.S. corporations have been guilty of negligence in monitoring and controlling the quality of working conditions in their overseas sweatshop operations, resulting in continued abuse and exploitation of workers.

NO: In testimony to a U.S. Senate subcommittee, Daniel Griswold, an expert scholar in labor issues for the Cato Institute, argues that anti-sweatshop legislation is unwise and contrary to the interests of both U.S. corporations and the citizens of the host countries.

$\mathbf{I}$n March of 2006, the National Labor Committee commissioned a Harris Poll to ascertain American attitudes toward various labor-related issues. Of particular interest was the finding that 75 percent of respondents agreed with the statement, "I want my Member of Congress to support legislation to protect human rights in the global economy by prohibiting the import or sale of sweatshop goods in the U.S. which were made under conditions violating internationally recognized worker rights standards" (http://www.nlcnet.org/article.php?id=75). In fact, the results of this poll were instrumental in the subsequent development of a bill currently on Capitol Hill. Although this bill, introduced in 2007 and known as the Decent Working Conditions and Fair Competition Act, has not as yet been turned into law, it does have the support of President Obama (Michigan Messenger, Feb. 15, 2008). His support coupled with a favorable public opinion virtually guarantee that the issue of whether U.S. corporations should be allowed to use cheap overseas labor will remain newsworthy for the foreseeable future.

Historically, the expression "sweatshop" is usually linked with the tremendous industrial growth of the American economy during the mid-nineteenth century. Originally associated with the apparel and garment industries, the use of the term eventually grew to describe any factory position in which employees—frequently, women and children—worked excessively long hours, often in unsanitary or unsafe working conditions, for barely subsistence-level wages. The massive influx of immigrants into the country during this time period resulted in low wage rates and provided corporations with little incentive to improve working conditions in their plants and factories. Social commentators and union activists at the turn of the century argued that sweatshops were exploitative and called for their abolition. Their efforts resulted in a series of successful labor strikes and legislative actions that helped to dramatically improve worker conditions in the United States.

In their current manifestation, sweatshops are portrayed as an inevitable outcome of economic globalization (see Issue 17 in this text for more on the subject of globalization) (National Labor Committee, 2006). Critics of globalization argue that sweatshops are inherently exploitative because multinational corporations take advantage of the low wages and poor working conditions characteristic of Third World countries. The developing countries must compete with each other to attract foreign firms; they do this by decreasing their labor standards. Thus, according to critics of globalization, multinational firms use the poverty and desperation of the developing countries to their advantage. Critics also point out that it is not just the workers in the sweatshops that are exploited—jobs in western countries are lost when firms decide to locate their operations overseas to take advantage of the low labor costs.

Many proponents of globalization note that most anti-sweatshop efforts actually hurt the very people they intend to help. Workers in developing countries usually have no other alternatives. Sweatshops represent the best of a bad situation. Shutting down sweatshops takes money out of their hands and sends the workers onto the street where, in many instances, they starve to death or turn to illegal activities, such as prostitution, to survive (Thomas DiLorenzo, "How 'sweatshops' help the poor," Ludwig von Mises Institute, http://www.mises.org, November 9, 2006). Proponents of globalization also note that virtually every industrialized First World economy capitalized on cheap labor early in its economic development. Consider that the rapid growth of Hong Kong and Singapore over the last quarter of the twentieth century was due in large measure to their willingness to use their comparative advantage of cheap labor early in their economic development.

The following selections are concerned with U.S. corporations employing cheap overseas labor. The first is from a special online issue of *BusinessWeek* and argues that many U.S. corporations have been guilty of negligence in monitoring and controlling the quality of working conditions in their overseas sweatshop operations. The result is continued abuse and exploitation of overseas workers by U.S. firms. In the second selection, we present Daniel Griswold's testimony to a U.S. Senate subcommittee considering anti-sweatshop legislation. Griswold covers much ground in arguing that anti-sweatshop legislation is unwise and contrary to the interests of both U.S. corporations and the citizens of the countries providing the cheap labor.

Secrets, Lies, and Sweatshops

Tang Yinghong was caught in an impossible squeeze. For years, his employer, Ningbo Beifa Group, had prospered as a top supplier of pens, mechanical pencils, and highlighters to Wal-Mart Stores (**WMT**) and other major retailers. But late last year, Tang learned that auditors from Wal-Mart, Beifa's biggest customer, were about to inspect labor conditions at the factory in the Chinese coastal city of Ningbo where he worked as an administrator. Wal-Mart had already on three occasions caught Beifa paying its 3,000 workers less than China's minimum wage and violating overtime rules, Tang says. Under the U.S. chain's labor rules, a fourth offense would end the relationship.

Help arrived suddenly in the form of an unexpected phone call from a man calling himself Lai Mingwei. The caller said he was with Shanghai Corporate Responsibility Management & Consulting Co., and for a $5,000 fee, he'd take care of Tang's Wal-Mart problem. "He promised us he could definitely get us a pass for the audit," Tang says.

Lai provided advice on how to create fake but authentic-looking records and suggested that Beifa hustle any workers with grievances out of the factory on the day of the audit, Tang recounts. The consultant also coached Beifa managers on what questions they could expect from Wal-Mart's inspectors, says Tang. After following much of Lai's advice, the Beifa factory in Ningbo passed the audit earlier this year, Tang says, even though the company didn't change any of its practices.

For more than a decade, major American retailers and name brands have answered accusations that they exploit "sweatshop" labor with elaborate codes of conduct and on-site monitoring. But in China many factories have just gotten better at concealing abuses. Internal industry documents reviewed by *BusinessWeek* reveal that numerous Chinese factories keep double sets of books to fool auditors and distribute scripts for employees to recite if they are questioned. And a new breed of Chinese consultant has sprung up to assist companies like Beifa in evading audits. "Tutoring and helping factories deal with audits has become an industry in China," says Tang, 34, who recently left Beifa of his own volition to start a Web site for workers.

A lawyer for Beifa, Zhou Jie, confirms that the company employed the Shanghai consulting firm but denies any dishonesty related to wages, hours, or outside monitoring. Past audits had "disclosed some problems, and we took necessary measures correspondingly," he explains in a letter responding to questions. The lawyer adds that Beifa has "become the target of accusations" by former employees "whose unreasonable demands have not been satisfied." Reached by cell phone, a man identifying himself as Lai says that the Shanghai consulting firm helps suppliers pass audits, but he declines to comment on his work for Beifa.

Wal-Mart spokeswoman Amy Wyatt says the giant retailer will investigate the allegations about Beifa brought to its attention by *BusinessWeek*. Wal-Mart has stepped up factory inspections, she adds, but it acknowledges that some suppliers are trying to undermine monitoring: "We recognize there is a problem. There are always improvements that need to be made, but we are confident that new procedures are improving conditions."

CHINESE EXPORT manufacturing is rife with tales of deception. The largest single source of American imports, China's factories this year are expected to ship goods to the U.S. worth $280 billion. American companies continually demand lower prices from their Chinese suppliers, allowing American consumers to enjoy inexpensive clothes, sneakers, and electronics. But factory managers in China complain in interviews that U.S. price pressure creates a powerful incentive to cheat on labor standards that American companies promote as a badge of responsible capitalism. These standards generally incorporate the official minimum wage, which is set by local or provincial governments and ranges from $45 to $101 a month. American companies also typically say they hew to the government-mandated workweek of 40 to 44 hours, beyond which higher overtime pay is required. These figures can be misleading, however, as the Beijing government has had only limited success in pushing local authorities to enforce Chinese labor laws. That's another reason abuses persist and factory oversight frequently fails.

Some American companies now concede that the cheating is far more pervasive than they had imagined. "We've come to realize that, while monitoring is crucial to measuring the performance of our suppliers, it doesn't per se lead to sustainable improvements," says Hannah Jones, Nike Inc.'s (NKE) vice-president for corporate responsibility. "We still have the same core problems."

This raises disturbing questions. Guarantees by multi-nationals that offshore suppliers are meeting widely accepted codes of conduct have been important to maintaining political support in the U.S. for growing trade ties with China, especially in the wake of protests by unions and antiglobalization activists. "For many retailers, audits are a way of covering themselves," says Auret van Heerden, chief executive of the Fair Labor Assn., a coalition of 20 apparel and sporting goods makers and retailers, including Nike, Adidas Group, Eddie Bauer, and Nordstrom (JWN). But can corporations successfully impose Western labor standards on a nation that lacks real unions and a meaningful rule of law?

Historically associated with sweatshop abuses but now trying to reform its suppliers, Nike says that one factory it caught falsifying records several years ago is the Zhi Qiao Garments Co. The dingy concrete-walled facility set near mango groves and rice paddies in the steamy southern city of Panyu employs 600 workers, most in their early 20s. They wear blue smocks and lean over stitching machines and large steam-blasting irons. Today the factory complies with labor-law requirements, Nike says, but Zhi Qiao's general manager, Peter

Wang, says it's not easy. "Before, we all played the cat-and-mouse game," but that has ended, he claims. "Any improvement you make costs more money." Providing for overtime wages is his biggest challenge, he says. By law, he is supposed to provide time-and-a-half pay after eight hours on weekdays and between double and triple pay for Saturdays, Sundays, and holidays. "The price [Nike pays] never increases one penny," Wang complains, "but compliance with labor codes definitely raises costs."

A Nike spokesman says in a written statement that the company, based in Beaverton, Ore., "believes wages are best set by the local marketplace in which a contract factory competes for its workforce." One way Nike and several other companies are seeking to improve labor conditions is teaching their suppliers more efficient production methods that reduce the need for overtime.

The problems in China aren't limited to garment factories, where labor activists have documented sweatshop conditions since the early 1990s. Widespread violations of Chinese labor laws are also surfacing in factories supplying everything from furniture and household appliances to electronics and computers. Hewlett-Packard (**HPQ**), Dell (**DELL**), and other companies that rely heavily on contractors in China to supply notebook PCs, digital cameras, and handheld devices have formed an industry alliance to combat the abuses.

A compliance manager for a major multinational company who has overseen many factory audits says that the percentage of Chinese suppliers caught submitting false payroll records has risen from 46% to 75% in the past four years. This manager, who requested anonymity, estimates that only 20% of Chinese suppliers comply with wage rules, while just 5% obey hour limitations.

A RECENT VISIT by the compliance manager to a toy manufacturer in Shenzhen illustrated the crude ways that some suppliers conceal mistreatment. The manager recalls smelling strong paint fumes in the poorly ventilated and aging factory building. Young women employees were hunched over die-injection molds, using spray guns to paint storybook figurines. The compliance manager discovered a second workshop behind a locked door that a factory official initially refused to open but eventually did. In the back room, a young woman, who appeared to be under the legal working age of 16, tried to hide behind her co-workers on the production line, the visiting compliance manager says. The Chinese factory official admitted he was violating various work rules.

The situation in China is hard to keep in perspective. For all the shortcomings in factory conditions and oversight, even some critics say that workers' circumstances are improving overall. However compromised, pressure from multinationals has curbed some of the most egregious abuses by outside suppliers. Factories owned directly by such corporations as Motorola Inc. (**MOT**) and General Electric Co. (**GE**) generally haven't been accused of mistreating their employees. And a booming economy and tightening labor supply in China have emboldened workers in some areas to demand better wages, frequently with success. Even so, many Chinese laborers, especially migrants from poor rural regions, still seek to work as many hours as possible, regardless of whether they are properly paid.

In this shifting, often murky environment, labor auditing has mush-roomed into a multimillion-dollar industry. Internal corporate investigators and such global auditing agencies as Cal Safety Compliance, sgs of Switzerland, and Bureau Veritas of France operate a convoluted and uncoordinated over-sight system. They follow varying corporate codes of conduct, resulting in some big Chinese factories having to post seven or eight different sets of rules. Some factories receive almost daily visits from inspection teams demanding payroll and production records, facility tours, and interviews with managers and workers. "McDonald's (**MCD**), Walt Disney (**DIS**), and Wal-Mart are doing thousands of audits a year that are not harmonized," says van Heerden of Fair Labor. Among factory managers, "audit fatigue sets in," he says.

Some companies that thought they were making dramatic progress are discovering otherwise. A study commissioned by Nike last year covered 569 factories it uses in China and around the world that employ more than 300,000 workers. It found labor-code violations in every single one. Some factories "hide their work practices by maintaining two or even three sets of books," by coaching workers to "mislead auditors about their work hours, and by sending portions of production to unauthorized contractors where we have no oversight," the Nike study found.

THE FAIR LABOR ASSN. released its own study last November based on unannounced audits of 88 of its members' supplier factories in 18 countries. It found an average of 18 violations per factory, including excessive hours, under-payment of wages, health and safety problems, and worker harassment. The actual violation rate is probably higher, the FLA said, because "factory person-nel have become sophisticated in concealing noncompliance related to wages. They often hide original documents and show monitors falsified books."

While recently auditing an apparel manufacturer in Dongguan that sup-plies American importers, the corporate compliance manager says he discussed wage levels with the factory's Hong Kong-based owner. The 2,000 employees who operate sewing and stitching machines in the multi-story complex often put in overtime but earn an average of only $125 a month, an amount the owner grudgingly acknowledged to the compliance manager doesn't meet Chi-nese overtime-pay requirements or corporate labor codes. "These goals are a fantasy," the owner said. "Maybe in two or three decades we can meet them."

Pinning down what Chinese production workers are paid can be tricky. Based on Chinese government figures, the average manufacturing wage in China is 64 cents an hour, according to the U.S. Bureau of Labor Statistics and demographer Judith Banister of Javelin Investments, a consulting firm in Bei-jing. That rate assumes a 40-hour week. In fact, 60- to 100-hour weeks are com-mon in China, meaning that the real manufacturing wage is far less. Based on his own calculations from plant inspections, the veteran compliance manager estimates that employees at garment, electronics, and other export factories typically work more than 80 hours a week and make only 42 cents an hour.

BusinessWeek reviewed summaries of 28 recent industry audits of Chinese factories serving U.S. customers. A few factories supplying Black & Decker (**BDK**), Williams-Sonoma, and other well-known brands turned up clean, the summaries show. But these facilities were the exceptions.

At most of the factories, auditors discovered records apparently meant to falsify payrolls and time sheets. One typical report concerns Zhongshan Tat Shing Toys Factory, which employs 650 people in the southern city of Zhongshan. The factory's main customers are Wal-Mart and Target (**TGT**). When an American-sponsored inspection team showed up this spring, factory managers produced time sheets showing each worker put in eight hours a day, Monday through Friday, and was paid double the local minimum wage of 43 cents per hour for eight hours on Saturday, according to an audit report.

But when auditors interviewed workers in one section, some said that they were paid less than the minimum wage and that most of them were obliged to work an extra three to five hours a day, without overtime pay, the report shows. Most toiled an entire month without a day off. Workers told auditors that the factory had a different set of records showing actual overtime hours, the report says. Factory officials claimed that some of the papers had been destroyed by fire.

Wal-Mart's Wyatt doesn't dispute the discrepancies but stresses that the company is getting more aggressive overall in its monitoring. Wal-Mart says it does more audits than any other company—13,600 reviews of 7,200 factories last year alone—and permanently banned 141 factories in 2005 as a result of serious infractions, such as using child labor. In a written statement, Target doesn't respond to the allegations but says that it "takes very seriously" the fair treatment of factory workers. It adds that it "is committed to taking corrective action—up to and including termination of the relationship for vendors" that violate local labor law or Target's code of conduct. The Zhongshan factory didn't respond to repeated requests for comment.

An audit late last year of Young Sun Lighting Co., a maker of lamps for Home Depot (**HD**), Sears (**SHLD**), and other retailers, highlighted similar inconsistencies. Every employee was on the job five days a week from 8 a.m. to 5:30 p.m., with a lunch break and no overtime hours, according to interviews with managers, as well as time sheets and payroll records provided by the 300-worker factory in Dongguan, an industrial city in Guangdong Province. But other records auditors found at the site and elsewhere—backed up by auditor interviews with workers—revealed that laborers worked an extra three to five hours a day with only one or two days a month off during peak production periods. Workers said they received overtime pay, but the "auditor strongly felt that these workers were coached," the audit report states.

Young Sun denies ever violating the rules set by its Western customers. In written answers to questions, the lighting manufacturer says that it doesn't coach employees on how to respond to auditors and that "at present, there are no" workers who are putting in three to five extra hours a day and getting only one or two days off each month. Young Sun says that it follows all local Chinese overtime rules.

Home Depot doesn't contest the inconsistencies in the audit reports about Young Sun and three other factories in China. "There is no perfect factory, I can guarantee you," a company spokeswoman says. Instead of cutting off wayward suppliers, Home Depot says that it works with factories on corrective actions. If the retailer becomes aware of severe offenses, such as the use of child labor, it terminates the supplier. A Sears spokesman declined to comment.

Coaching of workers and midlevel managers to mislead auditors is widespread, the auditing reports and *BusinessWeek* interviews show. A document obtained last year during an inspection at one Chinese fabric export factory in the southern city of Guangzhou instructed administrators to take these actions when faced with a surprise audit: "First notify underage trainees, underage full-time workers, and workers without identification to leave the manufacturing workshop through the back door. Order them not to loiter near the dormitory area. Secondly, immediately order the receptionist to gather all relevant documents and papers." Other pointers include instructing all workers to put on necessary protective equipment such as earplugs and face masks.

SOME U.S. RETAILERS SAY this evidence isn't representative and that their auditing efforts are working. *BusinessWeek* asked J.C. Penney Co. (**JCP**) about audit reports included among those the magazine reviewed that appear to show falsification of records to hide overtime and pay violations at two factories serving the large retailer. Penney spokeswoman Darcie M. Brossart says the company immediately investigated the factories, and its "auditors observed no evidence of any legal compliance issues."

In any case, the two factories are too small to be seen as typical, Penney executives argue. The chain has been consolidating its China supply base and says that 80% of its imports now come from factories with several thousand workers apiece, which are managed by large Hong Kong trading companies that employ their own auditors. Quality inspectors for Penney and other buyers are at their supplier sites constantly, so overtime violations are hard to hide, Brossart says.

Chinese factory officials say, however, that just because infractions are difficult to discern doesn't mean they're not occurring. "It's a challenge for us to meet these codes of conduct," says Ron Chang, the Taiwanese general manager of Nike supplier Shoetown Footwear Co., which employs 15,000 workers in Qingyuan, Guangdong. Given the fierce competition in China for foreign production work, "we can't ask Nike to increase our price," he says, so "how can we afford to pay the higher salary?" By reducing profit margins from 30% to 5% over the past 18 years, Shoetown has managed to stay in business and obey Nike's rules, he says.

But squeezing margins doesn't solve the larger social issue. Chang says he regularly loses skilled employees to rival factories that break the rules because many workers are eager to put in longer hours than he offers, regardless of whether they get paid overtime rates. Ultimately, the economics of global outsourcing may trump any system of oversight that Western companies attempt. And these harsh economic realities could make it exceedingly difficult to achieve both the low prices and the humane working conditions that U.S. consumers have been promised.

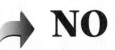 **NO**

Overseas Sweatshop Abuses, Their Impact on U.S. Workers, and the Need for Anti-Sweatshop Legislation

Mr. Chairman and members of the subcommittee, thank you for inviting the Cato Institute to testify today at this hearing on U.S. trade policy and global labor standards. My name is Dan Griswold, and I am director of the institute's Center for Trade Policy Studies.

The Cato Institute is a non-profit, non-partisan, voluntarily funded education institution. Through research and public events, we have worked for three decades now to broaden the parameters of public policy debate to allow consideration of the traditional American principles of limited government, individual liberty, free markets and peace among nations.

The constituents you represent have no reason to fear America's growing trade with people around the world, including trade with workers in developing countries. Expanding trade with developing countries not only promotes more U.S. exports, but just as importantly it provides a wider array of affordable products for American consumers—such as shoes, clothing, toys, and sporting goods. Tens of millions of American families benefit from more vigorous price competition in goods that make our lives better everyday at home and the office. Lower prices and more choice translate directly into higher real compensation and living standards for American workers.

There Is No 'Race to the Bottom'

American workers are not pitted in zero-sum competition with workers in poor countries. There is no global "race to the bottom" on labor standards. Through specialization, global incomes and working conditions can rise for workers in all countries that participate in the global economy. American workers can compete profitably in world markets because we are so much more productive. Because of our education, infrastructure, efficient domestic markets, the rule of law, political stability, and a generally open economy, American workers compete and prosper in a broad range of sectors. As our country has become more globalized in the past 25 years, American workers and their families have enjoyed significant increases in real incomes, compensation, and wealth.

U.S. Senate, February 14, 2007.

Nor has trade with developing countries undermined America's manufacturing base. According to the latest figures from the Federal Reserve Board, the output of America's factories in 2006 was more than 50 percent higher than in the early 1990s before NAFTA and the World Trade Organization came into being. American factories are producing more aircraft and pharmaceuticals, more sophisticated machinery and semiconductors, more chemicals and even more passenger vehicles and parts than 15 years ago. It is true that output of clothing, shoes and other low-tech goods has been declining, but those are not the industries of the future for the world's most sophisticated economy. U.S. factories can produce more with fewer workers because manufacturing productivity has been growing so rapidly.

If there were a "race to the bottom," then the lower wages and labor standards in less developed countries should be attracting large shares of global investment. Of course, developing countries attract foreign investment in those sectors in which they enjoy a comparative advantage, such as light manufacturing, but in fact, the large majority of manufacturing foreign direct investment (FDI) flows between rich countries.

When U.S. multinational companies look to invest abroad, their primary motivation is not a search for low wages and low standards. Far more important than lower costs are access to wealthy consumers, a skilled workforce, modern infrastructure, rule of law, political stability, and freedom to trade and repatriate profits. That is why most outward U.S. FDI flows to other high-income, high standard countries. Between 2003 and 2005, more than 80 percent of U.S. direct manufacturing abroad flowed to the European Union, Canada, Japan, South Korea, Taiwan, and Singapore.

Openness to trade and investment leads to faster growth, which leads to higher wages and labor standards, including so-called core worker rights. That is why the world's most developed economies, which account for most of the world's trade and attract most of its foreign direct investment, also pay the highest wages, and maintain the highest labor standards related to freedom of association, discrimination, forced labor, and child labor.

Trade and Globalization Are Raising Labor Standards in Developing Countries

Trade and globalization are lifting wages and working conditions for hundreds of millions of people in developing countries. The pay and conditions offered in foreign-owned factories are almost always far higher than those offered in the domestic economy. In fact, working for multinational companies that export are almost invariably the best jobs available in poor countries. Those jobs offer poor workers, especially young women, their best opportunity at financial independence and the simple pleasures and dignities of life we take for granted.

For example, apparel jobs are among the lowest paying manufacturing jobs in our country, but they are among the best paying in poor countries. A recent study from San Jose University found that the apparel industry actually pays its foreign workers well enough for them to rise above the poverty line in the countries where they invest. In Honduras, for example, where college protestors have targeted its alleged "sweatshops," the average apparel worker earns $13 per day, compared to the $2 a day or less earned by 44 percent of the country's population.

Rising levels of global trade have lifted hundreds of millions of people out of the worst kind of poverty and working conditions. According to the World Bank, the share of the world's population living in absolute poverty, defined as an income equivalent to one U.S. dollar per day or less, has been cut in half since 1981, from 40.4 percent to 19.4 percent. Poverty has fallen the most rapidly in those areas of the world that have globalized the most rapidly, especially China. It has fallen the least or actually increased in those regions that are the least touched by globalization, in particular sub-Saharan Africa.

Openness to trade and the growth it brings exert a positive impact on the welfare of children in less developed countries by reducing rates of child labor. The International Labor Organization recently reported that the number of children in the workforce rather than in school worldwide has dropped by 11 percent since its last report in 2002, to about 200 million. The number working in the most hazardous jobs has dropped even more steeply, by 26 percent.

Globalization is a major reason for the positive trend in child labor. As household incomes rise in developing countries, especially wages paid to adult females, fewer families face the economic necessity of sending their children to work. Studies confirm that labor force participation rates by children aged 10 to 14 decline significantly with rising GNP per capita.

The overwhelming majority of child laborers toiling in poor countries work in sectors far removed from the global economy. More than 80 percent work without pay, usually for their parents or other family members and typically in subsistence farming. Most other child laborers work for small-scale domestic enterprises, typically non-traded services such as shoe shining, newspaper delivery, and domestic service. A report by the U.S. Department of Labor found, "Only a very small percentage of all child workers, probably less than five percent, are employed in export industries in manufacturing and mining. And they are not commonly found in large enterprises; but rather in small and medium-sized firms and in neighborhood and home settings."

Parents in poor countries do not love their children any less than we love our own. When they succeed in rising above a subsistence income, the first thing they typically do is remove their children from working on the farm, domestic service, or factory and enroll them in school. By raising incomes in poor countries, free trade and globalization have helped to pull millions of kids out of the workforce and put them in school where they belong.

In Central America, trade liberalization and other reforms of the past two decades have spurred not only growth in incomes but also measurable social progress. According to the World Bank, literacy rates for men and women 15 and older have risen significantly in every one of the six DR-CAFTA countries since 1980. In fact, between 1980 and 2001, the average literacy rate in the region has increased from 67 percent to above 80 percent. At the same time, the percentage of children aged 10 to 14 who are in the workforce has been steadily declining in all six countries. The average share of children in the labor force across the six countries has dropped from 17.4 percent in 1980 to 10.0 percent in 2002. Expanding trade with the United States will likely accelerate those positive trends.

It is certainly true that working conditions in less developed countries can strike Western observers as unacceptable if not appalling. But two points need to be considered. First, wages and working conditions are likely to be even worse in non-trade-oriented sectors, such as services and subsistence agriculture, sectors that have been largely untouched by globalization. Second, poor working conditions in those countries are not a new development but have always been a chronic fact of life. "Sweatshop" conditions persist today not because of globalization, a relatively new phenomenon, but because of previous decades of protectionism, inflation, economic mismanagement, hostility to foreign investment, and a lack of legally defined property rights. Globalization is not the cause of bad working conditions but the best hope for improving them.

Punitive Tariffs Aimed at Sweatshops Will Only Hurt the People We Are Trying to Help

Perversely, withholding trade benefits because of allegedly low standards would in effect punish those countries for being poor. It would deprive them of the expanded market access that offers the best hope to raise incomes and standards. The use of trade sanctions would target the very export industries that typically pay the highest wages and maintain highest standards in those countries.

The effect of sanctions would be to shrink the more globally integrated sectors that are pulling standards upwards, forcing workers into informal, domestic sectors where wages, working conditions, and labor-rights protections are much lower. Lower wages paid to parents would make it more difficult for families on marginal incomes to keep children in school and out of fields or factories. "Tough" sanctions to allegedly enforce higher standards would be tough only on the poorest people in the world.

Demanding that poor countries eliminate child labor under threat of trade sanctions can easily backfire. In 1993, Congress seemed poised to pass the U.S. Child Labor Deterrence Act, which would have banned imports of textiles made by child workers. Anticipating its passage, the Bangladeshi textile industry dismissed 50,000 children from factories. Most of those children did not end up in school but instead fell into prostitution and other "occupations" far more degrading than weaving cloth in a factory.

America's trade policy is already biased against workers in poor countries without making it more so through "anti-sweatshop" legislation. The United States and other rich countries currently impose their highest trade barriers against products of most importance to poor countries: clothing, textiles, and agricultural products. In fact, our average tariff imposed on imports from poor countries is about four times higher than those imposed on imports from other rich countries.

Our regressive tariff system imposes punitive tariffs on workers in some of the poorest countries in the world. According to the Progressive Policy Institute, the U.S. government collects more tariff revenue on the $2 billion in mostly hats and t-shirts we import from Bangladesh in a year than on the $30 billion in planes, computers, medicines and wine we import from France. Imports from Cambodia face an average tariff of 16 percent, ten times higher than the average 1.6 percent we impose on all imports.

Our trade policies also hurt the world's poorest farmers and their children. A 2002 study for the National Bureau of Economic Research found that higher rice prices in Vietnam were associated with significant declines in child labor rates. Specifically, a 30 percent increase in rice prices accounted for a decrease of children in the workforce of 1 million, or 9 percent. The drop was most pronounced among girls aged 14 and 15. As the incomes of rice-growing families rose, they chose to use their additional resources to remove their children from work in the field and send them to school. If U.S. rice subsidies are indeed depressing global rice prices, as evidence confirms, then those same programs are plausibly responsible for keeping tens of thousands of young girls in Vietnam and other poor countries in the labor force rather than school.

Attempts to "enforce" labor and environmental standards through trade sanctions are not only unnecessary but also counterproductive. Sanctions deprive poor countries of the international trade and investment opportunities they need to raise overall living standards. Sanctions tend to strike at the very export industries in less developed countries that typically pay the highest wages and follow the highest standards, forcing production and employment into less-globalized sectors where wages and standards are almost always lower. The end result of sanctions is the very opposite of what their advocates claim to seek.

If members of Congress want to encourage higher labor standards abroad, they should support policies that encourage free trade and investment flows so that less developed nations can grow more rapidly. As a complementary policy, Congress could seek a more robust International Labor Organization that could systematically monitor and report on enforcement of labor rights in member countries. Meanwhile, civil society organizations are free to raise public awareness through campaigns and boycotts, while importers can cater to consumer preferences for higher standards through labeling and other promotions. The demand for trade sanctions as a tool to enforce labor standards confronts Americans with a false choice. In reality, the best policy for promoting economic growth at home and abroad—an economy open to global trade and investment—is also the best policy for promoting higher labor standards.

POSTSCRIPT

Is it Immoral for U.S. Corporations to Use Cheap Overseas Labor?

Opponents of global sweatshops argue that they are exploitative in two ways. First, as noted in the introduction to this debate, exploitation occurs when multinational corporations systematically single out countries with favorable labor conditions to produce their products at considerably lower expense than they could in their home country. In addition to this practical position, opponents of sweatshops argue from a moral perspective. In this view, derived from Immanuel Kant's categorical imperative, people are entitled to respect because they are moral beings possessed of dignity. Ethics scholars Denis Arnold and Norman Bowie quote Kant: "In Kant's words, 'Humanity itself is a dignity; for a man cannot be used merely as a means by any man . . . but must always be used at the same time as an end. It is just in this that his dignity . . . consists . . .'" (Arnold and Bowie, "Sweatshops and Respect for Persons", *Business Ethics Quarterly,* vol. 13, no. 2, 2003, p. 222). According to Arnold and Bowie, global sweatshops are inhumane and exploitative because they treat workers as means to an end and not as ends in and of themselves. The below-subsistence wage rates and dangerous, abusive working conditions in sweatshops more than testify to the truth of this assertion.

The standard defense of sweatshops consists primarily of practical observations and arguments, most of which Daniel Griswold noted in his testimony to Congress in 2007. But there is a philosophical justification as well. This line of defense argues that workers have a right to dispose of their labor in any manner they see fit. Granted, in most developing countries, workers have few options available in terms of deciding how to spend their labor; nevertheless, as long as they decide to work on their own volition, the sweatshops are not guilty of exploiting the workers. Indeed, it is the opponents of sweatshops who are guilty of immoral behavior because they want to take away—through the shutting down of sweatshops and the punishment of multinational firms that use them—the local worker's right to decide how to use his labor. This leads to a difficult question for the sweatshop critics: What right do you (the critic) have to go into another country and tell its people where they can and cannot work?

Suggested Readings

Denis Arnold and Norman Bowie, "Sweatshops and Respect for Persons,"
Business Ethics Quarterly (vol. 13, no. 2, April 2003)

National Labor Committee, "Harris Poll: Americans Want Legal Protections for Workers in the Global Economy," (2006). http://www.nlcnet.org/article.php?id=75

Ed Brayton, "Obama and Clinton Sponsor Anti-Sweatshop Legislation," *The Michigan Messenger* (Feb. 15, 2008). http://michiganmessenger.com/869/obama-and-clinton-sponsor-anti-sweatshop-legislation

Thomas J. DiLorenzo, "How 'Sweatshops' Help the Poor," *Mises Institute* (Nov. 9, 2006). http://www.mises.org/story/2384

Thomas Sowell, "Third World Sweatshops: Multinational Opportunity vs. Nihilistic Indignation," *Captalism Magazine* (January 28, 2004). http://www.capmag.com/article.asp?ID=3489

Benjamin Powell, "In Defense of Sweatshops," *Library of Economics and Liberty* (June 2, 2008). http://www.econlib.org/library/Columns/y2008/Powellsweatshops.html

ISSUE 3

Are U.S. CEOs Paid More Than They Deserve?

YES: Sarah Anderson, John Cavanagh, Chuck Collins, Mike Lapham, Sam Pizzigati, from "Executive Excess 2007," (Institute for Policy Studies, 2007). http://www.ips-dc.org/reports/#84

NO: Ira T. Kay, from "Don't Mess with CEO Pay," *Across the Board* (January/February 2006)

ISSUE SUMMARY

YES: Arguing that US CEOs are substantially overpaid in a 2008 study conducted for the Institute for Policy Studies are compensation expert and IPS Fellow Sarah Anderson and her colleagues.

NO: Ira Kay is an expert in executive compensation and a consultant at Watson Wyatt Worldwide. He argues persuasively that market forces play an important role in executive compensation, which is, on the whole, fair and equitable.

On February 4, 2009, in what must have been a tremendously rewarding moment for those who believe that American CEO pay is out of control, President Obama placed a ceiling on the amount of pay top executives at financial institutions receiving federal bailout funds can receive. Imposing a cap of $500,000 on top executive pay, Obama said Americans are angry "at executives being rewarded for failure." He also pointed out that "For top executives to award themselves these kinds of compensation packages in the midst of this economic crisis is not only in bad taste, it's a bad strategy—and I will not tolerate it as president." (*The Seattle Times*, February 5, 2009; http://seattletimes .nwsource.com/html/politics/2008709424_pay05.html).

Less than six weeks later, the issue of excessive CEO pay achieved even greater attention when it was reported that senior level executives at AIG—a huge US insurance company based in New York City—doled out more than $160 million in bonuses using funds they received as part of the federal government's massive bailout of the financial industry. Again, Obama expressed outrage, declaring that his administration would "pursue every single legal avenue to block those bonuses and make the American taxpayers whole." (Lynn Sweet, *Chicago Sun-Times*, March 17, 2009; http://blogs.suntimes .com/sweet/2009/03/obamas_aig_bonus_outrage_aig_u.html).

Clearly, the topic of US CEO compensation is one that invokes much emotion and, if President Obama's behaviors are any indication, a lot of political attention as well. And who doubts that the average American citizen believes that American CEOs are paid more than they deserve? Nevertheless, as is so often the case, closer scrutiny of this topic suggests that things are not so simple. In fact, even in the aftermath of the financial debacle of 2008, many academicians, public intellectuals, and business observers strongly believe that US CEO pay is not excessive. Furthermore, and as you shall soon learn, they have very compelling reasons for advocating this view. And because the purpose of this text is to have you decide where you stand on controversial issues in management, let's carry on and consider our next debate topic: Are US CEOs paid more than they deserve?

Those who argue that US CEOs are overpaid raise several interesting points in support of their position. One emotionally powerful point involves the apparent unfairness of paying a CEO millions of dollars while the firm is simultaneously reducing its workforce via layoffs and downsizing. Why should a CEO be rewarded for cutting the workforce? Additionally, some boards of directors have shown a willingness to award large bonuses not only to high-performing CEOs but also to CEOs whose organizations were clear under-performers the previous year. Such actions suggest that an individual CEO's pay may not be tied to how well he or she performs, a situation that most would agree is not fair. Perhaps the strongest argument put forth by those who think US CEOs are overpaid is based on a comparison of the CEO pay-to-worker pay ratio in America to that of other industrialized countries. Critics frequently point out that US executives typically make several hundred times more in annual income than the lowest paid employees in their firms. In other countries, however, the ratio is considerably smaller. In Japan, for example, the typical CEO makes only about 15 times the lowest worker, and many member countries of the European Union restrict top executive pay to around 20 times the lowest worker's pay.

On the other side of the debate, supporters of current US CEO pay levels argue that CEO pay is, like most jobs in America, subject to labor market influences. Currently, the market for quality CEOs is very tight, and wage-increasing bidding wars are the norm. Thus, CEO pay is clearly subject to labor market conditions. In response to the layoff issue, proponents of existing CEO pay levels argue that CEOs are paid to make and execute difficult decisions. They point out that often the alternative to downsizing and staying in business is not downsizing and going out of business entirely. Proponents also point out that US CEOs, in many instances, are actually *underpaid* because US CEOs and their organizations have created an incredible amount of wealth over the past two decades. In other words, when compared to the wealth US CEOs have made for shareholders, their compensation packages typically look very reasonable indeed.

The following selections represent opposite sides of our CEO pay debate. The affirmative position in this debate is provided by a 2008 study conducted for the Institute for Policy Studies by Sarah Anderson and her colleagues. The negative position, that is, arguing that CEOs are not paid more than they deserve is, Ira Kay, an expert in executive compensation and a consultant at Watson Wyatt Worldwide.

YES

Sarah Anderson et al.

Executive Excess 2007: The Staggering Social Cost of U.S. Business Leadership

I. Introduction

What's the "going rate" for leadership in the United States today?

This question would once have made little sense. Years ago, we didn't treat "leadership" as a marketable skills set. Today we do. We have academic centers that teach leadership, headhunters who search for it.

Our grand enterprises and institutions still sometimes hire their top leaders from within. But they feel no pressure to hire someone already deeply steeped in the specific work they do. They seek, or at least claim to seek, proven leadership ability, from individuals who have demonstrated a capacity to innovate and inspire, analyze and imagine.

A good leader, we have come to believe, can perform successfully almost anywhere. The CEO of Home Depot can become the head of Chrysler. A military general can become a school superintendent. You need not know how a particular industry operates to play a leadership role within it. You need only know how to lead. Leadership skills, and leadership skills alone, can make you eminently marketable.

Every market, of course, sports a "going rate." Try to collect significantly above that "going rate," if your skill be computer programming or selling real estate, and you'll likely get nowhere quick.

But the market for leadership doesn't seem to work that way. Some individuals with leadership skills in our contemporary United States—those individuals who sit atop America's business enterprises—are capturing far more compensation for their labors than individual leaders in other fields who appear to hold the same exact leadership skill set.

Indeed, our current pay gap between American business leaders and their leadership counterparts in other walks of American life today runs wider, often far wider, than the pay gap a generation ago between business leaders and average American workers.

Back around 1980, big-time corporate CEOs in the United States took home just over 40 times the pay of average American workers. Today's average

American CEO from a *Fortune* 500 company makes 364 times an average worker's pay and over 70 times the pay of a four-star Army general.

Another example of this growing leadership pay gap: Last year, the top 20 earners in the most lucrative corner of America's business sector, the private equity and hedge fund world, pocketed 680 times more in rewards for their labors than the nation's 20 highest-paid leaders of nonprofit institutions pocketed for theirs.

Most Americans, over recent years, have become aware that business leaders make enormously more than the workers they employ. The gap between business leaders and other leaders in our society has received considerably less attention. This report, our 14th annual examination of executive excess, seeks to remedy that situation.

But we will begin this year's report on more familiar ground, with a review of the current status of the gap between business leaders and their workers. That gap remains at unconscionably wide levels.

The CEOs of major American corporations, the data show, once again last year made as much in a day as average workers took in over the entire year. The 20 top kingpins of the private equity and hedge fund industry last year made more than average worker annual pay *every ten minutes.*

These numbers shock but do not surprise. We have come, as a society, to expect—and even accept—such phenomenally wide pay differentials between workers and business leaders. These differentials have come to appear as a given of modern economic life.

But modern economies, in reality, do not require excessive business executive pay to function. If they did, then the business executives that American executives compete against in the global marketplace would be just as excessively compensated as American executives. They aren't. Top executives of major European corporations, we show in this latest edition of *Executive Excess,* last year earned three times *less* than their American counterparts.

The vast rewards that go to business leaders in the United States represent, in short, not an inevitable unfolding of marketplace dynamics, but a marketplace failure.

Markets that fail need to be corrected, and, in generations past, Americans organized politically to make sure needed corrective action took place. These Americans broke up monopolies. They established a minimum wage. They regulated business behavior. *Executive Excess 2007* spotlights, in this historic spirit, a series of corrective initiatives we here today can take to restore a modicum of balance to modern American economic life.

We ignore initiatives like these at our peril. The outrageously massive rewards now attainable at the top of our economic ladder do our society no good. They ravage the enterprise teamwork that true leaders strive to nurture. They discourage individuals with leadership talent from entering less lucrative fields where their skills could make an important contribution to our common well-being.

In a democracy, we don't depend on leaders to fix problems like these. We citizens take leadership responsibilities onto ourselves. This year's *Executive Excess* aims to help this process along.

II. CEOs v. Workers

The CEO-Worker Pay Gap

Last year, CEOs of major U.S. companies collected as much money from one day on the job as average workers made over the entire year. These CEOs averaged $10.8 million in total compensation, according to an Associated Press survey of 386 *Fortune* 500 companies, the equivalent of over 364 times the pay of an average American worker.

Meanwhile, the private equity boom has pushed the pay ceiling for American business leaders further into the economic stratosphere. Pay data for the chiefs of these privately held firms remain difficult to obtain, but *Forbes* magazine estimates that the top 20 private equity and hedge fund managers, on average, took in $657.5 million last year, or 22,255 times the pay of the average U.S. worker.

These massive private equity take-homes have an enormous impact on inequality in the United States, at both ends of the economic ladder. Private equity managers, to extract such massive personal rewards out of the companies that sit in their portfolios, typically make decisions—on matters ranging from job cuts to pensions—that place steady downward pressure on U.S. working standards.

Astronomical pay packages for managing partners at privately held investment companies also serve to bump up the already overly ample pay of CEOs at publicly traded corporations. CEOs are now routinely leaving their corporate perches to take on far more remunerative leadership slots in the private equity world. Those who remain within publicly traded corporations, meanwhile, use the threat of exit to bargain even higher pay for their executive services.

To retain leadership talent, the argument goes, publicly traded companies must simply pay more. This past March, at a House Financial Services Committee hearing, one business professor cited massive private equity payoffs as evidence that CEOs "may even be underpaid at public companies."

Minimum Wage

This Labor Day, American workers can celebrate the first raise in the federal minimum wage in ten years. But the minimum wage increase that went into effect July 24 makes barely a dent in the gap between pay rates at the American economy's top and bottom. In the decade that ended in 2006, CEO pay rose roughly 45 percent, adjusted for inflation. The real value of the minimum wage, with this year's increase from $5.15 to $5.85, now stands 7 percent below the minimum wage's value in 1996.

Average worker pay has, over the past decade, also lagged far behind CEO compensation. In 2006, average American workers earned $29,544 per year, up 7 percent from 1996.

The Pension Gap

New federal corporate disclosure rules are shining a brighter light on the stark disparity between CEO and worker pensions. According to data available in proxy statements for the first time this year, large company CEOs last year enjoyed a $1.3 million average increase in the value of their pensions. The biggest CEO increase in pension account value—$10.7 million—went to Textron's Lewis B. Campbell. By contrast, the share of ordinary U.S. workers with any type of retirement account has declined in recent years.

According to the most recent Federal Reserve Board survey, only 58.5 percent of households headed by 45-to-54-year-olds had any type of retirement account in 2004, down from 64.3 percent in 2001. Of those in that age bracket who did have such funds, the average account value grew by only $11,325 over those same three years, or roughly $3,775 per year.

According to the Corporate Library, CEOs of S&P 500 companies retire with an average of $10.1 million in their Supplemental Executive Retirement Plan, just one type of special account large American companies regularly set up for their top executives. To place that number in perspective: In 2004, only 36.3 percent of American households headed by an individual 65 years or older held any type of retirement account at all.

Those over-65 households *with* pension protection in 2004, according to the Congressional Research Service, held an average of $173,552 in their retirement accounts, a miniscule 1.7 percent of the dollars in the supplemental accounts set aside for America's top CEOs. Looking at all American households, regardless of age, slightly more than half had retirement accounts in 2004. The average value of these accounts: $129,310.

Among the king-sized supplemental CEO pension stashes accumulated by the end of 2006: $91.3 million for William McGuire of the UnitedHealth Group. Edward Whitacre of AT&T followed closely behind with $84.7 million. Pfizer CEO Hank McKinnell accumulated $77.1 million in his supplemental retirement account before his ouster last year.

With even financially healthy U.S. companies, including IBM, Verizon, Motorola, Hewlett-Packard and Sears, slashing their worker pension benefits, the CEO-worker pension gap is likely to grow even wider.

III. U.S. Business Leaders vs. Other U.S. Leaders

Healthy democracies and dynamic economies require strong leadership, in every sector of society. But current pay practices in the United States send a quite different message: that only for-profit business leadership really matters.

Business leaders, our compensation patterns proclaim, add tens, hundreds, and even thousands of times more value to our society than the leaders we hold responsible for educating our youth, protecting our national security, providing essential public services, or crafting the laws that govern us.

Such extreme pay gaps undermine our future. These gaps siphon off talent from public service and create a nonstop revolving door between government and the business world that breeds conflict of interest and corruption and distorts our democracy.

Top leaders in non-business sectors of our society already earn comfortable incomes. These incomes do not need to be raised. To limit leadership pay gaps, we need to address the problem of excessive pay in the for-profit sector.

Private Equity and Hedge Funds

The top 20 highest-earning leaders of private equity and hedge funds collected an average of $657.5 million in 2006. The top four each pocketed over $1 billion. These men—and they are all white men—are leading a revival of the 1980s leveraged buyout phenomenon that hollowed out a variety of once-venerable companies, while enriching a precious few. Last year saw more than 1,000 corporate buyouts worldwide, with a total value estimated between $500 and $700 billion. Hedge funds now account for 30 to 60 percent of daily global turnover in financial markets.

Unlike companies that are publicly traded on Wall Street, private equity and hedge funds are not required to report executive compensation to the federal Securities and Exchange Commission. These funds also rely on different forms of compensation. Investment managers reap their rewards primarily from management fees and a share of the profits from fund investments, rather than from stock options, salary, and bonuses.

Private equity and hedge fund managing partners typically receive 20 percent of the profits their funds generate and an annual fee that equals 2 percent of the assets they manage. Some managers demand even higher rewards. For example, James Simons commands 44 percent of profits and 5 percent of assets from investors in his two hedge funds, Medallion and Renaissance Institutional. Last year, he raked in $1.1 billion from Medallion and $395 million from Renaissance. His total earnings: nearly $1.5 billion.

After Simons, Steven Cohen of SAC Capital scored the second-highest Wall Street investment fund windfall, with $1.2 billion. Cohen's wealth has proved a boon to art dealers. He recently acquired an Andy Warhol image of Marilyn Monroe, "Turquoise Marilyn," for an estimated $80 million, nearly three times the price garnered for a similar painting by the pop artist.

Cohen shared second place on the investment fund payday list with Kenneth Griffin, head of Citadel Investment Group. The 38-year-old Griffin has also made a name for himself as an art collector and will soon have his name etched on a section of the Art Institute of Chicago. For the site of his second wedding in 2003, Griffin chose Versailles, where the ill-fated King Louis XVI and Marie Antoinette also tied the knot.

Two of last year's 20 highest-paid hedge fund managers first became public figures as 1980s-era corporate raiders. T. Boone Pickens, for example, made a fortune two decades ago bidding for Gulf Oil and other big oil companies. His current hedge fund, BP Capital, invests almost exclusively in the energy industry and last year generated $1.1 billion in earnings for Pickens.

Another icon of the "greed is good" 1980s, Carl Icahn, cleared $350 million in 2006. Most notorious for his 1986 takeover of TWA, a company he left in bankruptcy, Icahn today heads the Icahn Partners fund, a two-year-old venture that manages about $2.5 billion in assets.

Publicly Traded Companies

The top 20 highest-paid executives of U.S. publicly traded companies raked in an average $36.4 million in 2006. The top earner: Yahoo's Terry Semel, whose $71.7 million in annual earnings consisted almost entirely of options grants estimated to be worth $71.4 million. The Internet services chief also cashed in $19 million in options last year. Semel stepped down as CEO in June, amid widespread shareholder concern over the company's sluggish performance.

The second- and third-highest-paid U.S. CEOs last year both hailed from the oil industry, a sector that continues to benefit from record-high world crude oil prices. Bob Simpson of Texas-based XTO Energy took in $59.5 million, including a $31 million cash bonus and $27 million worth of new options grants. He cleared another $39.8 million exercising previously awarded options.

XTO Energy last year also donated $6.8 million to Baylor University, Simpson's alma mater, for the construction of a sports complex. In exchange, the XTO proxy explains, the university will name the new athletic complex after Simpson—and provide him "access to certain sporting events."

The sixth-highest-paid CEO in 2006 was Angelo Mozilo of Countrywide Financial, with $42.9 million. In July 2007, the company's sub-prime mortgage woes drove its foreclosure rates to the highest level in more than five years and contributed to a global liquidity crisis.

Non-Profits

In 2005, the most current year with data available, the 20 highest-paid nonprofit leaders in the United States averaged $965,698 in compensation. The highest-paid—Harold Varmus, the chief executive of the Memorial Sloan-Kettering Cancer Center in New York—earned $2,491,450. Varmus won the 1989 Nobel Prize for his research on the genetic basis of cancer.

The lowest-paid of the 20 top nonprofit leaders, University of Pennsylvania President Amy Gutmann, collected $675,000 for her labors overseeing a school with nearly 24,000 students and 5,000 faculty members. UPenn's budget last year totaled $4.87 billion, more than the revenues of XTO Energy, whose CEO gathered up nearly $60 million in 2006. Five university presidents, besides Gutmann, appear on the top 20 nonprofit pay list.

Over the last several years, several scandals have taken down nonprofit leaders who seem to have yearned to live the same imperial lifestyles as their corporate counterparts. Lawrence Small, a former banker, stepped down as head of the Smithsonian Institution in early 2007 after reports that his lavish leadership style required $2 million worth of spending on chauffeured cars, private jets, and exclusive hotels. Benjamin Ladner lost his job as American University president in 2005 after news reports revealed he had spent university money on personal chefs, limousines, and extravagant family parties.

Federal Executive Branch

By law, the President of the United States earns the highest salary in the federal government, $400,000 last year. Vice President Richard Cheney, who accumulated enormous wealth in the private sector before entering the Bush White House, made a government salary of $208,575 in 2006. Rounding out the 20 highest-paid federal executive branch officials: 15 cabinet secretaries and other cabinet-level government executives who earn the top executive pay grade of $186,600.

Military Service

In 2006, 15 top brass earned $187,390, the highest military pay rate. These included the chair and vice chair of the Joint Chiefs of Staff, the heads of each branch of the military, as well as the chiefs of various specialized commands, such as John Abizaid, who retired this year as head of the Central Command. Abizaid oversaw some 250,000 U.S. troops in 27 countries, including Iraq and Afghanistan. High-ranking generals round out last year's military top 20. Their base pay: $152,000.

All these generals are operating in an increasingly privatized war-time environment where many basic operations that used to be direct Pentagon responsibilities have been contracted out to powerhouse defense industry corporations. The CEOs of the top six defense contractors last year each pulled in between $12 million and $24 million. These included the chief executives of Lockheed Martin ($24.4 million), Boeing ($13.8 million), Northrop Grumman ($18.6 million), General Dynamics ($15.7 million), Raytheon ($11.9 million), and Halliburton ($16.5 million). Each of these six business leaders last year made more in a week than any of the generals made in a year.

U.S. Congress

The two highest-paid members of the U.S. Congress—the House speaker and Senate majority leader—each earned $212,100 salaries in 2006. The minority leaders in both chambers earned $183,500. All rank-and-file senators and representatives received $165,200 in paychecks last year.

The lowest-paid corporate executive on last year's list of the 20 highest-paid CEOs in America—Viacom's Philippe Dauman—personally pocketed over seven times more compensation for his leadership labors than the 20 top leaders in Congress together.

The huge gaps between congressional and business pay levels keep the revolving door spinning between Capitol Hill and K Street lobby groups. According to Public Citizen, 43 percent of the members of Congress who left office between 1998 and mid-2005 eligible to lobby actually became lobbyists.

This revolving door threatens government integrity in two ways:

- Members of Congress who are hoping to land lucrative private sector jobs have an incentive to shape public policy to please potential future employers or clients.
- Lawmakers-turned-lobbyists have privileged access to their former colleagues that can give them undue influence to advance their clients' interests.

In late July, the House of Representatives passed new ethics legislation that chooses not to extend the ban on lobbying by former House members from one to two years after their congressional service ends.

IV. U.S. Business Leaders vs. European Business Leaders

American executives continue to leave their European counterparts in the compensation dust, even after recent increases in European executive pay levels. In 2006, the 20 highest-paid European managers made an average of $12.5 million, only one third as much as the 20 highest-earning U.S. executives. The Europeans earned less, despite leading larger firms. On average, the 20 European firms with the highest-paid executives on the continent had sales of $65.5 billion, compared to $46.5 billion for the 20 U.S. firms.

The gap between U.S. and European executives is actually running wider than the dollar-equivalence figures below suggest. The drastic fall in the value of the dollar against the euro serves to inflate the compensation European executives received last year.

French executives dominated the list, making up 10 of the 20 highest-paid European executives. The top-earning French executive, Carlos Ghosn of Renault, took in $45.5 million, mostly in stock options. This total does not include Ghosn's compensation from Nissan. Ghosn has been CEO of both Renault and Nissan since 2005. Once considered a hero of the auto industry for resuscitating the Japanese automaker, Ghosn has had to face angry shareholders of late as both firms have performed sluggishly. Ghosn recently gave up his post as head of Nissan's North American operations.

The top-ranked German executive, Josef Ackermann of Deutsche Bank, collected $12.4 million. Ackermann became a lightning rod figure in Germany's ongoing executive pay debate when he faced criminal charges for having helped approve, as a board member, massive bonuses for executives at another German company. Ackermann and five other board members at this company were charged with "breach of fiduciary trust." Ackermann's unapologetic defense of both the bonuses and his own massive paycheck provoked charges that the Swissborn banker was injecting a more ruthless style of American capitalism into a relatively egalitarian German society. The former head of the German Social Democratic Party called Ackermann's behavior "disastrous to the image of democracy.

V. Proposals for Change

This section highlights six practical initiatives that can rein in excessive executive pay. Five involve more equitable taxation, while one would use government contracting dollars to encourage more reasonable pay.

Recent polls suggest that these reforms would enjoy broad public support. The same July 2007 *Financial Times*/Harris poll that found widespread European support for capping executive pay found that 77 percent of Americans feel that corporate executives "earn too much." Only 11 percent admire "those who run" America's "largest companies" either "a great deal" or "quite a bit."

On top of that, Americans—by an overwhelming margin—want to see their nation's top income-earners pay more in taxes. Just 12 percent of Americans feel their country "correctly taxes those who earn the highest incomes." Five times that number, 61 percent, feel wealthy Americans "should be taxed more."

Proposals

Eliminate Tax Subsidies for Excessive CEO Pay

Under current law, corporations can deduct, as a "business expense," whatever excessive pay packages they hand their top executives, simply by defining that excess as a "performance incentive." This tax loophole essentially operates as an incentive for excessive compensation. The more corporations shell out in executive compensation, the less they pay in taxes. And the rest of us taxpayers wind up paying the bill.

Rep. Barbara Lee (D-Calif.) is promoting a reform that would cap the amount of executive compensation corporations are permitted to deduct to 25 times the pay of a company's lowest paid worker. Corporate boards would still be allowed to pay their executives as much as they wanted. They just wouldn't be able to deduct excessive amounts from their taxes.

If such a deductibility cap had been in place last year, the 386 companies included in the Associated Press pay survey would have paid as much as $1.4 billion more in 2006 taxes—just on their CEOs' compensation alone. That additional revenue, if earmarked for reducing class sizes in overcrowded schools, would have been enough to pay the annual salaries of 29,218 elementary school teachers.

And that's just the amount that would have been generated by capping the deductibility of CEO pay at these 386 firms. Rep. Lee's proposal, if enacted, would apply to all top management compensation within a company that exceeds the 25-to-1 ratio.

Down through the years, many noted figures in the business world have argued for reasonable ratios between executive and worker pay. A century ago, financier J. P. Morgan insisted on 20-to-1 ratios, a theme picked up in more recent times by Peter Drucker, the founder of modern management science.

End the Preferential Tax Treatment of Private Investment Company Executive Income

Rep. Sander Levin (D-Michigan) has introduced legislation that would plug the tax loophole that allows managers of the nation's private equity and hedge funds, individuals who often make hundreds of millions of dollars a year, to pay taxes at lower rates than average Americans.

These managers currently pay taxes on a substantial portion of their personal income at the 15 percent capital gains rate, not the 35 percent rate that would apply if their earnings were treated as ordinary income. Private investment managers earn an annual administrative fee (usually 2 percent) and carried interest on profits (usually 20 percent), often called a "carry." The tax code treats the carry portion of pay as capital gains, even though the investment manager is providing a professional service.

A recent Economic Policy Institute paper estimates that this loophole costs the federal treasury about $12.6 billion a year. This lost revenue, EPI notes, would be enough to fully fund a five-year, $35 billion expansion of SCHIP, the public health insurance program for America's low-income children.

Cap Tax-Free 'Deferred' Executive Pay

Most major corporations in the United States today—85 percent of the companies in the S&P 500—have created special "deferred pay" accounts for their top executives. Dollars in these accounts earn guaranteed interest, compounding on a tax-free basis, until the executives retire. Last year, according to an analysis by Equilar, a compensation analytics firm based in California, the median major company CEO deferred pay account held $3.7 million.

But this median understates the vast sums that some top executives have accumulated. The chief executive at retail giant Target, Robert Ulrich, held $133.5 million in his deferred pay account at year's end, all of this over and beyond the dollars in Ulrich's regular pension and 401 (k).

Standard 401 (k) plans, the only tax-deferral tool available to rank-and-file corporate employees, carry strict deferral limits. Workers under age 50 can this year defer from their taxes no more than $15,500 in 401 (k) contributions. Corporate executive deferred pay plans allow unlimited deferrals.

Senate Finance Committee chairman Max Baucus (D-Montana) and the panel's ranking minority member, Senator Charles Grassley (R-Iowa), earlier this year pushed all the way to a House-Senate conference committee legislation that would have limited annual executive pay deferrals to $1 million. The proposal, attacked fiercely by corporate interests, did not survive the conference committee deliberations. But Senator Baucus has pledged to revisit the initiative.

Eliminate the Tax Reporting Loophole on CEO Stock Options

Corporations are currently allowed to report one set of executive stock option compensation figures to investors on their financial statements and a completely different set of figures to the Internal Revenue Service (IRS) on their tax returns.

Corporations deduct the value of executive stock options, greatly reducing their taxes. At the same time, they often report a significantly lower stock option expense to their shareholders. The IRS examined corporate tax returns filed between December 2004 and June 2005 and identified a $43 billion discrepancy between deductions claimed to the IRS and option expenses reported to shareholders.

The U.S. Senate Permanent Subcommittee on Investigations examined the stock option tax deductions claimed by nine companies over five years. The deductions exceeded their reported stock option expenses by a total of more than $1 billion, or 575 percent. For example, of the 12 million stock options the Occidental Petroleum CEO exercised during the five-year period, the company claimed a $353 million tax deduction—12 times as much as the book expense that, under current accounting rules, would have totaled just $29 million.

This creative bookkeeping is not currently illegal. Senator Carl Levin, chairman of the U.S. Senate Permanent Subcommittee on Investigations, feels these companies "are benefiting from an outdated and overly generous stock option tax rule that produces tax deductions that often far exceed the companies' reported expenses."

Link Government Procurement to Executive Pay

Some of the most excessive executive pay packages over recent years have gone to CEOs whose companies take in much of their revenue from government contracts. Most of these contracts involve the defense industry.

Federal procurement law already limits the amount of pay that a company with a government contract can bill the government for executive compensation. But this "cap" only applies to direct federal dollars. Corporations whose profits or share prices soar after receiving a federal contract remain free to pay their top executives whatever company boards please.

A simple change could end these executive windfalls. The federal government could deny procurement contracts—or economic development subsidies or tax breaks—to all firms that pay their top executives over 25, 50, or even 100 times what their lowest-paid workers receive.

The federal government currently denies contracts to companies that increase, through discriminatory employment practices, racial or gender inequality in the United States. The same principle could be invoked to deny contracts to companies that, through excessive executive compensation, increase the nation's economic inequality.

Increase the Top Marginal Tax Rate on High Incomes

In 2006, not one of the compensation dollars collected by the business leaders discussed in this report faced a federal income tax rate higher than 35 percent.

Back in the 1950s, by contrast, earned income over $400,000—the equivalent of less than $3 million today—faced a top marginal tax rate of 91 percent.

These steeply graduated tax rates, in place for most of the mid-20th century, served to actively discourage excessive compensation. They sent a powerful cultural message that compensation beyond a certain lofty level serves no useful societal purpose.

Our contemporary CEO pay explosion began in the early 1980s, shortly after the Reagan administration sped through Congress legislation that dropped the top marginal tax rate from 70 percent, its level since 1964, down to 50 percent. The top rate has since dropped even lower. These lower rates may not have "caused" the executive pay cascade. But they opened the floodgates.

Any move to restore mid-20th century top marginal tax rates would raise substantial revenue for investments in education and other social programs that could significantly broaden economic opportunity. If the federal income tax rate on all annual income above $10 million were raised to 70 percent—and the tax rate on all income between $5 million and $10 million were raised to 50 percent—federal revenues in 2008 would increase by a stunning $105 billion.

Ira T. Kay   ➔ **NO**

Don't Mess With CEO Pay

For years, headlines have seized on dramatic accounts of outrageous amounts earned by executives—often of failing companies—and the financial tragedy that can befall both shareholders and employees when CEOs line their own pockets at the organization's expense. Images of lavish executive lifestyles are now engraved in the popular consciousness. The result: public support for political responses that include new regulatory measures and a long list of demands for greater shareholder or government control over executive compensation.

These images now overshadow the reality of thousands of successful companies with appropriately paid executives and conscientious boards. Instead, fresh accusations of CEOs collecting huge amounts of undeserved pay appear daily, fueling a full-blown mythology of a corporate America ruled by executive greed, fraud, and corruption.

This mythology consists of two related components: the myth of the failed pay-for-performance model and the myth of managerial power. The first myth hinges on the idea that the link between executive pay and corporate performance—if it ever existed—is irretrievably broken. The second myth accepts the idea of a failed pay-for-performance model and puts in its service the image of unchecked CEOs dominating subservient boards as the explanation for decisions resulting in excessive executive pay. The powerful combination of these two myths has captured newspaper headlines and shareholder agendas, regulatory attention and the public imagination.

This mythology has spilled over into the pages of *Across the Board,* where the September/October cover story links high levels of CEO pay to the country's growing income inequality and wonders why U.S. workers have not taken to the streets to protest "the blatant abuse of privilege" exercised by CEOs. In "The Revolution That Never Was," James Krohe Jr. manages to reference Marie Antoinette, Robespierre, Adam Smith, Alexis de Tocqueville, Andrew Jackson, Kim Jong II, Jack Welch, guerrilla warfare, "economic apartheid," and police brutality, in Selma, Ala., in an article that feeds virtually every conceivable element of the myth of executive pay and wonders why we have not yet witnessed calls for a revolution to quash the "financial frolics of today's corporate aristocrats."

In a very different *Across the Board* feature story published a few months earlier, the myth of managerial power finds support in an interview with one of the myth's creators, Harvard professor Lucian Bebchuk, who believes that the pay-for-performance model is broken and that executive control over boards is to blame. Bebchuk is a distinguished scholar who has significant insights into the executive-pay process, but he greatly overestimates the influence of managerial power in the boardroom and ignores empirical evidence that most companies still operate under an intact and explicit pay-for-performance model. And although he acknowledges in his interview with *ATB* editor A.J. Vogl that "American companies have been successful and executives deserve a great deal of credit," his arguments about managerial power run counter to the realities of this success.

Fueling the Fiction

These two articles, in different ways, contribute to what is now a dominant image of executives collecting unearned compensation and growing rich at the expense of shareholders, employees and the broader community. In recent years, dozens of reporters from business magazines and the major newspapers have called me and specifically asked for examples of companies in which CEOs received exorbitant compensation, approved by the board, while the company performed poorly. Not once have I been asked to comment on the vast majority of companies—those in which executives are appropriately rewarded for performance or in which boards have reduced compensation or even fired the CEO for poor performance.

I have spent hundreds of hours answering reporters' questions, providing extensive data and explaining the pay-for-performance model of executive compensation, but my efforts have had little impact: The resulting stories feature the same anecdotal reporting on those corporations for which the process has gone awry. The press accounts ignore solid research that shows that annual pay for most executives moves up and down significantly with the company's performance, both financial and stock-related. Corporate wrongdoings and outlandish executive pay packages make for lively headlines, but the reliance on purely anecdotal reporting and the highly prejudicial language adopted are a huge disservice to the companies, their executives and employees, investors, and the public. The likelihood of real economic damage to the U.S. economy grows daily.

For example, the mythology drives institutional investors and trade unions with the power to exert enormous pressure on regulators and executive and board practices. The California Public Employees' Retirement System—the nation's largest public pension fund—offers a typical example in its Nov. 15, 2004, announcement of a new campaign to rein in "abusive compensation practices in corporate America and hold directors and compensation committees more accountable for their actions."

The AFL-CIO's website offers another example of the claim that managerial power has destroyed the efficacy of the pay-for-performance model: "Each year, shocking new examples of CEO pay greed are made public. Investors are concerned not just about the growing size of executive compensation packages, but the fact that CEO pay levels show little apparent relationship to corporate profits, stock prices or executive performance. How do CEOs do it? For years, executives have relied on their shareholders to be passive absentee owners. CEOs have rigged their own compensation packages by packing their boards with conflicted or negligent directors."

The ROI of the CEO

As with all modern myths, there's a grain of truth in all the assumptions and newspaper stories. The myths of managerial power and of the failed pay-for-performance model find touchstones in real examples of companies where CEOs have collected huge sums in cash compensation and stock options while shareholder returns declined. (You know the names—there's no need to mention them again here.) Cases of overstated profits or even outright fraud have fueled the idea that executives regularly manipulate the measures of performance to justify higher pay while boards default on their oversight responsibilities. The ability of executives to time the exercise of their stock options and collect additional pay through covert means has worsened perceptions of the situation both within and outside of the world of business.

These exceptions in executive pay practices, however, are now commonly mistaken for the rule. And as Krohe's article demonstrates, highly paid CEOs have become the new whipping boys for social critics concerned about the general rise in income inequality and other broad socioeconomic problems. Never mind that these same CEOs stand at the center of a corporate model that has generated millions of jobs and trillions of dollars in shareholder earnings. Worse, using CEOs as scapegoats distracts from the real causes of and possible solutions for inequality.

The primary determinant of CEO pay is the same force that sets pay for all Americans: relatively free—if somewhat imperfect—labor markets, in which companies offer the levels of compensation necessary to attract and retain the employees who generate value for shareholders. Part of that pay for most executives consists of stock-based incentives. A 2003 study by Brian J. Hall and Kevin J. Murphy shows that the ratio of total CEO compensation to production workers' average earnings closely follows the Dow Jones Industrial Average. When the Dow soars, the gap between executive and non-executive compensation widens. The problem, it seems, is not that CEOs receive too much performance-driven, stock-based compensation, but that non-executives receive too little.

The key question is not the actual dollar amount paid to a CEO in total compensation or whether that amount represents a high multiple of pay of the average worker's salary but, rather, whether that CEO creates an adequate return on the company's investment in executive compensation. In virtually every area of business, directors routinely evaluate and adjust the amounts that companies invest in all inputs, and shareholders directly or indirectly endorse or challenge those decisions. Executive pay is no different.

Hard Realities

The corporate scandals of recent years laid bare the inner workings of a handful of public companies where, inarguably, the process for setting executive pay violated not only the principle of pay-for-performance but the extensive set of laws and regulations governing executive pay practices and the role of the board. But while I condemn illegal actions and criticize boards that reward executives who fail to produce positive financial results, I know that the vast majority of U.S. corporations do much better by their shareholders and the public. I have worked directly with more than a thousand publicly traded companies in the United States and attended thousands of compensation-committee meetings, and I have *never* witnessed board members straining to find a way to pay an executive more than he is worth.

In addition, at Watson Wyatt I work with a team of experts that has conducted extensive research at fifteen hundred of America's largest corporations and tracked the relationship between these pay practices and corporate performance over almost twenty years. In evaluating thousands of companies annually, yielding nearly twenty thousand "company years" of data, and pooling cross-sectional company data over multiple years, we have discovered that for both most companies and the "typical" company, there is substantial pay-for-performance sensitivity. That is, high performance generates high pay for executives and low performance generates low pay. Numerous empirical academic studies support our conclusions.

Our empirical evidence and evidence from other studies have produced the following key findings:

1. Executive pay is unquestionably high relative to low-level corporate positions, and it has risen dramatically over the past ten to fifteen years, faster than inflation and faster than average employee pay. But executive compensation generally tracks total returns to shareholders—even including the recent rise in pay.
2. Executive stock ownership has risen dramatically over the past ten to fifteen years. High levels of CEO stock ownership are correlated with and most likely the cause of companies' high financial and stock-market performance.
3. Executives are paid commensurate with the skills and talents that they bring to the organization. Underperforming executives routinely receive pay reductions or are terminated—far more often than press accounts imply.
4. CEOs who are recruited from outside a company and have little influence over its board receive compensation that is competitive with and often higher than the pay levels of CEOs who are promoted from within the company.
5. At the vast majority of companies, even extraordinarily high levels of CEO compensation represent a tiny fraction of the total value created by the corporation under that CEO's leadership. (Watson Wyatt has found that U.S. executives receive approximately 1 percent of the net income generated by the corporations they manage.) Well-run companies, it bears pointing out, produce significant shareholder returns and job security for millions of workers.

Extensive research demonstrates a high and positive correlation between executive pay and corporate performance. For example, high levels of executive stock ownership in 2000, created primarily through stock-option awards, correlated with higher stock-market valuation and long-term earnings per share over the subsequent five-year period. In general, high-performing companies are led by highly paid executives—with pay-for-performance in full effect. Executives at low-performing companies receive lower amounts of pay. Reams of data from other studies confirm these correlations.

Why CEOs Are Worth the Money

The huge gap between the realities of executive pay and the now-dominant mythology surrounding it has become even more evident in recent years. Empirical studies show that executive compensation has closely tracked corporate performance: Pay rose during the boom years of the 1990s, when U.S. corporations generated huge returns, declined during the 2001–03 profit slowdown, and increased in 2004 as profits improved. The myth of excessive executive pay continued to gain power, however, even as concrete, well-documented financial realities defied it.

The blind outrage over executive pay climbed even during the slowdown, as compensation dropped drastically. During this same period, in the aftermath of the corporate scandals, Congress and the U.S. regulatory agencies instituted far-reaching reforms in corporate governance and board composition, and companies spent millions to improve their governance and transparency. But the critics of executive pay and managerial power were only encouraged to raise their voices.

It might surprise those critics to learn that CEOs are not interchangeable and not chosen by lot; they are an extremely important asset to their companies and generally represent an excellent investment. The relative scarcity of CEO talent is manifested in many ways, including the frenetic behavior of boards charged with filling the top position when a CEO retires or departs. CEOs have significant, legitimate, market-driven bargaining power, and in pay negotiations, they use that power to obtain pay commensurate with their skills. Boards, as they should, use their own bargaining power to retain talent and maximize returns to company shareholders.

Boards understand the imperative of finding an excellent CEO and are willing to risk millions of dollars to secure the right talent. Their behavior is not only understandable but necessary to secure the company's future success. Any influence that CEOs might have over their directors is modest in comparison to the financial risk that CEOs assume when they leave other prospects and take on the extraordinarily difficult task of managing a major corporation, with a substantial portion of their short- and long-term compensation contingent on the organization's financial success.

Lucian Bebchuk and other critics underestimate the financial risk entailed in executive positions when they cite executives' large severance packages, derided as "golden parachutes." Top executive talent expects and can command financial protections commensurate with the level of risk they assume. Like any other element of compensation, boards should and generally do evaluate severance agreements as part of the package they create to attract and retain talent. In recent years, boards have become more aware of the damage done when executive benefits and perquisites are excessive and not aligned with non-executive programs, and are now reining in these elements.

Properly designed pay opportunities drive superior corporate performance and secure it for the future. And most importantly, many economists argue, the U.S. model of executive compensation is a significant source of competitive advantage for the nation's economy, driving higher productivity, profits, and stock prices.

Resetting the Debate

Companies design executive pay programs to accomplish the classic goals of any human-capital program. First, they must attract, retain, and motivate their human capital to perform at the highest levels. The motivational factor is the most important, because it addresses the question of how a company achieves the greatest return on its human-capital investment and rewards executives for making the right decisions to drive shareholder value. Incentive-pay and pay-at-risk programs are particularly effective, especially at the top of the house, in achieving this motivation goal.

Clearly, there are exceptions to the motivational element—base salaries, pensions, and other benefits, for example—that are more closely tied to retention goals and are an essential part of creating a balanced portfolio for the employee. The portfolio as a whole must address the need for income and security and the opportunity for creating significant asset appreciation.

A long list of pressures, including institutional-investor pushback, accounting changes, SEC investigations, and scrutiny from labor unions and the media, are forcing companies to rethink their executive-compensation programs, especially their stock-based incentives. The key now is to address the real problems in executive compensation without sacrificing the performance-based model and the huge returns that it has generated. Boards are struggling to achieve greater transparency and more rigorous execution of their pay practices—a positive move for all parties involved.

The real threat to U.S. economic growth, job creation, and higher living standards now comes from regulatory overreach as proponents of the mythology reject market forces and continue to push for government and institutional control over executive pay. To the extent that the mythology now surrounding executive pay leads to a rejection of the pay-for-performance model and restrictions on the risk-and-reward structure for setting executive compensation, American corporate performance will suffer.

There will be more pressure on boards to effectively reduce executive pay. This may meet the social desires of some constituents, but it will almost surely cause economic decline, for companies and the U.S. economy. We will see higher executive turnover and less talent in the executive suite as the most qualified job candidates move into other professions, as we saw in the 1970s, when top candidates moved into investment banking, venture-capital firms, and consulting, and corporate performance suffered as a result.

Our research demonstrates that aligning pay plans, incentive opportunities, and performance measures throughout an organization is key to financial success. Alignment means that executives and non-executives alike have the opportunity to increase their pay through performance-based incentives. As new regulations make it more difficult to execute the stock-based elements of the pay-for-performance model, for example, by reducing broad-based stock options, we will see even less alignment between executives' compensation and the pay packages of the rank-and-file. We are already witnessing the unintended consequences of the new requirement for stock-option expensing as companies cut the broad-based stock-option plans that have benefited millions of workers and given them a direct stake in the financial success of the companies for which they work.

Instead of changing executive pay plans to make them more like pay plans for employees, we should be reshaping employee pay to infuse it with the same incentives that drive performance in the company's upper ranks. A top-down regulatory approach to alignment will only damage the entire market-based, performance-management process that has worked so well for most companies and the economy as a whole. Instead of placing artificial limits on executive pay, we should focus squarely on increasing performance incentives and stock ownership for both executive and non-executive employees and rewarding high performers throughout the organization, from top to bottom. Within the context of a free-market economy, equal opportunity—not income equality by fiat—is the goal.

The short answer to James Krohe's question of why high levels of executive pay have not sparked a worker revolution is that the fundamental model works too well. Workers vote to support that model every day when they show up for work, perform well, and rely on corporate leadership to pursue a viable plan for meeting payroll and funding employee benefits. Shareholders vote to support the model every time they purchase shares or defeat one of the dozens of proposals submitted in recent years to curb executive compensation. Rejecting the pay-for-performance model for executive compensation means returning to the world of the CEO as caretaker. And caretakers—as shown by both evidence and common sense—do not create high value for shareholders or jobs for employees.

In some ways, the decidedly negative attention focused on executive pay has increased the pressure that executives, board members, HR staffs, and compensation consultants all feel when they enter into discussions about the most effective methods for tying pay to performance and ensuring the company's success. The managerial-power argument has contributed to meaningful discussions about corporate governance and raised the level of dialogue in boardrooms. These are positive developments.

When the argument is blown into mythological proportions, however, it skews thinking about the realities of corporate behavior and leads to fundamental misunderstandings about executives, their pay levels, and their role in building successful companies and a flourishing economy. Consequently, the mythology now surrounding executive compensation leads many to reject a pay model that works well and is critical to ongoing growth at both the corporate and the national economic level. We need to address excesses in executive pay without abandoning the core model, and to return the debate to a rational, informed discussion. And we can safely leave Marie Antoinette out of it.

POSTSCRIPT

Are U.S. CEOs Paid More Than They Deserve?

One reason the issue of CEO pay is so contentious is that both sides can easily cite data in support of their position. Even an issue as seemingly straightforward as determining actual CEO pay levels can be difficult. Consider the following case in point: In April of this year, the *Wall Street Journal*—a bastion of free-market capitalism and generally CEO-friendly—reported findings from an analysis of CEO compensation conducted for them by the Hay Group, a management consulting firm (Joann S. Lublin, "CEO pay sinks along with profits", *Wall Street Journal Online,* April 6, 2009; http://online.wsj.com/article/SB123870448211783759.html). Hay Group's study was limited to 200 very large corporations, defined as having more than $5 billion in yearly revenues. They found that for 2008, executive compensation fell 8.5 percent to an average salary-plus-bonuses compensation package of about $2.2 million. In light of these findings, the author of the article interprets this as evidence of a pay-performance link because, as a group, these 200 firms experienced either declines in profitability or outright losses during 2008. Under such difficult economic circumstances, the logic goes, if executive pay is affected by firm performance, then one would expect to see CEO pay take a hit, as is the case with this data.

On the other hand, consider the information found at the AFL-CIO's Executive PayWatch Web page (http://www.aflcio.org/corporatewatch/paywatch/). Here, the AFL-CIO—one of the most powerful unions in the world and most definitely not a supporter of large CEO pay—summarizes information from a study of the CEO compensation packages at the 500 corporations that comprise the S&P 500 stock market index. The results of this study, conducted by corporate governance research firm The Corporate Library, show that the average total compensation in 2008 for a CEO at a S&P 500 firm was approximately $10.4 million.

As the preceding example illustrates, finding common ground on even basic aspects of this topic is difficult. Consequently, it's not surprising that passions run high on both sides of this important management topic.

Suggested Readings

AFL-CIO, "2009 Executive PayWatch," http://www.aflcio.org/corporatewatch/paywatch/

Joann S. Lublin, "CEO Pay Sinks Along with Profits," *Wall Street Journal Online* (April 6, 2009). http://online.wsj.com/article/SB123870448211783759.html

Ted Balaker, "Nothing Wrong with CEOs Making Top Dollar," from the *Los Angeles Business Journal* (November 6, 2006). Article found at *Reason Foundation:* http://www.reason.org/news/show/122437.html

Yaron Brook, "Don't Cap CEO Pay: End Bailouts," *Ayn Rand Center for Individual Rights* (September 23, 2008). http://www.aynrand.org/site/News2?page=NewsArticle&id=21359&news_iv_ctrl=2528

Edward Lawler III, "Fixing Executive Compensation Excesses," *BusinessWeek* (February 5, 2009). http://www.businessweek.com/managing/content/feb2009/ca2009025_072667.htm

Chuck Jaffe, "Say On Pay Rules Won't Satisfy Public's Salary Bloodlust," *FoxBusiness* (April 1, 2009). http://www.foxbusiness.com/story/markets/industries/finance/say-pay-rules-wont-satisfy-publics-salary-bloodlust/

Madhukar Angur, "Executive Pay Isn't That Excessive and Some CEOs Really Deserve It," IBDeditorials (March 23, 2009). http://www.ibdeditorials.com/IBDArticles.aspx?id=322697364171124

ISSUE 4

Does an Employer's Need to Monitor Workers Trump Employee Privacy Concerns?

YES: Ian D. Meklinsky and Anne Ciesla Bancroft, from "Mindful Monitoring," *Security Management* (April 2007), http://www .securitymanagement.com/article/mindful-monitoring

NO: National Workrights Institute, from *Privacy Under Siege: Electronic Monitoring in the Workplace* (National Workrights Institute, 2005), http://www.workrights .org/issue_electronic.html

ISSUE SUMMARY

YES: Ian Meklinsky and Anne Ciesla Bancroft, experts in employment law, provide insightful analysis of this issue while explaining how, when, and why monitoring can and should be used in the workplace.

NO: The National Workrights Institute acknowledges that monitoring is legal for most employers most of the time but argues that more stringent laws should be enacted to provide more protection of employee rights.

One of the oldest sources of workplace conflict arises from the need of managers to monitor and control employee behavior at work. The trouble is that employees feel they have legitimate rights to privacy and that these rights are violated when management monitors workplace behavior. Although this issue is not new, over the past couple of decades, it has taken on increased importance as a result, primarily, of advances in electronic technology that allow for much closer monitoring of a much wider range of employee behaviors. Consequently, employees, now more than ever, feel that their rights are being violated. Employers and shareholders respond that their property rights are frequently violated by employees at the workplace. Thus, it is not surprising that they view monitoring employee behavior as a legitimate method of protecting their property.

An important study by the American Management Association in 2005 gives a good perspective on just how prevalent electronic monitoring in the workplace has become. The AMA surveyed more than 500 U.S. businesses, the majority of which had more than 2,500 employees. The results revealed that wide-ranging electronic monitoring methods were employed as a means to "manage productivity and protect resources" (American Management Association, *2005 Electronic Monitoring & Surveillance Survey: Many Companies Monitoring, Recording, Videotaping—and Firing—Employees,* May 18, 2005. http://www.amanet.org/press/amanews/ems05.htm). For example, 76 percent of surveyed firms monitor employee Web-surfing activities, and 65 percent use software designed to block access to unauthorized Internet locations. Over one-third (36%) of the firms monitor employee computer keystrokes, and 50 percent reported storing and reviewing employee e-mails. Also, over half (51%) reported using video surveillance to reduce theft and sabotage, while another 57 percent reported monitoring or restricting employee telephone behaviors, including the inappropriate use of voicemail.

To those supportive of employee monitoring policies, the results of the AMA survey are perfectly reasonable. Beyond the desire to reduce theft and to increase employee productivity, two additional arguments are frequently made in defense of employee monitoring. First is the fact that corporations can be held legally responsible for the behaviors of their employees at work. By way of example, consider an employee who causes an accident while under the influence of drugs at work. The employee not only causes property and human harm but also puts the organization into a legal bind because the firm can be held legally responsible for the employee's actions. As noted in Issue 6 in this text, businesses react to this threat by monitoring employee behavior via workplace drug testing. A second argument involves the issue of property rights. As noted earlier, shareholders have property rights in the organization and are legally allowed to defend and protect it. When an employee uses the organization's property (i.e., computers, telephones, etc.) improperly, the employee is not only violating his or her employment contract but is also, essentially, stealing from the company. Thus, from the shareholder's perspective, monitoring employee behavior is simply a way of protecting their property.

On the other side of this debate are those who claim that employees have rights in the workplace, including the right to privacy. Advocates of this perspective assert that monitoring all too often goes beyond tracking employee productivity and is used to gather personal information on employees. They point to numerous instances of management spying on employees with video cameras in restrooms and other non-work areas in the office. Another argument raised by supporters of employee rights is to note that many studies have shown little or no evidence that monitoring actually results in productivity gains, thereby undermining an important component of the pro-monitoring position. It should be noted, however, that despite the strong emotional appeal of the privacy rights position, it has not held up well in the courtroom. As noted in your "no" article for this topic, "And yet there are few, if any, legal protections for employees. There has been no attempt to balance employer demands with legitimate employee privacy concerns" (National Workrights Institute, *Privacy under siege: Electronic monitoring in the workplace,* http://www.workrights.org, 2005).

YES ⤶

Ian D. Meklinsky and
Anne Ciesla Bancroft

Mindful Monitoring

On January 30, 2001, Anthony Cochenour called the FBI with a tip. Cochenour's company, an Internet service provider, sold e-mail services to Frontline, an online payment processor. Cochenour told FBI Agent James Kennedy that a Frontline employee was accessing child pornography from his work computer. Kennedy contacted Frontline. As it turned out, the company's IT department was already monitoring the culprit, Brian Ziegler.

After talking with Kennedy, IT employees decided to go beyond monitoring Ziegler's computer activity remotely through the network. They obtained from HR a key to Ziegler's office, which he kept locked when he was not there. Staff then entered the office when he was away and made two copies of Ziegler's hard drive. The company, on advice of counsel, then turned Ziegler's computer over to the FBI. Forensic examiners found numerous images of child pornography.

In May 2003, Ziegler was indicted on three counts of receiving obscene material. He pled not guilty. He also filed a lawsuit seeking to suppress the evidence against him, claiming that it was obtained illegally.

According to Ziegler's suit, the government acted through Frontline to obtain the computer files and violated his Fourth Amendment right to privacy in the process. The U.S. District Court for the District of Montana held that Ziegler had no expectation of privacy in the files he accessed on the Internet, so those rights could not be violated by the government or his employer.

Ziegler appealed the decision. He argued that his computer files were the same as files in a desk drawer or a file cabinet. As proof, Ziegler noted that Frontline employees had to go through a locked door and access a password-protected account to get to the incriminating files.

The U.S. Court of Appeals for the Ninth Circuit ruled that Ziegler's expectations of privacy were not reasonable. The court noted that Frontline had an employee monitoring program and that employees were informed about it through training and a manual. Employees were specifically told that the computers were owned by the company and were not to be used for personal activities. In the written opinion of the case, the court noted that "employee monitoring is largely an assumed practice, and thus we think a disseminated computer-use policy is entirely sufficient to defeat any [privacy] expectation that an employee might harbor." (U.S. v. Ziegler, U.S. Court of Appeals for the Ninth Circuit, 2006)

Many organizations have resorted to monitoring their employees' use of e-mail and Internet systems to prevent abuses and to protect themselves and their employees. However, as the Ziegler case illustrates, employers must be mindful of employee privacy rights as they implement monitoring programs if they are to steer clear of liability.

Employee Protection

Employees may be protected from an employer's electronic monitoring under three categories. First, employees may seek protection under either the federal or a state constitution. Second, a federal or state statute may provide employees with protection. Third, employees may be able to find some common law precedent on which to base a claim that the company violated their privacy rights. Let's take a look at each of these protection categories.

Constitutional protections.   Privacy rights are not specifically mentioned in the U.S. Constitution, and while the Supreme Court has found a right of privacy in the Fourth Amendment, it applies only to actions carried out by governmental entities, not to the actions of private employers. In their state constitutions, many states, however, provide for a right of privacy that applies both to government and private sector actors.

Employers need to be aware of the constitutions of states in which they operate when developing monitoring policies. Public-sector employers, such as schools, must be cognizant of the federal privacy rights conferred by the Fourth Amendment as well as state constraints.

Statutory protections.   The statutes most directly applicable to electronic monitoring in the private-sector workplace are federal and state wiretapping laws. On the federal level, the Wiretap Act, as amended by the Electronic Communications Privacy Act of 1986 (ECPA), prohibits the interception, recording, and disclosure of "any wire, oral, or electronic communication" unless one of a few exceptions applies. The Stored Communications Act (SCA) prohibits unauthorized access to "the contents of a communication while [it is] in electronic storage" unless an exception applies.

Because the general rule is that an employer cannot intercept, access, record, or disclose an electronic communication, employers must qualify for one of the exceptions to these rules. The two most prevalent exceptions are the business extension exception and the consent exception.

Business extension.   The business extension exception pertains to certain types of interceptions. For example, if an employer uses equipment such as telephones, facilities, or related components furnished by a telephone service provider to a subscriber or user in the ordinary course of business, then the employer may intercept electronic communications that are business-related. An employer's telephone lines and facilities have been determined to fall within this exception. (As discussed later, the employer may not intercept personal communications.)

A business may not install tape recorders or other monitoring devices that are not acquired from a telephone service provider in the ordinary course of business to record conversations. (The government may not tape record conversations without a warrant.) However, employers may monitor the statistical aspects of employee telephone communications for data on the origin and destination of calls, call duration, and number of outgoing calls.

Under the exception, employers may monitor the content of employee communications only within certain contexts. To monitor the content of employee communications, an employer must have a reasonable business purpose, such as enforcing a no-private-calls policy or monitoring employee efficiency.

The methods and scope of interception must be reasonable. Under the exception, it is unreasonable for an employer to record all conversations in their entirety. The interception must terminate as soon as the monitored communication indicates that the message is personal.

Consent. Under the consent exception, it is legal for a person to intercept communications across state lines where one party has given prior consent. Also, interceptions are legal where the interceptor is a party to the communication. When both parties are in the same state, the law of that state prevails. For example, in Pennsylvania, all parties must consent.

This exception allows that consent may be implied where employers give appropriate notice to employees, and employees agree to the monitoring. However, a surreptitious or secret interception negates this consent.

The Federal Trade Commission has rules governing how companies must notify nonemployees if telephone communications will be taped. These involve issuing oral warnings that the conversations are being recorded or periodic tones that indicate taping.

An employer who is lackadaisical about establishing a proper and legal monitoring policy could face significant damage to its business, as well as liability. And the charges can go beyond the normal invasion-of-privacy claim. For example, an employer could be liable under the Sarbanes Oxley Act (SOX) for the release of confidential information of clients and customers.

States. Many states have adopted laws equivalent to the federal wiretap statute. In many respects, these laws track the federal law. However, some state courts have interpreted these statutes in different ways. For example, in Montana, a district court ruled that the use of a handheld recorder to record voicemail messages was not an interception, particularly where the person leaving the voicemail message consented to leaving the message in the first place. In contrast, a New Jersey district court ruled that the recording of phone conversations with a tape recorder and adapter is an interception. And, in a recent Pennsylvania case, a court ruled that searching a server and retrieving an employee's e-mails is not a violation of the ECPA or the SCA.

Numerous states have recently enacted identity theft protection laws. Under these provisions, employers have affirmative obligations to protect computerized records containing personal information and to report breaches of security to law enforcement and the individual whose information was accessed. These laws also impose requirements regarding the destruction of hard copies of such information, as well as restrictions on the use and dissemination of Social Security numbers.

Common law protection.   Employees seeking redress from electronic monitoring periodically assert an invasion of privacy claim. Most jurisdictions recognize this claim. In general, a party who intentionally intrudes, physically or otherwise, on the solitude or seclusion of another or on his private affairs or concerns is subject to liability for invasion of privacy if the intrusion would be highly offensive to a reasonable person.

Despite the availability of this type of claim, courts rarely find that employers have invaded the privacy of an employee through electronic monitoring. To be successful, an employee must overcome several hurdles. There must be an intrusion and the intrusion must be intentional. The employee must have a reasonable expectation of privacy in the matter intruded on and the intrusion must be highly offensive to a reasonable person.

Then, even if the employee satisfies all of these criteria, the employee may still be unsuccessful if the court finds that the employer had a legitimate business reason for engaging in the intrusion that outweighed the employee's privacy interest.

To further reduce the likelihood that an employee would prevail in this type of claim, employers should eliminate the employee's reasonable expectation of privacy by having a well-publicized policy and obtaining employee consent to monitoring.

Challenges

Employers frequently ask their legal counsel about their right to monitor employee use of e-mail and the Internet to detect, for example, excessive online shopping or visits to inappropriate Web sites. They want to understand their rights and obligations with respect to accessing an employee's e-mail or Web site history.

Employers have certain obligations that virtually mandate monitoring and review. For example, employers are required to investigate wrongdoing under federal antidiscrimination laws. While this legal obligation might be enough to protect an employer who must search an employee's e-mails and Web usage, properly drafted polices are still necessary. Companies should, therefore, maintain clear policies concerning the use of the systems by employees and the employer's right to monitor that use.

There have been various court challenges to company monitoring programs. A review of these cases can help companies understand which practices may withstand legal scrutiny.

In one case (Campbell v. Woodard Photographic, Inc., U.S. District Court for the Northern District of Ohio, 2006) a federal court found that an employer invaded an employee's privacy during a workplace investigation. In the case, Woodard Photographic had experienced a series of suspected thefts of cash and office equipment. An investigator claimed that he found a printout of items that Dwayne Campbell had listed for sale on eBay and that these items were identical to the missing equipment. This evidence, coupled with other facts that pointed to Campbell as the culprit, was used to terminate Campbell.

Campbell filed a lawsuit against the company, claiming invasion of privacy. He claimed that he did not print out the eBay listings and that the company must have accessed his password-protected eBay account to get the information. The company requested that the case be dismissed.

The court denied the company's request, finding that Campbell could pursue his invasion of privacy claim against the company and that if the company did obtain its information by accessing a password-protected account, it could be held liable. However, the court did note that if the company had established an employee monitoring policy and communicated that policy to its employees, Campbell would not have had an expectation of privacy and his lawsuit would have failed.

Why monitor? To avoid the potential liability that monitoring could create, companies might be inclined simply to avoid any oversight or investigation of employee activity. Yet this approach can land them in hot water as well, as the case of Doe v. XYZ (Superior Court of New Jersey, 2005) illustrates. (Names were sealed in the case to protect the victims.)

XYZ Corporation employed 250 workers in Somerset County, New Jersey. One of the employees, whom the courts called John, worked for the company as an accountant. He worked in a cubicle, which was located along a wall in a line of cubicles. The cubicles had no doors and opened onto a hallway.

In late 1998, the company's IT manager, whom the court called George, conducted a standard computer log review and noted that John had been visiting pornographic Web sites. George told John to stop visiting the sites but did not tell John's supervisor, called Keith in court documents, about the incidents.

Over the next three years, various employees raised questions about John's Internet use. Two investigations launched by his supervisors proved that John had visited child pornography sites from his work computer. John was warned to stop several times but repeatedly slipped back into his old habits.

In 2001, John began taking nude photos of his 10-year-old stepdaughter (called Jill in the case). He transmitted three of these photos over the Internet from his workplace computer to a child pornography site. He also threw some photos of Jill in the trash at work. Someone saw the photos and called police.

When the police searched John's work computer, they found more than 1,000 pornographic images stored on his computer, e-mails to pornographic Web sites, and e-mail discussions with others about child pornography. The police arrested John for possession and transfer of child pornography.

Jill's mother, named as Jane Doe, sued XYZ for negligence, claiming that it knew or should have known that John was using his computer to view and download child pornography. The lawsuit also alleged that, because of the nature of the offense, XYZ had a duty to report John's activities to the police. According to Doe, this negligence led to the continued exploitation of her daughter.

XYZ filed a motion for summary judgment—a hearing based on the facts of a case, without a trial. The trial court granted the summary judgment, ruling that there was no evidence that the company knew that John's conduct was dangerous to others. Further, according to the court, the company had no duty to investigate the private communications of its employees.

Because most of the exploitation of Jill occurred in the home, the court concluded, more rapid action on the part of XYZ would not have protected the child. Doe appealed the decision.

The New Jersey Superior Court disagreed with the lower court, finding that XYZ could be held liable. The court determined that XYZ could have implemented software to monitor employee activity on the Internet. It also found that the company could have conducted investigations into computer use.

The company had a written policy stating that the employee had no right to privacy in e-mail or Web searches at work and that those who used the system for "improper purposes" could be disciplined or discharged. All employees were supposed to read and sign the policy. There was no record of John signing the policy, but according to the court, there was no suggestion that he was unaware of the policy.

Solutions

Companies should implement and disseminate a comprehensive electronic monitoring policy, and it should be well publicized to ensure that employees have no expectation of privacy.

An electronic monitoring policy should state that the employment relationship is "at will" and that the policy does not create a contract of employment, either express or implied. The policy should be part of a more comprehensive employee handbook that has all of the necessary and properly drafted disclaimer notices required by the courts.

This disclaimer must clearly state that employees have no expectation of privacy when they use the computer equipment or other communication systems provided by the employer, including the Internet and e-mail systems. Also, the policy must include the notice that the continued use of the employer's systems constitutes an employee's consent to monitoring.

In the policy, employers must assert that the business computer systems are the sole property of the company and that the employer has the right to monitor and access all areas of the employee's computer files.

Similarly, the policy should state that the employer reserves the right to store e-mails that pass into or out of its systems and that it may review e-mails and disclose the contents of e-mails to third parties, with or without notice to employees. Some employers may wish to apply the policy to all company communications systems.

The policy should advise employees that they may be liable for submission of personal information or other sensitive data they send through interactive computer systems. It should also caution employees that e-mails should only contain content that would otherwise be included in a normal business memorandum or letter. The company should clearly prohibit e-mails containing defamatory, sexual, racist, abusive, harassing or other offensive material.

The policy should also clearly state that accessing offensive Internet sites or offensive use of e-mail is prohibited. Companies may want to include a reference to the employer's antiharassment and antidiscrimination policies.

Some companies have taken an additional step and included statements in the policy asserting that all messages composed, sent, or received on the e-mail system are and remain the property of the employer and are not property of the employee.

Another possible statement a company might want to use would assert that the e-mail system may not be used to solicit or proselytize for commercial ventures, religious or political causes, outside organizations, or other nonbusiness-related solicitations.

Companies should notify employees that the confidentiality of any message should not be assumed, that even when a message is erased, it is still possible to retrieve and read that message, and that the company retains the right to amend the policies at any time. The company should also set out guidelines for the reporting of policy violations and explain the disciplinary steps that will be taken if an employee violates the policy.

The employer should obtain a signed acknowledgment form relating to the policy and maintain the acknowledgment in each employee's personnel file. In addition to having this written policy, management may want to have the IT department set up banners or sign-in windows so that as employees log on to the computer system, they are reminded that they consented to monitoring.

Employers cannot afford to ignore the legal issues arising out of the introduction of technology into the workplace especially when coupled with the employers' interests in monitoring the use of that technology. By addressing the legal ramifications of monitoring, employers can maintain efficiency while also avoiding liability.

Synopsis

Many organizations monitor their employees' use of e-mail and Internet systems to prevent abuses and to protect themselves and their employees. However, employers must be mindful of employee privacy rights as they implement monitoring programs if they are to steer clear of liability.

Employees may be protected from an employer's electronic monitoring under three categories: First, employees may seek protection under either the federal or a state constitution. Second, a federal or state statute may provide employees with protection. Third, employees may be able to find some common law precedent on which to base a claim that the company violated their privacy rights.

Employees seeking redress from electronic monitoring periodically assert an invasion of privacy claim. Despite the availability of this type of claim, courts rarely find that employers have invaded the privacy of an employee through electronic monitoring. To be successful, an employee must overcome several hurdles. There must be an intrusion, and the intrusion must be intentional. The employee must have a reasonable expectation of privacy in the matter intruded on, and the intrusion must be highly offensive to a reasonable person.

To further reduce the likelihood that an employee would prevail in this type of claim, employers should eliminate the employee's reasonable expectation of privacy by having a well-publicized policy and obtaining employee consent to monitoring.

Privacy Under Siege: Electronic Monitoring in the Workplace

Introduction

Everyone in the office knew that Gail would change her clothes in her cubicle for the gym after the work day was done. When her employers installed a hidden camera to monitor the person in the neighboring cubicle's suspected illegal activities, her daily ritual was captured on film. The first few times could have been labeled as mistakes, but the filming of Gail changing her clothes over a five month period was inexcusable.

Electronic monitoring is a rapidly growing phenomenon in American businesses. Introduced in the early twentieth century for such limited uses as timing breaks and measuring hand-eye movements, systematic electronic monitoring has since grown into the very fabric of American business practice. As technologies become more powerful and easy and inexpensive to install and maintain, the rates of electronic monitoring in this country have skyrocketed. In 1999 the percentage of employers who electronically monitor their workers was 67%. Just two years later, in the year 2001 this number had increased to 78%. By 2003, 92% of employers were conducting some form of workplace monitoring. This rapid growth in monitoring has virtually destroyed any sense of privacy as we know it in the American workplace. Employers now conduct video surveillance, listen in on employee telephone calls, review employee computer use such as e-mail and the Internet and monitor their every move using GPS. But as legitimate work product is being monitored, so are the personal habits and lives of employees. As technology has proliferated in the workplace, it has become ever more penetrating and intrusive. And yet there are few, if any, legal protections for employees. There has been no attempt to balance employer demands with legitimate employee privacy concerns. Collection and use of personal information is a rampant byproduct of workplace monitoring and threatens the very freedoms that we cherish as Americans. Legislation is necessary to govern the practice of electronic monitoring in the workplace, protect employee privacy and return a sense of fundamental fairness and dignity to the American workplace.

Privacy and Intrusion Issues

While employers generally initiate electronic monitoring in response to legitimate business concerns, the results have been devastating to employee privacy. Virtually everything we do and say at work can be, and is, monitored by our employers. Our employers watch us on video cameras, read our e-mails, listen to our voice mail, review documents on our hard drives, and check every Web site we visit.

This would be bad enough if it involved only work related behavior and communication, but it doesn't. The advent of cell phones, pagers, and home computers is rapidly erasing the traditional wall between the home and the workplace. People now regularly receive communications from their employer at home. Maggie Jackson, former workplace correspondent for the Associated Press, estimates that the average professional or managerial employee now receives over 20 electronic messages from work every week. This new flexibility also means that personal communication increasingly occurs in the workplace. An employee who spent much of the weekend on a cell phone with her boss will not (and should not) consider it inappropriate to make a personal call from the office.

This means that employer monitoring systems frequently record personal communications. Often, this communication is not sensitive. But sometimes the messages are very personal. An employee who sends their spouse a romantic e-mail while eating lunch at his or her desk can find that their love letter has been read by their boss. Or a note to a psychiatrist stored in an employee's hard drive is disclosed.

Internet monitoring can be extremely invasive. People today turn to the Internet as their primary source of information, including sensitive subjects they would be uncomfortable communicating about on their office telephone or e-mail. In part, this is because of the efficiency of internet research. Even an untrained person can find information on the Web in minutes that would have taken hours or even days to find by traditional means (if they could find it at all). People also turn to the Internet for information because they can do so anonymously.

The result is that people turn to the Internet for information and help about the most sensitive subjects imaginable. Women who are victims of domestic abuse turn to the Internet for information about shelters and other forms of help. People also turn to the Web for information and help with drug and alcohol problems, financial difficulties, marital problems, and medical issues. Monitoring Web access gives an employer a picture window into employees' most sensitive personal problems.

Most invasive of all is video monitoring. Some cameras are appropriate. Security cameras in stairwells and parking garages make us all safer without intruding on privacy. But employers often install cameras in areas that are completely indefensible. Many employers have installed hidden video cameras in locker rooms and bathrooms, sometimes inside the stalls. No one should be subjected to sexual voyeurism on the job.

Such problems are made worse by the manner in which monitoring is often conducted. Most employers make no effort to avoid monitoring personal communications. The majority of employers install systems that make no distinction between business and personal messages, even when more discriminating systems are available.

In addition to official monitoring, IT employees often monitor their fellow employees for personal reasons. Most employers give such employees carte blanche access to employee communications. While it is possible to set up technical barriers to ensure that monitoring is confined to official programs, few employers use them. Many employers do not even have policies directing IT employees to restrict their monitoring to official programs. Even employers with such policies rarely have procedures to enforce them. As a result, employees involved in monitoring often read the messages of fellow employees for their own amusement.

The final indignity is that employees don't even know when they are being watched. While a majority of employers provide employees what is described as notice, still many do not and the information currently provided is generally useless. The standard employer notice states only that the company reserves the right to monitor anything at any time. Employees do not know whether it is their e-mail, voice mail, Web access, or hard drive that is monitored. They do not know whether the monitoring is continuous, random, or as needed. They do not even know whether they are being monitored at all. Such notice is almost worse than no notice at all.

As bad as the situation is today, it is likely to be far worse in the future. Many people today do work for their employer on their home computers. The most direct example of this is telecommuting. Approximately 20 million employees and independent contractors now work at home at least one day per month, and this number is growing rapidly. Millions more have linked their home computer to their office network so they can work from home informally on evenings and weekends.

When this occurs, people's home computers are subject to monitoring by their employer. Workplace computer monitoring systems monitor the entire network, including a home computer that is temporarily part of the network. This means that personal communications in our home computers will be revealed to our employers. Personal e-mail sent from or received by our home computers will be disclosed to our employers, along with personal letters, financial records, and any other personal information in our home computers. Not only is this possible, it is highly likely. When asked if they would be interested in having personal information from employees' home computers, corporate attorneys responded positively.

Monitoring and Productivity

Employers generally conduct electronic monitoring in order to increase productivity. It is far from clear, however, that monitoring achieves this goal. In fact, too much monitoring can actually decrease productivity by increasing employee stress and decreasing morale.

In a study conducted for Bell Canada it was reported that 55% of all long distance and directory assistance operators experienced added stress due to some form of monitoring. Increased stress can often lead to physical symptoms. In a study by the Department of Industrial Engineering, University of Wisconsin-Madison, higher levels of stress in monitored employees resulted in an increase in somatic complaints, including a 27% increase in occurrences of pain or stiffness in shoulders, a 23% increase in occurrences of neck pressure and a 21%

increase in back pain experienced by employees. Such stress and stress related symptoms can create medical expenses, lost time and absenteeism.

Studies have shown that the introduction of electronic monitoring into the workplace is likely to encourage employees to favor quantity of work produced over quality. Even employers who do not intend on placing production increases above quality may do so inadvertently, simply because quality is more difficult to monitor electronically. Pressure to increase productivity commonly has adverse effects on the quality of work produced. In two studies published in the National Productivity Review the authors found that "monitored employees were less willing to pursue complex customer inquiries than their unmonitored coworkers." Similar results were found in other productivity studies.

Trust between employee and employer is crucial to maintaining a high level of productivity and unnecessary and covert monitoring is harmful to this balance. A recent study conducted jointly by Microsoft and the London School of Economics found that "providing information in an environment of trust can greatly facilitate the coordination of work." Indeed "Mutual trust is not an added bonus of the mobile organization, it is an absolute core principle. . . Mistrust results in the perceived need to engage in activities only serving the purpose of demonstrating ability internally and not generating business value."

This does not mean that employers should never collect information about employees' work by electronic means. It does mean, however, that monitoring should not be employed based on a general idea that it will increase productivity. Before initiating any program of monitoring, employers should carefully consider:

1. Why they believe this specific monitoring program will increase efficiency.
2. The effect of the monitoring program on employee stress.
3. The effect of the program upon employee morale.
4. Whether the value of the increased efficiency outweighs the cost of increased stress and decreased morale.

As with any other important decision, employers should attempt to quantify these factors and conduct a cost-benefit analysis.

More Effective Solutions

Most employers are not voyeurs. More often than not, they would rather not know personal information about their employees that has no bearing on job performance. Yet there is rarely an attempt to be more discriminating in their practices or a balancing of employer needs with employee privacy concerns. There are a variety of ways that employers can address specific concerns without monitoring highly personal information. The following are a few suggestions.

- Businesses should properly train managers and supervisors to deal with employee issues and problems. Most businesses do not have managers that are properly trained to deal with sensitive employee subjects. These staffs need to be observant and reactive to employee needs. Properly trained managers are a company's best asset in terms of dealing directly with and correcting many of the concerns that prompt the adoption of electronic monitoring practices. Supervising staffs can set conduct guidelines, address concerns, mediate complaints, as well as monitor and deal individually with those employees that choose to abuse company resources.

- Businesses should always conduct an in-house assessment to identify whether electronic monitoring is even necessary. This seems like an obvious point, but many businesses adopt large scale monitoring programs on the assumption that they will add benefits to their workplace without identifying their own specific requirements and whether the adoption of an electronic monitoring program would meet those requirements.
- Before deciding to conduct monitoring, management should speak with employees about the productivity problem. Employees may suggest alternative ways of solving the problem. If monitoring is chosen, employees can participate in designing the monitoring program and its scope in a way that is acceptable to them.
- If monitoring is conducted, the scope should be as narrow as is consistent with achieving the desired objective. Employers should be especially careful to restrict the program to business related communications and avoid monitoring personal communications. Additionally they should utilize Web access software that eliminates the need for monitoring each individual Web site an employee visits.
- Consider monitoring on an "event basis." This involves conducting monitoring when it is known something inappropriate has occurred and confining the monitoring to dealing with that event.
- If a company does choose to adopt a program of electronic monitoring, proper notice should be given well in advance of any monitoring practices. This notice should explicitly state what would be monitored as well as when this monitoring would occur. The American Management Association has recommended that employers give notice of electronic monitoring since 1997.

The Numbers: Electronic Monitoring Has Become a Common Practice

Electronic monitoring in the American workplace has seen dramatic growth in recent years. Prior to 1980, electronic monitoring was virtually unknown. When the Congressional Office of Technology Assessment studied its use in 1987, only 7% of employees were affected. But in only 6 years, a MacWorld survey found that electronic monitoring had nearly tripled (to 20% of employees). In 2001, the American Management Association reported that the percentage of companies monitoring had risen to 78.4%. By 2003, 92% of employers were conducting workplace monitoring.

Even more troubling are the ways employers monitor:

- 75% of employers that monitor do so without individualized cause
- 50% of all employers that do have a monitoring policy do not train their employees about their monitoring policy

- 20% of employers do not have a written monitoring policy
- 25% of employers do not have in place any procedures or safeguards to ensure that the monitoring process is not abused

While the national debate over privacy rages, the unregulated growth of electronic monitoring in the American workplace shows no signs of abating.

Everyday People: Stories of Workplace Monitoring across America

California

At a Neiman-Marcus Store in Fashion Island Newport Beach, Kelly Pendleton, a two-time "employee of the year" discovered a hidden camera in the ceiling of the changing room used by female employees that was being monitored by male colleagues.

Employees of Consolidated Freightways were horrified to find that the company had installed hidden cameras in its restrooms—some cameras pointing directly at the urinals. Over a thousand hours of video records were made covering thousands of employees. "The guys were really shaken, and some of the women went home crying," says Joe Quilty, the dockworker who discovered the hidden cameras.

An AT&T employee received a formal reprimand for using the company e-mail system to send a love note to his wife, also an AT&T employee.

9th Circuit Court of Appeals Judges disabled computer monitoring software that had been installed by the Administrative Office of the U.S. Courts without notice or consent. Judge Alex Kozinski charged that the surveillance system was a needless invasion of privacy. Several members of Congress agreed, Rep. Howard Berman wrote "While it may be appropriate to monitor an employee's Internet use or e-mail in certain circumstances, I do not believe indiscriminate, systematic monitoring is appropriate. . . It is particularly inappropriate for the courts, which will inevitably be called on to rule in cases involving questions of employee privacy."

Alana Shoars was in charge of the Epson Torrance, California plant e-mail system. Ms. Shoars assured Epson employees that their e-mail was private. She discovered later that her supervisor was reading all employee e-mail in the Torrance plant.

Florida

An employee of Walt Disney World videotaped female employees in bathrooms and locker rooms. After several months, Disney security became aware of these activities, but did nothing to correct the situation for many months. Finally, Disney decided to conduct a sting operation by setting up its own video surveillance system. None of the female employees were informed so they could take measures to protect themselves and both the employees and the voyeur were videotaped hours in the dressing room area.

The general manager of the Apalachicola Times newspaper installed a hidden video camera in the employee bathroom and made 29 videotapes worth of recordings. Barbara Lynn Perry, one of several women who was regularly videotaped remarked "No one had my permission as far as surveillance. . . . I was never formally or informally asked for my permission. I had no idea there was a camera in the bathroom."

Georgia

Air force machinist Donald Thompson is placed under investigation by the Office of Special Counsel for forwarding an e-mail lampooning the president's qualifications. "To me, sending it was just an electronic version of water cooler chit chat" he said.

Female employees at a local plant in Pendergrass run by Atlas Cold Storage were regularly videotaped in the bathroom without their knowledge or consent. According to employees, the plant manager would regularly remind them that "there's not anywhere you can go where I can't see you."

Hawaii

Hawaiian airlines pilot Robert Konop sets up a personal, password protected website so that he and fellow pilots can have private discussions and freely criticize management. A Vice-President of the airline pressures a fellow pilot for the password and accesses the site.

Illinois

A technology professional was terminated after his boss listened in on a phone conversation he was having with his girlfriend after his shift ended.

An employee quits after his boss announces to the entire office the content of a personal e-mail that had been retrieved from the monitoring system.

Maryland

A 17-year-old woman, Jennifer Smith, testified before the Judiciary Committee of the Maryland House of Representatives that in her job as a lifeguard, she was videotaped changing into her bathing suit by her supervisor at the county swimming pool.

Massachusetts

At the Sheraton Boston Hotel hidden cameras were discovered in the employee changing room. Hours of tape of employees in different stages of undress were logged. One of the Sheraton workers, Jean L. Clement, stated that: "Learning about the secret videotaping made me very scared at work because I feel as though I'm being watched wherever I go, which is how I felt when I lived in Haiti."

Nebraska

Melissa Haines of Broken Bow, an employee of Mid-Nebraska Individual Services, discovered hidden monitors the employer had installed to record personal as well work related conversations. "My job has been awful. Is there anything I can do? What I say to a friend should be confidential," she remarked.

New Jersey

The City of Clinton Township, NJ installed GPS tracking devices behind the front grilles of patrol cars without notifying their officers.

A female employee logs onto an expectant mothers' Web site at her job during working hours. Just looking for information, the employee tells no one of her possible condition. Soon after, her immediate supervisor congratulates her on her pregnancy.

Heidi Arace and Norma Yetsko, two employees of the PNC Bank, were terminated after forwarding jokes on their company's e-mail. Such letters had been regularly sent in the past by fellow employees with the attention of the employer and they had previously never enforced any monitoring policies. As Arace puts it, "I was cold. I was frozen. It was like I lost everything in my life. You get a simple e-mail like this, you read it; you chuckle; forward it on, click. Done deal . . . everyone was doing it."

New York

Howard Boyle, president of a fire sprinkler installation company in Woodside, N.Y., presented his employees with cell phones to use without informing them that they were equipped with GPS. Mr. Boyle can find out where they are at all times including during breaks and while they are off duty. "They don't need to know," said Mr. Boyle. "I can call them and say, 'Where are you now?' while I'm looking at the screen and knowing exactly where they are."

Lourdes Rachel Arias and Louis J. Albero discovered that their employer, Mutual Central Alarm Service, was monitoring and recording all incoming and outgoing telephone calls including personal and private conversations without notice or consent.

Pennsylvania

Despite assurances from his employer that e-mail was confidential, that it would not be intercepted, and that it would not be used for the basis for discipline or discharge, Michael Smyth is terminated for sending an unprofessional message from his home over the company e-mail.

Tennessee

Joyce Carr and Bernice Christianson discovered that their employer, Northern Telecom, was secretly taping all incoming and outgoing private telephone conversations in a Nashville plant by means of hidden microphones. An investigation discovered systematic efforts by top management to wiretap public pay phones in the employee cafeteria and monitor conversations through microphones in the plant sprinkler system.

Texas

Microsoft, which had no monitoring policy at the time, opens the personal folders of employee Bill McLaren's office computer even though they are password protected.

Washington

At Washington's WJLA-TV station, tracking devices were installed in station vehicles supposedly to allow editors to know where the closest vehicle might be to a breaking story, but employees claimed that the devices had been used to monitor them. Employees recounted stories of managers phoning them to instruct them to drive slower or to question them about stopping at certain locations.

Electronic Monitoring of Employees a Lack of Legal Regulation

Federal Law

The only relevant federal legislation to protect employee privacy is the Omnibus Crime Control and Safe Streets Act of 1968, as amended by the Electronic Communications Privacy Act of 1986. The ECPA, with certain exceptions, prohibits the interception, disclosure, or use of a wire, oral or electronic communication. This protection applies to all businesses involved in interstate commerce and has also been interpreted to extend to most intrastate phone communications. It also applies to conversations between employees that employers may overhear because the employees are wearing headsets. The Act creates both criminal and civil causes of action. Civil remedies may include compensatory and punitive damages, as well as attorney's fees and other litigation costs.

There are three exceptions to this blanket prohibition. One exception allows wire and communications service providers (common carriers) to intercept communications if done for quality of service purposes. Under this exception, a telephone company can monitor its employees to ensure adequate job performance and supervise customer contacts.

A second exception allows interception when there is consent. A party to the communication may intercept the communication, or prior consent may be given by one of the parties to the communication. Generally, courts will not find implied consent. For instance, knowledge of the capability of monitoring alone will not substitute for actual consent. See Watkins v. L.M. Berry & Co., 704 F. 2d 577 (11th Cir. 1983). Consent will be implied where the employee is aware of a general monitoring program and uses a business-only phone to make a personal call when other phones are provided for that purpose. See Simmons v. Southwestern Bell Tel. Co., 452 F. Supp. 392 (W.D. Okla. 1978), aff'd., 611 F 2d 342 (10th Cir. 1979).

The third and primary exception allows for wire eavesdropping when done in the "ordinary course of business": context and content. Under a context analysis, emphasis is placed on the importance of the business policy served by the monitoring and extent to which the monitoring furthers that policy without unnecessarily interfering with employee privacy. Business units whose primary function involves customer contact via telephone have the strongest argument for the legitimacy of monitoring. The "unnecessary interference" element includes considerations of whether the monitoring was announced or covert and whether separate telephones were provided for personal calls. A content analysis focuses on whether the monitored call was personal or business in nature. Regardless of their chosen approach, the courts have consistently held that an employer violates the act when it continues to monitor a purely personal phone call after learning of its personal nature. See U.S. v. Harpel, 493 F. 2d 346 (10th Cir. 1974) and U.S. v. Axselle, 604 F. 2d 414 (5th Cir. 1980). The employer may be limited to a "reasonable" length of time to make this determination. Courts which have considered this question have defined "reasonable" as anywhere from 10 seconds to 5 minutes (See Watkins and Axselle).

ECPA does prohibit access to stored communications (Stored Communications Act) but this prohibition is also subject to severely weakening exceptions. There remain access exemptions for the person or entity providing a wire or electronic communications service and for the user of that service with respect to a communication of or intended for that user. Employers are likely to fall under one or both of such exceptions.

What limited protections ECPA does provide to employees have been greatly weakened because the statute has quickly become outdated. The ECPA does not apply to most common forms of monitoring technologies such as electronic mail monitoring, Internet monitoring and video surveillance. Since ECPA requires an "interception" of a communication, communications in a stored state are exempt. Additionally, as in the case of electronic mail, courts have so far found that company owned proprietary systems are exempt. See Shoars v. Epson, 90 SWC 112749 and 90 BC 7036 (Superior Court, Los Angeles County). Assurances by employers that monitored and stored employee e-mails are not reviewed by management is no guarantee that employers will not reprimand or terminate employees for the content of their e-mail messages. See Smyth v. Pillsbury & Co. 914 F. Supp. 97, 101 (E.D. Pa. 1996).

Additionally the ECPA does not require an employer to give notice of electronic monitoring practices, nor is there any other statute that requires an employer to give notice of monitoring practices, no matter how invasive the monitoring may be.

State Law

In addition to federal statute, employees sometimes also receive some privacy protection from various state constitutional, common law and statutory sources. Most states have a constitutional provision that reflects the proscriptions in the Fourth amendment regarding search and seizure. Some states have specific constitutional guarantees of privacy that extend beyond the Federal Constitution's privacy rights. Only California courts, however, have held that the state constitutional right of privacy applies with respect to both public and private employers. See Porten v. University of San Francisco, 134 Cal. Rptr. 839 (Cal Ct. App. 1976) In all other states, employees have successfully invoked the state constitutional right of privacy only after establishing the government as the employer. Some state courts, such as New Jersey and Alaska, have nevertheless determined that their state constitutions can form a basis for creating public policy arguments in favor of a private sector employee's right to privacy.

A majority of states do have statutes restricting the interception of wire communications by private individuals. These states, however, generally mirror the ECPA, and contain similar exceptions and exemptions. Although some states have shown a willingness to legislate in the employee privacy area, the efforts have only been piecemeal. Within the past year California has added a section to its Labor Code that prohibits an employer from monitoring, without a court order, employees in restrooms, locker rooms or other places designated by the employer for changing clothes. Labor Code, Sec 435 (a) to (c). Additionally, Connecticut added a section to its labor code requiring employers to give employees written notice of the types of monitoring which may occur. Conn. Gen. Stat. Sec 31-48d. Nevertheless, state governments have not addressed the issue comprehensively or uniformly, and in most cases have not addressed it at all.

Finally, some limited protections exist in the common law of torts. The tort that most plaintiffs use to challenge employer monitoring and surveillance is the intrusion-on-seclusion tort. The classic conception of this tort, recognized in every state, is that it is used to punish highly offensive privacy invasions. There has been an attempt to apply the tort in the employment context to challenge workplace monitoring abuses. Under present law, however, formidable obstacles face the employee who wishes to bring such a privacy claim.

First, the intrusion-on-seclusion tort requires the employee to establish that the monitoring conduct is highly objectionable to a reasonable person. Because routine monitoring can appear harmless from some perspectives (especially that of a third party), and because the negative effects of such monitoring are often gradual and incremental, this standard frequently forecloses an employee claim. In particular, when the monitoring complained of has been arguably linked to work-related activities, those challenges have been unsuccessful. See Barksdale v. IBM 620 F. Supp. 1380 (W.D.N.C. 1985). Additionally, courts have not been receptive to employee claims that their work environments contain sufficiently private spaces for an invasion of privacy to occur. See Ulrich v. K-Mart Corp., 858 F. Supp. 1087 (D. Kan. 1994). For example, an employee's office, desk or locker may be held to be the employer's property, and therefore not private. The combination of these elements typically defeats an employee's tort claim in all but the most egregious of circumstances, which usually involve monitoring in areas such as bathrooms or locker rooms. Even in such highly private areas, state court decisions are mixed. See, for example, Speer v. Department of Rehabilitation & Correction, 646 N. E. 2d 273 (Ohio Ct. Cl. 1994).

Questions and Answers

Is there a Need for Workplace Privacy Legislation?

Yes. The explosion of workplace surveillance in recent years has stripped Americans of virtually all their privacy on the job. Nearly 80% of employers now use electronic surveillance. Soon it will be universal. Employer monitoring practices often go well beyond specific and even legitimate management concerns. They are rarely tailored to meet individual employer demands or balanced with employee privacy concerns. Current laws are outdated, vague or more often silent on this issue. A balance between the legitimate concerns of business and employee privacy must be created.

Should Employers Give Notice of Monitoring?

Yes. Employers may need to conduct monitoring for quality control and other business reasons, but they do not need to do it in secret. Indeed, the American Management Association and most corporate counsels recommend that employers provide notice of monitoring programs. Legitimate monitoring programs do not need to be carried out behind employees' backs. Secret monitoring is not only unnecessary, it is counterproductive. The purpose of monitoring is to ensure that employees are following company policy regarding the use of electronic communications technology. If employees know that the company monitors e-mail or Internet access, they will be more careful to follow the rules. Most important, secret monitoring is ethically wrong. People have a right to know when they are being watched. Reading someone else's messages without telling them is both deceptive and a profound violation of their privacy.

In What Situations Should Monitoring be Limited?

Employers have legitimate reasons for many monitoring programs. Company e-mail systems have sometimes been used to send inappropriate material that contributes to a hostile environment. The seemingly endless level of information on the Internet has led some employees to spend excessive time at work Web surfing. Employers need to respond to these concerns. But, without limitation, employers' efforts to prevent abuse can often lead to serious invasions of privacy. People are not robots. They discuss the weather, sports, their families, and many other matters unrelated to their jobs while at work. While many of these non-work related conversations are innocuous, some are highly personal. An employee might tell her best friend about problems with her husband or share concerns about family financial problems, or their fear that their child may have a drug problem. Most employers are not voyeurs. More often than not, they would rather not know personal information about their employees that has no bearing on job performance. Yet there is rarely an attempt to separate personal from business related communications. An employer is well equipped to run an efficient and productive business without monitoring the content of personal communications.

Clearly the most invasive workplace monitoring practice; video surveillance of highly private areas such as bathrooms and locker rooms, is never conducted in the ordinary course of business and is ripe for abuse. Employees have a heightened expectation of privacy and personal autonomy in such areas. Such monitoring destroys the very essence of human dignity, is highly degrading and such activity disproportionately involves the secret photography of women. The decision to breach such highly sensitive areas and to what degree, is a decision better suited to the reasoned judgment of a court of law.

Why Should the Government be Entitled to Dictate How Private Management Can Run their Businesses?

The government at times must act to ensure that management treats its workers fairly and justly. In the past, Congress has passed numerous laws placing restrictions on private business activities. Such laws include actions prohibiting private businesses from hiring children, discriminating against women and minorities, and paying sub-minimum wages. In addition, legislation has been enacted to ensure employees' rights to organize unions, and to receive prior notice of expected plant closings. Today, in order to protect employees' right to privacy and dignity, restrictions on electronic monitoring by employers must be enacted.

Federal Legislative History

Congress has introduced two notable bills in the past fifteen years to protect employee privacy. These bills were endorsed by a variety of civil rights and labor organizations.

The Privacy for Consumers and Workers Act

On February 27, 1991, the late Senator Paul Simon and Representative Pat Williams introduced the PCWA. The bill would have required employers to clearly define their privacy policies and notify prospective employees of those practices that would affect them. It would have required that surveillance be limited to job related functions and would have prohibited such surveillance of personal communications. It would have prohibited video surveillance in highly personal places such as bathrooms (unless there was suspicion of illegal conduct) and would have required notification when telephone monitoring was taking place. Additionally, it would give employees access to records collected as a result of surveillance.

The Notice of Electronic Monitoring Act

A more limited version of PCWA was introduced by Senator Schumer on July 20, 2000. NEMA would have subjected an employer to liability for intentionally monitoring an employee without first having given the employee substantive notice that the employer was engaged in such a monitoring program. Notice fulfilling the requirements of the Act would include the type of monitoring taking place, the means, the type of information that would be gathered including non-work related information, the frequency of monitoring and how the information would be used. An exception to such notice was made if the employer had reasonable grounds to believe the employee was engaged in illegal conduct and surveillance would produce evidence of such. NEMA put no actual restrictions on an employer's ability to monitor as long as they complied with the notice provisions.

Workplace Privacy Act
A Bill

To amend title 18, United States Code, to authorize electronic monitoring conducted in the ordinary course of business, provide for the disclosure of electronic monitoring of employee communications and computer usage in the workplace and limit electronic monitoring in highly sensitive areas of the workplace.

Section 1. Short Title

This Act may be cited as the 'Workplace Privacy Act'

Section 2. Electronic Monitoring in the Workplace

(a) IN GENERAL—(1) Except as otherwise specifically provided in this section, an employer may, by any electronic means, read, listen to, or otherwise monitor any wire communication, oral communication, or electronic communication of an employee of the employer, or otherwise monitor the computer usage of an employee of the employer if the monitoring meets the requirements of sections (b) and (e) and—
   (A) The monitoring is conducted at the employer's premises and
   (B) The monitoring is conducted in the normal course of employment while the employee is engaged in any activity which is a necessary incident to the rendition of his service or to the protection of the rights or property of the employer.
(2) An employer who conducts monitoring in violation of this section shall be liable to the employee for relief as provided in subsection (f).

(b) IN GENERAL—(1) Except as provided in subsection (d), an employer who intentionally, by any electronic means, reads, listens to, or otherwise monitors any wire communication, oral communication, or electronic communication of an employee of the employer, or otherwise monitors the computer usage of an employee of the employer, without first having provided the employee notice meeting the requirements of subsection (b) shall be liable to the employee for relief as provided in subsection (f).
(2) Not later than one year after first providing notice of electronic monitoring under paragraph (1), and annually thereafter, an employer shall

provide notice meeting the requirements of subsection (b) to all employees of the employer who are subject to such electronic monitoring.

(3) Before implementing a material change in an electronic monitoring practice described in paragraph (1), an employer shall provide notice meeting the requirements of subsection (b) to all employees of the employer who are subject to electronic monitoring covered by that paragraph as a result of the change.

(c) NOTICE—A notice meeting the requirements of this subsection is a clear and conspicuous notice, in a manner reasonably calculated to provide actual notice, describing—

(1) the form of communication or computer usage that will be monitored;

(2) the means by which such monitoring will be accomplished and the kinds of information that will be obtained through such monitoring, including whether communications or computer usage not related to the employer's business are likely to be monitored;

(3) the frequency of such monitoring; and

(4) how information obtained by such monitoring will be stored, used, or disclosed.

(d) EXCEPTION—An employer may conduct electronic monitoring described in subsection (a) without the notice required by subsection (b) if the employer has reasonable grounds to believe that—

(1) a particular employee of the employer is engaged in conduct that—

(A) violates the legal rights of the employer or another person; and

(B) involves significant harm to the employer or such other person; and

(2) the electronic monitoring will produce evidence of such conduct.

(e) IN GENERAL—(1) No employer or agent of an employer may engage in video or audio monitoring of an employee in bathrooms, dressing rooms, locker rooms, or other areas where employees change clothing unless—

(A) Such monitoring is authorized by court order.

(2) An employer who conducts monitoring in violation of this section shall be liable to the employee for relief as provided in subsection (f).

(f) CIVIL ACTION—(1) Any person aggrieved by any act in violation of this section may bring an action in a United States district court.

(2) a court in an action under this section may award—

(A) actual damages, but not less than liquidated damages in the amount of $5,000;

(B) punitive damages;

(C) reasonable attorneys' fees and other litigation costs reasonably incurred; and

(D) such other preliminary and equitable relief as the court determines to be appropriate.

(g) ENFORCEMENT ACTION BY SECRETARY

(1) IN GENERAL—Any employer who violates this section shall be liable to the United States for a civil money penalty in an amount not to exceed $10,000 for each violation, except that, if the violation is knowing, the penalty for the violation may be up to $25,000.

(b) Written Notice and Opportunity for Hearing—The Secretary of Labor shall assess a civil penalty under subsection (a) by an order made on the record after opportunity for a hearing provided in accordance with section 554 of title 5, United States Code. In connection with the hearing, the Secretary may issue subpoenas requiring the attendance and testimony of witnesses and the production of evidence that relates to the subject matter of the hearing.

(c) Determination of Amount of Civil Money Penalty—In determining the amount of a civil money penalty under subsection (a), the Secretary shall take into account—

(1) the nature, circumstances, extent, and gravity of the violation or violations; and

(2) with respect to the violator, the ability to pay, effect on ability to continue to do business, any history of prior violations, the degree of culpability, and such other matters as justice may require.

(h) WAIVER OF RIGHTS—(1) The rights provided by this Act may not be waived by contract or otherwise, unless such waiver is part of a written settlement to a pending action or complaint.

(i) PREEMPTION—(1) Nothing in this Act shall be construed to preempt, modify, or amend any State, county, or local law, ordinance, or regulation providing greater protection to the privacy of employees.

POSTSCRIPT

Does an Employer's Need to Monitor Workers Trump Employee Privacy Concerns?

Advances in electronic and digital technology have increased the ability of employers to monitor employees' behavior at work. And, for the most part, courts have been sympathetic to employers' needs to protect their property from theft and vandalism and to monitor employee productivity. But this latitude is not without boundaries, as was clearly evident in the article by Meklinsky and Bancroft. And when legitimate monitoring crosses the line, it can cause tremendous damage to the employer–employee relationship. Kevin Curran, lead author of the Internet Technologies Research Group, details several examples of employers going too far:

> . . . postal workers in New York City were horrified to discover that management had installed video cameras in the restroom stalls. Female workers at a large North Eastern department store discovered a hidden video camera installed in an empty office space that was commonly used as a changing room. Waiters in a large Boston hotel were secretly videotaped dressing and undressing in their locker room. Although in each of these instances the employer claimed it was concerned about theft, no illegal acts were ever uncovered. But the employees were robbed of their dignity and personal privacy. (Curran et al., 2004)

As Curran notes, such behaviors are insensitive to legitimate employee privacy concerns and often result in negative attitudes toward management. They also have the potential of creating an atmosphere in which employees feel their every behavior is being watched and that they are being micro-managed. As Liz Ryan notes in her article, "Don't be an every minute manager," "too many bosses seek to control their employees' every nanosecond at work. But it only kills motivation and stresses everyone" (*BusinessWeek* Online, September 15, 2005).

Thus, it's a difficult situation for managers: Don't monitor and run the risk of employee theft, low productivity, and corporate liability, or monitor the workplace and potentially create an atmosphere of stress, distrust, and low company loyalty among employees. Fortunately, the task facing you, our reader, is much easier: Now that you have read both sides of the issue, do you support employee monitoring of the workplace?

Suggested Readings

G. Stoney Alder, Maureen L. Ambrose, & Terry W. Noel, "The Effect of Formal Advance Notice and Justification on Internet Monitoring Fairness:

Much about Nothing?" *Journal of Leadership and Organizational Studies,* vol. 13, no. 1 (2006).

Liz Ryan, "Don't be an Every Minute Manager," *BusinessWeek* Online (September 15, 2005). http://www.businessweek.com.

Kevin Curran, Steven McIntyre, Hugo Meenan, Francis McCloy, & Ciaran Heaney, "Civil Liberties and Computer Monitoring," *American Journal of Applied Sciences,* vol. 1, no. 3 (2004).

Chauncey M. Dupree, Jr. & Rebecca K. Jude, "Who's Reading Your email? Is That Legal?" *Strategic Finance* (April 2006).

American Management Association, "2005 Electronic Monitoring & Surveillance Survey: Many Companies Monitoring, Recording, Videotaping—and Firing—Employees," *American Management Association News* (2005). http://www.amanet.org/press/amanews/ems05.htm.

Internet References . . .

ProEnglish

ProEnglish is a member-supported, national, non-profit organization working to educate the public about the need to protect English as our common language and to make it the official language of the United States. Since its creation, ProEnglish has gained expertise and considerable experience in the rapidly evolving field of language law. As a result, ProEnglish has specialized in providing pro-bono legal assistance to public and private agencies facing litigation or regulatory actions over language.

http://www.proenglish.org/

Workplace Fairness

Workplace Fairness is a nonprofit organization that brings together employers, workers, policymakers and others to ensure and promote fairness in the workplace and employment relationships.

http://www.nerinet.org/

Partnership for a Drug-Free America

This website has much information on drug use by young adults as well as many links to related sites. Also features an updated news resource link.

http://www.drugfreeamerica.org/Home/default.asp?ws=PDFA&vol=1&grp=Home

Independent Women's Forum

Founded in 1992, IWF focuses on issues of concern to women, men, and families. Our mission is to rebuild civil society by advancing economic liberty, personal responsibility, and political freedom. IWF builds support for a greater respect for limited government, equality under the law, property rights, free markets, strong families, and a powerful and effective national defense and foreign policy.

http://iwf.org/about/

The Heritage Foundation

The Heritage Foundation is a research and educational institute whose mission is to formulate and promote conservative public policies based on the principles of free enterprise, limited government, individual freedom, traditional American values, and a strong national defense.

http://www.heritage.org/

Organizational Behavior and Human Resource Management

*A*ffirmative action has been with us for several decades. There can be no question that it has helped in obtaining more and better opportunities for minorities and females during this time. But, as some critics claim, has it become outdated? Do we still need it? Companies have the right to protect themselves from harm and to ensure a safe and drug-free workplace. But employees also have a right to privacy. Given this inherent conflict, perhaps not testing is a wise policy? In the late 1950s, women made about 40 percent less than did males. By 2008, the male-female wage gap had only shrunk to 23 percent. With the continued influx of immigrants into the United States, employers are increasingly using English-only policies in the workplace. Should they be allowed to do this? Is discrimination still responsible for this difference? Unit 2 explores these and other important questions for managers.

- Has Affirmative Action Outlived Its Usefulness in the Workplace?

- Is Workplace Drug Testing a Wise Corporate Policy?

- Is Gender Discrimination the Main Reason Women Are Paid Less Than Men?

- Should Employees Be Allowed to Vote by Secret Ballot When Deciding Whether to Support Unionization in the Workplace?

- Should Corporations Be Allowed to Implement English-Only Rules in the Workplace?

ISSUE 5

Has Affirmative Action Outlived Its Usefulness in the Workplace?

YES: Carl Cohen, from "Why Race Preference Is Wrong and Bad," *Affirmative Action and Racial Preference: A Debate* (Oxford University Press, 2003)

NO: Garth Massey, from "Thinking about Affirmative Action: Arguments Supporting Preferential Policies," *Review of Policy Research* (Wiley-Blackwell, 2004)

ISSUE SUMMARY

YES: Dr. Carl Cohen is a philosophy professor who believes that affirmative action is not only ineffective but also immoral. In addition to his charge of immorality, he presents three additional points against affirmative action.

NO: Garth Massey, Professor of Sociology and Director of the International Studies Program at the University of Wyoming, readily admits that traditional defenses of affirmative action are weak and counter-punches by presenting three unusual and "new" arguments in support of affirmative action.

In April 2009, possibly the most important affirmative action case to date was argued in front of the Supreme Court of the United States. A unique aspect of this case was that it involved allegations of reverse discrimination by city lawmakers against 19 New Haven, Connecticut fire department employees. These fire fighters, most of whom were white, had successfully completed and passed New Haven's promotions exam and expected to be promoted to a higher pay grade. However, no African-American test takers passed the exam. In response, city officials decided that the test was discriminatory against minorities, threw out the results of all 77 test takers, and promoted no one. This led to the group of 19 filing suit against New Haven, charging them with reverse discrimination. Finally, after spending time in the lower courts, the case was accepted by the Supreme Court and heard in April 2009. As of this writing, a decision had not been announced.

One of the most important ideas to come out of the 1960s, affirmative action is the "process in which employers identify needs and take positive steps to create and enhance opportunities for protected class members [i.e., minorities and females]" (Mathis and Jackson, 2007, *Human Resource Management,* Thompson South-Western Publishers). Four-and-a-half decades after the Civil Rights Act of 1964 formalized the concept, many detractors argue that it has accomplished its goals and is no longer needed. On the other hand, supporters contend that affirmative action has not yet met all its goals and because discrimination is still prevalent, it is still needed in the workplace.

One of the reasons for the intensity surrounding this issue is that there are several persuasive arguments on each side of the debate. Let us consider a couple in defense of affirmative action. Proponents believe that many of the current differences in racial and gender success in the workplace can be attributed to the effects of discrimination built up over many years. These effects cut both ways: women and minorities suffer unfair employment treatment while males and non-minorities have received preferential treatment. Not surprisingly, supporters argue that it is needed to overcome the effects of past discrimination. A second argument rests on the observation that social ills such as crime, drug abuse, and low educational attainment levels are most likely to occur among those at the lowest level of the socioeconomic ladder, a rung that consists primarily of minorities. Because economic disparities will be reduced as a result of the increased employment and economic opportunities provided by affirmative action, social problems could be expected to decline, thus benefiting all members of our society.

The other side of the debate also has several strong points to consider. For example, consider the concept of reverse discrimination. As shown in the account presented earlier in this introduction, when we give preferential treatment to any group of individuals, we necessarily discriminate against other groups. Critics of affirmative action argue that this occurs frequently, is reverse discrimination (usually against males and non-minorities), and requires adopting a "two wrongs make a right" viewpoint. Another line of reasoning against affirmative action involves the recognition that the overwhelming majority of non-protected class members have nothing to do with past discrimination—indeed, many were not even alive at the time—and yet it is exactly these individuals that are penalized by affirmative action programs. Opponents argue that it is patently unfair, unjust, and immoral for these individuals to be penalized for discrimination that occurred in the past and in which they played no part.

In the two selections that follow, the question of whether affirmative action has outlived its usefulness in the workplace is addressed. The "yes" selection is presented by Dr. Carl Cohen, a philosophy professor who believes that affirmative action as economic and social policy is not only ineffective but is also immoral. Indeed, he opens his four-pronged attack on affirmative action by arguing the immorality of affirmative action as a concept. Garth Massey's article is particularly intriguing in that he readily admits that traditional defenses of affirmative action are wanting. However, after briefly explaining why this is so, he counter-punches by presenting three unusual and "new" arguments supporting affirmative action. These he labels as "strong" arguments in contrast to the traditional "weak" arguments he dismissed previously.

YES

Carl Cohen

Why Race Preference Is Wrong and Bad

Race Preference Is Morally Wrong

1. The Principle of Equality

That *equals should be treated equally* is a fundamental principle of morality. Race preference is morally wrong because it violates this principle.

But who are equals? Identical treatment for everyone in all matters is certainly not just. Citizens have privileges and duties that aliens do not have; employers have opportunities and responsibilities that employees do not have; higher taxes may be rightly imposed upon those with higher incomes; the right to vote is withheld from the very young. Groups of persons may deserve different treatment because they *are* different in critical respects. But what respects are critical? Surely the poor or the elderly or the disabled may have special needs that justify community concern.

The principle of equality does not require that all be treated identically; but this much is clear: If some receive a public benefit that others do not receive, that preference will be unfair unless the advantages given can be justified by some feature of the group preferred. Unequal treatment by the state requires defense.

As a justification for unequal treatment some group characteristics are simply not relevant and not acceptable, all agree. Ancestry we reject. Better treatment for Americans of Irish descent than for those of Polish descent is wrong; we haven't any doubt about that. Sex we reject. Privileges to which men are entitled cannot be denied to women. Religion we reject. Opportunities open to Methodists must be open to Baptists. Color we reject. When the state favors white skins over black skins—a common practice for centuries—we are now properly outraged. Such categories cannot determine desert. This matter is morally settled: In dealings with the state, persons *may not be* preferred because of their race, or color, or religion, or sex, or national origin.

Bigots, of course, will draw distinctions by race (or nationality, and so on) in their private lives. But private opinions, however detestable, are not public business. Under rules to be enforced by our body politic, bigotry is forbidden. Persons of all colors, religions, and origins are equals with respect to their rights, equals in the eyes of the law. And equals must be treated equally. Race and nationality simply cannot serve, in our country, as the justification for unequal treatment.

This we do not learn from any book or document. These principles are not true because expressed in the Declaration of Independence, or laid down in the Constitution of the United States. The principles are found in those great documents because they are true. That "all men are created equal" is one way, perhaps the most famous way, of expressing the fundamental moral principle involved. A guarantee that the "equal protection of the laws" is not to be denied to any person by any state (as the Fourteenth Amendment to our Constitution provides) is one way of giving that moral principle political teeth. Our great documents *recognize* and *realize* moral truths grasped by persons everywhere: All the members of humankind are equally ends in themselves, all have equal *dignity*—and therefore all are entitled to equal respect from the community and its laws.

John Dewey, rightly thought of as the philosopher of democracy, put it this way:

> Equality does not mean mathematical equivalence. It means rather the inapplicability of considerations of . . . superior and inferior. It means that no matter how great the quantitative differences of ability, strength, position, wealth, such differences are negligible in comparison with something else—the fact of individuality, the manifestation of something irreplaceable. . . . It implies, so to speak, a metaphysical mathematics of the incommensurable in which each speaks for itself and demands consideration on its own behalf.

This recognition of the ultimate equality and fellowship of humans with one another is taught by great thinkers in every culture—by Buddha, and St. Francis, and Walt Whitman. At bottom we all recognize, as Walter Lippmann wrote, a "spiritual reality behind and independent of the visible character and behavior of a man. . . . We know, each of us, in a way too certain for doubting, that, after all the weighing and comparing and judging of us is done, there is something left over which is the heart of the matter."

This is the moral standard against which race preference must be judged. The principle of equality certainly entails at least this: It is wrong, always and everywhere, to give special advantages to any group simply on the basis of physical characteristics that have no relevance to the award given or to the burden imposed. To give or to take on the basis of skin color is manifestly unfair.

The most gruesome chapters in human history—the abomination of black slavery, the wholesale slaughter of the Jews—remind us that *racial* categories must never be allowed to serve as the foundation for official differentiation. Nations in which racial distinctions were once embedded in public law are forever shamed. Our own history is by such racism ineradicably stained. The lesson is this: Never again. Never, *ever* again.

What is today loosely called "affirmative action" sticks in our craw because it fails to respect that plain lesson. It uses categories that *must not* be used to distinguish among persons with respect to their entitlements in the community. Blacks and whites are equals, as blondes and brunettes are equals, as Catholics and Jews are equals, as Americans of every ancestry are equal. No matter who the beneficiaries may be or who the victims, preference on the basis of race is morally wrong. It was wrong in the distant past and in the recent past; it is wrong now; and it will always be wrong. Race preference violates the principle of human equality.

2. Race Preference Is Not Justified as Compensation

What about people who have been hurt because of their race, damaged or deprived because they were black or brown? Do they not deserve some redress? Of course they do. But it is the *injury* for which compensation is given in such cases, not the skin color.

But (some will respond) it is precisely the *injuries* so long done to minorities that justify special consideration for minorities now. Bearing the past in mind, deliberate preference for groups formerly oppressed reverses historical injustice, and thereby makes fair what would otherwise seem to be unfair. They argue that blacks, Native Americans, Hispanics, and other minorities have for many generations been the victims of outrageous discrimination, the sum of it almost too cruel to contemplate. Explicit preference to these minorities now makes up, in part, for past deprivation. Historical wrongs cannot be undone, but we can take some steps toward the restoration of moral balance. At this point in our history, advocates continue, equal treatment only appears to be just. Minorities have been so long shackled by discriminatory laws and economic deprivation that it is not fair to oblige them to compete now against a majority never burdened in that way. The visible shackles may be gone, but not the residual impact of their long imposition. We must *level the playing field* in the competition for employment and other goods. Only explicit race preference can do this, they contend; therefore, explicit race preference is just.

This is the essence of the argument in support of race preference upon which most of its advocates chiefly rely. It is an argument grounded in the demand for *compensation,* for redress. It seeks to turn the tables in the interests of justice. White males, so long the beneficiaries of preference, are now obliged to give preference to others. Past oppression must be paid for. Is turnabout not fair play?

No, it is not—not when the instrument turned about is essentially unjust. The compensatory argument is appealing but mistaken, because preference *by race* cannot serve as just compensation for earlier wrongs. It cannot do so because race, as a standard, is crude and morally blind. Color, national origin, and other accidents of birth have no moral weight. Historical injustices we now seek to redress were themselves a product of moral stupidity; they were inflicted because burdens and benefits were awarded on grounds entirely irrelevant to what was deserved. Blacks and other minorities were not injured by *being* black or brown. They were injured by treatment unfairly *based* on their being black or brown. Redress deserved is redress that goes to *them,* to persons injured, in the light of the injuries they suffered. Many are long dead and can never be compensated. Those ancient injuries are not remedied by bestowing benefits now upon other persons who happen to belong to the ethnic group of those injured.

Using race to award benefits now does injustice in precisely the way injustice was done originally, by giving moral weight to skin color in itself. The discriminatory use of racial classifications is no less unfair when directed at whites now than it was when directed at blacks then. A wrong is not redressed by inflicting that same wrong on others. By devising new varieties of race preference, moreover, we give legitimacy to the consideration of race, reinforcing the very injustice we seek to eradicate. We compound injustice with injustice, further embedding racial categories in public policy and law.

The moral blindness of race preference is exhibited from both sides: *the wrong people benefit, and the wrong people pay the price of that benefit.*

Consider first who benefits. Race preference gives rewards to some persons who deserve no rewards at all, and is thus over inclusive. Preferential systems are designed to give special consideration to *all* those having some physical or genetic feature, all those who are black, or female, or of some specified national origin. Hispanics, for example, receive the advantage because they have parents or grandparents (is one enough?) of certain national origins. But have all those of Hispanic origin been wrongly injured? Do all those of that single national origin deserve compensation now for earlier injuries? No one seriously believes that. Discrimination against Hispanics in our country has been (and remains) common, to be sure. But it is also true that many of Hispanic ancestry now enjoy here, and have long enjoyed, circumstances as decent and as well protected as those enjoyed by Americans of all other ethnicities. The same is true of African-Americans, some of whom are impoverished and some of whom are rich and powerful. Rewards distributed on the basis of ethnic membership assume that the damage suffered by some were suffered by all—an assumption that we know to be false. . . .

Race preference is morally defective also in being *under* inclusive, in that it fails to reward many who deserve compensation. If redress is at times in order, for what injuries might it be deserved? Inadequate education perhaps: teachers poorly qualified, books out of date or in short supply, buildings vermin-infested and deteriorating, schools rotten all around. High school graduates who come to the verge of college admission in spite of handicaps like these may indeed be thought worthy of special consideration—but that would be a consideration given them not because of the color of their skins, but because of what they have accomplished in spite of handicap. *Everyone* whose accomplishments are like those, whose determination has overcome great barriers, is entitled to whatever compensatory relief we think graduation from such inferior schools deserves. Everyone, no matter the color of her skin.

So race preference is morally faulty in what it does not do, as well as in what it does. Seeing only race we cannot see what may truly justify special regard. Blacks and Hispanics are not the only ones to have been burdened by bad schools, or undermined by poverty or neglect, or wounded by absent or malfunctioning families. But those with skins of other colors, however much they too may have been unfairly injured or deprived, get no support from race-based "affirmative action." They are simply left out.

Also left out are most of those blacks and Native Americans who really were seriously damaged by educational deprivation, but who fell so far behind in consequence that they cannot possibly compete for slots in professional schools, or for prestigious training programs, and therefore cannot benefit from the race preferences commonly given. So those most in need of help usually get none, and those equally entitled to help whose skins are the wrong color get absolutely none.

Whatever the community response to adversity ought to be, this much is clear: What is given must be given without regard to the race or sex or national origin of the recipients. It is the injury and not the ethnicity for which relief may be in order, and therefore relief cannot be justly restricted to some minorities only. If some injury or deprivation does justify compensatory redress, whites and blacks who have suffered that injury should be entitled to the same redress. Racial lenses obscure this truth.

A just apportionment of remedies should be designed to compensate most those who were injured most, and to compensate least, or not at all, those who were injured least, or not at all. Therefore a keen regard for the nature of the injury suffered, and the degree of suffering, is critical in giving redress. Remedy for injury is a complicated matter; naked race preference must fail as the instrument in providing remedy because by hypothesis it has no regard for variety or degree. How gravely injured are they who complete undergraduate studies and compete for admission to law school, or medical school? The daughter of a black physician who graduates from a fine college has been done no injury entitling her to preferential consideration in competitive admissions simply because she is black—but she will surely receive it. The principal beneficiaries of "affirmative action" in law schools and medical schools are the children of upper middle-class minority families, for the simple reason that they are the minority applicants most likely to be in a position to apply to such schools. Those whose personal histories of deprivation may in truth entitle them to some special consideration are rarely in a position even to hope for preference in such contexts. It is one of the great ironies of "affirmative action" that those among minority groups receiving its preferences are precisely those least likely to deserve them. . . .

In sum, race preference gives to those who don't deserve, and doesn't give to those who do. It gives more to those who deserve less, and less to those who deserve more. These failings are inescapable because the preferences in question are grounded not in earlier injury but in physical characteristics that cannot justly serve as grounds for advantage or disadvantage. Whatever is owed persons because of injuries they suffered is owed them without any regard to their ethnicity. Many who may now deserve remedy for past abuse are not minority group members; many who are minority group members deserve no remedy. Preference awarded only to persons in certain racial categories, and to all in those categories whatever their actual desert, invariably overrides the moral considerations that are genuinely relevant, and cannot be rightly defended as compensatory.

3. Race Preference Imposes Unfair Penalties upon Those Not Preferred

Not only the benefits, but also the *burdens* imposed by race-based preferences are distributed unfairly. By attending to skin color rather than to what should truly count, racial instruments invariably impose penalties upon those who deserve no penalty at all, persons entirely innocent of the earlier wrong for which the preference is allegedly given, but whose skin is of the wrong color.

Even if those receiving race preference now had been injured earlier because of their race, it is plainly false to suppose that those over whom they are now preferred were in any way responsible for the earlier injuries. A race-based system of penalty and reward is morally cockeyed.

In a competitive setting, advantages given must be paid for by disadvantages borne. If the goods are in short supply—as jobs and promotions and seats in a law school and the like are certainly in short supply—whatever is given to some by race is necessarily taken from others by race. If some are advantaged because of their color or sex, others must be disadvantaged because of their color or sex. This is a truth of logic that cannot be escaped. *There is no ethnic preference that can be "benign."*

Advocates of preference scoff at the alleged burden of race preferences, contending that their impact upon the majority is insignificant. The body of white job applicants, or white contractors, or white university applicants is large, while the number of minority applicants given preference is small. So if those preferences impose a burden, the advocates contend, it is at worst a trivial burden because of the great number over whom that burden is distributed. The complaint about unfairness, the advocates conclude, thus makes a mountain of a molehill. Preferences given to minority applicants are so greatly *diluted* by the size of the majority that their consequences are barely detectable.

This argument is deceptive and its conclusion is false. True it is that only some in the majority are directly affected, and true also that after such preferences are given we often cannot know precisely who among the majority would have been appointed or admitted if that preferential system had not been in place. But it is not true that, because the group from whom the benefits are taken is large, the burden of preference is diluted or rendered insignificant. The price must be paid, and some among that larger group must pay it. Some individual members of the majority must have been displaced, and upon them the burden is as heavy as it is unfair. Injustice is not made trivial because the names of its victims are not known. . . .

Getting a job, or keeping one, is no minor matter. Some folks lose out in their quest for employment *because of their race*. Some employees who might have been promoted in their workplace are passed over. Some who might have been admitted to fine colleges, or law schools, or medical schools, are not admitted because of their race, and must go elsewhere, or perhaps go nowhere. The white applicants squeezed out in this process are, ironically, often the children of first-generation Americans, the first members of their families pulling their way into universities and professional life. They, not the established rich, are the ones hit hardest by race preference. . . .

In deciding upon what is to be given by way of redress for injury, the properly critical moral consideration is the injury itself, its nature, and its degree—not the race or national origin of the persons compensated. When preference is given to persons because of their race alone, many who are in fact owed redress do not receive it (either because they had been too greatly damaged, or because they happen not to be members of the favored categories), while many who are members of the favored categories receive benefits although owed nothing in the way of redress. And those who bear the burden of the preferential award are totally innocent of wrongdoing, bearing no responsibility whatever for injuries that may have been done to persons of the race preferred. Because both benefits and burdens are a function of race, and are not determined by considerations having genuine moral weight, race preference is perfectly incapable of achieving the compensatory objective offered in its defense; such preference is inevitably unfair and morally wrong.

4. Race Preference Cannot Be Justified by the Quest for Diversity

Diversity is now widely offered as a justification of race preference. In universities, and where information or argument is reported or discussed, intellectual diversity is indeed a value worthy of pursuit. Among students, teachers, and journalists, a wide range of opinions and perspectives is certainly healthy. But the importance of diversity in these spheres is often greatly exaggerated, and its merits, even when they are substantial, cannot override the principle of equality. The quest for variety cannot justify the suspension of our moral duty not to discriminate by race.

In any case, the term "diversity" (as commonly used in this arena) does not actually mean variety of viewpoint and opinion; in practice it means variety among the *races* in their proper proportions. Colleges and universities that could greatly enrich their *intellectual* diversity do not work very hard at that, except so far as the variety they claim to seek is associated with minority ethnic groups. The almost complete homogeneity of political views on the faculties of major universities—one respect in which diversity would be particularly helpful—is extraordinary, but appears not to be a matter of great concern. And even ethnic diversity, if it does not satisfy the quest for more of those minorities thought to have been earlier oppressed, does not count for much. Diversity of religion, diversity of lifestyle, diversity along any one of many other dimensions that really could provide more genuine enrichment are commonly ignored. The only "diversity" that is said to justify preference is racial diversity, and the standard by which it is decided whether "diversity goals" have been adequately achieved is the *match* of the proportion of certain minorities entering college (or entering professional schools, owning radio or TV stations, and so on) to the proportion of those minorities in the population at large. "Diversity," as everyone well understands, is today no more than a euphemism for race proportionality. A candid demand for proportionality would require highly objectionable (and probably unlawful) racial quotas, so politically correct institutions insist that it is only "diversity" that they pursue—an objective with wide appeal that is superficially race neutral.

But even where the quest for diversity is honest, that quest cannot justify outright unfairness. Preference by race is plainly unfair, as we have seen, and the demand for ethnic diversity simply ignores that unfairness. Are the numbers of black students enrolled, or Hispanic faculty appointed, sufficiently large? Is the racial profile of those employed, or of those winning prizes, or of those going to prison proportionate to the profile of the larger population? *Proportionality* is the unquestioned standard of success in achieving diversity; the racial *numbers* are what count. But ethnicity has no bearing whatever in many spheres, and in such spheres percentages cannot justifiably govern or distort the selection process. The alleged but uncertain benefits of some desired racial distribution do not override moral principles requiring fair treatment.

Suppose we were confronted with very strong evidence that racially *segregated* classrooms improve learning and teaching. Suppose the evidence in support of segregated schools were far more impressive than the very thin materials now offered in support of ethnic diversity. Would we think that such evidence (supposing it reliable) provided a *justification* for the deliberate racial segregation of our classrooms? Of course we would not. On the contrary, we will condemn the imposition of racial discrimination by the state in any case; we will point out that *whatever* the evidence of its consequences may show, racial discrimination is unacceptable, *wrong,* and that any advantages that may flow from it could not begin to justify a policy that is intrinsically unjust. And that is what race preference is.

As it happens, the praises of diversity as an instrument of education are greatly overblown; there is serious doubt that racial diversity has any measurable impact upon the quality of learning or teaching in a university. But even if those claims of benefit had substantial merit, they would carry very little weight in a just society. Racial discrimination imposed by the state is despicable, we know. Whichever the race favored by some discriminatory policy, the policy itself is morally intolerable; no studies or scholarship aiming to persuade us of its educative benefits can make it acceptable.

Garth Massey  **NO**

Thinking about Affirmative Action: Arguments Supporting Preferential Policies

What Is Affirmative Action and Why Is It So Controversial?

> Affirmative action is a set of public policies, laws, and executive orders, as well as voluntary and court-ordered practices designed to promote fairness and diversity. (National Council for Research on Women, 1996)

Often described as a tool that seeks to level the playing field in an inequitable society where the idea of opportunity for all is widely embraced, affirmative action hardly appears controversial. Everyone knows the playing field is not level. Everyone believes equality of opportunity is a good thing. Nearly everyone roots for the little guy and is willing to give him a helping hand. So what is the reason for opposition to policies addressing this?

In the past forty years there have been few public issues more contentious than affirmative action. The range of opposition is wide. On the far right of the political spectrum, extreme conservatives reject the very idea that such a thing as socially structured inequality exists. For them, social inequality is a consequence of personal effort, parental foresight, or biology. From their perspective social inequality is the merit-based result of both natural and desirable processes predicated on individual differences, and SO cannot be considered unjust or even undesirable. In its less virulent form, social inequality is a fundamental feature of the good society, reflecting the complexities and varying needs of the modern social system. Any effort to change the circumstances in which it exists will only initiate injustice and chaos.

Conservatives less comfortable about inequality may be no less certain about its inevitability, but more for reasons of human design than the design of humans. That is, human designs—legislation, organization, and planning—are bound to fail or fall far short of achieving their goals. They are skeptical of any effort at social engineering, not only because they oppose the ideas of social reformers, but also because they doubt the possibility of planned

From *Review of Policy Research,* 21:6, November 2004, pp. 784–794 (excerpted). Copyright © 2004 by Policy Studies Organization and American Political Science Association. Reprinted by permission of Wiley-Blackwell.

social change. Any "absurd effort to make the world over," as the nineteenth-century social Darwinist, William Graham Sumner, said, can only bring about a worse situation than whatever failings presently exist in society. Modern-day conservatives point to the collapse of the Soviet system as proof of this, even while celebrating the genius of Thomas Jefferson and others who constructed the United States Constitution to guide an equally radical exercise in social engineering.

Ambiguous conservatives are a third category opposing affirmative action. Despite President Ronald Reagan's mantra, "Government is not the solution to our problem; government is the problem," the United States economy depends on and has benefited mightily from taxation, trade, investment, regulation, and the monetary policies of the federal government. The world's largest and most powerful military, the world's best institutions of higher education, and a remarkable interstate highway system were and remain planned public works. Not surprisingly, those parts of the country that have realized the least benefit from long-range planning—large portions of rural America generally and much of the Midwest and Rocky Mountain West—are the most hostile to government action, not because it has not worked, but because it has not worked for them. The same could be said about affirmative action.

Conservatives are not the only ones opposing affirmative action. A more centrist political viewpoint argues against affirmative action in less ideological and more personal terms. Its proponents give an assenting nod to the 1960s War on Poverty but wonder why it did not have greater effect. The simple and probably most accurate reason is that the War on Poverty was among the briefest wars in United States history. In the final analysis, centrists feared that sustained policies designed to make this country more equitable would have made them less comfortable. Altering class relations, acting seriously to eradicate poverty and substandard education, insuring health security and decent employment at a wage level that could actually support a family, creating social investments in areas abandoned by the private market, and possibly decentering the patriarchal family by giving women equal status and power is not without personal costs. It is neither inexpensive nor easy. And the direct benefits to them were not readily apparent. More likely, their piece of the pie would shrink from such a sustained effort.

Affirmative action policies are passe for moderate opponents who argue that those persons capable of benefiting from them already have. Whatever could be accomplished by affirmative action is now a reality. They point to the commendable growth of the black middle class and the wealthy elites and political clout of the Hispanic communities. The continued wage, employment, education, and political influence gap found in black/white comparisons are closing, or so it seems. The glass ceilings and walls women confront throughout the workplace, the male/female wage gap, the 97% of the Fortune 500 companies that are headed by men (nearly all of them white), and the growing portion of the poor who are in families headed by women—these are uncomfortable and acknowledged facts. But there has been progress, and there will continue to be progress in these areas. Affirmative action is either no longer needed or is unsupportable in terms of the benefits it can deliver versus the resentment it incurs.

The rejection of affirmative action by large portions of the United States population is periodically reported when a major court decision addresses preferential policies. In recent decades the most significant cases involved awarding a quota of contracts to minority-owned businesses, such as City of Richmond v. Croson in 1989, and challenges to college admissions practices, the most prominent of which is the 1978 Bakke case (Regents of the University of California v. Bakke). In that case the court ruled in favor of making race a factor in admissions decisions, but deemed as unconstitutional set-asides for specific categories of minorities. In 1996 the Fifth Circuit Court of Appeals ruled in Texas v. Hopwood that any admissions policy providing preference on the basis of race was unconstitutional. In 2003 the United States Supreme Court ruled (Gratz v. Bollinger) against the University of Michigan's undergraduate admissions policies on much the same grounds as the Hopwood ruling, but it affirmed (Grutter v. Bollinger) Michigan's law school admissions practice of considering "holistically" each applicant's record—including background factors and race—in order to increase diversity among the student body.

The popular, anti-affirmative-action view is that qualified nonminority students are turned away while less-qualified minority students are taking their seats in the country's best educational institutions. As well, scholarships are going to the wrong people: just because they are minorities. As Fischer and his colleagues have shown, this specious view cannot withstand statistical scrutiny. Empirical analysis of tuition reductions, legacy consideration, the increasing reliance on standardized test scores since the mid-1970s, and more recent "percent plans" offering admittance to the top percent of high school graduates—regardless of race or social class—show that whites and the more affluent continue to be favored. In fact, the biggest winners tend to be Asian Americans when affirmative action in university admissions is eliminated.

Still, there has been a subtle but significant shift in the justification of affirmative action, beginning with the Bakke case and Justice Lewis Powell's decisive vote in Bakke, which he justified in terms of diversity and not as a corrective to the injustices of American history. Powell's position rested on the determination by a university as to what best ensures the education of its students, as set forth in Justice Felix Frankfurter's 1957 opinion in Sweezy v. New Hampshire. Universities, including the University of Michigan, have responded by arguing that a diverse campus culture provides the kind of quality education and the preparation of leaders that best ensures the future of the nation.

Positive outcomes have resulted from affirmative action college-admissions policies, as shown in the most extensive study yet done on the impact of preferential admissions policies for ethnic minorities. William Bowen and Derek Bok—former presidents of Princeton and Harvard, respectively—evaluated the consequences of twenty-eight colleges and universities having provided affirmative action to more than forty-five thousand minority individuals between 1976 and 1989. They found overwhelming evidence that such policies have had a positive impact on the careers and accomplishments of minority persons. Contrary to the personal account of Stephen Carter in his Reflections of an Affirmative Action Baby, Bowen and Bok found that the vast majority of those benefiting from affirmative action, including those with the highest SAT scores, did not feel stigmatized or think they had been harmed by the fact that their schools had affirmative action policies. It was just the opposite.

Favorite stories of white police candidates rejected, male dental school applicants turned away, qualified white males passed over for promotions that go to less-qualified females or minority persons are legion, but when investigated they usually reveal an errant policy or the misapplication of a good policy. In most cases they show, ironically, what good affirmative action practices can and do look like and what they can accomplish.

Still, affirmative action remains highly controversial. This has brought forth several defenses of it. I describe three of these as "weak arguments" that do not convincingly deflect the weight of criticism and mobilized forces allied against affirmative action. Three other arguments, however, do meet this challenge. I call these "strong arguments," that individually and together provide the basis for a vigorous defense of preferential policies that will continue to keep the doors of opportunity open to those who have found their entrance blocked or obstructed by circumstances not of their making nor experienced by the traditionally privileged in this society. These strong arguments deserve to be well understood and used in defense of affirmative action in the twenty-first century.

Three Weak Affirmative Action Arguments

Payback or Reparations for Past Wrongs

The first weak argument seeks policies that compute and repay lost or stolen benefits to those who have been deprived of the full value of their labor, abilities, and rights as citizens. The clearest case is the cost of three hundred years of human bondage. The abolitionists' call for "forty acres and a mule" recognized that the wealth of the South had been created by slavery, as well as the need for freed slaves to have a means of self-sufficiency. Of course, reparations were not made and this country has lived with the consequences ever since.

While it seems only right to pay back people for past wrongs and deprivations, the counterarguments are sufficiently compelling. As a group claim, reparations may be sought by persons with no more connection to those wronged in the past than the color of one's skin. Those who would be asked to pay argue that it was not them, or even their ancestors, who committed the crimes of slavery. Dalton Conley (2003) is partially right that slavery is "an institution on which America's wealth was built," but this wealth is quite inequitably and only indirectly enjoyed by the majority of white people today. (Many whites also can find injustices committed against their own nationality that would seem to qualify for reparations.) In the end, it may be the statute of limitations that applies.

Give the Other Guy a Chance

The occasional voice of concern argues that people historically excluded from active participation in the social, economic, and political life of a nation should be given a special opportunity to be involved. This appeals to the sense of fair play, and while it is a commendable sentiment, the counterarguments are more likely to carry the day. "What's stopping them? This is a free country." People can choose to participate or not participate.

If women are underrepresented in Congress and state legislatures, maybe it is because they have better things to do. After all, when women run, they win as often as men. If millions of women are working part-time—without benefits and often at below-poverty wages—this is hardly evidence that there should be special policies to help them become more committed, career-oriented employees. Domestic responsibilities and the anchoring of women's identities to home and children should be respected, rather than pushing women into the stressful and demanding rat race their husbands face every day. Similarly, the idea of not being represented politically is countered by the observation that in the United States barely half the adult population casts a vote for president. Many people see political involvement as a personal choice, not a consequence of structural barriers or a political system that disadvantages some groups from being heard. Anybody can vote, if they want to.

Finally, the visibility of gay and lesbian groups lobbying, protesting, and capturing the public's attention with issues of bias, discrimination, and violence seems to contradict the notion that they or other groups need any special attention, let alone affirmative action policies. That gay activism has led to few changes in the personal security of gay men and lesbians or increased their workplace rights this to sway . . . those who oppose affirmative action. Though they may think the courts are wrong, these opponents will point to recent decisions allowing gay marriage and civil unions as evidence of the power of a group toward whom they may approve discriminatory policies. Who needs special attention?

A New Way of Doing Things

As the writer Virginia Woolf recognized nearly a century ago, a society controlled by and for white males sets the rules and establishes the criteria of merit on terms that benefit themselves, largely by valuing the things characteristic of white males in a patriarchal society. Whether it is the job expectations for junior executives, the athletic prowess celebrated by the sports entertainment industry, or the physical demands of modern warfare, in order to qualify women are expected to be "like men" or "better than men at being men." The features valued in women, like those valued in minority cultures and subcultures, are frequently devalued in the dominant society. The third weak argument for affirmative action contends that these values and styles should be respected, but more so they should become respected criteria used to evaluate applicants, candidates, and participants.

Perhaps the clearest example of this is the conduct of international relations. Feminists argue that there is a masculine style of making international claims, facing off, negotiating, and resorting to violence that should be radically altered. If women were more involved, the entire framework of international relations would be different. Similarly, the highly direct, competitive style of dominant American culture is perhaps less able to listen to others, find mutual respect, and reach a consensual solution to issues and problems than the more indirect, circuitous, respectful style of some regional or ethnic minority groups. Those practicing this style should be the ones seeking solutions, not the muscular, testosterone-driven leaders and negotiators who rule the world and its multinational corporations.

Though one may sympathize with a less confrontational or in-your-face approach to problem solving and decision making, this is easily dismissed as "unrealistic." The counterargument generally takes existing organizational procedures and institutional practices as given, then points out "what it takes to get things done." The idea that fundamental practices and organizational cultures need affirmative action to provide an infusion of new ideas and approaches is hard, if not impossible, to sell to people who are in the thick of power and policy, and who are benefiting from their ability to operate in this style.

They are quick to argue that women, too, can be successful in these environments, and have been for decades, if not centuries. Similarly, it is fine for minorities to maintain their cultural styles, but in the dominant society they need to be able to speak, act, and present themselves in the way the system expects. Thousands of minorities have done this and succeeded. Affirmative action would only make them less competitive, less able to stand the rigors required of them. And besides, what kind of a contest would it be if the soft, nonconfrontational approach was applied to global business and politics? We would be crushed!

Three Strong Affirmative Action Arguments
Community Choice

The first strong argument, that rationality is not always the best guide to action, seems an unlikely candidate in support of affirmative action and preferential policies in matters affecting the workplace, education, and citizenship. If being rational is not right, then what is? Emotion? Intuition? Reason is the foundation for the rule of law that limits arbitrary authority and protects the less powerful from oppression. Emotion is the guiding force for prejudice. Reason is the antidote to hysterical arguments that get us nowhere.

The "community choice" argument does not seek to replace reasoned decisions with emotional appeals. Rather, it recognizes the limitations of rational procedures and suggests a healthy supplanting of the logical conclusions of bureaucratic process with deliberate, corrective measures most reasonable people would endorse. Consider the following.

A company needs to increase its sales in order to remain competitive. At a staff meeting the director of public relations reminds everyone that most clients are middle-aged white males who have a preference for working with affable, attractive staff younger than themselves. When hiring is done, a rational decision would be to exclude persons over age thirty-five and applicants with any physical blemishes or who are plain looking (or just plain ugly). Affirmative action policies would prohibit the company from practicing such hiring discrimination, and most people recognize this as a good thing.

Let us examine this a bit more closely. The rational choice approach to decision making is predicated on an individual's gains and losses, largely irrespective of the needs or good of others or the larger community of which the individual is a part. Any policy that hinders the unfettered choice of individuals to maximize their own gain with a minimum of cost would appear to be anathema to conclusions reached by rational people. The rational choice view is that the larger good of the community and society are built on just such choices of individuals to benefit themselves. Sometimes they are, and sometimes they are not.

To set the background for rational choice theory, it is useful to review briefly what Mancur Olson calls the "logic of collective action" and the "free-rider problem" of the public good—the public good being something that would make everyone (the community) better off. In such cases everyone should be expected to contribute to the realization of a public good if they expect to benefit from this good. It is often the case, however, that the inability to exclude nonparticipants from benefiting makes it rational for them to not contribute.

By way of illustration, take an example of a lighthouse that will ensure safer navigation. Imagine a fishing village, some of whose inhabitants have been killed every year when they crash on the rocky shoals as they approach the harbor in darkness or a blinding storm. Fed up with this, the village council decides that every adult should contribute four days of labor and $100 in materials to build a lighthouse. Most agree, and others will go along in the spirit of civic duty. But not everyone.

The village offers no penalties for noncompliance. There can be "free-riders," and they are the rational ones, despite the sound logic applied by the village council. The rational individual will reason that, because no one can withhold the light (and enhanced safety of travel) from them, they too will share the public good whether or not they contribute. Of course, if everyone took this tact the public good (the lighthouse) would not be built. The rational individual assumes that others will not act so self-interestedly, but knows if they do he or she will be no worse off than before in terms of expenditures, having put no effort or money into the project.

Philosophically, this view is the foundation of laissez faire capitalism. Many economists, however, question the idea that market behavior rewards the individual who acts rationally solely to benefit him- or herself. They point to the many examples of state regulation, corporate collusion, price fixing, and other practices that benefit those who cooperate rather than compete. They also reject the attention free-market economic theory gives to instrumental rationality (emphasizing tactics for short-term and immediate gains), to the exclusion of substantive rationality (emphasizing strategic actions, long-term gains and losses, and benefits for the community). A healthy economy and the accumulation of personal wealth require more than personal self-interest.

Economic conservatives, infatuated with the logic of the market, counter that competition ultimately rewards the most efficient producer, whether this efficiency is measured in terms of the wise use of resources or the most profitable expenditure for human capital. They do not deny the reality of discrimination, but argue that discrimination will ultimately penalize the discriminator by raising the cost of human capital and thus the cost of production. This occurs because the discriminator, with prejudice toward a category of persons, will overlook potentially productive employees and so be forced to hire persons of lesser quality. Such discrimination creates a market disadvantage and ultimately the firm that does not discriminate will out-compete the discriminator. It is this point that Christopher Jencks challenges in explaining the need for affirmative action.

As Jencks shows, the self-interested firm will be rewarded for practicing discrimination in a society that assigns different measures of social honor and social stigma on the basis of ethnicity or race, gender, sexual orientation, and the like. It does make sense to act (like a free rider) in terms of rational self-interest, so long as others do not. And this is the basis for the argument favoring affirmative action.

Three types of discrimination are most likely to be found in the economy: consumer-driven, worker-driven, and statistical discrimination. Prejudiced consumers—whether they be airline passengers, restaurant goers, or buyers of new cars—may be uncomfortable being served by a person of a deprecated group. For decades, airlines catered to passenger preference by employing young, attractive white females to serve meals and drinks on flights. Prejudiced whites may avoid a restaurant where they can expect to be served by an African American. People will shop for a car at Dealer A if they believe the Hispanic salespersons at Dealer B are more likely to give them false information to make a sale. The rational thing for an airline, restaurant manager, or car dealer to do is avoid hiring people of the "offending" group. The skills required are not in short supply, so the penalty of discriminating in the form of not hiring qualified employees is surely less than the loss of customers.

The second form of discrimination is similar to the first. Worker-driven discrimination results from an employer accommodating the prejudices of his or her employees. Women as well as minorities, gays, and lesbians experience this, both in the hiring process where they are rejected and on the job site where they may be ostracized, harassed, and passed over for promotion. At the risk of losing experienced, prejudiced employees, having a disruptive workplace, or incurring an employer-training cost by having a disgruntled minority person or woman quit (and possibly sue the offending firm), the rational choice is to not hire them in the first place, a practice William Julius Wilson (1996) has well documented.

The third form of discrimination, statistical discrimination, provides an advantage to the discriminator who acts in terms of statistical probability based on past cases. If women are, in fact, more likely to leave a job due to family responsibilities, even if this is only by a factor of 10%, it may be rational not to hire women. If, in fact, young Hispanic males occupy 5% of the vehicles on a major highway but are twice as likely to be transporting illegal drugs than any other identifiable group, it may be rational for the highway patrol to stop them without probable cause. It might be rational to act in an offensively discriminatory way.

In all of these cases—consumer-driven, worker-driven, and statistical discrimination—the inescapable conclusion is that discrimination is not always penalized by the "market" in goods, services, and perpetrators. And the loser is the public good of fair treatment for all. The market does, in fact, favor the free rider. That is why taxes are levied and penalties are applied for noncompliance—in order to get lighthouses built. Similarly, to discriminate is often a sensible, rational choice of individuals and firms.

The lessening of these forms of discrimination can only occur if there is affirmative action. That is, if "fairness" is guaranteed by building it into laws, procedures, guidelines, and organizational practices that explicitly prohibit consumer, worker, and statistical discrimination. That is what affirmative action means.

Rawlsian Fairness

The second strong argument is a derivative of John Rawls's seminal work, A Theory of Justice. In what is arguably the most important contribution to contract theory since Rousseau's Social Contract, Rawls invites each of us to set forth our own principles of a just society. Rather than compelling, exhorting, or shaming people to adopt specific practices that value fair treatment, Rawls believes that the average person can, in most cases, come to agreement with others about basic principles of what is fair and reasonable. These principles should and can guide the society and its laws—and they are principles included in affirmative action.

Rawls asks us to engage in an imaginative experiment. Imagine you can determine the rules by which your society will operate. Knowing there are limited amounts of all valued goods—material and nonmaterial—ask yourself, "What principles should be used in the distribution of these values?" Not only how much, but how wide a range of differences should there be, and according to what rules should the distribution take place? Should some live in comfort and safety that is two, three, or three hundred times greater than that of someone else in the society? Should this difference be a consequence of hard work, intelligence, birth, or luck?

There is one basic condition for your thinking about these things: You must decide on the range of differences as well as the rules and the principles of distribution behind a "veil of ignorance." That is, you imagine yourself living in this world, but you have no knowledge of your own statuses or personal characteristics. Will you be male or female? Old or young? Black or white? Clever and quick, or slow and easily perplexed? Born in Gabon or Coral Gables? Sexually attracted to those of your own sex or the opposite sex? You do not know.

Rawls's contention is that reasonable people can agree on principles of fairness under these conditions. In point of fact, these principles will be, prima facie, just. These principles will very often include public policies and criteria for receiving benefits that we usually refer to as affirmative action. Using Rawls's imaginative experiment, reasonable people will endorse affirmative action as a requirement of the just society.

Not everyone is a gifted or even a competent teacher of children. Should those who are more gifted or competent be rewarded more highly than those without this gift or competence? How high on the pecking order should they be? We all know that some children learn more readily than others. How much should this advantage be rewarded? If I am willing to work day and night,

Sunday to Sunday, should I not live in a larger house than you? Should I be the first to receive a heart transplant? Should the law treat me differently than the lethargic, shirking, intemperate, procrastinating fellow down the street?

In any city you can sit at night and see the women of color moving about in the office buildings, cleaning up after the white professionals and preparing their workplace for the next day. Should skin color and gender be criteria for who works at night and who works by day? Travel across any city and see the dramatic change in neighborhoods, from rotting tenements to expensive and expensively furnished apartments, from crowded neighborhoods to spacious estates, from dangerous and crime-filled streets to secure, regularly patrolled residential boulevards that invite a late-night stroll. In our current society, those born of fortune must struggle mightily to avoid relieving themselves of this inherited advantage. Almost no one born rich dies poor. Almost no one born poor dies rich.

Few of us would recommend complete equality, but most of us would wish for a lessening of deprivation, a reduction in differences, a greater openness of opportunity and lesser penalties for mistakes or bad choices—recognizing that we all are human and, on occasion, fallible. Also, we are not all the same; we are neither equal in physical stamina nor mental acumen. If we are fortunate, we will grow old in our own time. Some of us will be lucky to know a lifetime of trust, while others of us will know betrayal. A few of us will act decisively and benefit, while others of us will suffer for our haste. Deciding about the principles that should govern the advantages of age, birth, intelligence, luck, and hard work means deciding on the ways those less advantaged of us should be treated. That is the role of affirmative action.

Under the veil of ignorance we can imagine the just expenditure of funds to make education accessible to everyone, regardless of gender, race, ethnicity, or physical condition. We recognize that some decisions should be on the basis of need, such as handicap accessibility, public transportation, and classroom aids. We would probably endorse measures that counter disadvantages of birth, thus making loans, job opportunities, adult retraining, and dental and optical care available without prejudice. In a democratic society, the veil of ignorance would recommend that, regardless of who we are in the society, we would not be barred from political participation and public service, nor should barriers be placed in our way because of sexual orientation or religion. The laws, guidelines, and procedures that would be proposed under a veil of ignorance recognize unavoidable and inevitable differences and seek not only to level the playing field, but also to maximize the quality of life for everyone. These laws, guidelines, and procedures are affirmative action.

The Good Society

The third argument comes from many sources, but perhaps the best articulation of it is by Ruth Sidel in her book, On Her Own: Growing up in the Shadow of the American Dream. In the concluding chapter she asks quite simply, what kind of a world do we want for our grandchildren? If we think about the contours of this world, most of us can agree on the kinds of things we would not want our grandchildren to face. War, hunger, ignorance, brutality, indoctrination, injustice—the list may be endless, but it is a list worth compiling. Caring about those who will come after us, especially those we love, motivates us to do more, to be involved, to care about what is happening today and its consequences for the future.

But there will be costs involved, sacrifices made, and immediate opportunities lost. What price are we willing to pay for the kind of future we want? The price can be thought of in two ways: as that which we pay in making a purchase and the cost to us of a tax. While most individuals think of their taxes as going elsewhere and benefiting the other guy, most people see a purchase as a price paid for something wanted, something of benefit, something that will make life better for them. It is not unreasonable to think of affirmative action as the price we pay to purchase the future we want, and not as a tax that benefits only the other guy.

As we calculate the price we must pay for the kind of benefit we want; many people have concluded that the costs of affirmative action are not too high a price. Admittedly, not everyone makes the same calculation. A case in point is the retired professor whom I once heard arguing in favor of carrying concealed weapons. This man likes to walk about in the mountains accompanied by his dog. He contends that his old dog is vulnerable to attack by porcupines and needs his master's protection. To do this requires carrying a gun. Because it is often wintry when he treks in porcupine country, he must wear a large bulky coat, precluding his wearing a visible gun belt. And he is too old and frail to be toting a heavy shotgun. The only solution is to carry a pistol under his coat, a concealed weapon. Hence his opposition to any law that would make it more difficult to carry concealed weapons. While he recognizes that fewer concealed weapons translates into fewer gun accidents, fewer uses of guns in anger, and a net reduction in loss of life and injury, the price he would incur with a restriction on his own behavior is not worth paying. Not everyone is willing to pay the cost of affirmative action, but there is reason to believe that most of us think it is worth paying.

Many people balk at the notion that affirmative action translates into the kind of future they desire. Yet as Brent Staples has written, "Even hardcore conservatives were shaken to see Black and Hispanic students disappear from California's elite campuses after Proposition 209 outlawed race-sensitive admissions policies there in 1996." Thirty-five years of affirmative action provide ample evidence that the price of preferential policies can, in fact, help buy the future we seek. Not only do individuals benefit, but the institutions and organizations in which they are now involved are more reflective of a wide and vital range of talents, perspectives, and experiences as a result of affirmative action.

The appeal to a future for those who come after us rests on a belief that we can make a better future. Support for affirmative action rests, in part, on the view that different cultures enrich a society, that women's experiences are as valid as men's, that vital imagination and creativity have many sources, and that a society can be richer, more resourceful, and more at peace with itself when everyone is included, when everyone can make a contribution.

Affirmative action requires that some people in previously privileged positions, often advantaged in ways they scarcely recognize, not only give up some of their privileges, but also shift a portion of them to others.

This is what universities have done in insisting that qualified female candidates and qualified minority candidates be interviewed for positions ahead of similarly qualified white male candidates. This is the only way that my own university has been able to address the wide gender gap that existed when I was first hired. The candidates first considered were qualified. The successful candidates brought perspectives and backgrounds long absent from the classrooms, and the classrooms of my university are now better learning environments for students. The affirmative action policy that made this possible was necessary.

As Ronald Dworkin describes this view, "affirmative action . . . has a forward-looking, not a backward-looking justification. [I]t is justified in order to improve society in ways that benefit practically everyone". Affirmative action is a fair price to pay, a down-payment on a better future.

POSTSCRIPT

Has Affirmative Action Outlived Its Usefulness in the Workplace?

In the 1960s, America was a society polarized across racial lines. Dr. Martin Luther King, in his famous "I have a dream" speech, presented his vision of an American society where skin color plays no role in securing economic and social opportunities. His hope was that harmony between the races would be possible if all were afforded the same opportunities to succeed. And, although he did not live long enough to see its emergence, there can be no doubt that King's civil rights activities helped pave the way for the development of affirmative action as an important vehicle for promoting a more diverse American workplace. But in a cruel twist of fate, it seems that affirmative action has given rise to the very scenario it was intended to alleviate. Consider these comments from Dr. Onkar Ghate, a widely respected resident fellow at the influential Libertarian think tank, the Ayn Rand Institute: "The consequence of the spread of racial quotas [i.e., affirmative action] and multiculturalist ideas hasn't been harmony, but a precipitous rise in racial hatred throughout America, particularly in the classroom and the workplace."

Those are certainly powerful words, but they still leave one wondering if abandoning affirmative action is a wise move at this point in time. As you've just read, Dr. Cohen attacks affirmative action on four fronts, but it's his assertion that it is immoral that may be most problematic for supporters of affirmative action. Indeed, many might reasonably conclude that if an action is immoral, it should cease immediately, regardless of circumstances. On the other hand, Dr. Massey has weighed into the debate by offering some decidedly unique defenses of affirmative action. So now that you have finished these selections, the onus is on you to decide—has affirmative action outlived its usefulness in the workplace?

Suggested Readings

Marie Gryphon, "The Affirmative Action Myth," *The Cato Institute* (July 10, 2004). http://www.cato.org/dailys/07-10-04.html

Public Broadcasting Service, "Attacking Affirmative Action," *Now* (August 29, 2008). http://www.pbs.org/now/shows/434/index.html

Charles L. Geshekter, "The Effects of Proposition 209 on California: Higher Education, Public Employment, and Contracting," *National Association of Scholars* (September 25, 2008). http://www.nas.org/polArticles.cfm?doc_id=351

Prue Burns and Jan Shapper, "The Ethical Case for Affirmative Action," *Journal of Business Ethics* (vol. 83, no. 3: 369–379, 2008).

David Kelley, "Ban Government Racism, Not Discrimination," *The Atlas Society* (February 28, 2003). http://www.objectivistcenter.org/cth—579-Ban_Government_Racism_Not_Discrimination.aspx

Affirmative Action and Diversity Project, "The Affirmative Action and Diversity Project: A Webpage for Research (2004)". http://aad.english.ucsb.edu/

ISSUE 6

Is Workplace Drug Testing a Wise Corporate Policy?

YES: Elaine Davis and Stacie Hueller, from "Strengthening the Case for Workplace Drug-Testing," *S.A.M. Advanced Management Journal* (Summer 2006, vol. 71, no. 3)

NO: Russ Belville, from "Drug Testing Does No Good," *The Oregon Herald* (April 20, 2005). http://www.oregonherald.com/n/radicalruss/20050420_workplace-drug-testing.html

ISSUE SUMMARY

YES: Scholars Elaine Davis and Stacie Hueller provide an analysis on how and why businesses should address the growing use of methamphetamines in the workplace.

NO: Former talk radio host and social commentator Russ Belville cites results of several studies questioning the effectiveness of workplace drug testing. He further argues that given their expense, drug-testing policies are not sound strategic initiatives.

Substance abuse costs employers tens of millions of dollars every year as a result of the increased levels of absenteeism, work-related accidents, health care costs, and theft. The National Institute on Drug Abuse reports that 75 percent of illegal drug users are employed, and approximately 20 percent of 18 to 25-year-olds use drugs at the workplace (*National Institute on Drug Abuse*; http://www. NIDA.nih.gov). It's not surprising, then, that private employers across the country have adopted various types of drug-testing policies as a way of fighting back. The federal government is also involved in the battle, having entered with the passage of the Drug-free Workplace Act of 1988. This act requires all government agencies and firms with governmental contracts to take action toward eliminating drugs from the workplace.

Despite society's apparent acceptance of drug testing at work, there is considerable resistance to the policy of testing employees. Central to the opposition's position is the issue of employee privacy rights. Notwithstanding the indisputable fact that corporations have a right to protect themselves, critics of workplace drug testing fear that it infringes on employee privacy rights. Critics also point to studies that call into question the degree to which employee productivity is truly affected by workplace drug use.

Responses to the employee privacy issue have generally fallen into one of three categories and can be thought of as comprising a continuum of viewpoints: at one end are those who are against drug testing in the workplace under any and all circumstances. They typically invoke a rights-based argument in contending that individual rights always trump organizational rights. America is a country founded on the belief in the supremacy of individual rights and, because drug testing violates an individual's right to privacy, organizations should not be allowed to implement them under any condition.

At the opposite end of our continuum reside the pro-testing advocates. The view here is that organizations are actually a collection of individuals who share common ownership of the firm and have a right to protect themselves and their property. Inasmuch as they can be held accountable for the moral and legal violations committed by their employees, they should be allowed to exercise reasonable control over the workplace. Thus, taking into account the tremendous damage drug abuse can inflict on an organization, workplace drug testing would appear to be a reasonable managerial policy.

Perhaps the most commonly accepted view, representing the midpoint of our continuum, is that corporations should hold employee privacy as an important corporate principle. Testing can be done, but all effort should be made to protect employee privacy throughout the process, and it should be implemented only in cases with reasonable grounds for suspicion. Thus, determining employee drug use is fair game only when there is evidence that it results in undesirable behaviors such as lower productivity or increasing the likelihood of safety violations.

Before you read the following articles and develop your own opinion, some facts should be presented. It is important to know that the courts have consistently sided with the rights of corporations to test employees provided there is no evidence of discrimination in its implementation or unwarranted targeting of specific individuals for testing. Also, courts have been particularly supportive when the job in question is of a sensitive nature.

Indeed, the fact that workplace drug testing is legal accounts in large measure for its widespread use by employers. Recent surveys of major American corporations indicate that nearly 90 percent of the firms use some form of drug testing. Almost all firms surveyed use tests as part of the applicant process and eliminate from consideration those individuals that fail (Gray and Brown, *Perspectives in Business Ethics*, 2nd ed., Laura P. Hartman, ed., McGraw-Hill, 2002, p. 433). Thus, workplace drug testing is both legal and widespread; nevertheless, the question remains, does that make it good corporate policy?

Supporting the view that workplace drug testing makes business sense are scholars Elaine Davis and Stacie Hueller. They focus attention on the growing problem of methamphetamine use both in society and in the workplace. After providing background on the drug and the threat it poses in the workplace, the authors detail appropriate steps for management to take to curb its use. Russ Belville disagrees. He cites results of several studies that suggest drug testing does not lead to either increases in employee productivity or to a great number of workplace accidents resulting from unsafe employee behaviors.

YES

**Elaine Davis
and Stacie Hueller**

Strengthening the Case for Workplace Drug Testing: The Growing Problem of Methamphetamines

Introduction and Background

According to the National Institute on Drug Abuse (NIDA), an estimated 75% of illegal drug users are employed and one out of five workers in the 18–25 age bracket uses drugs at the worksite. Methamphetamine (meth) use, in particular, is causing growing alarm for employers across the U.S. In a 2004 summary report by Quest Diagnostics Inc. that analyzed all drug test results performed by the company, positive tests for meth increased 68% over a one-year period. The resulting negative workplace behaviors have caused many companies to increase drug screenings. According to Quest Diagnostics, the country's largest drug-testing company, the number of workers and applicants testing positive for meth has been rapidly increasing in the general workforce, led by southeastern states such as Georgia and Alabama. In addition, U.S. police raids of meth labs increased as much as 500%. Police nationwide rank methamphetamine the No. 1 drug they battle today: in a survey of 500 law-enforcement agencies in 45 states released in July of 2005 by the National Association of Counties, 58% said meth is their biggest drug problem. According to the World Health Organization, the drug is more abused worldwide than cocaine and heroin and is increasingly popular with workers in highly industrialized economies. Future projections indicate that meth use will surpass cocaine as the illegal stimulant of choice.

Implications for employers are great. The U.S. Department of Labor estimates annual workplace losses due to drug use of over $100 billion. Meth abuse losses are from accidents, health insurance and medical costs, absenteeism, tardiness, sick leave abuse, grievances, disability payments, lowered productivity, lowered co-worker morale, turnover, equipment damage, damage to public image, threats to public safety, worksite security and theft. According to the U.S. Center for Substance Abuse Prevention, National Clearinghouse for Alcohol and Drug Information (NCADI), drug users consume

From *Advanced Management Journal*, 71:3, Summer 2006, pp. 4-9. Copyright © 2006 by Society for Advancement of Management. Reprinted by permission.

almost twice the employment benefits as nonusers, are absent 50% more often, and file more than twice as many workers' compensation claims.

The University of Arkansas Center for Business and Economic Research conducted an economic impact study in Benton County, Arkansas. According to the findings, meth use costs employers an estimated $42,000 per meth-using-worker each year. This number does not include treatment, law enforcement, or other drug related expenditures. The Center identified five categories in which meth use most notably affects the workplace. The first and largest impact is on employee absenteeism; employees who use meth are five times more likely to miss work than non-using co-workers. Second, meth users are less productive; it takes four meth users to do the job of three non-meth users. Third, employee theft is more likely. Fourth, health insurance premiums are higher with meth users in the workplace. Lastly, employers pay more in workers' compensation costs because meth users are more likely to file claims and the claim is typically more expensive.

Meth use has moved across socio-economic levels. Once exclusively the choice of low-income people, truckers, and bikers, it is now being used by overworked secretaries, stressed teachers, soldiers on long battle missions, attorneys in law firms, and workers in the medical profession, all in attempts to boost concentration, stamina, and deal with the increasing work pressure of longer hours and need for greater productivity. Furthermore, meth is different from other illegal drugs used in the workplace. It causes more damage to the employee's brain, is more likely to cause mental illness in those who are predisposed, including psychosis, and increases the propensity to aggressive behavior and violence.

Alarm over meth use has intensified in the workplace and organizations are struggling with ways to handle the significant risks of employee abuse. This has led many companies that previously did not have drug policies to implement them and those with policies to revisit and clarify them. A drug-free workplace with well thought out drug-testing procedures, supervisor and staff training, and establishment of an Employee Assistance Program are key elements for organizations to ward off meth's effects. Many companies whose drug problems cannot be remedied using drug-free policies alone have enlisted the help of local law enforcement, and some evidence shows this has helped scale back the problem in the workplace.

Methamphetamine Overview

The drug. Use of amphetamines and their methyl subgroup methamphetamines has been widely documented, as early as the first German synthesis in 1887. They were used to treat asthma, low blood pressure, weight loss, depression, and as a stimulant, but over-the-counter sales were banned in the 1970s due to increasing abuses. The more potent meth is a highly addictive synthetic drug that stimulates the central nervous system with effects similar to the drug "speed." Meth can be taken orally, smoked, injected, or snorted. Known by names such as "ice," "Tina," "glass," and "crystal," meth users experience a high immediately after taking the drug, which lasts for 8 to 14 hours. During this time, users exhibit high energy behavior and usually do not eat or sleep. Meth-amphetamines work by blocking the brain's ability to rid itself of the euphoria-causing neurotransmitter dopamine. Meth is very similar to cocaine, but cocaine is metabolized more quickly in the body. Thus, the high achieved from meth last hours, compared to a cocaine high which lasts only 30–45 minutes; users often identify the long high as its main attraction. The hours-long meth high is also more suitable to people punching time clocks than the 30-minute cocaine high. Workers can't be running to the bathroom every half hour to get high on cocaine; if an employee does meth in the morning, he or she is good until noon. Meth is also often referred to as the "poor man's cocaine."

Short-term effects of meth use include increased attention and decreased fatigue, increased activity, decreased appetite, euphoria or rush, increased respiration, and hyperthermia. While short-term effects are mostly physical, long-term effects are both physical and psychological and include dependence and addiction, psychosis (paranoia, hallucinations, and mood disturbances), stroke, and severe weight loss. Chronic use can result in inflammation of the heart lining, episodes of violent behavior, extreme paranoia, anxiety, confusion, insomnia, and lead poisoning. Acute lead poisoning occurs because production requires lead acetate as a reagent. Errors during production can lead to drug contamination, which inevitably can poison users.

Continued meth use can damage areas of the brain related to cognition and memory which may persist even years after discontinuation of use. Meth addiction causes long-term, sometimes irreversible behavioral, cognitive, and psychological problems that can continue throughout life. According to Paul Thompson, a brain-mapping expert at UCLA, regular meth users lose about 1% of their brain cells every year, which is comparable to the loss experienced by people with Alzheimer's disease, stroke, and epilepsy. The long-term effects of meth are unusually harsh compared with other drugs.

- **Meth crime.** Because meth is relatively easy to make, abusers eventually attempt to make it themselves. With the advent of the Internet, meth recipes and ingredients are very accessible. Labs are typically found in rural areas; close proximity to farms and distant neighbors make obtaining chemicals necessary for production easy and detection less likely. In Minnesota, the Department of Corrections (DOC) reports that compared to other criminal offenses (which tend to be concentrated in large urban areas) meth has been largely a rural phenomenon, with 72% of the meth offenders incarcerated outside metro counties. This rural overrepresentation is even greater for those imprisoned for the manufacture and sale of meth, with 87% of the offenders coming from rural Minnesota. The Minnesota DOC also reports that as of July 1, 2005, meth inmates constituted 49% of drug offenders in Minnesota prisons. Statistics from the Minnesota Department of Public Safety reveal that meth lab seizures rose more than 700 percent between 1998 and 2003. Minnesota's experience is not unlike that of neighboring states, with Iowa particularly hard hit. Missouri tops the list with more than 8,000 labs, equipment caches, and toxic dumps seized between 2002 and 2004.

- **Company culture.** Employees are being asked by their employers to do more, and meth seems to provide a good solution to busy work schedules and demanding bosses. Many occupations demand long hours of repetitive work, such as construction and manufacturing, and, as a result, these are the most common workplaces where employees use methamphetamines. However, methamphetamine is increasingly a white-collar drug as well; its use is growing in the entertainment, sales, retail, and legal professions. The California Bar Association revealed that one in four lawyers who are admitted voluntarily to drug rehabilitation are addicted to methamphetamines.

In pursuit of increased products and profits, it is easy for corporations and managers to remain unaware of methamphetamine abuse. Although the increasing us of meth consistently makes headlines, part of corporate America doesn't recognize it as a serious problem. Researchers, counselors, and government officials say employers have done little to address the erratic behavior, accidents, increased sick days, and health costs attributed to or associated with its use. According to former workers and addicts at a recreational vehicle manufacturing facility in South Bend, Indiana, their employer was aware of the prevalent meth use, but did nothing about it. According to these workers, employers benefit from allowing employees to use meth. It allows them to be more productive by working faster and avoiding accidents because of their increased state of alertness. This contradicts earlier statistics citing the heavy financial cost of meth use.

Further examples of complacent corporations are those with employees known as "maintenance users." Maintenance users are hard to recognize because "many of the drug's initial characteristics, increased concentration and the ability to work longer hours are traits valued by managers and unlikely to be seen as a problem." Initially, the drug does increase performance. In defense of corporations, some users can hide their methamphetamine use for a very long time and not have altered performance.

Prevention and Solutions: Creating a Drug Free Workplace

According to the Department of Labor and the Department of Health and Human Services Drug Free Workplace Guidelines, a drug-free workplace adheres to a program of policies and activities that discourage alcohol and drug abuse and encourages treatment, recovery, and return to work. The Substance Abuse and Mental Health Services Administration (SAMHSA), a division of the Department of Health and Human Services, advocates six components for a drug-free workplace program: assessment, policy, education and training, EAPs, and drug testing. . . .

Needs assessment involves assessing the current state of drug addiction in your workplace, determining areas needing focused attention and the means by which to evaluate any newly implemented programs. Quantifiable measures of success could include lower absenteeism, reduced turnover, and fewer accidents and workers' compensation claims.

Policy development is the foundation of a drug-free workplace. A written policy tells employees the organization's position on drug abuse and explains what will happen if the policy is violated. Consultation with an attorney is warranted to ensure compliance with state and federal law, particularly with nonregulated industries outside the scope of the Drug-Free Workplace Act of 1988, which mandates a drug-free workplace for recipients of federal contracts and grants. Because each state's laws governing drug testing in the workplace are different, establishing a well-written policy will help companies comply with state and federal laws and meet legal challenges.

Employers should determine which types of drugs they will be testing for, since different tests target specific drugs. Employers' policies should also state what will happen to employees or new hires if they test positive for drug use, such as termination or the chance to enter a company-sponsored drug treatment program. Some states mandate rehabilitation and do not allow dismissal. Employers in states without such mandates must decide what they are willing to pay for, since meth treatment can last as long as a year and is very costly. In addition, the policy should set limits on when employees are eligible for rehire after drug-related termination. A drug-free policy must be clear to employees and must be applied consistently from executives to entry-level employees. It is also important for U.S. companies that conduct business internationally to have a standard drug testing policy, because other countries are also feeling the effect of methamphetamines in the workplace. . . .

Employee education is vital and must be more than sending an e-mail to all employees outlining the policy and requiring their adherence. Essential education includes the policy, how to get assistance and referrals, how employee performance problems will be evaluated, appeal provisions, procedures of drug testing if testing is included, confidentiality, and other employee protections in the policy. Companies that proactively advertise a drug-free workplace and offer education to employees, can help deter substance abuse in the workplace. Not only does education help employees understand the effects of substance abuse on their company, it also helps employees identify the common signs of abuse. Corporations who sponsor programs for a drug-free workplace will also display goodwill towards their communities in helping the fight against methamphetamines.

Supervisor training is essential so they know the signs and symptoms of meth abuse and know company policy so they can explain it to other employees. They also need to understand their role, which is not to diagnose addiction but to rate employee performance. The quickest way to spot potential problems is to know your employee's performance. If it starts to decline, steps should be taken to find out why. Supervisors should have comprehensive detailed training about the specifics of the policy. They should learn how to assess situations appropriately and act in the event employees violate the policy. The mandatory training should be documented to prove that supervisors attended and the policy was covered in detail.

Employee Assistance Programs (EAP) offer help to employees and their families with drug and alcohol abuse problems, in addition to personal and work-related problems such as health, finances, and marital and social issues. As part of these programs it is important to address the needs of employees who are not abusers themselves but may face these problems due to a loved one's addiction. EAP enrollment has increased steadily over the past 10 years. EAP play a key role in the fight against meth abuse, providing necessary counseling to employees.

Drug testing serves as a deterrent to continued use of illicit substances and provides a means to detect and identify employees or job applicants who are using meth. Through detection and identification, employers may be able to assist employees in recognizing and admitting their abuse problems so that they may obtain necessary treatment. The American Management Association reports that 60% of employers test employees and new hires.

According to the Joseph Rowntree Foundation, the four fundamental reasons for employing drug testing in the workplace are safety, organizational efficiency, reputation risk, and employee welfare. Employees under the influence of meth at work pose a risk to themselves and others, and employers have a duty to their employees to maintain a safe working environment. Drug testing allows organizations to remain efficient by "weeding out" users who are unproductive, have high rates of absenteeism, and cause high turnover rates. Furthermore, some companies drug test solely because they are concerned about potential damage to their reputations by drug users.

Four common programs are used by companies to test current and prospective employees for drug abuse: random testing, reasonable suspicion testing, post-accident testing, and return-to-work testing. Many states discourage or restrict random testing. Employers have the right to test based on reasonable suspicion, but must have documentation supporting their suspicions. They must provide transportation to and from the testing facility to keep the suspected user from driving under the influence. Post-accident testing is common in many workplaces when human error may be the cause of accidents. A positive post-accident test may prevent employees from collecting workers' compensation or unemployment benefits.

Return-to-work testing is often a stipulation for employees after participating in a drug treatment program. Employees often sign "contracts" with their employers outlining the procedures they must follow to return to work. Elements of the contract often include ongoing rehabilitation programs, passing drug tests upon returning to work, and submitting to unannounced, repeated drug testing. The contracts also state that if the employee fails to follow any of the procedures, employment will be terminated.

While urine and blood testing are the most prevalent, they are also the easiest methods for which users can submit fraudulent specimens. Hair, sweat, and saliva cannot be tampered with as easily; however, a simple Web search for "drug testing" lists numerous Web sites touting advice and selling kits to help drug users pass any type of drug screenings. Recent arrests of some high-profile athletes and movie actors have focused attention on The Whizzinator, a product worn inside pants to conceal a tampered urine sample. As companies get more aggressive in their drug testing and enforcement, more products will be marketed to beat the tests.

Examples of companies who are successfully dealing with meth are numerous. Creative Memories, a large scrapbook manufacturer in St. Cloud, Minnesota, became aggressive with drug testing, policy enforcement, and creating a rehabilitation culture that encourages employees to seek help. The company has seen positive results. HR Director Cindy Mason-Sebastian has been so impressed with the results that she now takes one of her employees, formerly addicted to meth, with her to make team presentations to other organizations on how to control meth in the workplace. One employee tells groups that "getting caught by Creative Memories was the best thing that ever happened to me." Matson Navigation Co., a shipping company in Hawaii, added an educational film to their training lineup. It had been made specifically for the shipping industry and showed maritime workers using meth, which is particularly dangerous in that industry. The impact on employees of seeing co-workers on screen was profound.

Alternatives. Although drug testing and drug-free workplace policies are the two most common methods of handling drug use, there are other alternatives. For most companies, policies that include drug testing, education, and training will be comprehensive enough to curtail most of employee drug use. However, some companies find they need stronger measures. A harsher measure for drug prevention is establishing an undercover operation in conjunction with local law enforcement. Such operations are being undertaken by more organizations with systemic meth problems. Although time intensive (nearly 15 months at a plant in Baltimore), undercover operations are often successful, especially when meth use is widespread or sales are occurring on site. An undercover officer applies for a position, typically a janitor or position that allows mobility throughout the workplace, and then infiltrates a group of users or dealers. After building trust and sometimes simulating drug use with the offenders, the officer collects data that eventually lead to arrests. To maintain confidentiality at the company, only corporate security and Human Resource executives are aware of the investigation until completion. At a GM plant in Baltimore, undercover agents worked for 15 months to collect evidence that led to the arrest of 24 people.

Conclusion

Methamphetamine abuse is a growing problem across the United States and has grave implications for companies, especially major employers in rural areas. Employers see their labor pool shrink as potential employees are passed over due to a positive drug test, or existing employees begin using and are fired for excessive absences, low productivity, or other costly behaviors. Employers have been forced to spend thousands of dollars to implement drug testing to maintain a safe environment. Meth abuse brings a multitude of problems to corporations, and their Human Resources departments may the frontlines of this dilemma.

Meth use may continue, but employers, communities, and law enforcement can work collaboratively at least to stop continued growth in usage. To control this increasing problem, companies need to develop a drug-free policy, educate employees, train supervisors, perform drug tests regularly, and assist employees who need help with abuse. Developing a comprehensive drug-free workplace is a huge undertaking, but the costs of not doing so are even greater. Companies cannot afford to be complacent.

Russ Belville

Drug Testing Does No Good

Recently, an RV manufacturing plant in Goshen, Indiana, made headlines because they had drug tested all 120 of their employees and found that nearly a third of them tested positive for some illicit substance.

What caused the company to drug test all of their employees? Was there a rash of accidents? Had productivity dropped significantly? Were there increasing incidents of absenteeism and illness? Did a supervisor notice any drug use occurring at the plant, or notice an employee obviously under the influence of drugs?

No. The only reason the plant spent the time, effort, and money to test their employees was due to a police tip that there was a drug problem at the plant. In other words, there was no reason for the company to believe they had a drug problem.

You would think that running a manufacturing plant with one third of your employees working under the influence would lead to some obvious problems. You'd be right. The problem is that a positive drug test does not indicate that a person is under the influence of drugs. It only indicates that a person has done drugs in the past.

The methods of drug testing have evolved over the past decade. Once, businesses, schools, and government could only test a person's urine. These tests were so easily defeated that the tests only detect whether you're too dumb to fool the test. But new methods of testing the blood, saliva, and hair have made fooling a drug test much harder.

With the urine test, evidence of past use of cocaine, amphetamines, and other hard drugs can be detected for 72 hours after use. Thus, a worker testing positive for these drugs could have ingested these substances on a Friday evening and be completely sober for work on Monday. Likewise, a person seeking a new job need only abstain from these substances for three days.

Ironically, the one drug with the lowest potential for abuse and harm, marijuana, remains detectable in a person's urine for 30 to 45 days. It is odd to consider that for two employees passing a urine test, one may have been abstaining from smoking pot last month while the other may have been smoking crack all of last month up until three days ago.

The newer testing does a better job of detecting drug use; some tests can indicate the use of any illicit substance for up to three months prior to the test. However, all that means is that problem drug users who wish to go straight and re-enter the workforce have a longer wait before they can apply for work.

Updated version of essay originally published at www.RadicalRuss.com and seen in *The Oregon Herald,* April 20, 2005. Copyright © 2009 by Au Gratin Productions, Inc. Reprinted by permission of Russ Belville, NORML Outreach Coordinator.

Without gainful employment, how much harder is it for a recovering addict to stay sober?

There must be a good reason for American businesses spending up to $1 billion per year on drug testing. One of the usual reasons for this expenditure is workforce productivity.

However, when independent researchers analyzed the statistics on drug testing and productivity, they found some surprising results. According to The Committee on Drug Use in the Workplace (CDUW) assembled by the government's own National Institute of Drug Abuse, "The empirical results suggest that drug testing programs do not succeed in improving productivity. Surprisingly, companies adopting drug testing programs are found to exhibit lower levels of productivity than their counterparts that do not."

How could a company actually lose productivity by drug testing workers? CDUW suggests four possible reasons:

1. Drug testing is expensive. Tests cost around $50 per worker. A congressional committee estimated that the cost of each positive result in government testing was $77,000 because the positive rate was only 0.5%. Then there's the costs of administration, medical review, follow-up tests for positive results, treatment or discipline for the worker, or searching, hiring, and training a new worker.

2. Drug testing lowers employee morale. An overwhelming majority of workers find drug testing to be an invasion of privacy. They consider drug testing unfair when it is only detecting prior use, not current impairment. They find it profoundly unfair that these tests do not consider the abuse of alcohol, which is a more significant factor in workplace safety and productivity. The lowered morale causes employees to show less loyalty to a company, not work as hard, and good workers may seek other jobs with non-drug testing firms.

3. Drug use may actually increase productivity for some people. The CDUW found that moderate use of drugs or alcohol had either a positive effect or no effect on worker productivity. Numerous studies have found that moderate marijuana use actually increased productivity. Furthermore, marijuana users who are treating pain, cancer, AIDS, multiple sclerosis, glaucoma, arthritis, migraines, or even depression are much more productive than they would be without treatment.

4. Drug testing may lead marijuana smokers (by far the largest segment of the drug using population) to using harder drugs. Since most workplaces still choose the cheaper urine testing over the other tests, marijuana smokers may instead use harder drugs or alcohol, all of which are flushed quickly from the system. Marijuana's low addictiveness allows a casual user to remain healthy and productive, while the high addictiveness of the harder drugs make it more likely for the person to slip from casual use to the severe abuse that causes the illness, absenteeism, safety risks, and low productivity the drug tests were meant to alleviate in the first place.

Another excuse offered for drug testing is workplace safety. We don't want to have drug-impaired workers operating heavy machinery, public transportation, or any other industry where safety is of paramount concern. Of course, this reasoning falls flat when we recall that drug testing does not detect impairment. But perhaps one could assume that someone who has used drugs in the past may be more likely to use them on the job and endanger fellow employees and the public.

Unfortunately, the data do not support that assumption. Many companies use some form of impairment testing, a system that does not test for drugs, but rather hand-eye coordination, concentration, and reaction times. Those companies that have used these systems have found that severe fatigue and illness, not drug or alcohol use, are the most common causes of workplace accidents.

One added advantage of these tests is that they do reduce the level of workplace accidents. Also, workers are much more accepting of impairment tests, as they do not violate privacy and are perceived to be fairer than drug testing. Also, the impairment tests are much cheaper to administer and they actually detect the problem that drug testing does not—worker impairment.

The final nail in the coffin of any workplace drug testing argument is the fact that casual drug users (once per week or less) are just as likely to find employment and hold down a job as their non-drug using counterparts. Our drug testing regime has not kept casual drug users out of the workplace at all, and those users are not adversely affecting productivity, safety, or their own career goals.

Businesses and government aren't the only entities routinely testing for drugs. Our schools are now testing our children for evidence of illicit drug use. In a series of controversial rulings, the Supreme Court has steadily added to the number of our children being drug tested.

First they allowed students to be tested for cause; if a student was suspected of using or possessing drugs on campus, he or she could be tested. Next they ruled that students involved with extracurricular athletics could be tested randomly, citing the need for safety in potentially dangerous sports activities.

Most recently, the justices have decided that students in any extracurricular activity, from band to chess club, could be tested randomly. Justice Clarence Thomas expressed the opinion of the slim 5-4 majority stating that children involved in after-school activities voluntarily give up some of their rights to privacy.

Many of the same issues of safety and productivity are raised in support of drug testing students, and they are met with the same evidence found in the workplace. No significant differences in accidents or performance are found between schools that drug test and those that do not, nor between students who pass drug tests and those who fail.

However, with the student population there are other arguments that are stated: we need to send a message to students that drug use will not be tolerated and we need to provide disincentives for students to stop using drugs.

This argument also falls flat when confronted with the evidence. A federally funded study in 2003 of over 76,000 students in almost 900 schools found no correlation between drug testing and student drug use. Kids were just as likely to use drugs at the drug testing schools as the non-drug testing schools.

Moreover, just as workplace drug testing has the unintended consequence of lowering morale and productivity, school drug testing has its unintended consequences. Kids who might be falling in with the wrong crowd are discouraged from joining the after-school sports or clubs that would provide a healthier environment. Kids already enrolled in extra-curricular activities must sacrifice their privacy and discover that their word and their achievements are not trusted.

Of course, like workplace drug testing, there's the added expense of operating such a program, a cost that weighs heavily against chronically insufficient school budgets. The cost of one positive drug test result could have bought new instruments for the band, computers for the classroom, or equipment for the team.

Further compounding the futility of all drug testing is the fact that there is no perfect drug test. Every test gives a significant amount of false-positives and false-negatives. Many common over-the-counter medications can show up as an illicit drug. Cold tablets containing pseudoephedrine may be detected as amphetamines (speed). Cold remedies with dextromethorphan can register positive for opiates (heroin). Naproxen/ibuprofen-based pain relievers give positives for cannabis (marijuana). Nasal sprays sometimes indicate for MDMA (ecstasy).

Even some common foods can cause a failed drug test. Poppy seeds that you ingest from muffins or bagels can register as heroin. Large amounts of riboflavin (vitamin B-2) and perfectly legal (and incredibly healthy) hemp seed oil can register as marijuana.

Then of course there are many prescription drugs that can lead to a false positive. Amoxicillin, the antibiotic most prescribed for those allergic to penicillin, can show up as cocaine. Many asthma medications register as ecstasy or amphetamines. Even in the absence of these pharmaceuticals, some medical conditions can register a false positive. Kidney infection, liver disease, and diabetes can all lead to false positives for cocaine, ecstasy, opiates, or amphetamines.

Worst of all, you may fail a drug test through no fault of your own. A small fraction of people excrete larger amounts of certain enzymes in their urine that may produce a false positive. One researcher hypothesizes that the higher levels of melanin (the pigment producing cell) found in darker-skinned people may lead to positives for marijuana, because melanin and THC metabolites share a similar molecular structure.

For every false positive there is a person who has suffered the indignity of the accusation, the suspicion of family, co-workers, and friends, the threat of job loss or school suspension, and the burden of proving themselves innocent of a crime they did not commit. For every false negative there is the time, money, and effort wasted failing to discover someone who is actually using drugs.

But beyond the obvious futility and waste involved, there is one superseding argument against drug testing: it is un-American.

Our Founding Fathers laid out our basic liberties in the Bill of Rights. Drug testing violates at least two of our most sacred liberties.

Our 5th Amendment lays out two basic legal concepts: that we cannot be compelled to testify against ourselves and that we are innocent until proven guilty. Drug testing assumes that you are guilty until your body proves you to be innocent. Being compelled to provide urine, hair, saliva, or blood is a testimony against yourself. The Founders were clearly against compelling the citizenry toward self-incrimination; they had seen the results of tyrants using these techniques throughout history. It's a shame our courts haven't been as wise.

Our 4th Amendment is the basis for our right to privacy and freedom from government investigations and seizures without warrant and probable cause. Drug testing is certainly an invasion of privacy; it's hard to imagine how a stranger watching you urinate isn't an invasion of privacy. If there is no probable cause to believe you have committed a crime, there is no good reason to seize your bodily fluids.

Sadly, courts have decided that going to work or school is a voluntary activity, that you exchange some of your expectation to privacy in getting a job or an education, and that employers and educators are not the police or government. It's hard for me to imagine how work or education is truly voluntary; I guess that homelessness and ignorance are a viable choice in their minds; a choice I think would lead to more drug abuse, not less.

For many people, there is no choice but to swallow their pride, surrender their rights, face the embarrassment, risk the false positive, and take the drug test. Almost half of all employers perform some sort of drug testing. The farther down the socio-economic scale, the more likely a worker will face a pre-employment drug test. Around 36% of financial, business, and professional services test their new hires, compared to more than three-fourths of manufacturing and more than 60% of wholesale, retail, and other services. Yet rates of illicit drug use remain fairly constant among all segments of society.

The cash-strapped schools are less likely to be testing for drugs. In 2003, some 19% of schools had drug testing for cause, only 5% tested student-athletes, and only 4% tested participants in all extra-curricular activities. But for the student at these schools, unlike the worker, attendance is compulsory and there aren't many other options available. Their choices are to either avoid all extracurricular activities (which can be determining factors in college selection and future career) or suffer the same risks and indignities as their parents in the workforce.

Drug testing is but one of the many failures in our government's war on casual drug users, and its failure to achieve its stated goals is one of the easiest to prove. Fortunately, many companies are coming to recognize this fact—rates of workplace and school drug testing have declined steadily since 1990. But there remains a federal government with a strong inclination toward abrogating the rights of citizens to look "tough on crime," and many industries that stand to gain from increased drug testing.

Personally, I just try to imagine what possible argument could have convinced hemp farmers Thomas Jefferson and George Washington to pee in a cup in order to get a job.

POSTSCRIPT

Is Workplace Drug Testing a Wise Corporate Policy?

Beyond the right-to-privacy argument, drug-testing opponents have raised a host of concerns. Foremost among these is the accuracy of the tests themselves. Critics point out that the repercussions from inaccurate test scores can be devastating not only to the specific individuals involved but also to the rest of the workforce. Employee confidence in management's neutrality as well as the appropriateness of testing can be severely eroded if innocent individuals are punished or guilty employees go undetected. Testing also seems to send a message of distrust from management to employees regardless of whether such a perception is accurate. As Russ Belville notes in his article, another important concern is the expense of drug testing. There is, not surprisingly, a cost/accuracy tradeoff: Cheap tests are notoriously undependable, and highly accurate tests are extremely expensive. Small firms may have little choice but to use inexpensive tests while large firms with thousands of employees might find the costs to be prohibitive. Finally, critics worry about the information obtained from the tests and the manner in which management uses it. They fear that employers will use the information to target employees for dismissal on grounds that are completely unrelated to job performance.

Despite the valid points raised by the opposing side, supporters of drug testing policies note that, often, those individuals who have a reason to fear drug tests are the ones that are the most vocal against their use. Consider the results of an interesting study: Human resource scholars found that students that had never used drugs were much more likely to support workplace drug testing programs than were students that had used drugs in the past (Murphy, Thornton, & Reynolds, 1990, in *Perspectives in Business Ethics*, 2nd ed., Laura P. Hartman, editor, McGraw-Hill Irwin, 2002).

So, after having read both sides of this debate, where do you stand? For some of you this question will become very tangible in the near future when you enter the workforce to pursue your career. How will *you* feel if you are called on to submit to a drug test?

Suggested Readings

Robert L. Mathis and John H. Jackson, *Human Resource Management,* 11th ed. (Thompson South-Western, 2007).

Gary Dressler, *Human Resource Management,* 11th ed. (Pearson Prentice-Hall, 2008).

American Civil Liberties Union, "Second Federal Court in Two Weeks Halts Suspicionless Drug Testing of Teachers," *American Civil Liberties Union* (2009). http://www.aclu.org/drugpolicy/testing/38356prs20090115.html

Karen E. Klein, "Establishing a Drug-Free Workplace," *BusinessWeek*, (September 1, 2007). http://www.businessweek.com/smallbiz/content/aug2007/sb2007081_883800.htm

Ken D. Tunnell, "Pissing on Demand: Workplace Drug-Testing and the Rise of the Detox Industry," (NYU Press, 2004).

U.S. Department of Health and Human Services (USHHS), Substance Abuse and Mental Health Services Administration (SAMHSA), "Reasons for Drug-Testing," (USDHH, SAMHSA Division of Workplace Programs, 2005) http://www.workplace.samhsa.gov/DrugTesting/DTesting.aspx

ISSUE 7

Is Gender Discrimination the Main Reason Women Are Paid Less Than Men?

YES: Stephen J. Rose and Heidi I. Hartmann, from "Still a Man's Labor Market: The Long-Term Earnings Gap," *Institute for Women's Policy Research* (2004)

NO: Frank S. Zepezauer, from "The Feminist Crusades" (Author-House, 2007)

ISSUE SUMMARY

YES: Stephen J. Rose and Heidi I. Hartmann, scholars at the Institute for Women's Policy Research, argue in their 2004 study that discrimination is still the main reason for the persistence in the gender gap.

NO: Frank Zepezaur strongly disagrees with the position taken by Rose and Hartmann. Zepezaur, an English graduate from the University of Chicago and a prominent influence in the men's rights movement, marshals considerable data in support of his view that there are many factors that contribute to the wage gap.

During the 1950s, female workers in the United States earned about 59 cents for every dollar males earned. Not surprisingly, the differential in pay between women and men—the "gender wage gap"—was assumed to be the result of sexual discrimination in the workplace. Critics and social reformers at this time made the issue of wage discrimination—gender, racial, or any other type—an integral part of the overall civil rights movement that was sweeping the country in the first part of the 1960s. As a result, two critically important laws were passed that directly addressed the issue of discrimination and the wage gaps allegedly produced by it. The Equal Pay Act of 1963 requires employers to pay equivalent rates for similar work regardless of gender. Similar pay must occur for jobs requiring equal skill, equal effort, equal responsibility, or jobs with similar working conditions (Mathis and Jackson, *Human Resource Management*. Thomson South-Western, 2006, p.106). In 1964, the Civil Rights Act was passed, which, among other things, further solidified the basis of the Equal Pay Act as a discrimination barrier in the workplace. Over the next three decades, the gender wage gap slowly, but consistently, declined as women gained access to jobs and pay levels typically reserved for men. By the mid-1990s, women, on average, earned 70 cents on the male dollar, a fact generally interpreted as evidence that the legislative actions of the 1960s were having the desired effect on workplace gender discrimination. Recent Department of Labor data show that, on average, women's earnings are 77 percent of men's in the United States (from Independent Women's Forum, August 20, 2008; http://www.iwf.org/campus/show/20604.html).

Although there is no dispute about the existence of the gender wage gap, there is most definitely a difference of opinion as to its cause. On one side are those that believe the answer is pretty straightforward—the persistence of the wage gap is due to gender discrimination, be it subtle or direct, intentional or not. As noted previously, such a view has informed social and political initiatives, resulting in various employment laws and regulations.

Opposing this view are those who argue other factors are more important than discrimination in accounting for the gender wage gap. Chief among these factors are the choices that people make. For example, it seems fair to note that women frequently make different workplace-related choices than men. Many of these choices—dropping out of the workforce to raise children, choosing part-time over full-time work more often than men, and opting not to pursue higher paying careers in the sciences, to name a few—and their effects on the wage gap have been well documented, if not actually accepted by supporters of the discrimination narrative. Of particular interest here, and definitely less frequently mentioned, is that choices men make also play a role in the wage gap. Consider this observation by Allison Kasic, columnist at Townhall.com, "The choices that men make matter too. The truth is that more men, on average, are willing to take on jobs that are dirty, dangerous, and distasteful to most women. Men's willingness to perform more dangerous jobs is one of the reasons that more than 9 out of 10 workplace deaths is of a male worker. Why would men take on such risks? To make more money. Men also work more hours per week, on average, than full-time working women do. Again, add all these factors up and you get a wage gap. It's hardly cause for concern. . ." (Townhall.com, April 28, 2009).

In the following selections, we look at the issue of whether or not gender discrimination is the primary factor responsible for the gender wage gap. Stephen Rose and Heidi Hartmann, scholars at the Institute for Women's Policy Research, argue in their 2004 study that discrimination is still the main reason for the persistence in the gender gap. Frank Zepezaur strongly disagrees with the position taken by Rose and Hartman. Zepezaur, an English graduate from the University of Chicago and a prominent influence in the men's rights movement, marshals considerable data in support of his view that there are many factors that contribute to the wage gap. Indeed, he considers several of these variables, each taken independently, as contributing more to the wage gap than does gender discrimination. Do you find his data persuasive? Do you agree with Allison Kasic that there is really is "no cause for concern"?

YES ↵

Stephen J. Rose and
Heidi I. Hartmann

Still a Man's Labor Market:
The Long-Term Earnings Gap

Many argue that women's prospects in the labor market have steadily increased and that any small remaining gap in earnings between women and men is not significant. They see the remaining differences as resulting from women's own choices. Others believe that with women now graduating from college at a higher rate than men and with the economy continuing its shift toward services, work and earnings differences between women and men may disappear entirely.

Although the wage gap, measured by conventional methods, *has* narrowed in the last several decades, with women who work full-time full-year now earning 77 percent of what men earn (compared with 59 cents on the male dollar 40 years ago), its sweeping effects are largely unacknowledged because its measurement is limited to a single year and restricted to only a portion of the workforce. *When accumulated over many years for all men and women workers, the losses to women and their families due to the wage gap are large and can be devastating.*

For many families, the quality of children's care and education suffers from women's low earnings throughout their child rearing years. Even with increased time in the labor market after their children are grown, women cannot make up the loss in lifetime earnings. Moreover, most women enter retirement without pensions, either from their own or their husband's employment, and thus lack security in old age.

A New Measure Highlights Wage Gap Understatement

The conventional way of measuring the differences in earnings and labor force experience between women and men is misleading because it fails to capture the difference in men's and women's total lifetime earnings. The more commonly cited wage ratio is based on comparing the annual earnings of women and men who work full-time, full-year in a given year. Using a more inclusive 15-year time frame (1983–1998), and taking into account women's lower work hours and their years with zero earnings due to family care, this study finds that women workers, in their prime earning years, make only 38 percent of what men earn. *Across the 15 years of the study, the average prime age working*

From *IWPR Report*, #C355, 2004, pp. iii–v, 33–36. Copyright © 2004 by Institute for Women's Policy Research. Reprinted by permission.

woman earned only $273,592 while the average working man earned $722,693 (in 1999 dollars). This gap of 62 percent is more than twice as large as the 23 percent gap commonly reported.

This new measure of the long-term earnings gap is based on comparing the average annual earnings, across 15 years, of prime-age workers between the ages of 26 and 59 years, regardless of how many hours they worked or how many years they had earnings. The data used are from the Panel Study of Income Dynamics, a longitudinal data set that tracks the same groups of women and men over many years. *Compared with men, women are more likely to work part-time, less likely to work year-round, and more likely to have entire years out of the labor force.* Thus, the conventional 77-cent comparison underplays all of these factors by focusing only on the earnings of the approximately half of women and the 85 percent of men who work full-time for at least 50 weeks in a given year. To measure the access women and men have to economic resources through working, earnings for all prime-age women and men is a more relevant statistic.

Across 15 years, the majority (52 percent) of women but just 16 percent of men have at least one complete calendar year without any earnings. A career interruption like this has a large effect on the earnings of both men and women independent of their education and previous experience, and such interruptions partially account for women's lower life-time earnings. But even among men and women who have earnings in all 15 years, men's average annual earnings are $49,068 while women's are $29,507, or 57 cents on the dollar. Again, this figure is considerably below the commonly cited 77-cent comparison.

Women Are More Likely to Be Long-Term Low Earners

Women's lower average earnings mean that women are much more likely than men to be low earners overall. Even among those who have earnings every year in the 15-year study, 17 percent of women but only 1 percent of men average less than $15,000 per year in earnings—just above the poverty line for a family of three. Women are less likely than men to move up and out of low-wage work. In fact, more than 90 percent of long-term low earners among prime-age adults are women. Furthermore, in the new economy, one's educational background plays more of a role than ever before. Yet, women with a bachelor's degree earn less than men with only a high school diploma or less (even when the comparison is restricted to those with earnings in all 15 study years).

Again when only committed workers, those with earnings in all 15 years, are considered, the earnings range of $25,000–$49,999 annually is the most common earnings range for both men and women with nearly half of both sexes earning in that range. But for men, that range is effectively the bottom, since 42 percent of men earn more than $50,000 annually, while for women it is effectively the top, since only 9 percent of women average above that amount.

Gender Segregation in the Labor Market Results in Lower Pay for Women

One major reason for the gender gap in earnings is that women work in 'women's jobs'—jobs that are predominantly done by women, while men work in 'men's jobs'—those predominantly done by men. This phenomenon is known as the gender segregation of the labor market.

In this report, we develop a three-tier schema of elite, good, and less-skilled jobs; within each tier, there is a set of occupations that are predominantly male and a set that are predominantly female. In the elite tier, women are concentrated in teaching and nursing while men are business executives, scientists, doctors, and lawyers; in middle tier jobs, women are secretaries while men are skilled blue collar workers, police, and fire fighters; and in the lowest tier, women are sales clerks and personal service workers while men work in factory jobs. Among prime-age workers who are continuously employed (have earnings every year in the 15-year study period), nearly 60 percent are employed consistently at least 12 of 15 years in one of these six occupational clusters.

Within each of the six gender-tier categories, at least 75 percent of the workers are of one gender. In each tier, women's jobs pay significantly less than those of their male counterparts even though both sets of occupations tend to require the same level of educational preparation.

Perhaps largely because of the generally low pay scales in the female career occupations, only 8 percent of men work in them. In contrast, 15 percent of continuously employed women, apparently more eager to seek higher-paying male jobs, work consistently in male occupations. These women, however, earn one-third less than their male counterparts in male elite and less-skilled jobs. Among the few women who make it into the middle tier of good male jobs (the skilled, blue collar jobs), the more formal wage structures (due to unions and civil service regulations) mean that their pay lags men's by only one-fifth. Increasing women's entry into this tier of male good jobs would thus increase their earnings substantially.

For the preponderance of women who remain in the female sector of each tier, earnings are strikingly low. In general, even restricting the comparison to women who work full-time, women in women's jobs earn less than men in men's jobs one tier below: women in female elite jobs earn less than men in male good jobs, and women in female good jobs earn less than men in male less-skilled jobs.

Time Spent in Family Care Limits Women's Own Earnings

Women's working experience is conditioned on their experience in families, where they often do most of the child and elder care and family and household maintenance. Because the United States lags behind many other countries in providing subsidized childcare and paid family leave, families are left to their own resources to meet the challenges of combining family care and paid work.

Most women spend the majority of their prime-age years married. As a result, women's average standard of living (as measured by average household income over 15 years, assuming that all family members share equally in this income) lags men's by only 10 percent (despite women's much lower earnings). For married women, it is still their connection to men that insulates them at least partially from their own low earnings. For women with few years of marriage, however, their family income lags men's with similar marital histories by more than 25 percent.

Women's lack of own earning power limits their options (in the worst case, they may feel forced to stay in an abusive relationship) and exposes them to great risk of poverty and near poverty when they divorce or if they never marry (especially if there are children present). Women who never experienced a year as a single parent during the 15-year study period had an average annual income of $70,200, compared with women who experienced single parenthood in at least 5 of 15 years, who had an average annual income of less than $35,800. Moreover, after the prime earnings years observed in this study, approximately half of women enter the retirement years alone, no longer married even if they once were. Women's low earnings come home to roost in old age, when widowed, divorced, and never married women all share high poverty rates of approximately 20 percent.

The Gendered Division of Labor Is Self-Reinforcing But Increasingly Unstable

Another major reason for the gender gap in cumulative earnings is the self-reinforcing gendered division of labor in the family and its implications for women's labor market time. First, families need childcare and other activities to be performed. Second, since the husband usually earns more than his wife, less income is lost if the lower earner cuts back on her labor force participation. Third, employers, fearing that women will leave their jobs for family responsibilities, are reluctant to train or promote them and may take advantage of women's limited opportunities by paying them less than they would comparable men. Fourth, a set of jobs evolves with little wage growth or promotion opportunities but part-time hours and these jobs are mainly held by women. Fifth, an ideology develops that proclaims this the natural order, resulting in many more men in men's jobs with higher pay and long work hours and many more women working in women's jobs with lower pay and spending considerable time on family care. Women without men particularly suffer from this ideology since they often support themselves and their families on jobs that pay women's wages.

This self-reinforcing arrangement, while long lasting, is also increasingly unstable. Women are demanding more independence and greater economic security throughout the life cycle, whether single or married. Many women and men believe that women's talents are being underutilized and undercompensated.

In the United States, the flipside of women typically being the caregivers and men typically the breadwinners has led to very high working hours, especially for men. Compared with other advanced countries, the United States has developed a set of institutions that leads to significantly longer labor market hours and considerably less leisure.

Policy Changes Can Bring Improvement

Several policy recommendations are offered to help move U.S. institutions toward supporting greater equity between women and men. Among them are: strengthening enforcement of existing equal opportunity laws, increasing access to education and training in high paying fields in which women are currently underrepresented, developing new legal remedies for the comparable worth problem (the tendency of 'women's jobs' to pay less at least partly because women do them), making work places more 'family friendly' through more flexible hours, providing more job-guaranteed and paid leaves of absence for sickness and family care, encouraging men to use family leave more, increasing subsidies for childcare and early education, encouraging the development of more part-time jobs that pay well and also have good benefits, and improving outcomes for mothers and children after divorce. Certainly, the United States should be able to develop a better way to share responsibility for family care and work, resulting in increased gender equity in earnings, family work, and leisure and greater long-term economic security for both women and men.

꧁ᘖꙥ꧂

Policy Implications

While experts disagree about the significance that should be attributed to the remaining differences found in women's and men's work experiences in and out of the labor market, we argue in this report that they are significant for many reasons.

- First, the gender gap in earnings has a major influence on families' life choices and poverty rates, on older women's retirement security, and on single mothers' ability to provide for their children's care and education. More and more women, both single mothers and married women, are contributing to their family's income through their paid work. Nearly all families with women earners or would-be earners would have a higher standard of living if women's wages and lifetime earnings were higher.
- Second, there is ample evidence that women's low earnings are not primarily the result of their preferences for low-wage work. Rather women face discrimination in the labor market and in pre-labor market preparation as well. The degree of sex segregation in the labor market is striking and women's jobs at all educational levels pay less than men's jobs at the same level. Women's access to the better paying jobs and occupations is still constrained. Women deserve equal opportunity in the labor market.

- Third, while many women spend more time on family care than many men, the choices women and men make in allocating their time between work and family are heavily constrained. The lack of societal provisions for family care such as subsidized child and elder care means that most families have to fend for themselves. Women's lower earnings, of course, make it more practical for the family to sacrifice the woman's rather than the man's earnings and, given the loss of the woman's earnings, the man often works even more hours.

- Thus, a kind of perverse internal logic perpetuates a system with a rigid division of labor both in the workplace and in the home. Employers may feel justified in discriminating against women workers if they think they will be less devoted to their jobs because of family responsibilities. They may structure jobs as part-time and dead-end for this reason and many women may accept them because they cannot find better-paying jobs. Labor market discrimination means lower earnings for women; women's low earnings mean women spend more time in family care; women's commitments to family care contribute to discrimination against them. Single mothers especially suffer as they must attempt to support their families on women's lower wage levels.

- Finally, such a system surely fails to use human talent productively. How much total output is lost to society because the skills of women are not developed and put to work in the most productive way? To what extent are economic resources misallocated because of the constraints noted above? To what extent are both men and women denied the opportunity to allocate their time between home and work as they would most prefer? . . .

As this study demonstrates, the pay gap remains quite large and is bigger than many people think. Women still retain primary responsibility for family care in many families, making it difficult for women workers to compete equally with their male counterparts. Ideological attacks on women's equality also seem to be growing (or in any case not abating). Every few years, the media reassert that working moms may be hurting their children and wearing themselves out under the strain of the double burden.[1] In late 2002, Allison Pearson's *I Don't Know How She Does It: The Life of Kate Reddy, Working Mother* (Anchor Books) provided an example of this trend. And in late 2003 Lisa Belkin in "The Opt-Out Revolution" (*New York Times Magazine,* October 26) argued that highly educated and high earning women (with high earning husbands) are increasingly stepping off the fast track voluntarily, without presenting much evidence to support an actual increase. Her article also seemed to downplay the evidence she had collected in her interviews of this small, select group, showing that several of the women dropped out only because their employers would not offer more family friendly work schedules. The cultural war over the demands of childrearing and work represents a real dilemma that society must face. The critics of working mothers and the champions of at-home mothers, however, tacitly assume that it is primarily the responsibility of women alone to solve the problem.

The genie is out of the bottle. Women, even those with young children, are working for significant portions of their lives. And, despite the economic slow-down and the continuing critique of women's increased employment, women continue to devote more and more hours to work and fewer to family care. They don't appear to be changing their minds and going back home.[2] While many married women are partially insulated from the effects of their own lower earnings by living with higher earning men, overall women are acting to reduce their economic dependence on husbands and to protect themselves from the vulnerabilities of divorce. Women are choosing the path to greater independence, arranging childcare, balancing their work and care giving tasks as best they can, and trying to get their partners to put in their fair share of housework and care giving.[3] Women are spending less of their adult lives in marriage, marrying later, and having fewer children. One third of prime age working women have at least one year as a single parent. Women's needs for equal earnings are increasing as they spend less time living with men.

The current system also places a burden on American men, who have the longest work hours in the advanced industrialized world, and the least leisure. The relative lack of infrastructure to support working parents in the United States (subsidized childcare, paid family leave) means that families are left to cope on their own. Most do so by increasing male work hours, enabling women to work less and spend more time on family care in the short run, but increasing women's economic vulnerability in the long run.

And to the extent that women's unequal pay contributes to poverty, it places a strain on our social safety net. The cumulative effect of years of lower earnings for women raises the cost to our welfare system, and reduces tax revenues.

Can the system change to become more conducive to women's equality? Certainly nothing is fixed in the long run, but many barriers remain in the United States. If women in the United States hope to improve their economic standing and achieve greater economic parity with male workers, there must be a systematic change in both practices and policies with regard to work and family life. Among the policy strategies that are needed are the following:

- Strengthening equal employment opportunity (EEO) enforcement, by increasing federal support for government oversight agencies, both the Equal Employment Opportunity Commission (EEOC) and the Office for Federal Contract Compliance Programs (OFCCP). Complaints could be resolved more quickly with more resources, and, if more cases were resolved in the plaintiffs' favor, due to stronger and more timely enforcement efforts, employers would have larger incentives to improve their employment practices. The OFCCP could target federal contractors in egregious industries (e.g., construction) to encourage them to adhere to their affirmative action plans, much like mining and banking were targeted in the 1970s. One promising approach might be to audit many large employers regularly for discrimination, much the way large federal contractors have their financial transactions continu-ally monitored by on-site auditors. Women's greater entry into pre-dominately male jobs in the middle tier—in fire fighting, police work, or skilled trades—would be especially important in raising women's wages since women's jobs in this tier are particularly underpaid relative to men's jobs.

- Opening up educational and job training opportunities. Unfortunately there are still too many women who have been discouraged from pursuing higher education and/or job training for occupations that are not traditionally held by women. Jobs in the skilled trades and in the computer industry, for example, frequently require pre-job preparation that women are less likely to have access to. Programs that help women get to the starting gate with equal skills will benefit women tremendously.

- Developing new EEO remedies to address unequal pay for jobs of comparable worth (the tendency for jobs done disproportionately by women to pay less than jobs that require similar skill, effort, and responsibility but are traditionally held by men). Employers could be required to show that comparable jobs are paid fairly, using tools such as job evaluation systems that measure job content on many dimensions. Both men and women in jobs that are underpaid because they are done predominantly by women would stand to gain from comparable worth implementation.

- Improving workers' bargaining power in the workplace, such as through encouraging increased unionization in unorganized sectors and raising the minimum wage, especially since women are over-represented among the non-unionized and low-wage work force. Living wage campaigns and efforts to tie the federal or state minimum wages to cost of living increases all raise public awareness about the importance of setting a reasonable wage floor. A reasonable wage floor disproportionately benefits women workers and the children they support.

- Creating more good part-time jobs that provide decent pay, benefits, and promotion opportunities. A less than optimal equilibrium may have formed in the labor market where many good jobs require more than 40 hours of work per week. This prevents workers from entering such jobs if they want to work fewer hours, and employers miss the opportunity to learn whether part-time workers in these jobs can contribute equally (on a per hour basis). Career part-time jobs could be fostered by public sector employers and, if successful, private sector employers could be encouraged to follow suit. Single parents would also be especially helped by the greater availability of part-time jobs with good hourly pay and benefits since their family care responsibilities generally limit their hours to less than full-time.

- Making work places 'family friendly'—including flexible hours, parental and other family care leave (including paid leave), and paid sick leave. Too often it is the lowest-paid workers who have the least access to these benefits since they are not legally required of most employers. Yet if such leaves were made more available and if they were used equally by both sexes, new workplace norms would be developed that recognize that all workers, male or female, have responsibilities to others that sometimes take them away from their jobs. Such paid leave programs could be provided through social insurance schemes, such as the recent expansion of the Temporary Disability Insurance system in California to include paid leave for family care. More wide spread use of leaves should, over time, reduce the earnings penalties observed for time out of the labor market.

- Providing more high quality, affordable childcare, through subsidized childcare centers at workplaces and in the community, and more public subsidies for higher education as well. Since well-reared and well-educated children are an asset to the whole society it makes no economic sense that most parents shoulder the financial responsibility for children's care and education alone. This arrangement disadvantages single mothers particularly since they have only one wage, and a lower one at that, with which to provide for their children.

- Encouraging men to be full participants in family care. Such sharing can be encouraged by government requirements for both parents to share available parental leave (as is done in the Nordic countries) and by utilizing the bully pulpit to educate employers and the public about the positive benefits of encouraging men to exercise options for flexible work arrangements when available and spend more time with children and less time working. A full-scale public education campaign against the double-standard in parenting, in which mothers seem to be expected to meet a higher standard of care than fathers, is needed.

- Reducing income tax rates on secondary earners, most often women, and reducing the 'marriage penalty' for dual earner couples. Higher tax rates for married couples are found up and down the income scale and they generally depress the work effort of the lower earning member of the couple.

- Improving access to non-custodial fathers' incomes or otherwise raising incomes in single mother families. Since single mothers and their children suffer disproportionately from poverty and near-poverty, even when the mother works (as the mothers in this study do), additional measures are needed to improve their income and support their work effort. In addition to paid leave and other family-friendly benefits, benefits such as subsidized housing or child care should be extended further up the income scale. Child support should be increased and income and property settlements at divorce should be more generous to the custodial parent. A strong safety net and work supports are necessary for low-income parents to maintain their employment and enable them to gain from long-term, steady employment.

- Democratizing the 'old boy' network. Since many positions in the economy depend on strong social interactions, these seemingly non-work relationships have economic consequences. The refusal of the Augusta National Golf Club to admit women in the spring of 2003 is one example of a principal location where the 'old boy' network remains intact. More surprising, perhaps, is the failure of male corporate leaders to resign from the club quickly once its exclusive membership policies became generally known. Federal EEO regulations and tax laws could be strengthened to clarify that employer support of such networks is discriminatory and not allowable as a business related tax deduction.

- Reducing working time norms. As long work hours increasingly become the standard, women can be more easily excluded because they are less likely to be able to meet this requirement. Most European countries manage to both provide more public support for parenting and have lower working hours on average. Reducing work hour norms, perhaps through eliminating or setting a cap on mandatory overtime, increasing the required premium paid for overtime work, or reducing the standard work week to 35 hours could spread the work and jobs more equitably across all members of society, increase gender equality in family care time, and increase the time available for leisure and civic engagement.

Achieving equality in the work place will likely require several more decades. The important thing is to keep the momentum going and prevent backsliding toward the reestablishment of the feminine mystique or 1950s family values. Instead, we must continue the progress our society has been making toward equal opportunity and fair compensation for women in the labor market and the more equitable sharing of family care between women and men.

Notes

1. Interestingly, research shows that mothers today, despite spending much more time working for pay, spend about as much time directly interacting with their children as mothers a generation ago (Bianchi 2000).

2. While data show a small drop from 1998–2002 in the labor force participation of mothers with infants (children less than one year of age), at approximately the same time the economic recession and slow recovery reduced labor force participation generally. The long-run trend in the labor force participation of mothers has been one of considerable increase. For mothers of infants, for example, the proportion in the labor force increased from 31 percent in 1976 to 55 percent in 1995, roughly the same as the 2002 figure of 54.6 percent (U.S. Census Bureau 2003b: Figure 2).

3. In an overview of changes in women's well-being, Blau (1998) shows that housework time decreased for almost everyone between 1978 and 1988. Married men were the only group to increase their housework time, indicating that married women were having some success in getting household tasks reallocated.

Frank S. Zepezauer   ➡ **NO**

The Feminist Crusades: Making Myths and Building Bureaucracies

The Crusade Against Workplace Inequality

> Feminism today is not a campaign to end inequality for women. It is a business and a bureaucracy whose mission is as much about organizational survival as it is about securing rights for women.

Feminists believed that women suffered from second class status in the health care and the educational systems. To end these outrages, they launched two of their biggest and longest crusades, each rivaling the other in shock and awe.

What is even more awesome is that while they two crusades went on the march, feminists were in the middle of still another crusade even bigger and longer. It sought to end another long-lasting outrage: in the economic system women were second class citizens. Complaints about this condition also prompted one of feminism's biggest lobbying campaigns, a four decade crusade against what they perceived as workplace inequality. Feminists regarded as evidence of this condition any deviation from their rigid and simplistic definition of equality: 50/50 across the board, as many women as men at every level of every occupation in both public and private employment. Because they found such deviations wherever they looked, they felt they had smoking gun proof for their claim of economic injustice, enough to energize one of their most passionate crusades.

It was their signature operation. Pressed to explain what feminism is about, their shortest answer is that it is simply about equality. In an egalitarian age it therefore becomes their most widely supported crusade. Whatever quibbles people might have with feminist excesses in their other crusades they nevertheless conceded that these ideologues have opened up workplace opportunities for women. When Sally Ride, the first female astronaut, headed for space, her mother said, "Thank you, Gloria Steinem." Most women agreed. In a survey 94 percent of them identified pay equity as the most important of all issues.

In spite of this supportive consensus, the crusade against workplace inequality has, according to a long succession of critics, taken its rationale from one of feminism's most famous and most enduring myths. It is that "women have not enjoyed the full fruits of the economic system." The myth itself has been symbolized by one of feminism's most widely propagated advocacy numbers: 59¢. That figure represented what women earned in contrast to their male counterparts. Men earned one dollar; women earned "only" 59¢. Warren Farrell reported that when he served on NOW's New York chapter during the early 1970s, he sported a badge on his lapel that read, simply, "59 cents." It was all that needed to be said about the supposedly outrageous wage gap between the genders and all that society needed to know about feminism's primary economic goal. Feminists would not rest until the government reported that the female dollar exactly matched the male dollar. Nor would they rest until in every occupation the number of women exactly matched the number of men, particularly at upper management levels.

This goal, incidentally, put the lie to the frequently repeated assertion that feminism was essentially about options for women: whether, for example, to choose full time housewifery or full time out-of-home career or some combination of the two. On that question the radical position has been that women should not have the option to begin with. Founding mother Simone deBeauvoir made that clear when she said, "No woman should be authorized to stay at home to raise her children. . . . Women should not have that choice, precisely because if there is such a choice, too many women will make that one." In 1981, University of Illinois Professor Vivian Gornick re-asserted the feminist position: "Being a housewife is an illegitimate profession. . . . The choice to serve and be protected and plan towards being a family-maker is a choice that shouldn't be. The heart of radical feminism is to change that." In 2004, radicals were still attacking the housewife choice. University of Texas professor of Gender Studies Gretchen Ritter declared that "full-time mothering is . . . bad for children [and] . . . bad for society." Radicals kept saying to the public that feminism is simply about equality and choice. Among themselves they kept saying "Damn the choices and get all women into the workforce."

Most critics of the crusade have therefore understood that, with regard to the woman's movement, more was at stake than simple economic reform. The critics have nevertheless focused on the movement's symbolic issue, the wage gap. Over the years they have produced an extensive rebuttal literature, more than enough to demonstrate that the gap was a myth created by partisan finagling with numbers. One of the earliest of these critics was Mary Mainland, a Stanford University School of Law graduate and the mother of three children. In a 1984 article, "Feminist Myths Reconsidered," Mainland pointed out the primary error behind the wage gap myth: that it was based on comparing the average wages of all men to those of all women while ignoring the gender-specific factors that accounted for the differences. The most significant of these was marital status. Married women on average made less than married men because women made career choices that enabled them to balance occupational with family obligations. "Married women average about 25 percent as much income as married men," Mainland wrote. "However, single women earn about 91 percent as much as single men, even though substantially fewer women are in such highly paid occupations as the construction skilled trade and medicine. . . ." Moreover, "married women are more likely to work part time and to drop out of the labor force for extended periods of time. . . . Women's career choices have tended to reflect their role as the primary caretaker of children."

Mainland then observed that most of the agitation for boosting the average female wage came from upper middle class women, the class that would most obviously profit from the changes. "An indeterminate number of women have unquestionably benefitted from the movement: lawyers appointed to the bench sooner than male colleagues of similar age and experience; medical students now permitted to interrupt their training to take maternity leaves; academics teaching in newly created women's studies departments; appointees to influential government commissions; leaders of organizations such as NOW who have derived power and prestige from politicians' courtship of the female vote and organizational funds. . . . These women enjoy a status virtually indistinguishable from that of upper-class males." The same benefits have not as predicted, "trickled down" to lower class women. "During the same period that the percentage of women in law and medicine nearly doubled, female-headed households came to account for almost half of all those living below the poverty line."

There is irony in the class privileges that elite women have enjoyed because radical feminism is essentially a neo-Marxist ideology that uses the women's rights issue to leverage a communist society. Mainland quotes one of the radicals, Rosemary Ruether, who calls for the dismantling of "'sexist and class hierarchies,'" and the restoration of "'ownership and management of work to the base communities of workers themselves who then create networks of economic and political relationships." Marching behind the banner of women's rights has worked for Marxists because, in spite of feminist complaints about a commanding male elite, male politicians are deferential to women to the point of obsequiousness. They scurry to accommodate angry women because of the demands of chivalry and the power of the female vote. "There is no mystery as to why politicians of either sex are reluctant to state that the feminist empress has no clothes. Seldom are they prepared to alienate any articulate and well-organized interest group. Nor is it reasonable to expect those women who have profited from their allegedly disadvantaged status to blow the whistle. . . . Women are no less inclined than men to further their own self-interest." Mainland said that in 1984 when the economic justice branch of the feminist lobby was already a big time outfit.

The same points were made 17 years later, in 2001, by Diane Furchtgott-Roth and Christine Stolba in *The Feminist Dilemma: When Success Is Not Enough*. The "dilemma" these two writers spoke of concerned the feminist problem of having to poor mouth American women in the face of enormous economic gains wrought by three decades of feminist wage gap agitation. As the word "success" in their sub-title indicates, the agitators themselves have had trouble portraying themselves as beleaguered, financially strapped advocates for an economic underclass. Furchtgott-Roth and Stolba spoke of them as "professional feminists" many of whom worked full-time in governmental or foundation subsidized institutions. They now were, say the writers, "a special interest group [that] has achieved their agenda through bureaucratic stealth" and which now pursued policies "that ensures their existence." The massive media support they enjoyed has enabled them to so "thoroughly invade popular culture that is taken for granted that women do not receive equal pay." They are consequently in open pursuit of "preferential programs for women and of discrimination against men" and are insouciant about accusations of their sexism. In regard to the gender quota system they have helped to establish, for example, one of them said, " 'It's unfair but so is life. The overall goal . . . is important enough that perhaps we can be unfair temporarily.'" The feminist movement had thus become in the 1990s what the labor movement had become in the 1950s, a powerful interest group that commanded the respectful attention of the Democrats and the worried deference of the Republicans. Crossing them on any of their many "women's" issues became for elected officials the third rail in American politics.

Paramount among them was economic justice for women. As Furchtgott-Roth and Stolba pointed out, this had in fact become a non-issue because of feminist successes. Three/fourths of American women were now in the labor market, for example, and paid employment for women had become the norm. The top two economic sectors expected to grow significantly between 1990 and 2005 were female-dominated occupations: service and retail trade, finance, insurance, and real estate. "For many women workers, the 'pink-collar ghetto' will be a boon–not the bane that feminists claim it is." And the pay gap had shrunk from 41¢ (59% of the male dollar) to 27¢ (73% of the male dollar). Even so, it has remained a misleading indicator of relative earning power. When all relevant factors are considered, particularly the significant differences in career choices between men and women, the wage gap disappears where it did not in fact favor women.

None of this has deterred feminism's now large and formidable economic justice industry from pressing their claims of pervasive female suffering in the labor market. They have managed this scam by removing one of the horns of the dilemma from which Furchgott-Roth and Stolba said they were dangling, their impressive economic successes. This they accomplished by insisting that all parties accept their definition of equality, the simplistic 50-50 distribution of females and males throughout the workforce. They thus demanded "equality of outcomes and statistical parity between men and women rather than equality of opportunity." In pursuit of this goal, "they pursue a numbers game that sees discrimination against women in any area in which they constitute less the 50 percent of participants." Like earlier critics, these two writers saw a radical agenda behind these goals. The 50-50 standard, they said, "is insidious, for it cannot be achieved without substantial social engineering. It also rejects individual choice and freedom, which bring with them unpredictability." They thus join the long list of critics who when analyzing the feminist economic justice program, see a Marxist agenda, operating in the background.

In 2005, Warren Farrell, the one-time male feminist who became feminism's most trenchant critic, wrote the most comprehensive of all wage-gap myth rebuttals: *Why Men Earn More: The Startling Truth Behind the Pay Gap— and What Women Can do About It*. Except for the fact that feminists still enjoy solid support in academedia, Farrell's carefully researched book should have been enough to permanently demolish the myth. He provided, for example, the most thorough demonstration of why comparing the average wage of two entire genders leads to a meaningless advocacy number. It was 59¢ when Farrell belonged to the New York Chapter of NOW, 79¢ in the 1990s, 89¢ by the turn of the century and was still cited as a spur to outrage in 2005. Farrell repeated what other critics had been saying for three decades: that women's career choices rather than sexist discrimination accounted for the wage differentials, that when these figures were factored in the wage gap not only disappeared but, in an increasing number of occupations, actually *favored* women. He specified twenty-five of these female choices, pointing out that if in each case women were to choose differently, they could boost their wages.

Farrell introduced his readers to a number of surprising assertions:

- Thirty-nine large fields have more than a five percent pay advantage for women. In sales engineering, for example, women make 142 percent of the male income. There are 26 occupations in which women with B.A.s receive starting offers greater than men's. There are 29 college majors for which women were offered higher starting salaries than men. There are 80 occupational fields in which women earn more than men, 39 of which they earn at least five percent more.

- When women executives were surveyed nationwide to see if their career or their husband's had progressed better, the women executives were more than seven times as likely to feel their own careers had progressed better than their husband's. The women executives were almost six times as likely to feel their careers progressed faster than their husband's, four-and-a-half times as likely to feel their careers had been financially more rewarding than their husband's, and almost twice as likely to feel their careers had also been more rewarding in other ways. . . . Prior to age 40, women are 15 times more likely to become top executives. . . . Even so, one-third of female executives had left their jobs to not work or thought about it.

- Economics majors outnumber women's studies majors by 10 to 1, but 54 of 55 universities offer more courses in women's studies than in economics. Women are 53 times more likely to go for a master's degree in education than in physical sciences.

- There are 29 college majors in which women are offered higher starting salaries than men. There are 26 occupations in which women with B.A.s receive starting offers greater than men.

- Male university professors in more than 500 universities publish more in both peer-reviewed and non-peer-reviewed journals than women professors, which is one reason they are paid more. However men professors whose productivity equaled women's earned the same or just slightly less than their female counterparts. Women professors who are never married and have never published make 145 percent of what men in similar situations earn, 45 *percent more.*

- Men working full time average 45 hours a week on the job; women 42 hours. Women are less than half as likely as men to work more than 50 hours a week. A person who works 45 hours a week earns 44 percent more than a person working 40 hours a week.

- Female physicians earn more than men when the subfields of psychiatry, dermatology, neurology, aerospace medicine, general preventive medicine, physical medicine and rehabilitation, public health, occupational medicine, and radiation oncology are aggregated.
- Of 21 of the worst jobs, determined by degree of risk and unpleasant working conditions, 20 of them are male dominated. Jobs in dirty, unpleasant environments with little people contact—like auto mechanic, steelworker, sewer maintenance, plumbing, fumigating and short-order cook—are often avoided by women, but in most cases women who choose to [do] them actually earn more than their male counterparts. The same applies for highly hazardous jobs, all of which are heavily male-dominated, which is why over *97 percent* of workers killed on the job are male. In general women who are willing to risk their comfort or their physical and emotional well-being will earn more for the same kind of work than men. This fact also helps account for the seven year gap in longevity. . . .
- In the Iraq war, although women comprise 15 percent of active-duty military personnel, they make up only 2.6 percent of the deaths. Such discrepancies apply also to journalists. The death rate for journalists in the Iraq war was about 10 times as high as for soldiers in 2003, approximately one-tenth of one percent for solders versus one percent for reporters. Yet, though 38 percent of the journalists in the world are female, only seven percent of journalists killed were female.
- In high-tech jobs wages for women have been increasing faster than for men. Specifically the wages of young women who took high-tech jobs went up 23 percent as opposed to nine percent for their male counterparts. Among young African-American women, who enjoy double dip affirmative actions, wages increased 42 percent.
- Part-time working women earn $1.10 for every dollar male part-time workers make.

Farrell summarized these points with four statements:

- Women now make more money than men for the same work.
- Many other women make the same money men make for fewer sacrifices.
- Many unskilled women have jobs rarely made available to men.
- Many skilled women have careers in which it is much more difficult for equally qualified men to find employment.

To these Farrell added the comment: "It is not necessarily desirable to change all these inequities, but is disingenuous to cry victim without acknowledging any of them." Thus "the focus on the pay gap" has been "a sexist focus. It does not account for the full amount of each sex's income power, but especially neglects women's income power."

POSTSCRIPT

Is Gender Discrimination the Main Reason Women Are Paid Less Than Men?

Another way of viewing the wage gap debate understands it as an "equality of outcome" versus "equality of opportunity" issue. The goal of the former approach is equality in the sense that people are economically, socially, and legally equal. Regardless of where they start, this view holds that equity exists only when everyone enjoys the same results. Persistent differences in outcomes are indicative of discriminatory forces and can only be remedied through social initiatives designed to provide redress to victims. At the workplace, this approach argues that, within reason, all groups should be equally represented at each level of the organization. There should also be no persistent differences in pay between males and females. To the extent that there is, gender discrimination is presumed to be the cause. And, as researchers Stephen Rose and Heidi Hartmann note in their article here, women's access to high-paying career paths is constricted, thus indicating that "women face discrimination in the labor market and in the pre-labor market preparation as well."

Those that believe our societal obligations extend no further than providing everyone with a level playing field argue from a perspective of equal opportunity. Advocates of this view recognize that differences in women and men's pay and other indicators of corporate success have less to do with discrimination than with factors such as motivation levels, skill differences, and willingness to work hard. As feminist scholar Naomi Lopez makes clear: "These advocates [equality of outcome supporters] presume that unequal outcomes are due to discrimination, ignoring individual choices, preferences, and personal decisions. This, in turn, undermines opportunity, however unequal, which has been the cornerstone of women's achievements throughout this century" (Lopez, 1999).

There is a third possible explanation for the wage gap. It's not particularly insightful—it simply recognizes that both sides may have it partially correct. No doubt gender discrimination still exists in the workplace, and no doubt it partially accounts for the wage gap. On the other hand, career-path choices, willingness to work, and personal skills and motivation are just as likely to account for differences in pay as well.

Suggested Readings

Naomi Lopez, "Free Markets, Free Choices II: Smashing the Wage Gap and Glass Ceiling Myths," *Pacific Research Institute* (1999)

Independent Women's Forum, "Get the Facts: The Wage Gap," *Independent Women's Forum* (August 20, 2008). http://www.iwf.org/campus/show/20604.html

Arrah Neilson, "Gender Wage Gap Is Feminist Fiction," *Independent Women's Forum* (April 15, 2005). http://www.iwf.org/campus/show/18948.html

Doug Snover, "Gender Wage Gap Still Exists, Author Asserts," *Wrangler News* (September 23, 2006). http://www.wranglernews.com/author092306.htm

Allison Kasic, "Don't Celebrate Equal Pay Day; Celebrate Economic Opportunity," Townhall.com (April 28, 2009). http://townhall.com/columnists/AllisonKasic/2009/04/28/don't_celebrate_equal_pay_day;_celebrate_economic_opportunity

ISSUE 8

Should Employees Be Allowed to Vote by Secret Ballot When Deciding Whether to Support Unionization in the Workplace?

YES: F. Vincent Vernuccio, from "Card Check Double Standard, *CEI On Point* (March 24, 2009). http://cei.org/on-point/2009/03/24/card-check-double-standard

NO: Ross Eisenbrey and David Kusnet, from "The Employee Free Choice Act: Questions and Answers," Economic Policy Institute, Issue Brief 249 (January 29, 2009). http://www.epi.org/publications/entry/ib249/

ISSUE SUMMARY

YES: F. Vincent Vernuccio, a labor expert and scholar at the Competitive Enterprise Institute, argues that EFCA is unconstitutional because it does away with the secret ballot in the union creation process. He also shows that it is self-contradictory because other provisions of the bill actually allow for the use of secret ballot voting.

NO: Ross Eisenbrey and David Kusnet, scholars writing for the Economic Policy Institute, argue that much of the criticism of the EFCA is based on misunderstandings and incomplete analysis. In their defense of the bill, they address common complaints and questions about the EFCA.

In terms of the American labor force, union membership reached its zenith in the 1940s when slightly more than one of every three workers belonged to a union. Since that time however, union membership has declined steadily to the point where, in 2008, only one in eight workers were union members (Bureau of Labor Statistics, News: January 2009; http://www.bls.gov/cps/). Supporters of unions have seen not only a decrease in membership during this period but also a decline in unions' political clout in Washington D.C. But, as the saying goes, It's "The times they are a-changin'". Indeed, union advocates are decidedly optimistic about the future. That optimism is the result, primarily, of the election of Barack Obama as President and the expansion of the Democratic Party's control over both houses of Congress in 2008. Obama has made increasing union membership and strengthening organized labor's power base high priorities of his administration, a fact made clear in his strong support for the Employee Free Choice Act (EFCA).

The EFCA, often referred to as the "card check" bill, is highly controversial because its primary purpose is to make unionizing the workplace easier. Although the bill contains several provisions important to union supporters, the most controversial aspect of the legislation concerns the manner in which employees communicate their intentions to unionize (or not). The EFCA seeks to replace the traditional secret ballot voting process with a new method. Under the proposed approach, a union would be recognized when a majority of employees check a union card indicating support. This process is done publically, thus by passing the privacy protection inherent in secret ballot elections. Not surprisingly, this proposed change has union critics seeing red. But for our purposes here, the controversy is a good thing as it provides us with a very interesting question: Should employees be allowed to vote by secret ballot when deciding whether to support unionization in the workplace?

Those opposed to the "card check" bill offer a variety of reasons for their position. They point out that the secret ballot has been the method used to communicate workers' support (or not) of unions for more than 70 years. Indeed, the secret ballot is a fundamental pillar of American democracy and absolutely necessary to protect the rights of US citizens to vote according to their conscience, both in and out of the workplace. As feminist commentator Allison Kasic points out, the secret ballot ". . . ensures that individuals can vote their conscience with a shield of privacy. . . . But the Employee Free Choice Act aims to rob workers of this essential protection." (Allison Kasic, "Card Check Will Harm, Not Help, American Workers," *Independent Women's Forum*, Policy #17, February 26, 2009; http://www.iwf.org/publications/show/21200.html). Critics worry that without the protection of the secret ballot, employees will be harassed and intimidated into supporting unionization. Critics also claim that union supporters are hypocritical on this issue because they openly support the use of secret ballots in labor union activities other than organizing, a point well-made in the "yes" article that follows.

Those advocating passage of the EFCA believe that it is necessary to restore employee rights and power that presumably accompanied the substantial decline in union membership that commenced in the 1950s and continued for the rest of the twentieth century. Union supporters place most of the blame for diminished union membership and power on management anti-union behaviors and activities, many of which they claim are illegal but go unpunished. The EFCA is seen as the vehicle for restoring employee rights because it will make it considerably easier for workplaces to become unionized.

YES ↵   F. Vincent Vernuccio

Card Check Double Standard

The greatest controversy surrounding the so-called Employee Free Choice Act (EFCA, H.R. 1409, S. 560)—introduced on March 10, 2009, by Rep. George Miller (D-Calif.) and Sen. Tom Harkin (D-IA)—centers on its first provision, known as "card check," which would empower unions—and unions alone—to determine the method by which to organize workers at a given company. The Act's card check provision would effectively eliminate the secret ballot in union certification elections.

It would do so by requiring the National Labor Relations Board (NLRB) to recognize a union as the exclusive bargaining agent for all employees at a company once the union has collected signatures from a majority of the employees. Employees are asked to sign the cards out in the open, exposing them to high-pressure tactics—without time to reflect on their decision or make a private judgment.

Union leaders see the Employee Free Choice Act as an opportunity to stem decades of private sector membership decline. Thus, organized labor has made EFCA its top legislative priority. To see it enacted, unions gave heavily to Democrats during the 2008 election and now expect the politicians they have supported to support the union agenda. President Obama, his Secretary of Labor, and most congressional Democrats have supported EFCA.

However, many card check advocates have conveyed selective support for secret ballots in other contexts, including labor union matters other than organizing, both today and in the past. Indeed, many of the nation's top unions have secret ballot provisions in their constitutions and bylaws governing internal elections, and unions have insisted on secret ballot elections when their own employees have tried to organize. Moreover, EFCA sponsor Rep. George Miller (D-Calif.) and other supporters of the bill in Congress have even urged foreign government officials to use the secret ballot in union certification elections. Secretary of Labor Hilda Solis has fought for the secret ballot in the Congressional Hispanic Caucus, and sponsored legislation in California protecting the secret ballot for workers deciding their employers' overtime policies.

The Act itself is inconsistent. EFCA would leave in place many provisions of the National Labor Relations Act (NLRA) and Labor-Management Relations and Disclosure Act (LMRDA) that require the secret ballot in union elections

From *CEI On Point,* March 24, 2009, (notes omitted). Copyright © 2009 by F. Vincent Vernuccio. Reprinted by permission of the author.

other than certification, including decertification of a union and the election of local officers.

The Current Process

Under the National Labor Relations Act, a union can organize workers in two ways: by a secret ballot election or by card check. The union must turn in to the National Labor Relations Board cards signed by at least 30 percent of employees voicing their support for a union in order to request a secret ballot. It may also turn in 50 percent-plus-one to ask for immediate recognition, if the employer agrees. In the majority of cases, the employer will demand a secret ballot election. The NLRB supervises the secret ballot election, usually six to seven weeks after the union requests to be recognized. During the election process the union has decisive advantages.

The first advantage for the union is speech. An employer cannot make any promise or show any detriment to its employees that either could affect, or is contingent on, whether the company unionizes or not. The employer can only make vague generalizations of what has happened to other companies that have gone the union route. The union is not bound by the same speech limitations and can make promises—and even insinuate threats—to voting employees. This is what supporters of EFCA refer to as "management controlling the information."

Another advantage the union enjoys is its ability to control the timing of when a petition will be filed and the size of the bargaining unit. For example, if a union does not think that it can unionize an entire company, it will try to organize only one department. Moreover, the union retains sole possession of the signed cards, which include the names and home addresses of all potential members. On the day of the election, both the union and the employer are allowed to monitor the election for irregularities. Company and union monitors can keep tally of which employees vote but not of *how* they vote—which is crucial for minimizing coercion and intimidation.

The Process under EFCA

EFCA supporters claim that they are simply giving workers the choice of opting for card check, without taking away the right to a secret ballot. Labor consultant Steve Rosenthal, on the blog of the Service Employee International Union (SEIU), claims that EFCA "will not eliminate secret ballots in union representation elections (period)." Such claims rely on a verbal sleight of hand. EFCA mandates that the NLRB will certify a union to represent a collective bargaining unit if it finds that a majority of the employees have signed cards. However, it is not up to the workers whether to opt for a secret ballot election or go through a card check procedure—that decision is up to the union organizers.

In most cases, workers do not spontaneously request to join a particular union. Rather, an outside labor organization attempts to recruit the workers. Some labor organizations, including the AFL-CIO, even hold schools to train new professional organizers. These organizations spend a great deal of money and resources on organizing campaigns because they stand to increase their membership and gain substantial sums of revenue in dues if a new local union is created.

Card check usually weighs heavily in favor of the union, so much so that unions rarely settle for a simple majority if they know that there will be a secret ballot election. Unions advise their organizers to wait until they have gotten 60 to 70 percent of the workers to sign cards before they submit them to the NLRB. This is because erosion of support is practically inevitable, so the union stands a better chance of winning an election if it goes into it with a substantial margin for error. Organizers know that workers may change their mind or sign cards only so organizers will leave them alone.

Most employers expect union organizers to use sales gimmicks and pressure tactics to obtain the requisite number of cards. Therefore, the employer usually demands a secret ballot election run by the NLRB to ensure a fraud-and coercion-free process. For these same reasons, unions know that their best chance at organizing is through card check, and therefore prefer to avoid holding a secret ballot election which could jeopardize their campaign.

If EFCA is passed, and card check becomes the norm, workers will, in almost all cases, lose secret ballot organizing elections as an option. They will be subject to high-pressure sales techniques and possibly even coercion by union organizers. While EFCA does not explicitly outlaw the secret ballot in union recognition elections, it makes secret ballots a dead letter by allowing unions to determine the procedure for recognition. The Act states:

> If the Board finds that a majority of the employees in a unit appropriate for bargaining has signed valid authorizations designating the individual or labor organization specified in the petition as their bargaining representative and that no other individual or labor organization is currently certified or recognized as the exclusive representative of any of the employees in the unit, the Board shall not direct an election but shall certify the individual or labor organization as the representative described in subsection (a).

Under EFCA, union organizers would decide how long to continue collecting signatures. Since they can go back to ask employees again and again, unions would have no incentive to turn in cards to the NLRB until they have gotten to the 50 percent-plus-one threshold—which they could obtain by just wearing down resisting employees—at which point the NLRB is expressly prohibited from holding an election, and must certify the union as exclusive bargaining agent.

Secret Ballot Provisions for Union Issues Left Unchanged by EFCA

The Employee Free Choice Act would not eliminate the secret ballot from all union elections. It leaves several provisions of the National Labor Relations Act unchanged. While EFCA supporters would like to all but eliminate the secret ballot in union certification elections, they have not sought to eliminate it in decertification elections. The NLRA currently requires—and will continue to require if EFCA passes—a secret ballot election in order to decertify or disband a union.

Similarly, the Labor-Management Relations and Disclosure Act requires that secret ballots be used in the elections of—and impeachment proceedings for—local union officers. If the law will continue to require secret ballots to be used to decertify or dissolve a union and to elect local officers, why then is it not appropriate to certify a union as the exclusive bargaining agent for a group of employees?

Unions' use of the Secret Ballot

A majority of Americans and union members support the secret ballot. A January poll conducted by *McLaughlin & Associates* found that 86 percent of those surveyed supported keeping union recognition elections private, 40 percent of those surveyed were union members with 88 percent in favor of keeping the process private. With or without the secret ballot, the vast majority of Americans do not wish to join a union. A March poll by *Rasmussen Reports* found only 9 percent of non-union members would join a union if they could, and 81 percent would not. Under EFCA, union organizers will have complete control over whether to use the secret ballot or card check in organizing, with employers having no say in this aspect of their business

Many major unions have codified the secret ballot into their internal governing structures. Most of America's top unions have provisions in their constitutions and bylaws requiring the secret ballot for elections of officers and delegates and for deciding whether to go on strike. The chart on the next page highlights some of America's top unions and how they utilize the secret ballot. If the secret ballot is good enough for electing the people who run a union, why then is it not good enough to determine if a union should exist at all?

A survey by the consultancy PTI Labor Research shows that since 2000, union employees—not union members employed with private companies but a union's own staff—filed 162 petitions for an election to the NLRB. Under the current process, workers only need to file a petition to the NLRB if an employer demands a secret ballot election rather than take cards supporting a union at face value and recognize a new bargaining unit. According to the survey, unions have denied card check organizing petitions from their own staff 162 times since 2000 and instead favored the secret ballot. If unions object to card check for unionizing their own employees, then why do they seek to impose it on everybody else through the Employee Free Choice Act?

Congressional Card Check Advocates' Secret Ballot Double Standard

Rep. George Miller (D-Calif.), who introduced the Employee Free Choice Act in the House of Representatives on March 10, had a curiously different view of secret ballot union elections a few years ago. On August 29, 2001, Rep.

America's Top Unions' Use of the Secret Ballot

Union	Date	Title	Strike	Officer	Dissolution	Description
American Federation of Government Employees (AFGE)	August 2000	AFGE Constitution		✓		Art VI § 8 delegates elected by secret ballot; Art VIII § 1 election of officers by secret ballot
Communication Workers of America (CWA)	January 2008	CWA Constitution	✓	✓		Art XVIII. § 6.b strike vote by secret ballot; Art XIII. § 9.k delegates elected by secret ballot; Art XV. election of officers by secret ballot
International Association of Machinists (IAM)	June 2002	IAM Constitution	✓	✓		Art, XVI § 2 strike vote by secret ballot; Art, XXII § 7 election of officers by secret ballot
International Brotherhood of Electrical Workers (IBEW)	September 2001	IBEW Constitution Workers (IBEW)		✓		Art 2 § 10 delegates elected by secret ballot; Art III § 3 election of officers by secret ballot
Laborers International Union of North American (LIUNA)	September 2001	LIUNA International Constitution		✓		Art V§ 9 delegates elected by secret ballot; Art VII; election of officers by secret ballot; Local polices for secret ballot for strike
Service Employees International Union (SEIU)	June 2004	SEIU Constitution and Bylaws	✓		✓	Art 18 § 5 delegates elected by secret ballot; Art XXV dissolution by secret ballot; strikes left to locals see local 902 Art 19 §1 secret ballot for strike vote
Teamsters	June 2006	Teamsters Constitution	✓	✓		Art III § 5. delegates elected by secret ballot; Art IV § 2. election of officers by secret ballot; Art XII may use secret ballot for strike vote
United Association of Plumbers and Pipe Fitters (UA)	August 2006	UA Constitution	✓	✓	✓	§ 15 delegates elected by secret ballot; § 31 secret ballot to hold a convention; § 98 dissolution by secret ballot; § 122 election of officers by secret ballot; § 174 strike vote by secret ballot; § 213 referendum by secret ballot
United Auto Workers (UAW)	June 2006	UAW Constitution	✓			Art 8 § 4 special convention by secret ballot; Art 8 § 23 delegates elected by secret ballot; Art 50 § 1 (a) strike vote by secret ballot
United Brotherhood of Carpenters and Joiners (UBC)	August 2007	UBC Constitution		✓		§ 9 election of officers by secret ballot; § 17 delegates elected by secret ballot;
United Food and Commercial Workers (UFCW)	October 2005	UFCW Constitution			✓	Art 8 § (I) 3 delegates elected by secret ballot; Art 31 § (C) secret ballot for dissolution;

*Note: Local union officer elections ere mandated to be done by secret ballot by § 401 (b) Labor-Management Reporting Disclosure Act of 1959. All references above to officers are for officers at the national or international level.

Miller and 15 other members of Congress wrote to the Local Conciliation and Arbitration Board (*Junta Local de Conciliación y Arbitraje*) of the Mexican state of Puebla, urging the board to adopt the secret ballot for union recognition elections. The letter stated:

> We are writing to encourage you to use the secret ballot in all union recognition elections . . . We understand the secret ballot is allowed for but not required by Mexican labor law. However we feel that the secret ballot is absolutely necessary in order to ensure that workers are not intimidated into voting for a union they might not otherwise choose.

Every signer of the letter who is currently in office in the 111th Congress has co-sponsored EFCA. Of course, Mexican labor law is different than American labor law, but as in the United States, in Mexico the secret ballot is an option for union recognition. In their letter, the 16 members of Congress pointed out the "absolute necessity of the secret ballot" to avoid intimidation and urged Mexican officials to require the use of the secret ballot. Why, then, did the 12 members who are still in office change their mind from defending the secret ballot and urging Mexican officials to require it to co-sponsoring a bill that would make it a dead letter?

Political pressure from organized labor is one possible explanation. In 2008, the Service Employees International Union, one of America's largest unions, alone gave over $85 million in campaign contributions, mostly to Democrats and had 2,000 members take time off to work for the Obama campaign. What does Big Labor want for all this? American Federation of State, County and Municipal Employees President Gerald McEntee has plainly stated: "The payback would be the Employee Free Choice Act." And if the politicians they have supported do not deliver? SEIU President Andy Stern, when interviewed on EFCA by CNN, was asked [if "elected] officials should be afraid of him."? He replied that, "Everyone should be scared [of not living up to the promises they have made]."

Labor Secretary Hilda Solis' Support of the Secret Ballot

Throughout her career, Secretary of Labor Hilda Solis has supported the secret ballot. While still a State Senator in California, she proposed legislation mandating the secret ballot for workers deciding their employers' overtime policies. The bill specifically required that "only secret ballots may be cast by affected employees at any election held pursuant to [over time selection]." After being elected to Congress, Solis became involved in a fight over the Chairmanship of the Congressional Hispanic Caucus. In 2007, she and other women on the Caucus signed a letter protesting the election of Chairman of Rep. Joe Baca, (D-Calif.) because it was not done by secret ballot. The letter called for the secret ballot, stating, "as we prepare for the 110th Congress in which the Congressional Hispanic Caucus will have the opportunity to play a more prominent role, we believe it is imperative that our Caucus' integrity be unquestioned." Further, in an individual statement Solis wrote:

> Votes by secret ballot were in order but never taken. We therefore believe that we need to follow proper rules of procedure and hold a vote by secret ballot . . . It is important that the integrity of the CHC be unquestioned and above reproach.

So does this mean that a union that is certified as an exclusive bargaining agent through card check rather than a secret ballot election would be questionable and reproachable? If Secretary Solis has found the secret ballot to be so important, why was she a cosponsor of EFCA when she was in Congress?

To date, her attempts at explanation have been as incoherent as her positions have been inconsistent. During her Senate confirmation hearing for Labor Secretary, when questioned by Sen. Johnny Isakson (R-Ga.) about her sponsorship of the California overtime legislation, she claimed that, in California, "collective bargaining is much more advanced than other parts of the country." As with many other questions she soon demurred, saying only that being a nominee "doesn't . . . afford me the ability to provide you with an opinion at this time," and "I don't believe that I am qualified to address that at this time."

She was not as coy in her 2001 victory speech in El Monte, California, when she was first elected to Congress, when she stated: "I wouldn't be here, were it not for my friends in the labor movement." Indeed, labor organizations have given her $903,550 in campaign contributions throughout her career. And 15 of her top 20 campaign donors during the 2008 election cycle were unions. It would be a difficult position for someone who has been so reliant on support from organized labor in the past to oppose the union agenda. However, as Labor Secretary, her role is to function as a disinterested arbiter, not an advocate for a constituency she is supposed to oversee. Unfortunately, the Obama Administration does not seem to have made much effort to reinforce the former role.

Conclusion

No matter what organized labor and its congressional advocates claim, the Employee Free Choice Act will take away the use of the secret ballot in union recognition elections. The secret ballot as an option will be a mere legal technicality, and in practice it will become extremely rare, if not extinct. Unions will simply have no incentive to risk losing an election by allowing the workers to vote by secret ballot when card check is always an option, and they can keep going back to ask workers to sign cards time and again until they reach a majority. Make no mistake: Passage of EFCA will result in near-universal use of card check in union organizing and the high-pressure tactics and intimidation that go with it.

Doing away with the secret ballot in labor organizing only is not only opportunistic, but hypocritical. Many of EFCA's most ardent supporters—from members of Congress to the Secretary of Labor to unions themselves—have supported the secret ballot in the past and continue to do so in contexts other than union organizing elections. Laws such as the Labor-Management Relations and Disclosure Act and National Labor Relations Act would still require the secret ballot in other contexts, but not in the most important decision workers make vis-à-vis labor unions: whether to join in the first place.

Ross Eisenbrey and
David Kusnet

→ **NO**

The Employee Free Choice Act:
Questions and Answers

For more than 70 years, the nation's labor laws have proclaimed that working Americans' right to join a union is a fundamental freedom, just like the rights to speak or worship. Indeed the freedoms to form unions and bargain with employers follow from other basic American rights—freedom of association and petitioning for the redress of grievances.

But, over the years, this basic American right has been eroded by employers' interference in the process by which working Americans once were able to decide for themselves whether to form unions. In order to restore this right, bipartisan legislation—the Employee Free Choice Act—has been introduced by Sen. Edward Kennedy (D-Mass.) and Reps. George Miller (D-Calif.) and Peter King (R-N.Y.).

On March 1, 2007, a bipartisan majority of the U.S. House of Representatives passed the Employee Free Choice Act by 241-185. On June 26, 2007, the proposed law gained majority support in the U.S. Senate but was blocked by the threat of a filibuster.

In 2009, the newly elected Congress will consider the Employee Free Choice Act once again. There are strong economic arguments for a law that will empower working Americans to revive the economy by restoring their purchasing power. However, this compelling case has been challenged by false procedural points, including the claim that, by empowering working Americans to form unions through majority sign-up, the bill would outlaw secret ballot elections about union representation. Therefore, these questions and answers address the procedural issues, so that the debate can return to the real issues of how working Americans can share in the gains of their growing productivity and how the nation can build an economic recovery on paychecks, not bubbles.

Why Do the Nation's Labor Laws Need to Be Reformed?

The nation's labor laws are broken and need to be fixed.

The basic labor law—the National Labor Relations Act (NLRA)—was intended to protect workers' rights to organize and join unions and bargain with their employers for better pay, benefits, and working conditions. But it has been distorted by decades of hostile amendments, lax enforcement, and corporate tactics that bend or break the law.

Originally, the NLRA encouraged workers to form unions freely without interference by the employers who control their livelihoods. But now, elections administered by the National Labor Relations Board (NLRB) offer overwhelming advantages to anti-union employers. These companies can campaign on their premises, while workers who support the union cannot campaign on the worksites. During these anti-union campaigns, employers routinely intimidate, harass, coerce, and even free employees who support unions—and a weakened NLRB and watered-down labor laws can do little or nothing to stop them. In the event that workers succeed in voting to be represented by a union, companies can delay negotiations for the first union contract by challenging the results and then refusing to bargain in good faith, and existing labor laws are powerless to stop these stalling tactics.

How Was the National Labor Relations Act Intended to Work?

The National Labor Relations Act (NLRA) was originally intended to encourage the formation of unions and the process of collective bargaining. Enacted in 1935, in the midst of a national economic emergency with disturbing similarities to the current crisis, the NLRA's Findings and Declaration of Policy explains:

> The inequality of bargaining power between employees who do not possess full freedom of association or actual liberty of contract, and employers who are organized in the corporate or other forms of ownership association substantially burdens and affects the flow of commerce, and tends to aggravate recurrent business depressions, by depressing wage rates and the purchasing power of wage earners.

The law created the National Labor Relations Board (NLRB) to administer a simple democratic procedure for workers to decide on their own whether to be represented by a union. Workers would sign cards authorizing a union to represent them. The NLRB would verify the validity of these cards. If a majority of the employees at a workplace expressed their support, the NLRB would "certify" the union as their "exclusive representative." If there were a legitimate question about whether the majority of workers wanted union representation, the NLRB would conduct an election where the employees would choose between the union and "no representative."

Employers were expected to stay out of this process. Because employers control their employees' livelihoods, the NLRA's authors believed that any efforts on their part to discourage workers from forming unions would have the effect of coercing the employees. This concern even trumped traditional considerations of free speech, since employer involvement in the process could intimidate, not inform, the employees. This view was expressed in a 1941 decision by the legendary civil libertarian, Judge Learned Hand: "Language may serve to enlighten a hearer . . . but the light it sheds will in some degree be clouded if the hearer has no power . . . What to an outsider will be no more than the vigorous presentation of a conviction, to an employee may be the manifestation of a determination which is not safe to thwart."

How Did Labor Law Change?

Our nation's labor laws no longer fulfill their express purpose of protecting workers' rights to join together and bargain with their employers to improve their living standards and working conditions.

Leading business journalists recognize this reality. *Fortune* magazine senior writer Marc Gunther explains: "By law, American workers have the right to form unions and bargain over wages and working conditions. Trying to exercise those rights is another matter entirely—workers are routinely discriminated against for supporting unions, most employers hire anti-union consultants to block organizing drives, and some go so far as to close down work sites when employees vote for a union". As *Washington Post* business columnist Steven Pearlstein writes: "Over the years [the right to form unions and bargain collectively] has been whittled away by legislation, poked with holes by appeals courts, and reduced to irrelevance by a well-meaning bureaucracy that has let itself be intimidated by political and legal thuggery."

With the passage of the Taft-Hartley Act in 1947, the NLRA was amended to give employers effective veto power over their employees' decisions to be represented by unions. Under the new rules, even if 100% of the employees sign cards declaring that they want to be represented by a union, the employer can demand that the NLRB conduct an election. The Taft-Hartley amendments also give employers the right to campaign against the union as long as they do not threaten employees with reprisals for their union activities or promise benefits in return for opposing the union.

The new rules encouraged employers to conduct anti-union campaigns when their employees try to organize. By the 1980s, a $300 million-a-year industry emerged of lawyers, public relations experts, and management consultants who run companies' anti-union campaigns.

How Are Union Representation Elections Conducted by the National Labor Relations Board Different from Elections for Public Office?

Supervised by the NLRB but conducted at the very workplaces that employers own and manage, union representation elections are unlike any democratic elections held anywhere else in the United States. Quite simply, one side—the anti-union employer—has all the power. In large measure, this is because employers control employees' jobs, paychecks, and livelihoods.

The one-sidedness of these elections also results from the special circumstances of campaigns conducted on an employer's premises and during the employees' work-hours. As Professor Gordon Lafer, a political scientist at the

University of Oregon, explains, these elections fall short of four standards for free elections:

1. *Free speech, with equal access to the media and the voters:* Anti-union managers can campaign with every worker, throughout the workplace, and around-the-clock. Pro-union employees can campaign only on break time. Management can require employees to attend "captive audience" anti-union meetings. Pro-union workers can be forced to attend—but denied the opportunity to speak out. Management can post anti-union messages on the workplace's walls and bulletin boards. But pro-union employees cannot make use of these facilities.
2. *Freedom from coercion:* Because the nation's laws recognize that voters are vulnerable to economic coercion, it is illegal for private companies to tell their employees to support particular candidates in elections for federal offices, such as the Congress or the presidency. But, in union representation elections, supervisors—who manage workers and can fire, promote, demote, or reassign them—can hold one-on-one meetings with their employees to instruct them to oppose the union.
3. *Campaign finance regulation:* In federal elections, there are limits on how much money candidates can raise and spend. But, in union representation elections, there are no limits on how much money companies can spend to defeat the union, including their fees to the anti-union lawyers and consultants.
4. *Timely implementation of the voters' will:* In democratic elections, the winning candidates usually take office just two months after Election Day. But, with union representation elections, employers can appeal the result to five different levels for several years: the regional NLRB office, an administrative law judge, the entire NLRB, a federal appeals court and the Supreme Court. Then the employer can engage in delaying tactics during the negotiations over the first union contract.

As the former general counsel of the NLRB, Fred Feinstein, explains: "The inherent power of employers, combined with the potential for delay in the enforcement of NLRA rights and procedures, makes union success in a traditional NLRA campaign largely dependent on employer mistakes".

What Would It Be Like If a Political Campaign Were Conducted under the Same Rules as NLRB Elections?

NLRB election campaigns more closely resemble sham elections in totalitarian countries than elections for public office in the United States or any other democracy.

Imagine an election where an incumbent president, governor, or mayor can:

- Force voters to attend his campaign rallies.
- Treaten to fire his opponent's supporters or deny them raises.
- Prevent his opponent from campaigning in the daytime.

- And, if an opponent wins the election anyway, delay that person from taking office.

Even if this campaign concluded with a secret ballot, few if any Americans would say that this was a free election.

Do Employers Really Try to Intimidate Workers Before Union Representation Elections Conducted by the NLRB?

Employers' anti-union campaigns often violate even the watered-down protections of current labor law. For instance, Harvard Law Professor Paul Weiler estimates that 1 in 20 union supporters—an average of approximately 10,000 workers a year—is fired by their employers during union organizing campaigns. Similarly, in a study of 400 elections on union representation conducted by the National Labor Relations Board, Dr. Kate Bronfenbrenner of Cornell University found that 50% of the employers threatened to close the office or plant and 32% fired workers who actively supported the union. These findings are confirmed by the NLRB annual report for 2007: During that year, more than 29,000 people—one worker every 18 minutes—were disciplined or even fired for union activity.

These actions are in violation of the NLRA's provisions prohibiting employers from firing, harassing, or threatening employers who seek to organize unions. But, as the journalist Michael Kinsley once said of campaign finance, when it comes to employer opposition to workers' organizing efforts, the real scandal is not what is illegal but rather what is legal. Because of spotty enforcement by over-burdened federal officials, and slick tactics by the lawyers, publicists, and employee-relations specialists who earn an estimated $300 million a year advising employers how to defeat organizing drives, tactics that skirt the law have become commonplace.

All in all, according to Bronfenbrenner, 80% of employers who face employee organizing efforts hire consultants to help them conduct anti-union campaigns. And their tactics make a mockery of the NLRA's promise that workers are guaranteed "the right to self-organization, to form, join, or assist labor organizations, to bargain collectively through representatives of their own choosing, and to engage in concerted activities for the purpose of collective bargaining or other mutual aid or protection."

Bronfenbrenner found another, uglier reality. In addition to the 32% of employers who break the law by firing pro-union workers and the 50% who skirt the law by threatening to close down the workplace, others use legal but hardball tactics:

- Ninety-one percent of employers facing organizing efforts force employees to attend anti-union meetings;
- Seventy-seven percent distribute anti-union leaflets; and
- Fifty-eight percent show anti-union videos.

In addition to these efforts, employers can also get away with these tactics:

- Firing employees who refuse to attend the antiunion meetings or who insist on asking embarrassing questions;
- Excluding known union supporters from these meetings;
- And barring union representatives from the workplaces during the weeks before the federally supervised elections where workers decide whether to be represented by a union.

These conditions resemble sham elections in totalitarian countries. In fact, they violate international conventions that the United States has signed protecting freedom of association—a right that is a close cousin to the U.S. Constitution's guarantees of free speech and freedom of assembly. According to a recent study by the international watchdog group, Human Rights Watch: "Workers' freedom of association is under sustained attack in the United States, and the government is often failing in its responsibility under international human rights standards to deter such attacks and protect workers' rights."

Are Workers' Votes in Current NLRB Elections Really "Private"?

Workers' immediate supervisors often meet individually with employees to urge them to oppose their co-workers' efforts to form a union. Frequently, supervisors keep tallies of whether individual workers support the union and report back to higher-ups about individual employees' views on union representation. Therefore, even if there is a secret ballot election, individual employees' views are often anything but "private."

What Does the Employee Free Choice Act Do?

As Ed Kilgore, vice president of the centrist Democratic Leadership Council writes, the Employee Free Choice Act "is an example of how it is sometimes essential to amend the letter of the law to preserve its spirit." The Employee Free Choice Act keeps the original promises of the NLRA through three reforms:

First, the Employee Free Choice Act restores working Americans' rights to make their own decisions about whether to form and join unions. It provides that if a majority of the employees sign union authorization cards—and after the NLRB validates the cards—the company must recognize and bargain with the union. This short-circuits the current management-dominated election process where companies can coerce employees not to support the union. But if a majority of employees prefer instead to hold an election, they will have that right.

Second, the Employee Free Choice Act provides real penalties for companies that break the law during organizing campaigns and negotiations for the first contract. Currently, companies break the law with impunity during organizing campaigns and negotiations for first contracts because they think they can get away with it—or can afford to pay the penalties. That is why the Employee Free Choice Act provides tougher penalties to protect workers' rights:

- Up to $20,000 per violation for companies found to have willfully or repeatedly violated employees' rights during organizing campaigns or frst contract negotiations.
- Triple back pay for employees who are discharged or discriminated against for supporting unions during organizing campaigns.
- A requirement that the NLRB seek federal court injunctions when there is reason to believe that a company has discharged or discriminated against union supporters, threatened to do so, or engaged in other conduct that endangers employees' rights during organizing campaigns or frst contract negotiations.

Third, the Employee Free Choice Act makes sure that employers and employees negotiate a first contract after workers form a union. When an employer and a new union are unable to negotiate a frst contract within 90 days, either party can request mediation by the Federal Mediation and Conciliation Service (FMCS). If no agreement is reached after 30 days of mediation, there is binding arbitration. Both timelines can be extended if the employer and the union agree.

What Is Majority Sign-up ("Card-Check")?

With majority sign-up, a majority of the employees at a company sign cards declaring that they want to be represented by a union. Then the National Labor Relations Board determines whether the cards are valid. After the NLRB determines that the union represents a majority of the workforce, the employer is required to recognize and bargain with the employees' union.

Is Majority Sign-up a New Procedure?

In the years after the National Labor Relations Act went into effect, majority sign-up was one of the major methods by which working Americans formed unions. As Professor Harley Shaiken of the University of California at Berkeley writes: "During this early period, the NLRB and the courts found it illegal for an employer presented with signed authorization cards or other such evidence of majority support not to recognize the union. The Board directed elections take place only when a genuine question arose as to whether a majority of employees supported a union". During 1938 and 1939, almost a third of all union certifications took place as a result of majority sign-up, rather than an NLRB election.

As labor laws were weakened, majority sign-up as a method of forming unions became less common. Over the past decade, there has been renewed interest in majority sign-up among working Americans, employers, public officials, and unions. Twenty-two laws in 12 states now grant public and private employees the right to form unions through majority sign-up. In 2004, Oklahoma granted municipal employees the right to majority sign-up to encourage "labor peace."

Since 2003, more than half-a-million American workers formed unions through majority sign-up. Among many others, these workers include:

- 64,000 hotel and casino workers
- 46,000 home care providers
- 11,000 UPS freight workers
- 5,800 public school teachers and aides
- 225 reporters and editors at Dow Jones
- 162 nuclear engineers at Pacifc Gas & Electric
- 8,000 farmworkers jointly employed by Mount Olive Pickle and the North Carolina Growers Association

Does Majority Sign-up Work?

Growing numbers of employers—including the leading wireless phone company AT & T Mobility and the huge chain of hospitals and health plans Kaiser Permanente— have agreed to remain neutral in organizing campaigns and recognize unions through majority sign-up. As Kaiser Permanente explained in a brief filed with the NLRB, the health care giant agreed to majority sign-up because it "recognized that the protracted and often adversarial NLRB election processes frequently undermined the ability of everyone involved to focus on the primary mission of providing quality health care."

Why Can't the NLRB Election Process Be Fixed?

In theory, the NLRB election process could be fixed, but the reforms required would be quite radical and virtually impossible to enforce, so fixing the NLRB election process is not a practical solution.

The chief problems with the NLRB election process are:

- excessive delays,
- unlawful firings of union advocates during a campaign, and
- unequal access

The first two, excessive delays and unlawful firings, are relatively easy to fix, and EFCA provides means of doing so. But the third, unequal access, is the most serious, and the most impractical to fix.

Today, elections conducted by the NLRB have no resemblance to free elections of any kind. Jimmy Carter, who conducts election oversight around the world, would not find that NLRB elections meet any of the standards we expect of elections even in the most politically backward of countries. An analogy would be a political election where only one party was permitted to use radio, only one party was permitted to use television, only one party was given public voter lists for mailings, and where leaders of the other party were exiled until the election was over. Most of the public discussion about NLRB elections today concerns the last item in this analogy (exile, that is firing of union supporters during election campaigns), but this is actually the least important impediment to free elections. More damaging are the one-sided campaign rights.

During a union election campaign, workers are frequently subject to an ongoing campaign of employer terror and intimidation during their work time, with advocates of union representation having no opportunity to respond. Employers can lawfully hold "captive audience meetings" during work time during which sophisticated consultant-produced presentations threaten workers with loss of employment, reduction of wages, and loss of benefits and security if they should vote for union representation. Employers and their representatives (usually, outside consultants) pull workers off their jobs for individual meetings where similar threats and intimidation take place. Meanwhile, an employer is not even required to provide a name and address list of eligible voters (workers) to a union until about two weeks before the election (which can take place as much as a year or more after the campaign starts). The address list itself need not give the union any practical way of contacting workers—no phone numbers need be provided, many addresses may be incorrect or incomplete (e.g., only post office box numbers)—so while the employer is conducting daily "captive audience" meetings and individual supervisory conferences, union representatives (who are now not even permitted access to an employer parking lot) have no viable way to meet with employees to present an alternative point of view.

Prior to the Taft-Hartley amendments to the NLRA in 1947, employers were prohibited from campaigning against union representation during election campaigns. Taft-Hartley, however, protected employers' rights to campaign against unions, provided only that they did not threaten employees with reprisals for supporting unionization, or promise material rewards for opposing unionization.

Pre-election campaigns, therefore, take place in the following context:

1. Supervisors can (and do) campaign against unionization continuously during working hours, whereas union representatives are prohibited from entering the workplace and union supporters are prohibited from discussing unionization among themselves during working time, and can lawfully be discharged for doing so.
2. Although direct threats and promises by supervisors are prohibited, this prohibition is impossible to enforce, for two reasons:
   a. there are usually no witnesses to one-on-one conversations between supervisors and employees;
   b. it is practically impossible for employees to distinguish between prohibited threats and permitted expressions of opinion (e.g., it is prohibited for a supervisor to say that a facility will close after a union wins an election, but it is permitted for a supervisor to say that a facility could close after a union wins an election and that many other facilities have closed).

An even more serious problem, however, is that employer campaigning is inherently coercive, even in the absence of explicit or implicit threats, because of the power relationship that is inherent in the employer-employee relationship. We have a sophisticated understanding of these power relationships outside the union context. For example, we understand that there is no such thing as a non-coercive sexual approach ("pass") by a supervisor to a worker, even though such an approach would be perfectly appropriate in a non-workplace situation. We deem such appropriate non-workplace behavior to be "harassment" in the workplace, and have made such behavior unlawful, solely because we recognize that the power relationships in a workplace, where one party has the power over another's livelihood, make otherwise innocuous behavior improper. Similarly, there is no such thing as a non-coercive expression of opinion by a supervisor regarding unionization. Prior to Taft-Hartley, this was recognized, and such expression was prohibited.

This becomes especially difficult to fix because the Taft-Hartley amendments codified an earlier Supreme Court decision protecting employers' rights to "free speech" regarding the desirability of union representation. Therefore, it is possible that attempts to reverse this Taft-Hartley provision would be unconstitutional. As long as union election campaigns are permitted, it might arguably be constitutionally impossible to control employer exercise of "free speech" in an election campaign. The only solution is to permit unions to avoid long, one-sided, and inherently coercive employer campaigns by demanding recognition, based on majority support.

One suggestion has been that EFCA could grant unions equal rights to those enjoyed by employers; that is, employers, if they wish, can refrain from campaigning against unionization in the workplace, but if they choose to campaign, then union representatives must be granted equivalent rights. Such a provision, however, would be practically impossible to implement and enforce. As noted above, there are usually no witnesses to supervisory campaigning, so it would be difficult, if not impossible, for unions to establish their right to equivalent access. If "equal rights" to campaign were granted, it would likely spur endless litigation about whether the rights were equal. Because of typically high supervisor-to-employee ratios, unions could not practically have the resources to conduct equivalently intensive campaigns inside a workplace.

The only practical solution to all this is to eliminate the campaign period altogether, by permitting unions to make their majority status known, and requiring employers to recognize it.

Does the Employee Free Choice Act "Silence Employers" or Require That They Remain Neutral About the Election?

With the Employee Free Choice Act, employers are still free to express their opinions about unions as long as they do not threaten or intimidate employees.

In fact, employers can always express their views about unions—and many exercise this opportunity from their employees' frst days on their jobs. Companies frequently force new employees to watch anti-union videos during their orientations. Also, companies often place anti-union materials on their bulletin boards. When workers try to form unions, companies can send employees anti-union letters and emails.

Therefore, when deciding whether to organize, most workers believe they already have enough information about their employers' opposition toward the union. According to a survey of workers who signed cards in a majority sign-up recognition, 73% said they had enough information about management's attitude toward the union. In the same survey, 70% said they had enough information about the union, and 81% had enough information about the union recognition process.

Will Employees Be Pressured into Signing Union Authorization Cards?

It is illegal now for unions or their agents to coerce employees to sign a union authorization card. With the Employee Free Choice Act, it will still be illegal—and any person who breaks the law will face serious penalties.

Academic studies show that, with majority sign-up as compared to NLRB election campaigns, employees report less pressure from co-workers to support the union and less pressure from employers to oppose the union. In the first 70 years of the National Labor Relations Act, only 42 cases found fraud or coercion by unions in the submittal of authorization cards. By contrast, there were 29,000 documented cases of intimidation or coercion by employers in 2007 alone.

If Employees Could Decide for Themselves, Would Many More Working Americans Form and Join Unions?

While only 12% of working Americans and 7.4% of private-sector workers were union members in 2006, public opinion surveys show that much larger numbers would join unions if they could choose freely without interference and intimidation by their employers.

In a survey conducted in December 2006 by Peter D. Hart Research Associates, 58% of non-managerial working Americans indicated that they would join a union if they could.

While this finding represents a record level of interest, recent surveys show steadily increasing support for forming and joining unions. As Professor Richard Freeman of Harvard University wrote in 2007: "The proportion of workers who want unions has risen substantially over the last 10 years, and a majority of nonunion workers in 2005 would vote for union representation if they could. This is up from the roughly 30% who would vote for representation in the mid-1980s, and the 32% to 39% in the mid-1990s, depending on the survey."

Given a free and fair choice, millions more working Americans would form and join unions. But as currently amended, interpreted, and laxly enforced, the nation's labor laws do not allow most workers a free and fair choice. That is why the Employee Free Choice Act is needed now—to keep the promise that working Americans can exercise "the right to self-organization, to form, join, or assist labor organizations, to bargain collectively through representatives of their own choosing, and to engage in concerted activities for the purpose of collective bargaining or other mutual aid or protection."

POSTSCRIPT

Should Employees Be Allowed to Vote by Secret Ballot When Deciding Whether to Support Unionization in the Workplace?

The Employee Free Choice Act is highly controversial; indeed, supporters *and* detractors from *both* sides of the political spectrum are speaking out publically about the bill. Although the bill failed to become law in 2007, supporters are very optimistic that they have the votes necessary for passage in the current Congress. On the other hand, opponents are both active and vocal, and not likely to give up. In 2007, a band of mostly Republican senators supported an opposition bill known as the Secret Ballot Protection Act, and, in the summer of 2008, the Democratic Party was shocked when former Democratic presidential candidate George S. McGovern strongly derided the EFCA in the *Wall Street Journal*:

> To my friends supporting EFCA I say this: We cannot be a party that strips working Americans of the right to a secret-ballot election. We are the party that has always defended the rights of the working class. To fail to ensure the right to vote free of intimidation and coercion from all sides would be a betrayal of what we have always championed. (*Wall Street Journal*, August 8, 2008).

It's interesting to note that though supporters appear to have the upper hand in the power corridors of Washington D.C., the general public seems to be much less supportive of the bill. The results of a January 2009 poll conducted by consulting firm McLaughlin & Associates indicated that nearly 3 out of 4 (74%) voters were against eliminating the secret ballot from the union organizing process. More importantly, their data also indicated that 74 percent of *union* households were opposed to the EFCA. On the other hand, the results of a March 2009 Gallup survey provided some ammunition for union supporters. Fifty-three percent of respondents in the poll gave a favorable response to the question "Generally speaking, would you favor or oppose a new law that would make it easier for labor unions to organize workers?" Critics were quick to point out, however, that the generic nature of the question hides the controversial secret ballot removal aspect of the bill, thus somewhat undermining the validity of the results.

In any event, there you have our eighth debate topic. Were you persuaded by either of the arguments?

Suggested Readings

Allison Kasic, "Card Check Will Harm, Not Help, American Workers," *Independent Women's Forum*, Policy #17 (February 26, 2009). http://www.iwf.org/publications/show/21200.html

Doug Bandow, "When Workers Say No," *Cato Institute* (March 30, 2009). http://www.cato.org/pub_display.php?pub_id=10077

George S. McGovern, "The 'Free Choice' Act Is Anything But," *Wall Street Journal* (May 7, 2009). http://online.wsj.com/article/SB124165379013293871.html

Jagdish Bhagwati, "Check It," *The New Republic* (April 1, 2009). http://www.tnr.com/politics/story.html?id=a4edc34f-7670-4e85-a43d-16f3023f2b35&p=2

Donald Lambro, "Obama Supports Union Ploy to Drop Secret Ballots," *Townhall.com* (August 8, 2008). http://townhall.com/columnists/Donald-Lambro/2008/08/08/obama_supports_union_ploy_to_drop_secret_ballots

Thomas Frank, "It's Time to Give Voters the Liberalism They Want," *Wall Street Journal* (November 19, 2008). http://online.wsj.com/article/SB122705706314639537.html

ISSUE 9

Should Corporations Be Allowed to Implement English-Only Rules in the Workplace?

YES: K. C. McAlpin, Testimony before the U. S. Commission on Civil Rights Hearing on Specifying English as the Common Language of the Workplace (December 12, 2008). http://www.proenglish.org/news/USCCRTestimony.html

NO: Amy Crowe, from "May I Speak? Issues Raised by Employers' English-Only Policies," *Journal of Corporation Law* (April 2005). http://findarticles.com/p/articles/mi_hb5847/is_200504/ai_n23804796/

ISSUE SUMMARY

YES: K. C. McAlpin, the Executive Director of ProEnglish, a national organization that supports English-only rules for the workplace, defends his position primarily through his attack on the EEOC and its rationale and methods of prosecuting US firms that employ English-only rules.

NO: Legal scholar Amy Crowe provides a detailed analysis of the relationship between the US courts and the EEOC as it pertains to English-only policies and, in so doing, supports the EEOC and its rationale and methods for identifying and prosecuting discrimination in the workplace resulting from the implementation of English-only rules.

O ne of the more controversial issues stemming from the broader immigration reform topic concerns the implementation of English-only language rules in the workplace. Given the increased importance of the immigration issue to American society in recent years, it is not surprising to learn that the Equal Employment Opportunity Commission (EEOC) reported a 400-percent increase in the number of English-only–based discrimination cases during the 10-year period from 1996 to 2006 (Tresa Baldras, *The National Law Journal,* June 18, 2007). Part of the increase in these types of discrimination cases is likely due, in part, to the anti-English-only position the EEOC has adopted. Specifically, the EEOC policy on English-only in the workplace *assumes* that such a rule is itself a violation of Title VII of the 1964 Civil Rights Act and, is therefore, discriminatory. Interestingly, this approach has met with limited success in the courtroom as judges have mostly sided with businesses in allowing English-only workplace rules. However, this judicial support is not unconditional, and the case law in this area has identified the situations in which English-only rules do not violate protected class members' rights and are, therefore, legal.

In general, the courts have been supportive of English-only policies to the extent that they can be shown to constitute a "business necessity." As labor and employment lawyer Marc Scheiner explains, "The key is business necessity. If you could point to some business necessity that justifies the policy, that's really the hook" (Tresa Baldras, *The National Law Journal,* June 18, 2007). Court cases and legal decisions have helped to identify those situations in which English-only rules are considered to be appropriate. Situations involving safety concerns, for example, are fair game for such rules because the ability to communicate clearly, quickly, and reliably in safety-threatening circumstances is of paramount importance. Another common business activity where English-only rules are deemed legal involves the customer service function. Customers frequently complain that they feel uncomfortable when employees speak in front of them in a non-English language. Courts have been sympathetic to consumer's feelings in this regard, allowing the use of English-only rules in instances where employees, supervisors, or customers only speak English. A third situation in which English-only rules are acceptable involves group work activities that require high levels of cooperation among members for the group to function efficiently. Because a business has the right to pursue profit and to try and ensure its survival, it can implement English-only rules as a means of avoiding and eliminating potentially costly language-related sources of inefficiency.

On the other side of the debate are those who believe that English-only workplace rules are inherently discriminatory, a view explicitly endorsed by the EEOC. Indeed, in 1980, the EEOC released its formal policy regarding English-only rules, the basis of which was the *presumption* that such rules "have a disparate impact on the basis of national origin and therefore violate Title VII's ban on national origin discrimination." (K. C. McAlpin, Testimony to the US Commission on Civil Rights, December 2008). And although courts have sided with business more often than with the EEOC, anti-English-only proponents have helped to highlight business practices that have been ruled discriminatory. For example, a rule that demanded employees speak English during non-work times or in non-work areas is discriminatory. Detractors of English-only policies also argue that, frequently, what passes for business necessity is really discrimination in disguise. And, as you will learn from the "no" side article in this text, most of the situations described here as representing business necessity defenses can be addressed satisfactorily without having to resort to implementing English-only rules. The implication, therefore, is that businesses turn to English-only rules more out of discriminatory motives than from a desire to address legitimate business concerns.

YES

K.C. McAlpin

Hearing on Specifying English as the Common Language of the Workplace

Introduction

Good morning. My name is K.C. McAlpin. I am the executive director of Pro-English, a national organization that advocates making English the official language of government and other policies to protect the role of English as the common unifying language of our country. ProEnglish relies on voluntary contributions from the public for our support.

I want to thank you for giving us the opportunity to comment on language in the workplace polices and specifically on the Equal Employment Opportunity Commission's ("EEOC") policy of targeting employers with English language workplace rules for prosecution under Title VII of the Civil Rights Act.

Background & Definitions

In 1980 without prior notice, consultation with, or authorization by Congress, the EEOC adopted guidelines that *presume* employers' English-on-the-job rules have a disparate impact on the basis of national origin and therefore violate Title VII's ban on national origin discrimination.

The EEOC formulated its Guidelines despite a 1973 court decision, *Espinoza v. Farah Mfg. Co.*, which defined national origin as referring "to the country where a person was born, or more broadly, the country from which his or her ancestors came." Moreover the same year they were issued the EEOC included its Guidelines in briefs before the Fifth Circuit U.S. Court of Appeals, which immediately rejected them twice. In *Garcia v. Gloor* (1980) the Fifth Circuit held that "national origin must not be confused with ethnic or socio-cultural traits" and concluded the Equal Employment Opportunity Act does not support an interpretation that equates the language an employee prefers to speak with national origin. And, in 1981, in *Vasquez v. McAllen Bay & Supply Co.*, the Fifth Circuit again rejected the Guidelines'

US Commission on Civil Rights, December 12, 2008.

formula that *language equals national origin* and upheld an English-on-the-job rule for truck drivers.

But let's step back for a moment and apply some common sense. We don't need the courts to tell us that the language someone speaks and their national origin are distinct and different characteristics. Someone who speaks Spanish or Chinese as their native language may have been born in any number of different countries. On the other hand, someone could have a national origin of Nigeria or India, and speak any one of dozens of different languages as their native language. The equation of language and national origin is so over and under inclusive as to render it meaningless. More than one quarter of the member countries of the United Nations have designated English as an official language. The EEOC's claim that there is a "close connection" between language and national origin is absolute nonsense.

Yet despite this, and despite more than twenty court cases that explicitly reject the EEOC Guidelines, the EEOC continues to act on its corrupt definition and target employers that have English language workplace rules for investigation, prosecution, and harassment.

The EEOC attempts to justify its illegal anti-English policy by using carefully worded half-truths, evasions, and distortions. Thus on its website, under the heading: Discriminatory Practices—National Origin Discrimination, the EEOC states that "It is illegal to discriminate against an individual because of birthplace, ancestry, *culture, or linguistic characteristics common to a specific ethnic group*" (emphasis added). Thus the EEOC adds broad and incomprehensible terminology to the accepted and well defined meaning of national origin, and substitutes "linguistic characteristics" for the clearly defined term "language," which could be easily rebutted.

In another example, EEOC policy guidance on English language workplace policies state, "The primary language of an individual is often an essential national origin characteristic." While that may have been true 500 years ago, in today's world a person's primary language is *rarely* an essential national origin characteristic. The fact is that language and national origin are distinct and almost entirely unrelated characteristics.

The EEOC Is Abusing Its Statutory Authority

The EEOC Guidelines presume that employer English-on-the-job rules "when applied at all times" are a burdensome condition of employment that violate Title VII's ban on national origin discrimination. But the definition of national origin the EEOC is using is totally flawed. It makes no difference whether such a rule is applied at all times or only at certain times because the EEOC: (1) has no basis to assert any violation of Title VII where language is concerned; and (2) even less right to *presume* an employer's English workplace policy violates Title VII.

The EEOC Guidelines go on to say that even if an employer's English language policy is applied only at certain times the employer must still show that the rule is justified by "business necessity." The effect of this qualification is to give the agency the discretion to attack any English-on-the-job rule and burden the employer with having to demonstrate business necessity in court.

So, for example, when the EEOC sued the Sephora cosmetics store chain, the fact that Sephora's policy was both narrowly tailored and limited did not stop the agency from filing suit [*EEOC v. Sephora*].

In fact, the EEOC has been filing language discrimination cases against employers that do not even have an English-on-the-job policy. *EEOC v. Spring Sheet Metal* is a case in point. In *EEOC v. Spring Sheet Metal* the false allegations of an employee sent home for a display of out of control temper (after being instructed by a foreman about what tool to use), was sufficient to trigger an EEOC lawsuit alleging national origin (language) discrimination.

But court proceedings lag far behind the accompanying EEOC publicity campaigns that allege employers with language policies are guilty of civil rights violations. As the agency knows, such campaigns inflict serious damage to an employer's reputation in their community and undermine their will to defend themselves in court.

In examining language in the workplace cases brought by the EEOC both the 5th Circuit and the 9th Circuit Courts of Appeals have ruled that the EEOC was acting *ultra vires* (i.e. outside the scope of its statutory authority), or in layman's terms, illegally. But the EEOC apparently thinks it is an agency unaccountable to congressional oversight and judicial authority. In a letter to Colorado Congressman Tom Tancredo dated Jan. 21, 2000, the EEOC says it "disagrees with the [9th Circuit] decision in Spun Steak," and simply declared it was empowered to act as a court and make its own statutory interpretations. In a breathtaking display of bureaucratic arrogance, the EEOC goes on to parse words, cite minority court opinions, and even cite selectively from adverse court decisions in order to justify its actions.

Here is the bottom line. In thirty-five years of court rulings right up to the present there has not been one English language court decision favoring the EEOC that was ultimately upheld or which is controlling: not a single one that supports the EEOC's *language equals national origin* formulation. And there have been only two instances in which a U.S. District Court agreed with the EEOC as compared to over twenty instances at the state, federal, and federal circuit courts, in which courts and judges have *rejected* the EEOC arguments.

The EEOC Is Trampling on Employers' & Employees' Rights

Courts have long recognized an employer's right to set the conditions of employment, including what employees can say on the job. That right is also protected by Title VII, itself.

By singling out employers with English language workplace policies for investigation and illegitimate civil rights prosecution the EEOC is violating an employer's fundamental right to run their business successfully and in the best interests of themselves, their customers, and their employees. Certainly, in these trying times of economic uncertainty and high unemployment, employers must be free to make optimal business decisions without fear of unwarranted prosecution by an out-of-control federal agency.

In fact, if the EEOC's *language equals national origin* formulation were true, the EEOC itself would be guilty of national origin discrimination because its Guidelines presume that only English language workplace policies are violations of Title VII. Thus, the EEOC claimed the Spun Steak Company's English language policy on its dayshift was a violation. But the Spanish language policy on its nightshift *was not*.

You have heard (or will hear) from Richard Kidman, the owner of RD's Drive-In Restaurant, and the story of the EEOC's unethical and unwarranted attack on this small business owner. I am familiar with the Kidmans' case because ProEnglish was involved in helping the Kidmans defend themselves against an EEOC lawsuit.

You need to eat a green chili cheeseburger at RD's Drive-In to understand the absurd lengths that the EEOC will go to pursue their illegitimate policy. Richard and his wife Shauna are small business heroes. Their drive-in restaurant, which grosses barely $700,000 a year, holds its own in the small town of Page, Arizona against competition from fast food giants like McDonalds, Burger King, and Taco Bell.

In 30 years of being in business RD's has employed hundreds of local residents, the vast majority of whom have been Navajo. But in the year 2000, to protect their employees from harassment, including sexual harassment, they had no choice except to implement an English-language workplace policy. In so doing, they never guessed they would run afoul of a huge federal agency like the EEOC, with its thousands of employees and an annual budget of hundreds of million of dollars.

Here is a summary of what happened to the Kidmans after they put their language policy in place.

- The EEOC conducted a one-sided investigation in which investigators asked leading questions, attempted to intimidate RD's employees, and showed scant interest in evidence or testimony that would have justified the restaurant's policy.
- Without notifying the Kidmans of the results of the investigation or giving them an opportunity to voluntarily remedy the alleged defects in their policy, the EEOC filed a discrimination lawsuit against them in federal court. The suit sought monetary damages including back pay and interest, as well as compensatory and punitive damages that could have personally bankrupted the Kidmans because their business was unincorporated.
- The EEOC issued a press release under the headline ". . . national origin bias against Navajos and other Native Americans," and ballyhooing its case as "The First-Ever English-Only Lawsuit [by the EEOC] on Behalf of Native Americans." In its release Phoenix EEOC Office Director Charles Burtner announced the EEOC verdict before any trial took place. "We found that [the Kidmans'] policy and its implementation is a form of national origin discrimination."
- The EEOC rejected subsequent efforts by the Kidmans' attorney to modify their English-on-the-job policy to meet the agency's objections.

- The EEOC unleashed a public relations attack on the Kidmans consisting of public statements to reporters and letters to newspapers. These attacks inflamed local passions along ethnic lines and had a substantial negative economic impact on RD's business. The low point was EEOC Phoenix Office Director Burtner's Nov. 25, 2002 letter to *The Navajo Times* newspaper in which he wrote that the EEOC's case against the Kidmans "involves *an assault* on employees who speak Navajo in the work place . . ." (emphasis added).
- The EEOC public relations campaign also generated negative news stories about the Kidmans in local newspapers as well as national media like *CNN* and the *New York Times*.
- After the Kidmans felt compelled by the pressure of huge unpaid legal bills to attempt to negotiate a good faith settlement of the dispute, EEOC lawyers betrayed the Kidmans' trust by trying to insert provisions detrimental to the Kidmans and alter the proposed settlement in ways that had been specifically rejected. The EEOC's underhanded and unethical conduct was so offensive that it drew a formal reprimand from the judge handling the case.

The Kidmans' litigation was not finally resolved until six years later in November 2006. By the terms of a court imposed settlement the Kidmans' admitted no guilt but were required to rescind their existing policy. However they retained the option of reissuing an English language workplace policy subject to EEOC review. They did this and today I'm happy to say that RD's Drive-In Restaurant has a legal English language workplace policy in effect. In the meantime, the problems with employee on employee harassment they had previously experienced, as well as sky-high turnover and difficulty retaining employees have all but disappeared. And perhaps best of all, the people of Page Arizona, can continue eating and enjoying RD's green chili cheeseburgers.

In the end, the EEOC accomplished nothing by all its bullying, attacks, and unethical treatment of the Kidmans as employers and private citizens, not to mention the expenditure of hundreds of thousands of taxpayer dollars.

Unfortunately the Kidmans' case is not an isolated example. It conforms to a clear pattern of intimidation, misuse of taxpayer money, and heavy-handed behavior that the agency uses again and again to enforce its illegitimate anti-English agenda.

Employers have many valid and compelling business reasons for implementing an English language workplace policy. They include:

- promoting safety
- protecting employees from ethnic slurs and other forms of harassment
- effectively supervising employees at work
- providing a friendly and courteous atmosphere for customers
- maintaining a non-hostile work environment for employees
- protecting against employee theft, substance abuse, and other forms of crime
- insuring compliance with employer policies

Employers like the Kidmans are caught in an impossible situation. If they fail to take effective action to stop harassment including ethnic slurs and sexual harassment in languages other than English, they can be sued under Title VII for maintaining a hostile work environment. But if they take the common sense approach of implementing an English-on-the-job policy, they run the risk of attacks and prosecution by the EEOC.

And even if they fight the EEOC and win their case in court, they are unlikely to recover their legal expenses. Ken Bertlesen, the owner of the Spun Steak Company estimates it cost him and his brother $400,000 in legal fees and expenses to successfully defend themselves against the EEOC all the way through their 9th Circuit appeal.

The EEOC *modus operandi* is this. (1) Find a plaintiff. (2) Conduct a one-sided investigation that assumes the employer is guilty. (3) Negotiate a settlement in which the employer admits no guilt but lets the EEOC claim victory and issue a news release to the media ballyhooing its accomplishment. (4) If the employer resists, file a lawsuit and issue a headline-grabbing press release alleging national origin discrimination by the employer. (5) Bully the employer and wear down their will to resist by running up the employer's legal bills and waging a public relations campaign attacking the employer as a "discriminator." (6) Ultimately negotiate a settlement in which the employer admits no guilt but lets the EEOC claim the "victory" it wants.

In the rare instances in which an employer has the resources and determination to fight the EEOC, the EEOC either loses at trial or agrees to settle the case on terms that vindicate the employer's policy. Such was the case with the Sephora (cosmetics) Company whose English language workplace policy was upheld by a federal court in September 2005. And just recently, the EEOC was forced to back down and accept a humiliating settlement of its lawsuit against the Salvation Army that effectively recognizes the Army's legal English-on-the-job policy.

But far more often, due to its vastly superior resources, the EEOC prevails—especially in actions against small employers— and is able to impose burdensome and costly settlements on employers who in actuality are in full compliance with the civil rights laws.

This should not happen in a free society. The EEOC is acting like a multicultural police force—writing its own laws, defying the courts, and using coercive tactics to impose its agenda on law-abiding employers, and chilling their freedom to manage their own businesses.

By doing so, the EEOC is not only trampling on the rights of employers. It also is violating the civil rights of employees to work in a non-hostile environment, in which they are protected from racial and ethnic slurs and all forms of harassment including sexual harassment.

In conclusion we urge the Commissioners to condemn the actions of the EEOC which are infringing upon civil rights and which are especially dangerous because they are being committed by a government agency—the very agency created by Congress to safeguard the civil rights of all employees.

Thank you for the opportunity to present our views.

Amy Crowe

➔ **NO**

May I Speak? Issues Raised by Employers' English-Only Policies

I. Introduction to English-Only Cases

Imagine relocating to a foreign country due to economic depression and polit-ical strife in your home country. Because of your limited knowledge of the language of the host country, you are only able to obtain work as an unskilled laborer in a factory. You feel fortunate because some of your co-workers are from your home country as well, and you speak to them regularly during breaks, at lunch, and outside of work in your native tongue. Now imagine your employer instituting a policy that employees may speak only the host country's language during work time. The employer claims this policy will promote workplace harmony and safety. But does this policy really promote these goals? Or, do you feel targeted? One slip of the tongue, such as saying 'good morning' in your native language to a co-worker and friend, may result in a reprimand or your termination from the job that you need to support your family. Further, you are uncomfortable raising questions or concerns about workplace safety to your co-workers, because you lack the language skills to speak to them in the host country's language.

Now imagine being the child of this worker. Although you were born and raised in America, your first exposure to English was in kindergarten. To augment your American public school education, your parents send you to after-school and summer school programs every year where you study your native language and heritage. Through your studies, you earn a high school equivalency diploma recognized by your parents' native country. Your parents are proud that you speak both English and their native language flawlessly.

Although you do not identify yourself as an American, most people assume by virtue of your skin color that you are American. You and your family have incorporated various English terms that lack an adequate trans-lation into the language you speak at home. Likewise, at work, you occasion-ally pause because a word comes to you in your native language but there is not an appropriate English translation. Sometimes a phrase from your native language slips into your conversation when you speak to a co-worker. Now imagine that your employer institutes an English-only policy in your workplace.

From *Journal of Corporation Law*, April 2005, pp. 593–608 (references omitted). Copyright © 2005 by Amy Crowe. Reprinted by permission of the author.

Considering himself to be sensitive, your employer will not require you to speak English during breaks or lunch. As one of the few bilingual employees in the office, how would you feel?

Over the years, a variety of United States employers have instituted English-only policies in the workplace. These policies affect not only immigrants to the United States, but also native-born Americans raised in bilingual households. Plaintiffs have sought to enjoin these policies claiming that English-only policies constitute a form of disparate impact prohibited by Title VII. As the U.S. and its workforce continue to diversify, the issues raised by English-only cases become more pressing. Currently, the Supreme Court has not yet addressed these issues, although a ruling would end a split in the courts.

This Note will explore the history of disparate impact suits, the Equal Employment Opportunity Commission's (EEOC) guidelines on English-only policies and national origin discrimination, and caselaw on English-only policies. Next, this Note will explore three significant issues raised by English-only cases: (1) whether language implicates national origin; (2) whether courts should defer to the EEOC's guidelines on English-only policies; and (3) whether employers have a legitimate business necessity defense for English-only policies. Finally, this Note will consider recommendations to alter Title VII to address English-only policies.

II. Background

English-only cases constitute one member of a family of cases falling under the rubric of disparate impact suits. This family of cases can trace its origins to the Supreme Court's landmark decision in *Griggs v. Duke Power Company*. This section will explore the development of disparate impact cases beginning with *Griggs*, Congress's codification of the *Griggs* holding in the Civil Rights Act of 1991, and the application of the disparate impact theory by the courts. Finally, this section will provide an overview of English-only cases, guidelines promulgated by the EEOC, and the issues that have arisen since the promulgation of these guidelines.

A. Facts of *Griggs v. Duke Power Company*

In 1964, Congress enacted Title VII of the 1964 Civil Rights Act which prohibits an employer from hiring, firing, discriminating in terms or conditions of employment, or segregating individuals on the basis of their race, color, religion, sex, or national origin. In *Griggs*, employees of Duke Power Company brought a Title VII challenge against Duke Power's policy requiring a high school education or the passing of an intelligence test as a condition of hire or transfer. The appellate court held that the policy did not violate Title VII because it was facially neutral and there was no showing of discriminatory intent. In a landmark decision, the Supreme Court reversed, stating that under Title VII employment practices that are "neutral on their face, and even neutral in terms of intent, cannot be maintained if they operate to 'freeze' the status quo of prior discriminatory employment practices." *Griggs* thus marked the beginning of disparate impact cases.

B. The Development of the Burden-Shifting Test

Through *Griggs* and subsequent cases, the Supreme Court fleshed out the burden-shifting test of disparate impact. First, the plaintiff must show that the employer's policy significantly and adversely affects a protected group. The burden then shifts to the employer to provide a "business necessity" for its policy. If the employer is able to establish a business necessity, the burden shifts back to the plaintiff to prove that the employer could have used other nondiscriminatory means to satisfy the same business necessity. If the employer could have used nondiscriminatory means, the employer is deemed to have used the policy as a "pretext" for discriminating.

In *Wards Cove Packing Co. v. Atonio*, the Supreme Court lightened the employer's burden as set out in *Griggs*. Rather than having the burden of persuasion, the employer now only had the burden of production in justifying an employment policy. Therefore, the burden of persuasion remained with the *plaintiff* throughout the case.

C. The Civil Rights Act of 1991

In direct response to the Supreme Court's decision in *Wards Cove*, Congress enacted the Civil Rights Act of 1991. Congress stated that "the decision of the Supreme Court in *Wards Cove Packing Co. v. Atonio*, had weakened the scope and effectiveness of Federal civil rights protections. . . ." The Civil Rights Act of 1991 reinstated the burden-shifting test found in *Griggs*.

D. The Evolution of Disparate Impact Cases

Shortly following *Griggs*, the Supreme Court recognized that the theory of disparate impact applied to on-the-job policies as well as hiring and promotional policies. In the years succeeding these early Supreme Court cases and Congress's codification of the *Griggs* burden-shifting test, plaintiffs have brought disparate impact claims against a broad range of employers' policies with varying degrees of success. Employees and applicants have challenged employers' screening tests requiring applicants to run 1.5 miles in twelve minutes, promotional examinations, and pay policies. Although most disparate impact claims allege race or gender discrimination under Title VII, plaintiffs have also alleged disparate impact under the Age Discrimination in Employment Act (ADEA) and the Pregnancy Discrimination Act (PDA).

E. The EEOC's Guidelines on National Origin

Determining what constitutes national origin and discrimination based upon it is subject to debate. In 1970, the EEOC published *Guidelines on Discrimination Because of National Origin,* which defined national origin discrimination to include discrimination based on physical, cultural, or linguistic characteristics of a national origin group. The EEOC has since expanded this definition of national origin to encompass:

> the denial of equal employment opportunity because of an individual's, or his or her ancestor's, place of origin; or because an individual has the physical, cultural or linguistic characteristics of a national origin group . . . [and] for reasons which are grounded in national origin considerations, such as (a) marriage to or association with persons of a national origin group; (b) membership in, or association with an organization identified with or seeking to promote the interests of national origin groups; (c) attendance or participation in schools, churches, temples or mosques, generally used by persons of a national origin group; and (d) because an individual's name or spouse's name is associated with a national origin group.

Generally, the EEOC has identified four forms of national origin discrimination: (1) rules requiring employees to speak English at all times on the job; (2) an employer's refusal to hire an applicant because of the applicant's accent or manner of speaking; (3) harassment in the form of ethnic slurs or physical conduct because of an employee's national origin that create a hostile work environment; and (4) singling out applicants of a particular national origin and requiring only them to provide employment verification. According to the EEOC, its office received more than 8000 charges of national origin discrimination in 2001, and these charging parties in the aggregate obtained $48.1 million from settlements alone.

F. The EEOC's Guidelines on English-Only Policies

In its 1970 Guidelines to National Origin Discrimination, the EEOC recognized that English-only rules "create an atmosphere of inferiority, isolation and intimidation." In 1987, the EEOC supplemented its guidelines, stating that English-only rules that require employees to speak English at all times are presumed to violate Title VII. However, an employer may require employees to speak only English at specified times where the employer can show that there is a business justification for the requirement. For example, an employer cannot institute a policy requiring its employees to speak English at all times including breaks and lunches. However, the employer could require English be spoken where the health and safety of employees is at risk.

G. Caselaw on English-Only Policies

Courts have shown some reluctance to defer to the EEOC's guidelines. In the first decision by a federal appellate court, the Fifth Circuit held in *Garcia v. Gloor* that an employer's policy requiring employees to speak English unless working with Spanish-speaking customers did not constitute discrimination on the basis of national origin. In *Gloor,* the employee, a native-born American of Mexican descent, was discharged for responding in Spanish about a customer's order to another Mexican-American employee. The employee alleged that he found the employer's English-only policy difficult to follow, because Spanish was his primary language and he always spoke Spanish in his home. The Fifth Circuit concluded that because the employee was bilingual, speaking Spanish was a choice and therefore could not be equated to national origin.

Similarly, in *Jurado v. Eleven-Fifty Corp.*, the Ninth Circuit stated "[a]n employer can properly enforce a limited, reasonable and business-related English-only rule against an employee who can readily comply with the rule and who voluntarily chooses not to observe it as 'a matter of individual preference.'" However, the Ninth Circuit later deferred to the EEOC guidelines and recognized that an employer's English-only policy constituted disparate impact on the basis of national origin in *Gutierrez v. Municipal Court.* Nevertheless, in *Garcia v. Spun Steak Co.,* the Ninth Circuit concluded that its decision in *Gutierrez* had no precedential value because the Supreme Court had vacated it as moot. The court quoted its decision in *Jurado,* stating that an employer's rule has no disparate impact "if the rule is one that the affected employee can readily observe and nonobservance is a matter of individual preference." The court refused to defer to the EEOC, because its guidelines presume an English-only policy has a disparate impact without proof. The court stated that the guidelines failed to balance the prevention of discrimination with the preservation of the employer's independence.

Currently, no appellate court has deferred to the EEOC's guidelines. *Gloor* was decided before the guidelines were issued, so the court based its decision on the language of the statute itself. In *Gonzalez v. Salvation Army,* the court made no mention of the EEOC's guidelines despite their existence. Finally, *Spun Steak* expressly rejected the EEOC guidelines.

Recently, however, district courts have deferred to these guidelines in cases brought by the EEOC. For example, in *EEOC v. Synchro-Start Products, Inc.,* the court cited as the reason for its deference the difficulty a plaintiff would have in proving that an English-only policy had a disparate impact. These decisions appear to be supported in part by new psycho-linguistic studies suggesting that language is not a matter of choice. Because of these district court decisions, the courts are clearly divided on whether to defer to EEOC guidelines. Further, decided cases do not fully reflect the amount of litigation currently happening in the English-only arena. The EEOC has also settled several claims for large amounts.

At this juncture, the Supreme Court has not decided whether the EEOC acted within its power by promulgating the guidelines on English-only policies. This issue has been greatly debated in the legal community, and most scholars conclude that courts should defer to the guidelines. According to the Supreme Court, courts should show great deference to EEOC guidelines absent "compelling indications that [the guidelines] are wrong." The rationale for this deference is that the administrative agency, rather than a court, is in a better position to understand the intricacies of the workplace environment and policies. Most scholars contend that the EEOC was within its power when it promulgated its guidelines on English-only policies. Assuming the courts should defer to the EEOC, the question remains whether employers can establish an affirmative business necessity defense.

III. Analysis

This section will explore the three main issues surrounding English-only cases: (1) whether language implicates national origin; (2) whether the EEOC acted within its power in promulgating the regulations on English-only policies; and (3) whether businesses have a legitimate business necessity for maintaining English-only policies. Not all English-only cases explicitly raise these issues. However, to resolve the splits between courts, these issues will need to be resolved.

A. Language and Its Implication on National Origin

An important issue is whether language implicates national origin for the purposes of Title VII. Early cases have held that language is not a form of national origin. These courts rejected the argument that language implicates national origin, because they viewed the language a plaintiff spoke as a matter of choice.

However, recent psycho-linguistic studies suggest that language is not a matter of choice. These studies indicate that bilingual speakers unconsciously switch between English and their original language when speaking with members of their cultural group. This phenomenon, known as code-switching, is unconscious, and speakers will generally continue to speak in the same language most recently spoken. Therefore, it will be particularly difficult for Hispanic workers specifically hired to assist Spanish-speaking customers to comply with an English-only policy.

Because code-switching is not a matter of individual choice, bilingual employees face the risk of reprimand and termination for failure to comply with the employer's English-only policy. In contrast, monolingual English speakers are not subject to the same threat of reprimand and termination, because they can easily comply with the policy. Therefore, English-only policies have a disparate impact on bilingual employees.

B. The EEOC's Authority

It is uncertain whether the EEOC acted within its power when it promulgated its guidelines that (1) an English-only policy that applies at all times in the workplace including breaks and lunch periods will create a presumption of discrimination and (2) an English-only policy that does not apply at all times is valid if the employer can show there is a business necessity for the rule. Courts should defer to the EEOC guidelines if the EEOC acted within its regulatory power by promulgating the guidelines. In *Chevron U.S.A., Inc. v. Natural Resources Defense Council, Inc.,* the Supreme Court held:

> If Congress has explicitly left a gap for the agency to fill, there is an express delegation of authority to the agency to elucidate a specific provision of the statute by regulation. Such legislative regulations are given controlling weight unless they are arbitrary, capricious, or manifestly contrary to the statute.

However, the EEOC guidelines do not qualify for *Chevron*-style deference, because the Supreme Court has recognized that Congress did not confer upon the EEOC the power to promulgate regulations pursuant to Title VII. Still, according to the Court, courts should grant "great deference" to the EEOC guidelines unless there are "compelling indications" that the guidelines are wrong.

Courts generally cite three rationales for not deferring to the EEOC's guidelines: (1) language does not implicate national origin; (2) bilingual individuals can easily comply with the rule and therefore do not need protection; and (3) lack of congressional intent. As previously discussed, language does implicate national origin and, due to language processing, bilingual individuals will find it difficult to comply with English-only policies. Therefore, the first two arguments do not provide a compelling indication that the guidelines are wrong.

Congressional intent also does not provide a compelling indication that the EEOC guidelines are wrong. In *Spun Steak,* the court refused to defer to the EEOC guidelines because "nothing in the plain language of 703(a)(1) supports the EEOC's English-only guideline." However, it is hard to see how a lack of support in the plain language provides a compelling indication that the EEOC's guidelines are wrong. Concepts of race, gender, and national origin are ever shifting and intersecting. For instance, only a hundred years ago individuals of Irish descent were considered black. It would be impossible for Congress to predict the multitude of discriminatory policies that employers might adopt and the many protected groups that these policies might adversely affect. Rather, the language of statutes must be broad enough to change with the times. An argument that the plain language of the statute does not include English-only policies fails to provide a compelling indication that the EEOC guidelines are undeserving of deference.

In fact, legislative intent may suggest that the EEOC's English-only guidelines comport with the legislation. The Supreme Court has recognized that Congress "considered the policy against discrimination to be of the 'highest priority.'" It follows that guidelines established to end discrimination comports with the congressional intent behind Title VII. As the dissent recognized in *Spun Steak,* it would be almost impossible for an employee in an English-only case to establish a prima facie case of disparate impact. Therefore, a guideline requiring a plaintiff to maintain this insurmountable burden would go against the Supreme Court's interpretation of the congressional intent behind Title VII.

Further, when Congress enacted the Civil Rights Act of 1991, it discussed the EEOC's English-only guidelines. In congressional discussion, Senator Kennedy said that the EEOC's guidelines on English-only policies had worked effectively and that the new legislation would not affect them. Thus, Congress approved of the EEOC's guidelines.

C. Business Necessity

Assuming courts continue to hold that language is a form of national origin discrimination and to defer to the EEOC's guidelines on English-only policies, the question still remains whether businesses can provide a legitimate business defense. Under section 1606.7(b) of the guidelines, an employer may institute an English-only policy if it has a legitimate business necessity for the policy. Because initial caselaw held that English-only policies did not consti- tute national origin discrimination, employers were not required to provide a business necessity defense. In the ensuing years, employers have claimed two rationales for an English-only policy: workplace harmony and safety. Gener- ally, these English-only rules require the employees to speak English at the workplace, except during breaks and lunches, when they may speak the lan- guage of their choice. However, it is questionable whether either justification is a sufficient rationale for an English-only policy, especially for a policy that requires an employee to speak English at all times while at work.

1. Workplace Harmony

Employers often cite the desire to promote workplace harmony as a justifica- tion for an English-only policy. In *EEOC v. RD's Drive In*, the owner of the restaurant instituted a No-Navajo policy in response to complaints by mono- lingual English customers and coworkers that bilingual Navajo workers were making racial comments in Navajo. Similarly, one factory manager instituted an English-only policy in his plant after co-workers complained that some of the Hispanic workers were making racially hurtful comments in Spanish. An employer's English-only policy in such circumstances may be well intended. Nevertheless, the English-only policies appear to have the opposite effect. Rather than promoting workplace harmony, they serve to dichotomize the workplace between monolingual English speakers and bilingual speakers because they make bilingual speakers feel unnecessarily targeted and subject to reprimand or termination. The vast amount of litigation in this area suggests that English-only policies do not promote workplace harmony.

 Another problem with this workplace harmony justification is that it is overreaching in cases where employees are required to speak English at all times except during breaks or at lunch. It is hard to imagine how two maids cleaning a hotel floor with no other workers around will promote workplace harmony by speaking English rather than Spanish. Rather, if neither maid is very fluent in English, the policy may decrease workplace harmony because the employees will be unable to communicate with each other.

 Ultimately, the greatest problem with establishing an English-only policy to promote workplace harmony is that the policy does not address the under- lying racial or ethnic tension that compels an employer to institute an English- only policy. An English-only policy would not prevent workers from using code words or hand signals to communicate derogatory comments. Therefore, rather than an English-only policy, an employer should contend with the underlying racial or ethnic problems in the workplace.

2. Safety

Safety appears to be a more legitimate rationale for an English-only policy. However, a policy requiring employees to speak English at all times, while working, is too broad. The EEOC's Compliance Manual states that an English- only rule must be narrowly tailored to the specific circumstances in the workplace. Other than in a factory where safety may always be at issue, a rule requiring employees to speak English at all times, except during breaks, will be overbroad because employees will not always be faced with safety issues. The EEOC's Compliance Manual provides the following example of a narrowly tailored English-only requirement:

> XYZ Petroleum Corp. operates an oil refinery and has a rule requiring all employees to speak only English during an emergency. The rule also requires that employees speak in English while performing job duties in laboratories and processing areas where there is the danger of fire or explosion. The rule does not apply to casual conversations between employees in the laboratory or processing areas when they are not performing a job duty.

Such a policy would allow bilingual speakers to speak in Spanish when safety was not at issue. However, given psycho-linguistic studies, employees should also be given leniency in true emergency situations. In an unexpected emergency, the natural response would be to respond in the language most familiar to the speaker.

IV. Recommendation

An employer may wish to consider a number of alternative and less controversial measures rather than resorting to an English-only policy. To address issues of workplace harmony, a more appropriate measure than an English-only rule would be for the employer to institute stricter harassment training programs. Such measures would ensure that an employer is addressing the underlying racial or ethnic tensions existing in the workplace rather than targeting a particular group of individuals. An employer should also consider translating harassment manuals into languages other than English.

Similarly, an employer could consider translating safety manuals into languages other than English. An employer could also hire occupational safety workers who are fluent in multiple languages. Finally, an employer could institute protocols for responding to emergency situations in ways that do not use language, for example by sounding an alarm.

Several scholars have proposed that Congress amend Title VII to include language. This would ensure that courts would have to treat English-only policies as a form of disparate impact. However, such a solution might introduce unnecessary complications. For instance, what constitutes "language?" Should dialects such as Black-English be protected as well? Black-English could be perceived as a grammatically incorrect form of English; however, some scholars suggest Black-English is a distinct language by itself and should be recognized as such by society.

Further, a language amendment would not end the ongoing debate over how much courts should defer to the EEOC. Although a language amendment would resolve the question for English-only policies, the EEOC is constantly responding to the changing dynamics and intersections of race, gender, and religion. For instance, is a policy requiring a transgender employee to use a separate bathroom a form of sex discrimination within the meaning of Title VII?

V. Conclusion

Ultimately, society as a whole rather than the courts will resolve the issues raised by an ever-diversifying workforce. However, until society resolves these debates, courts should hold that employers' English-only policies are a form of national origin discrimination within the meaning of Title VII. Specifically, courts should recognize that: (1) language implicates national origin as shown by psycho-linguistic studies; (2) the EEOC acted within its power in promulgating the regulations on English-only policies; and (3) businesses can address their legitimate business concerns with less discriminatory measures.

POSTSCRIPT

Should Corporations Be Allowed to Implement English-Only Rules in the Workplace?

K.C. McAlprin, in his testimony to the US Commission on Civil Rights, raises many troubling questions and concerns regarding the Equal Employment Opportunity Commission's enforcement of English-only workplace discrimination. Particularly noteworthy, however, is a very dangerous unintended consequence of aggressive EEOC prosecution. McAlprin explains,

> Employers like the Kidmans are caught in an impossible situation. If they fail to take effective action to stop harassment including ethnic slurs and sexual harassment in languages other than English, they can be sued under Title VII for maintaining a hostile work environment. But if they take the common sense approach of implementing an English-on-the-job policy, they run the risk of attacks and prosecution by the EEOC.

Employers can be caught in a Catch-22 situation because failure to protect employees from ethnic harassment can lead to discrimination charges and EEOC investigation while, on the other hand, implementing an English-only workplace policy runs the risk of being accused by the EEOC of violating employee rights. And though putting employers in this type of dilemma is, of course, not the intention of the EEOC, one wonders how much that really matters. After all, as the famous proverb reminds us: "the road to hell is paved with good intentions."

Amy Crowe, most likely, would not be sympathetic to McAlprin's fears about the EEOC. She maintains that many of the concerns employers try to address through English-only rules can be effectively dealt with by other measures. She suggests stronger, more comprehensive harassment sensitivity programs and translating harassment-related materials into non-English languages as a means of reducing underlying ethnic tensions in the workplace. To address safety issues, Crowe advises employers to consider hiring safety specialists fluent in more than just English. Here, too, non-English language translations of safety manuals could be beneficial.

The question of whether or not employers should be allowed to use English-only rules in the workplace is one that is not likely to go away anytime soon. Indeed, at some point in the not-too-distant future, the larger immigration reform issue will move back to the center of the political stage as it was just a few years ago. And when it does, you will be ready to contribute to the debate having read both sides of the issue in this text.

Suggested Readings

Tresa Baldas, "English-Only Workplace Policies Trigger Lawsuits" *The National Law Journal* (June 18, 2007). http://www.law.com/jsp/ihc/PubArticleIHC.jsp?id=1182194749541

William P. Burns, "English-Only in a Diverse Workplace: One Language, Different Realities," *FindLaw* (December 1, 1998). http://library.findlaw.com/1998/Dec/1/129118.html

Michael H. Roffer and Nicholas J. Sanservino, Jr., "Holding Employee's Native Tongues: English-Only Workplace Rules," *HR Magazine* (September 2000). http://findarticles.com/p/articles/mi_m3495/is_9_45/ai_65578689/pg_3/

Wall Street Journal, "English-Only Showdown: Does Nancy Pelosi Really Object to a Common Language in the Workplace?" *WSJ Opinion Archives* (November 28, 2007). http://www.opinionjournal.com/diary/?id=110010917

Internet References . . .

ProEnglish

ProEnglish is a member-supported, national, non-profit organization working to educate the public about the need to protect English as our common language and to make it the official language of the United States. Since its creation, ProEnglish has gained expertise and considerable experience in the rapidly evolving field of language law. As a result, ProEnglish has specialized in providing pro-bono legal assistance to public and private agencies facing litigation or regulatory actions over language.

http://www.proenglish.org/

Workplace Fairness

Workplace Fairness is a nonprofit organization that brings together employers, workers, policymakers and others to ensure and promote fairness in the workplace and employment relationships.

http://www.nerinet.org/

Partnership for a Drug-Free America

This Web site has much information on drug use by young adults as well as many links to related sites. Also features an updated news resource link.

http://www.drugfreeamerica.org/Home/
default.asp?ws=PDFA&vol=1&grp=Home

Independent Women's Forum

Founded in 1992, IWF focuses on issues of concern to women, men, and families. Our mission is to rebuild civil society by advancing economic liberty, personal responsibility, and political freedom. IWF builds support for a greater respect for limited government, equality under the law, property rights, free markets, strong families, and a powerful and effective national defense and foreign policy.

http://iwf.org/about/

The Heritage Foundation

The Heritage Foundation is a research and educational institute whose mission is to formulate and promote conservative public policies based on the principles of free enterprise, limited government, individual freedom, traditional American values, and a strong national defense.

http://www.heritage.org/

UNIT 3

Strategic Management

*M*ost investors and executives do their utmost to help their firms grow and to increase profits. It seems obvious: Successful firms are growing firms. So why would highly knowledgeable and respected business scholars and observers argue that growth is not necessary for a firm to be successful? Speaking of growth, consider the issue of mergers and acquisitions. Would you be surprised to learn that, frequently, firms that engage in these behaviors actually experience a loss in corporate value? So why are mergers and acquisitions (M&As) so popular? For answers to these and other emotionally charged questions, dive into the five topics comprising the third section of this text.

- Is Downsizing a Sound Strategic Initiative?
- Is Outsourcing a Wise Corporate Strategy?
- Does Expanding via Mergers and Acquisitions Make for Sound Corporate Strategy?
- Is First-to-Market a Successful Strategy?
- Is Growth Always an Inherent Corporate Value?

ISSUE 10

Is Downsizing a Sound Strategic Initiative?

YES: Andrew Simone and Brian H. Kleiner, from" Workforce Reduction Guidelines," *Southern Business Review* (Spring 2004)

NO: Kenneth Levitt, Terry Wilson, and Edna Gilligan, from "Corporate Downsizing: An Examination of the Survivors," *Journal of Global Business Issues* (Summer 2008)

ISSUE SUMMARY

YES: Authors Andrew Simone and Brian Kleiner acknowledge that downsizing carries significant risks, but they believe that, if implemented correctly, downsizing can be an invaluable strategic program. They offer insightful suggestions to help ensure a successful downsizing initiative.

NO: East Stroudsburg University researchers Kenneth Levitt, Terry Wilson, and Edna Gilligan examine the effects of downsizing on those that "survive" the layoffs. Their results indicate that survivors are subject to several negative effects, thereby undermining the effectiveness of the downsizing intervention itself.

Corporate downsizing is the strategic action of reducing the size of an organization's workforce in the hope of achieving greater efficiency and productivity through the reduction in labour costs. Although academic discussion of the concept can be traced back to the 1950s, it wasn't until the early 1980s that the idea of using downsizing as a strategic tool found expression in the marketplace of corporate America. The accelerated growth of international and global competition during the 1980s forced American businesses to reduce costs and focus on increasing organizational efficiency. An obvious way to quickly lower costs and trim waste is to reduce the size of the workforce. This line of thinking, coupled with the growing competitive pressures, proved irresistible to thousands of corporations of all sizes and financial conditions. The result? Millions of employees were laid off as corporate America embraced the notion of downsizing as a valuable managerial weapon. By the time the 1990s were over, the acceptance of downsizing as an effective and dependable arrow in the corporate quiver was complete. And in the aftermath of the financial meltdown of

2008 and the concomitant economic recession, large corporations across a wide range of industries are once again laying off employees by the thousands.

On the surface, it seems reasonable to think that downsizing must be smart strategy—otherwise, why would it be such a widely used approach to cost cutting? However, this issue is more complicated than is often realized at first glance. Indeed, many savvy business commentators and scholars argue very persuasively against downsizing, thus providing the position of the controversial question: Is downsizing a sound strategic initiative?

For organizations facing fierce competition or struggling financially, downsizing represents a relatively fast, effective method of reducing costs and, often, avoiding bankruptcy. From an employer's perspective, laying off workers not only reduces direct financial compensation but also saves employee benefits costs, an area that has seen explosive growth over the past two or three decades. Supporters of downsizing also point out that it allows firms to reallocate resources to more productive areas of the organization as well as helping them become more streamlined. This, in turn, helps the organization to be more efficient and competitive. Business owner Hugh Aaron makes exactly this point:

> The cost of these [employee] benefits, which seemed negligible when they were adopted, had grown stealthily over the years. In most cases, they had increased an employee's effective wage by one third to one half. Only after we began cutting back did we appreciate this fact. Our new awareness of what an employee really costs guided our employment policy from then on. As business improved, we strove not to return to the excesses of the fat years. We purchased new, more efficient equipment. We hired part-timers and temporary workers, who received no benefits. Management also struck a bargain with the workers: in return for a willingness to work overtime in good times, the company would guarantee steady employment in bad times. In short, we avoided having to hire more permanent people unless absolutely necessary." (Hugh Aaron, "Downsizing for profit in a recession," *All About Business,* February 19, 2009. http://businesswisdom.blogspot.com/2009/02/downsizing-for-profit-in-recession.html)

Skeptics of downsizing are not impressed by such arguments. They are fond of noting that the research evidence is on their side: in general, downsizing firms show only a slight, temporary increase in their stock prices and other performance measures. And typically, this benefit disappears within a year of the layoffs. This, skeptics argue, is due to the fact that in most cases, the trouble goes deeper than high labor costs. Indeed, often the source of problem lies with management itself, not with the employees. Firing a bunch of employees may reduce costs in the near-term and give the appearance that management is on top of things, but if the problem is managerial in nature, downsizing will prove fruitless in the long run. Opponents also argue that downsizing is immoral because it violates the implied psychological contract between employer and employee. The view here is that employees should be able to keep their jobs as long as they live up to the terms of their employment contract; downsizing violates this agreement.

YES ↵

Andrew Simone and
Brian H. Kleiner

Workforce Reduction Guidelines

Now, more than ever, companies are taking part in workforce reductions. Workforce reduction can go by many names—reduction in force, downsizing, rightsizing, eliminating redundancy, lay-offs, cutting staff, or reengineering. Most people would choose to blame the poor condition of the U.S. economy. While this may be true in some cases, organizations undertake lay-offs for many different reasons. No matter what an organization chooses to call it, this objective can be accomplished in either effective or ineffective ways.

Lay-offs of a significant proportion generally suggest a considerable reduction in business. Usually, it is prudent to search for any other alternatives available before proceeding with a workforce reduction. If a workforce reduction is deemed the only course of action capable of meeting an organization's objectives, thorough planning, organization, and implementation need to be prearranged before any action is taken. The consequences of an ineffective workforce reduction strategy can be devastating.

Reasons Companies Need Workforce Reductions

The decision to undertake a workforce reduction is not made lightly. Companies require reductions in the workforce for many reasons, including poor economic environment, technology making functions obsolete, foreign competition, slumping sales, mergers, plant closures, bankruptcy, or even over-staffing.

To explore just one example, when the technology revolution began back in the 1980s, many jobs were eliminated by technological advancements in information technology (IT); however, by 1997, a Harvard study of 250 insurance companies noted that IT improvements that automated low-level job functions in the industry might have finally run their course (Leibs & Carrillo, 1997: 7). This demonstrates the unpredictability that technology places upon workforce makeup.

Organizations can hope to achieve several goals through a workforce reduction. These include increasing efficiency, improving customer service, improving quality, increasing profitability, as well as reducing costs and eliminating unproductive positions. Gaining an edge on the competition may be achieved with the right realignment of a workforce.

Importance of Doing It Correctly and Avoiding Common Mistakes

Many companies have learned through experience that downsizing is a process loaded with potential litigation. Government statutes supply employees with various methods of legal retribution. Any suit filed, regardless of its legitimacy, will create financial burdens for an employer. Obtaining qualified legal counsel, paying for the case preparation, filing motions, depositions, etc., are unavoidable expenditures whose costs must be considered. Sensible employers are aware of the frequency of litigation and take steps to minimize the liability. Without following careful steps to workforce reduction, businesses often fall short of their original objectives. One study showed that "two-thirds of the downsized organizations experience no increase in productivity and 50 percent see no improvement in profits" (Jane, 1997: 1).

Evaluating overall worker contributions and employee notification are multifaceted, legal, and, frequently, emotional processes for any organization. Short-term savings may be recognized through lay-offs, but any large-scale reduction in the workforce involves hidden costs from issues such as discrimination claims, class action suits, and wrongful discharge lawsuits. When economic conditions improve and growth returns, replacing employees who were laid-off can also prove to be difficult and costly.

One common mistake businesses make in reducing their workforces is to cut administrators and managers without reducing professional staff. A Harvard study of 250 insurance companies showed that

> [c]ompanies that do better (in reducing workforce) first scrutinize their professional staffs closely (Leibs & Carrillo, 1997: 2).

It is important to restructure the entire workforce of an organization to provide consistency with the corporate vision. Lay-offs should not be tactical but instead strategic. The makeup of a workforce after the reduction is critical for its success.

Other common mistakes identified when interviewing local executives include cutting too many employees, choosing the wrong employees to cut, poor timing, and a bad decision-making process. Surprisingly, the biggest mistake mentioned by executives was allowing emotions to get involved.

Steps of an Effective Workforce Reduction

The following steps are designed to minimize potential legal and financial ramifications. Failure to take extreme precaution will likely result in an unsuccessful workforce reduction.

Identifying the Reasons the Workforce Reduction Is Necessary

The business justification for a reduction in workforce should be put in writing. In doing this, employers can show evidence that all alternatives were considered, which can be extremely beneficial in demonstrating to a jury that only business reasons were relevant in the decision-making process. Alternatives to be considered include hiring or wage freezes; allowing for natural attrition; creating early retirement incentives; eliminating temporary workers; reducing hours, pay rates, or fringe benefits; or making employee transfers. Businesses can save money using any of these techniques, and an effort should be made to fully evaluate the potential savings of such actions. Human resources executives Carie Bennett of Velocitel, Inc., and Naomi Buenaflor of Young's Market Company, Inc., both stated that the first step in the process is to "identify future needs" (Bennett 2002: 1 & Buenaflor 2002: 1).

Evaluate Policy or Practice for Terminations and Reductions

While many companies do not have written procedures and policies, past practices and policies should be reviewed to determine if they apply to workforce reduction. Previous severance packages and the length of notice given to employees can be deemed as precedent. What was given in the past must be evaluated because employees who are laid-off may be entitled to the same benefits in addition to any special severance.

Determining the Scope of the Reduction

Employers must determine if the downsizing will involve individual departments, business units, or the entire company. Closing a facility or location during a lay-off presents some additional issues to be addressed. The timing should be determined, as well as the key personnel involved in implementing the workforce reduction.

Selecting Employees to be Discharged

Using objective measures to determine which employees will be laid-off is critical. Some criteria to be considered are seniority, elimination of functions, bargaining vs. non-bargaining employees, measured quantity of production, performance, and skill-level. Seniority and elimination of job functions are the most objective measures. Terminating employees based on performance without written documentation of evaluations will likely result in wrongful termination or discrimination suits. Written criteria outlining the decision-making process will avoid or minimize subjectivity. The primary objective is to be left with the best-qualified workforce after a reduction in force.

Studying the Workforce Profile

Discrimination claims against employers are usually related to age, sex, or race. Employers should have statistics showing the percentage makeup of the workforce before and after a reduction is undertaken. These data can be used to demonstrate that no statistically significant impact affected a particular protected class of employees. This analysis should be completed before any final decisions are made.

Weighing the Potential Costs

One of the main goals of most reductions in force is to decrease costs, but completing a workforce reduction usually results in a short-term increase. Litigation costs, attorneys' fees, severance pay, unemployment claims, and decreased productivity from remaining employees are likely to result. Analyzing the effects of these issues should be done in advance to determine whether a lay-off would actually achieve the objective of reducing costs.

Determining Contractual Commitments

Employers with collective-bargaining agreements are usually required to perform systematic lay-offs based on some criteria, such as seniority. Naomi Buenaflor, senior vice president of human resources at Young's Market Co., refers to this as "effects bargaining" (Buenaflor, 2002). In this example, union contracts spell out the reduction protocol from the union's negotiations with employees chosen by either seniority or qualifications. Other contract criteria may require that lay-offs first be on a voluntary basis or require a reduction in hours for all employees before reducing the workforce. Ms. Buenaflor warns that "bargaining employees must be evaluated strictly by the terms of the written contract or legal action will most assuredly follow" (Buenaflor, 2002).

Considering Employees with Lengthy Service or on Leave

Employees who have a long service record with a company tend to be very sympathetic litigants and are the most likely employees to file wrongful termination or discrimination lawsuits. Special consideration should be given to these employees because their attachment to an organization is stronger than a newer employee.

Legal counsel should be consulted regarding employees on worker's compensation, disability, family, or medical leave. Including these employees in a reduction should be carefully managed to limit exposure to legal claims.

Considering Legal Statutes/Issues

Worker Adjustment Retraining and Notification Act (WARN) requirements apply to employers with 100 or more employees. In the case of a mass lay-off or plant closing, 60 days notification is required. A mass lay-off is a reduction of at least 33 percent of the employees but not less than 50 total employees at a single site. A plant closing is a shutdown of a single site, or one or more operating units at a site, resulting in a reduction of 50 or more employees. These calculations include the previous 30 to 90 days, so any recent prior reductions need to be included.

The Older Workers Benefit Protection Act (OWBPA) concerns older employees. To obtain a release of claims from an employee more than 40 years of age, special requirements must be met. First, the release must be clearly written and must specifically make mention of the employee's rights under the Age Discrimination in Employment Act (ADEA) that are being waived. Next, the release must be in exchange for something of more value than the employee is already entitled. For example, if two weeks severance is being given to each employee in the reduction, something additional must be given to employees covered under OWBPA. The employer must advise these employees to seek legal counsel before signing the agreement. The release must also allow for a seven-day period in which the employee may revoke the agreement after it is signed. In addition, employees must be given between 21 and 45 days to consider the release agreement.

Employee Retirement Income Security Act (ERISA), Section 510 is another legal challenge that must be considered. It prevents employers from terminating an employee to prevent vesting of benefits offered in the company's plan.

> In 1993, the United States Supreme Court held that an employer does not necessarily violate the ADEA by interfering with an older employee's pension benefits where vesting rights were determined not by age but by the employee's years of service (Erwin, Macaulay and Stuckey, 1999: 6).

Therefore, if vesting is determined by age, older employees may be protected.

Creating a Termination Checklist

A checklist is helpful to managers who are not experienced in undergoing lay-offs. Being in a position to discharge a large number of subordinates can be very difficult for a supervisor. The checklist can also be beneficial to human resources professionals who are handling a large volume of lay-offs. Items on the checklist can include vacation due and owed, Consolidated Omnibus Budget Reconciliation Act (COBRA) information, money due from the employee, equipment the employee has outstanding, and required state pamphlets regarding unemployment.

Developing a Severance Package in Exchange for a Release

Businesses must determine if severance pay will be given. If a company has undergone previous workforce reductions, severance pay from those should be reviewed. If severance pay will be given, the employer should prepare with legal counsel a severance policy that limits it to this particular lay-off. This allows companies to make independent decisions for future reductions. It also limits future employees from receiving severance pay should the company decide it would not be including a severance package. Having departing employees sign a written release in exchange for severance pay dramatically helps to protect the business from future litigation. Items offered in a severance package can include severance pay, company paid COBRA, transitional funds, retraining, outplacement counseling, and unemployment information.

Preparing a Separation Letter

Every employee who is impacted should be given a separation letter. This letter should impart the company's regret that the current conditions make the workforce reduction necessary but should not mention any criteria used in selecting employees. The letter should also inform the employee that his or her final paycheck, severance pay, and accrued vacation are all being paid at that time. A description of all benefits available, including COBRA, should be covered in the separation letter, as well as details regarding stock options and 401k vesting. Also necessary is a statement that no other compensation or benefits will be provided except what is covered in the letter and that the employee has no rights regarding being recalled. Employees should also be reminded of their obligations under any nondisclosure or confidentiality agreements previously made. Finally, any transition assistance programs should be outlined, if available. By including each of these issues in the letter, little ambiguity will arise in the future, and the company can protect itself from as much litigation as possible.

Developing a Script

Instructions are usually helpful to managers involved in laying-off a number of employees. Providing a script may lessen the stress and difficulty for managers who are at a loss for words and can also help shield the company from managers making statements that could later be used in a court of law. It is important that these instructions include suggestions such as not belittling the departing employee or using negative attitudes in termination interviews.

Undertaking a Voluntary Reduction

One method of minimizing the legal exposure and difficult decision-making process is offering employees a voluntary severance package. Early retirement incentive plans are one method of accomplishing this. Employees close to retirement may welcome early retirement, provided they receive some additional severance benefits to which they are not yet entitled. Another method is offering packages for employees to take voluntarily. These packages are more generous than what the employee would otherwise receive if he or she were involuntarily downsized. The reason both of these plans are beneficial to the company is because, since they are voluntary, they greatly reduce any chance of claims being filed. Written releases should be signed in exchange for the severance packages being offered.

Completing Termination Interviews

A company should begin termination meetings by informing the employee of the company's decision and of the decision's finality. Next, the company outlines what the employee can expect to happen over the following week and explains the employee's rights while allowing him or her to respond and let out his or her frustration. The separation letter is discussed with the employee, and any questions the employee may have are answered while protecting the company's interests. By offering laid-off employees as much as possible, the company will benefit from survivors' morale and keeping the company's reputation intact. Because employees may have outbursts when informed of the company's decision, having a third person in the room and ensuring that an exit is nearby are both advisable. If a company suspects that an employee may become violent, it is necessary to notify the police of the situation beforehand. Being terminated can be very embarrassing for an employee, so offering the person an alternative time to pick up his or her belongings when the office is empty is a considerate option. If the terminated employee decides to gather his or her belongings, the employer should give him or her a time limit and escort him or her to gather his or her things and say goodbye to co-workers.

Implementing Survivor Plans

The poorly executed workforce reduction's biggest impact may be on the surviving employees. Seeing friends and co-workers leave is very difficult. If remaining employees feel the company did not treat them well or handled the situation poorly, their future performance and willingness to rise to the occasion may be compromised. A great deal of effort goes into a downsizing, but even more effort needs to be invested in the employees who remain. The goal should be to boost morale despite the loss, minimize damage to trust, aid renewal, and fuel increased productivity. Leadership is critical at this time, and top executives should be visible and open to communication. A company memo from the president with a positive tone is often used to boost morale once the reduction is complete. Carie Bennett, vice president of human resources at Velocitel, Inc., suggests "discouraging the leaders from hiding in their offices in the days following a reduction" (Bennett, 2002).

Managers should meet with survivors individually to demonstrate their value to the company and their contribution to the workplace. Because their trust in the organization may be damaged, it is necessary to reassure remaining employees of their job security and their future with the organization. Common reactions by survivors may include fears related to learning a new job or an increasing workload with more responsibilities, as well as feelings of victimization. Some employees find this exciting, while others find it difficult, and so it is important to recognize this time period as a transitional phase.

Thinking creatively after a workforce reduction is very important for managers. It is important for companies to streamline or eliminate as many non-value-added activities as possible. Ensuring that employees are focused on achieving the company's objectives is the most important corporate goal. Because employees may be feeling depleted, it is important that companies focus on making them feel that they are valued contributors. Career development discussions are invaluable during these times. Discussion of training and resources that remaining staff members need to excel should be encouraged, enabling them to feel confident and capable of great things.

In conclusion, following the recommendations outlined will greatly improve the effectiveness of any organizations' workforce reduction. While individual cases vary, the laws and statues that companies are most concerned about are almost universal. Emotions play an important role and may be the most difficult obstacle for management to overcome in downsizing, but every effort should be made to make terminations as smooth as possible. Using this practical guide to workforce reduction will limit liability and result in meeting the objectives set forth by the reduction.

Kenneth Levitt, Terry Wilson,
and Edna Gilligan

→ **NO**

Corporate Downsizing:
An Examination of the Survivors

Introduction

Corporate downsizing is more than a buzzword in today's business environment. It appears corporations have embraced the strategy of downsizing into their business as a regular practice, evidenced by the daily barrage of layoff announcements in the media. Downsizing is no longer viewed as a last course of action to be considered when a company is "in trouble" or needs to reduce operating expenses; rather, according to the literature, it has become a favored strategy by which a company can improve corporate efficiency and competitiveness (Godkin, St. Pierre, & Valentine, 2002).

While the ultimate effectiveness and benefits downsizing has for a corporation in the short and long term is in debate, there is a definite human impact. Robert Shaw believes "no other single factor has had as dramatic an impact on the erosion of trust in corporate America as the massive downsizings of the past decade" (Guiniven, 2001, p. 53). The most obvious human impact is to the people who have been laid off. According to the literature, these individuals are often known as the "victims of downsizing due to research that document's the devastation of job loss, focusing on negative consequences in terms of psychological and physical well being" (Collins-Nakai, Devine, Reay, & Stainton, 2003, p. 110). But what of those left behind, the survivors?

Until recently the "survivors" of corporate downsizing were considered the lucky ones. Little if any attention had been paid to the survivors, given the general consensus was the survivors would or should be grateful to have kept their jobs. Moreover, corporations believed the survivors would work harder and more efficiently to keep their jobs so as not to become the next casualty. This opinion appears naive in the sense that only positive expectations and impacts of the survivors were considered.

This paper will focus its investigation on the impacts massive corporate downsizing has on those left behind, the survivors. The importance of understanding how corporate downsizing impacts the survivors is essential since these are the very people the company will rely on to move forward. Are survivors really the loyal soldiers grateful to have kept their jobs? Have their attitudes changed? Does downsizing place additional stress on the survivors? By understanding the attitudes, emotions and viewpoints of the survivors, a clear

From *Journal of Global Business Issues*, 2:2, Summer 2008, pp. 13–19. Copyright © 2008 by Journal of Global Business Issues (JGBI). Reprinted by permission.

perspective on the true short and long-term benefits, gains or losses of downsizing for corporations can be derived.

Why Do Corporations Downsize?

The most common reason corporations downsize is to improve profits. Ranganathan and Samant provide the following explanation: "Facing competitive pressures, a slowed down economy and dwindling business performance, many firms downsized their personnel in an attempt to reduce costs and improve profitability" (2003, p. 239). Guiniven offers, corporations downsize for economic reasons (2001). Godkin, Valentine and St. Pierre stated, "Downsizing is widely used to improve corporate efficiency and competitiveness" (2002, p. 57). Lastly, Cummings and Worley believe downsizing is "generally a response to one or more of the following conditions: 1) mergers and acquisitions; 2) loss of revenues and market share through technological and industrial change; 3) the implementation of a new organizational structure; and 4) the belief and social pressures that smaller is better" (2005, p. 290).

Regardless of the reason, a review of the literature indicates there are significant effects not only to "who" are considered to be the "victims" of downsizing, but also to the "survivors", those who remain may in the long run be greater to both the individual survivors and the company.

How Are the Survivors of Downsizing Affected?

Within the past few years a number of articles have been written and studies performed on the "survivors" of downsizing. The literature suggests "downsizing may provide a decrease in operating expenses in the near term, but the long term impacts may not be so positive" (DiFrances, 2002, p. 49). The literature suggests the negative impacts or consequences of downsizing that could hinder the corporations growth are "1) lack of recallable employees; 2) poor morale and lack of trust among younger employees; 3) loss of knowledge and experience base; 4) loss of corporate culture and available mentors for existing and new employees; and 5) loss of established customer service and customer contacts" (Di Frances, 2002, p. 249). Guiniven further indicates downsizing when communicated in economic terms creates serious problems among employees who survive the layoffs. "Disloyalty, disaffection, increased absenteeism, and even acts of sabotage are growing among workers who view downsizing as a social, not economic issue" (Guiniven, 2001, p. 53). Rusaw simply states, "Cutting personnel weakens organizational performance" (2005, p. 482–483).

Why Are Survivors Dissatisfied?

The question becomes, why are the "survivors" of downsizing dissatisfied and distrust their company? Is it poor communication or is there a deeper explanation? How survivors view the company's motivation or reasons behind downsizing efforts can be a key indicator of employee's negative or positive reactions. Cascio and Wynn indicate, "Restructuring, including downsizing, often leads to predictable effects—diminished loyalty from employees" (2004, p. 427). The literature further suggests, "this breach of the unwritten rules that constitute the 'psychological contract' between employer and employee leads to a rise in stress and a decrease in satisfaction, commitment, intentions to stay, and perceptions of an organization's trustworthiness, honesty, and caring about its employees" (Casico & Wynn, 2004, p. 427–428).

Amundson, Borgen, Erlebach and Jordan document, "Of primary importance in understanding the survivors' experience is the changing relationship between the individual and the organization" (2004, p. 257). The literature suggests a condition referred to as "survivor syndrome", or a "set of attitudes, feelings and perceptions that occur in employees who remain in organizational systems following involuntary employee reductions" (Collins-Nakai, Devine, Stainton & Reay, 2003, p. 109–110). Survivor syndrome is defined by some human resource professionals as being the "mixed bag of behaviors and emotions often exhibited by remaining employees following an organizational downsizing" (Appelbaum, Close & Klasa, 1999, p. 424–436). "Consistent with the terminology of a syndrome, this collection of symptoms includes anger, depression, fear, distrust, and guilt"(Collins-Nakai, Devine, Stainton & Reay 2003, p. 110).

While the exact definitions of why survivors of downsizing differ slightly, the general consensus of the literature suggests the survivors of downsizing are not the happy campers, grateful to have their jobs, but rather that surviving is so difficult that continuing employees experience higher levels of stress than displaced employees (Collins-Nakai, Devine, Stainton & Reay, 2003). Kennedy suggests the reasons for such dissatisfaction is increased workloads, adjustment to a new order, self-doubt, loss of faith in management, guilt unsettled organizational politics and loss of respect for the organization (2005).

In a study conducted by Amundson, Borgen, Erlebach and Jordan, survivor's experience increased stress, decreased motivation, reduced performance with extra workload, distrust and withdrawal of managers and/or leaders, and experiencing the emotions of anger, sadness, guilt, insecurity and fear (2004). These feelings or behaviors were viewed as transitional, whereby the participant's view and emotions changed over time. The reactions and feelings were also impacted by how the company communicated and managed the downsizing activities (Amundson, Borgen, Erlebach & Jordan, 2004).

How Do Organizations View Survivors?

Regardless of the definition, downsizing is personal to both survivor and victim. Typically, victims of downsizing are offered support to help them transition. The literature states, "Organizations have underestimated the negative effects of downsizing and do not take into account the difficulties of motivating a surviving workforce emotionally damaged by watching others lose their jobs. Yet, motivating survivors to achieve greater productivity is essential for company success and employee job security" (Applebaum, Close & Klasa, 1999, p. 424–436).

Corporations do not fully understand the "survivor syndrome" theory evidenced by the continued lack of support for the survivors. Corporations do understand the survivors are the people the company will rely on to perform all the work moving forward and make the company profitable; companies understand the survivors must pick up the slack and perform the tasks previously performed by those individuals let go. Yet, there appears to be a disconnect between this understanding and how the company does or should "deal" with survivors. The literature states, "All organizations now say routinely, people are our greatest asset. Yet few practice what they preach, let alone truly believe it. Most still believe, though perhaps not consciously, what nineteenth-century employers believed, people need us more than we need them" (Guinven, 2001, p. 53–55).

DeYoung and Mariable assert, "symptoms of survivor syndrome pose a real threat to performance and productivity with new roles and additional tasks required for each employee as a result of a smaller workforce restructured to perform an increasing number of responsibilities. The consequences are undeniable, when an organization finds itself dealing with a workforce that is willing to assume fewer risks at the expense of productivity" (2005, p. 41).

Impact of Communication

The Amundson, Borgen, Erlebach and Jordan study concluded that in time of downsizing, there is a real need for clear and open communication during all stages of the process, including the top-down vision with the bottom-up input (2004). Kleiner and Simone suggest, corporations need to invest in the employees who remain (2004). "The goal should be to boost moral despite the loss, minimize damage to trust, aid renewal, and fuel increased productivity" (Kleiner & Simone, 2004, p. 20). The literature states, "How the organization communicated with its employees around downsizing was crucial to the success of the transition" (Amundson, Borgen, Erlebach & Jordan, 2004, p. 260). Amundson, Borgen, Erlebach and Jordan go on to state, "Unfortunately, at a time when communication was most needed, existing communication systems were often breaking down. Survivors commented that communication from the organization decreased as downsizing proceeded" (2004, p. 260).

Literature Summation

In reviewing the literature, a number of aspects of downsizing appear clear: 1) experts and corporations alike are just beginning to understand the effects downsizing has on the "survivors"; 2) survivors view downsizing as a breach of trust between employee and employer; 3) this breach of trust and increased or new expectations of the employee by the corporation leads to increased stress, decreased loyalty and negative or hostile feelings toward the company; 4) how the corporation communicates with the employee before, during and after the downsizing effort may lead to negative or positive feelings on behalf of the employee; and 5) the negative aspects of downsizing on the survivors may be transitional, in that the feelings may change over time. It is with this very information in mind that the methods and interview criteria and questions were structured.

Methodology
Research, Setting and Participants

Employees of a large insurance company were the focus of the investigation. The company was selected primarily due to large scale downsizing initiatives experienced during the past two years; approximately 25,000 positions have been eliminated to date and continue today. The company's downsizing and restructuring efforts were undertaken to improve efficiency and streamline operations, deemed necessary to compete in the marketplace.

All participants have been present for the numerous downsizing and restructuring initiatives. Three of the participants are female; the fourth participant is male. The participant's ages ranged from early 30s to early 60s. Job tenure ranged from 5 to 20 years. All four participants have four-year college degrees, hold middle management positions and had previously managed people; however, none of the participants currently have any direct reports. Two of the four participants had personal experience in laying off direct reports in previous job roles within the company.

The participants agreed to be interviewed with the understanding that all information provided would be kept confidential. The interviews took place within one year of the last large-scale downsizing effort. However, it should be noted that small-scale downsizing continues. All four participants were part of re-organization efforts within their respective divisions within the past 6 months.

Designing the Interview Question and Data Collection

The interview questions were developed and formulated based upon research to gain an understanding of the participant's feelings, impressions, perceived stress levels and commitment before, during and, after the large-scale downsizing initiatives. The participants were asked a standard set of 26 questions, 10 questions were based on the participant's feelings, stress and trust levels, how they felt about the company and opportunities available to them prior to the advent of the downsizing initiatives. Four questions were based on the participants' feelings and impressions of the corporation's communication style and the substance of the communications relating to the downsizing efforts over time. The remaining 12 questions were based on the participant's feelings, stress and trust levels, how they feel about the company, the opportunities available to them, and any effects the downsizing experience has had on them personally, since the downsizing began. Additional probing questions were asked when additional elaboration was deemed appropriate....

The interviewer documented the participant's response to each question. Additional notes were made to capture the participant's non-verbal response (face to face interviews only). Overall demeanor and any variation in tone or mood were captured in all of the interviews. The interviewer allowed the participants to verbalize until they had completed their response, at no point were the participants interrupted. Clarifying questions were asked at the discretion of the interviewer.

The interview questions were formulated to gather information and gain understanding of the survivor's feelings, impressions of the company, their perceived value to the company, and overall view of the company before and after the downsizing occurred. The thrust of the interviews were to gather information in an attempt to validate a number of hypotheses formulated as a result of the research conducted for this paper: 1) large-scale corporate downsizing is viewed as a breach of trust by the survivors, diminishing loyalty and commitment and creating negative feelings toward the company; 2) survivors experience an increase in stress levels after downsizing and restructuring then they had previously; 3) how the company communicates and what a company communicates to employees (a.k.a., the survivors) can negatively or positively impact how employees view the company and the employee's performance levels; 4) the negative aspects of downsizing on the survivors may be transitional, in that feelings may change over time.

Results

Large-Scale Downsizing Is Viewed as a Breach of Trust

The results of the interview questions relating to the participant's general feeling about and toward the company, and their loyalty and devotion to the company prior to downsizing were consistent with expectation. Participants reported positive feelings toward the company, indicating that while the company was large and successful, there was a good atmosphere and a real sense of team. All participants felt comfortable in their roles and believed they could advance and grow within the company. All participants reported high levels of trust and devotion to the company, indicating they would 'do what ever was necessary to get the job done'. Participants commonly cited the long work hours experienced during this period of time, yet they felt a vested interest in the business outcome and were willing to sacrifice time with their families in order to achieve company goals.

The interview results relating to the participants' feelings about and toward the company, their loyalty and devotion to the company today, post-downsizing was also consistent with expectation. Participants reported neutral to negative feelings toward the company indicating the atmosphere is one of apathy, fear, distrust and anger. These characteristics are consistent with what had been defined as "survivor syndrome" earlier in the paper (Collin-Nakai, Devine, Stainton & Reay, 2003).

All participants reported extremely low levels of trust and absolutely no devotion to the company. Participants indicated, they no longer strive to achieve, feel little to no desire to come to work and are "only here to collect a paycheck". None of the participants felt they had a vested interest in the outcome of the business decisions and were no longer willing to sacrifice time with their families in order to achieve company goals. Additionally, all participants reported they now worked a standard 40-hour workweek; seldom working overtime even though they believe it is needed.

Survivors Experience Increased Stress Levels After Downsizing

In response to the prior to downsizing questions, participants indicated stress levels in the medium to high range. Participants felt stress relative to the workloads and senior managements desire for only good news. While stress levels appear to be relatively high during this period of time, the stress was predominately isolated to the work at hand and did not extend beyond the workloads to any other facet of the participants working or personal relationships. In fact, most reported strong bonds with coworkers, subordinates and managers during this time period.

Participants reported similar stress levels post-downsizing as prior to downsizing, in the medium to high range. However, the type of stress felt was no longer isolated to the workloads. Participants reported being stressed about the ever-looming possibility of losing their jobs. While none of the participants had any indication of any immediate plans to eliminate their current positions, all believed they could be eliminated at any moment. Participants indicated they felt stress relative to the constant organizational changes, participants reported having between three and five managers within the last two years. The managerial changes were all in relation to changes in the organizational structure.

Participants felt stress in working relationships; there was a feeling of less overall ownership, and that people looked out only for themselves. The combination of these stress factors appears to have spilled over into the participant's personal relationships, causing friction and additional stress. One participant reported she is currently under a doctor's care and is taking medication to control her anxiety and stress. The literature states "Failure to acknowledge the mental strain employees experienced during downsizing and failure to support employee mental health were described as damaging by survivors" (Amundson, Borgen, Erlebach & Jordan, 2004, p. 261). The participants from the insurance company reported little to no support from the company, further supporting the research.

Survivors' Feelings Were Transitional

In response to the prior to downsizing questions, participants expressed a relatively high level of trust in and devotion to the company. The sense that direct managers and senior managers cared about the welfare of the employees was strongly portrayed. One participant cited the company provided employees with free massages, nap rooms, formal mentoring and career advancement programs and other on-site services to assist employees, thus demonstrating concern for employee well-being. Hard work and devotion to the company was both expected and rewarded. Participants believed as long as they did their job, there would be a place for them in the company. Commitment to the company was extremely high as was the sense of future career opportunities. All participants indicated they felt they would remain with the company for the balance of their careers.

The responses to the post-downsizing questions relative to the participants' feelings about the company provide further evidence that once the psychological contract is broken; it often leads to diminished loyalty from employees (Cascio & Wynn, 2004). However, interestingly enough the low levels of trust and zero level of devotion in the company reported by the participants appears to have occurred over time. The participants reported these feelings evolved over time, as a result of the ongoing downsizing and restructuring and what is perceived to be random and arbitrary staff reductions.

The participants believed early in the process that only low performers were let go, however, they believe performance is no longer the criteria. Participants now believe hard work and devotion to the company is no longer rewarded. The results of a study conducted in 2001 indicated "Employees learned that performers were as much at risk for job loss as non-performers. This resulted in reduced commitment to the organization and heighten commitment to one's own self-interest" (Guiniven, 2001, p. 53–72).

Participants expressed a general sense of apathy in relation to their jobs and had a distant relationship with their immediate managers. They also expressed anger that they no longer felt driven to succeed. This anger was predominately directed toward senior management, indicating they had no goal, no vision, believed they are only in it for the money and cared nothing for the employees of the company. The participants blamed senior management for their feelings of distrust and lack of devotion to the company in general. These reactions are consistent with the results of other studies, the literature states "Few top executives can even imagine the hatred, contempt and fury that has been created. . . . There will be retribution" (Guiniven, 2001, p. 59–60). Commitment to the company is extremely low; there is a sense of little to no career opportunities. This feeling is supported by the literature, "Downsizing has not only reduced the possibility of continuously learning and developing on the job, but it has also lowered expectations for a long-term career" (Rusaw, 2005, p. 485). All the participants indicated they did not expect to remain with the company for longer than three years.

How and What Is Communicated Matters

Participants believed early communication from the company was open and honest relative to downsizing. The communication provided information on which offices were targeted to be closed, and which departments were at risk. The participants believed early communication provided people with a sense of who may or may not be affected. The communication clearly provided valid business reasons for the downsizing efforts, which all participants supported and agreed, were necessary for the long-term success of the company. The responses are consistent with the research in that how an organization communicates with its employees around downsizing is crucial to the success of the transition (Amundson, Borgen, Erlebach, & Jordan, 2004).

Participants indicated the company's communication style has changed dramatically during the past year to year and a half. All indicated the company now provides little to no communication and when information is forthcoming it is carefully crafted. This lack of communication has led participants to further distrust the company and supports for them the feeling the company does not care about its employees. Again this was consistent with the results of a 2004 study indicating, "Confidence in the organization was hampered by vague communication or lack of communication. Organizations attempts to 'soft-pedal' their downsizing plans only increased anxiety" (Amundson, Borgen, Erlebach & Jordan, 2004, p. 260). Lastly, the participants indicated the lack of communication has created an ever-increasing gossip network, which can and does consume a fair amount of their time.

Discussion

Large-Scale Corporate Downsizing Diminishes Loyalty and Commitment

The results of the interviews and review of the literature provide support for the first hypothesis that large-scale corporate downsizing diminishes loyalty and commitment of the survivors to the company. The participants had expressed high levels of loyalty and commitment to the company prior to downsizing activities. Loyalty and commitment levels remained intact, at least initially. The participants indicated they felt they understood the reasons for downsizing and were supportive of the company's decision. However, these feelings changed dramatically over time, as all the participants reported no loyalty or commitment to the company today. The feelings of diminished loyalty and commitment, anger, fear and distrust are consistent with the literature's description of 'survivors syndrome' discussed in the literature review (Collins-Nikai, Devine, Stainton & Reay, 2003).

Survivors may be pleased to not have lost their job, however they are not grateful soldiers willing to work harder in gratitude. The converse appears to be true—survivors no longer feel obligated to perform above and beyond the call of duty, and no longer do so. The literature states, "this breach of the unwritten rules that constitute the 'psychological contract' between employer and employee leads to a rise in stress and a decrease in satisfaction, commitment, intentions to stay, and perceptions of an organizations trustworthiness, honesty, and caring about its employees" (Casico & Wynn, 2004, p. 427–428). The results from the interviews with the insurance company employees are consistent with the literature.

Survivors Experience Increased Stress Levels

Support for the second hypothesis, survivor's experience an increase in stress levels after downsizing and restructuring than they had previously, appears valid. While the stress levels reported by the participants were similar to prior stress levels, the type of stress currently felt by the participants is much wider in scope. Previous stress levels were reported to be relatively isolated to workloads; in contrast, current stress levels are reported in nearly all aspects of the participants' work and home life. These results are consistent with the research. The literature indicates, "in layoff situations, both victims and survivors lose control over their employment status, which either creates or exacerbates a potential stressor" (Collins-Nakai, Devine, Stainton & Reay, 2003, p. 111).

Communication Is Key

The interviews and research supports the third hypothesis, how the company communicates and what a company communicates to employees (a.k.a., the survivors) can negatively or positively impact how employees view the company and the employee's performance levels. The participants believed initially communication was open and honest, and as a result they remained committed. Participants believed they understood the business reasons for the downsizing efforts and supported the decisions. The literature supports this notion indicating employees need to know the "bigger picture" and the specifics of downsizing plans if they are going to pay a role in creating the new organization (Amundson, Borgen, Erlebach & Jordan, 2004). The participants stated that as the downsizing continued over time, communication slowed and participants began to feel a disconnect with the company and became distrustful. The literature indicates that confidence in organizations is indeed hampered by vague communication or lack of communication; that failure to communicate creates the impression that senior managers do not want to communicate or simply do not respect employees (Amundson, Borgen, Eriebach & Jordan, 2004).

The survivors of downsizing lose their spark and enthusiasm over time, this is especially true when the organization limits open communication and continues downsizing for extended periods of time. Amundson, Borgen, Erlebach and Jordan state, "Unfortunately, at a time when communication was most needed, existing communication systems were often breaking down. Survivors commented that communication from the organization decreased as downsizing proceeded" (2004, p. 260). This notion certainly rings true with the Health Care employees interviewed.

Survivors' Feelings Were Transitional

There is support for the fourth hypothesis; aspects of downsizing on the survivors may be transitional, in that feelings may change over time. The participants clearly provided evidence of transitional changes in their feelings over time; however, these changes or transitions were predominately positive to negative. Participants reported positive feelings initially that changed or transitioned to negative feelings. These negative feelings toward the company continued to grow over time. The expectation that feelings would transition over time led to the assumption these would result in both positive and negative feelings. This was not the case; the participants clearly transitioned in a linier fashion from one end of the spectrum (positive feelings) to the other end (negative feelings).

Closing Statement

Downsizing is often unsuccessful in achieving the goals sought by organizations. Recent empirical evidence has shown, as do the results of the interviews conducted for this paper, that downsizing as a means to improve organizational efficiency and solve long-term problems does not always prove adequate (Applebaum, Close & Klasa, 1999). While the company has achieved fewer numbers (of staff), it has lost something greater—dedicated and devoted employees. The survivors no longer feel a sense of team or purpose, put forth limited effort, operate at high stress levels, feel little job satisfaction, distrust the company and feel no devotion. In essence, the company has lost its heart and soul and the survivors continue to do just that, survive.

POSTSCRIPT

Is Downsizing a Sound Strategic Initiative?

Predicting the future is always a difficult thing to do. A little more than two years ago, the economy was humming along nicely, the housing market showed no signs of slowing, and the Dow was continuing its trend of setting new daily highs. Who, then, would have imagined our country would be in the economic mess it's in now? The point is that the future is uncertain. Nevertheless, when it comes to business, there is one thing that seems a sure bet: Global competition is here to stay and is likely to become even more intense in the foreseeable future. As a result, we can expect US firms will continue to be exposed to intense competitive pressures from both domestic and international businesses. As a means of reacting to these pressures, we also expect downsizing to remain a popular strategic initiative for reducing labor costs and increasing organizational efficiency.

Beyond the excellent points made in the article by the scholars at East Stroudsburg University, there are at least two additional considerations managers would be wise to acknowledge when deciding whether to downsize or not. First, it has the potential to impede innovation within the firm. Innovation is typically the result of contributions from many employees who are, frequently, spread across different departments and functions of the organization. Often, innovation "travels" along the linkages established by these workers. Downsizing has the very real possibility of interfering with these creative linkages, either directly through the elimination of jobs, or indirectly by the negative psychological impact survivors experience in the aftermath of the downsizing.

Another negative outcome of downsizing is the effect it has on an organization's reputation. Scholars have long appreciated the importance of corporate reputation; thus, actions that have the potential to reflect negatively on the firm need to be examined very carefully. Firms that have a reputation for being quick to downsize, for example, are likely to be viewed less favorably in the labor market (not to mention the stock market!) than are firms that are perceived as being more pro-employee. This is important because it not only reduces the labor market pool for the downsizing firm but also results in having to pay a premium (relative to firms without a negative downsizing reputation) for quality employees.

Although it is clear that downsizing will remain popular for the foreseeable future, whether it is a wise strategy is considerably less clear. Now that you have read both sides of the debate, what do you think?

Suggested Readings

E. Geoffrey Love & Matthew Kraatz, "Character, Conformity, or the Bottom Line? How and Why Downsizing Affected Corporate Reputation," *Academy of Management Journal* (vol. 52, no. 2: 314–335, 2009).

Don Minnick, "Why Downsizing Is a Good Thing," The Business Maker Radio Show (April 24, 2009). http://www.thebusinessmakers.com/special-features/don-minnick/why-downsizing-is-a-good-thing.html

Jeffrey Baumgartner, "Downsizing Workforce Downsizes Innovation," Jbp.com (2009). http://www.jpb.com/creative/downsizing_dangers.php

Shiv Dhawan, "Corporations Can Survive Bad Times Without Downsizing," Jansamachar.net (February 26, 2009). http://www.jansamachar.net/display.php3?id=&num=26375&lang=English

Hugh Aaron, "Downsizing for a Profit in a Recession," BusinessWisdom.blogspot.com (February 19, 2009). http://businesswisdom.blogspot.com/2009/02/downsizing-for-profit-in-recession.html

W. J. Baumol, A. S. Blinder, & E. N. Wolff, "Downsizing in America: Reality, Causes, and Consequences," (Sage Publishing, 2003)

ISSUE 11

Is Outsourcing a Wise Corporate Strategy?

YES: *BusinessWeek,* from "The Future of Outsourcing," *Business-Week* Special Report: Outsourcing (January 30, 2006), http://www .businessweek.com/magazine/content/06_05/b3969401.htm

NO: Ephraim Schwartz, from "Painful Lessons from IT Outsourcing Gone Bad," InfoWorld.com (August 25, 2008), http://www.infoworld .com/d/adventures-in-it/painful-lessons-it-outsourcing-gone-bad-032

ISSUE SUMMARY

YES: *BusinessWeek* writers argue that outsourcing is likely to become even more important to corporate America in the near future. Indeed, they suggest that it has the potential to transform whole industries.

NO: *InfoWorld* columnist Ephraim Schwartz explores the often-overlooked costs associated with failed outsourcing initiatives. His analysis consists of four brief case studies of outsourcing initiatives that turned out badly.

Based on the past two presidential elections, it would appear that one of the most contentious issues in American society is the outsourcing question. In 2004, the Democratic nominee, John Kerry, repeatedly expressed his disdain for US firms that "sent jobs overseas" and promised, if elected, to punish those businesses that engaged in outsourcing. In 2008, while on the campaign trail, then-Democratic presidential nominee Barack Obama said, "Unlike John McCain, I will stop giving tax breaks to corporations that ship jobs overseas, and I will start giving them to companies that create good jobs right here in America." (Dan T. Griswold, "Shipping Jobs Overseas or Reaching New Customers? Why Congress Should Not Tax Reinvested Earnings Abroad," *Center for Trade Policy Studies,* Free Trade Bulletin, January 13, 2009; http://www.freetrade.org/node/926). And speaking in front of a joint session of Congress on February 24, 2009, President Obama made this statement: "We will restore a sense of fairness and balance to our tax code by finally ending the tax breaks for corporations that ship our jobs overseas." (Daniel Ikenson, "The Outsourcing Canard," Cato at Liberty.org, February 25, 2009; http://www.cato-at-liberty.org/2009/02/25/the-outsourcing-canard/).

Part of the reason this topic is so controversial is because it overlaps with several other contentious issues. Some critics claim that outsourcing encourages the development of sweatshops in Third World countries (see Issue 2 in this text). On the other hand, supporters often claim that increased competition from globalization virtually requires outsourcing as a business strategy (see Issue 17). And depending on which side of the protectionism issue is being considered, outsourcing is presented as either pro- or anti-American (see Issue 18). Given the antagonism toward outsourcing that exists in the minds of many, one might reasonably question whether outsourcing is a wise course of action for a firm to follow.

Proponents of outsourcing have strong points on their side of the issue. The call to end outsourcing is, in their view, merely protectionism in disguise, a concept entirely at odds with traditional American political and economic principles. American capitalism and prosperity were built on free trade; forcing American firms to forego cheap overseas labor in the name of patriotism will ultimately cause US firms, and society, to suffer. In terms of the exploitation of foreign labor argument, supporters respond that it is not exploitation at all. According to Edwin Locke, Dean's Professor of Leadership and Motivation at the University of Maryland and a contributing author to the Ayn Rand Institute, an influential think tank:

> . . . the claim that multinational companies [e.g., American firms] exploit workers in poor countries by paying lower wages than they would pay in their home countries. Well, what is the alternative? It is: no wages! The comparative advantage of poorer countries is precisely that their wages are low, thus reducing the costs of production. If multinational corporations had to pay the same wages as in their home countries, they would not bother to invest in poorer countries at all and millions of people would lose their livelihoods.

Supporters also point out that the United States has the second highest corporate tax rate in the world, thus incentivizing firms to both make investments and move operations overseas.

On the other hand, those who argue that outsourcing is bad business generally rely on several lines of attack. The first and most obvious argument is that outsourcing moves jobs out of America and into foreign countries. And make no mistake, this is no small trend: Millions of jobs have left American shores in recent years, and many millions more are vulnerable. Critics also point to the growth of outsourcing in the service sector as an alarming trend. The historical justification for outsourcing was built on the belief that jobs lost in manufacturing would be replaced by jobs in the service sector as the United States shifted from an industrial- to a service-based economy. Because the current outsourcing wave is primarily service based, the concern is that outsourcing will accelerate further as we continue to move toward a service-oriented society. Finally, consistent with our comments earlier about the sweatshop issue, many charge that outsourcing is nothing more than American firms exploiting cheaper labor in other countries to increase profits.

In the selections that follow, you will be exposed to both sides of this interesting topic. In the first article, *BusinessWeek* writers argue that outsourcing is likely to become even more important to corporate America in the near future. In the "no" article, *InfoWorld* columnist Ephraim explores the often-overlooked costs associated with failed outsourcing initiatives by analyzing four brief case studies of outsourcing initiatives that turned out badly.

YES ⤶

The Future of Outsourcing: How It's Transforming Whole Industries and Changing the Way We Work

Globalization has been brutal to midwestern manufacturers like the Paper Converting Machine Co. For decades, PCMC's Green Bay (Wis.) factory, its oiled wooden factory floors worn smooth by work boots, thrived by making ever-more-complex equipment to weave, fold, and print packaging for everything from potato chips to baby wipes.

But PCMC has fallen on hard times. First came the 2001 recession. Then, two years ago, one of the company's biggest customers told it to slash its machinery prices by 40% and urged it to move production to China. Last year, a St. Louis holding company, Barry-Wehmiller Cos., acquired the manufacturer and promptly cut workers and nonunion pay. In five years sales have plunged by 40%, to $170 million, and the workforce has shrunk from 2,000 to 1,100. Employees have been traumatized, says operations manager Craig Compton, a muscular former hockey player. "All you hear about is China and all these companies closing or taking their operations overseas."

But now, Compton says, he is "probably the most optimistic I've been in five years." Hope is coming from an unusual source. As part of its turnaround strategy, Barry-Wehmiller plans to shift some design work to its 160-engineer center in Chennai, India. By having U.S. and Indian designers collaborate 24/7, explains Vasant Bennett, president of Barry-Wehmiller's engineering services unit, PCMC hopes to slash development costs and time, win orders it often missed due to engineering constraints—and keep production in Green Bay. Barry-Wehmiller says the strategy already has boosted profits at some of the 32 other midsize U.S. machinery makers it has bought. "We can compete and create great American jobs," vows CEO Robert Chapman. "But not without offshoring."

Come again? Ever since the offshore shift of skilled work sparked widespread debate and a political firestorm three years ago, it has been portrayed as the killer of good-paying American jobs. "Benedict Arnold CEOs" hire software engineers, computer help staff, and credit-card bill collectors to exploit the low wages of poor nations. U.S. workers suddenly face a grave new threat, with even highly educated tech and service professionals having to compete against

From *BusinessWeek*, January 30, 2006, pp. 50, 55–58. Copyright © 2006 by BusinessWeek. Reprinted by permission of the McGraw-Hill Companies.

legions of hungry college grads in India, China, and the Philippines willing to work twice as hard for one-fifth the pay.

Workers' fears have some grounding in fact. The prime motive of most corporate bean counters jumping on the offshoring bandwagon has been to take advantage of such "labor arbitrage"—the huge wage gap between industrialized and developing nations. And without doubt, big layoffs often accompany big outsourcing deals.

The changes can be harsh and deep. But a more enlightened, strategic view of global sourcing is starting to emerge as managers get a better fix on its potential. The new buzzword is "transformational outsourcing." Many executives are discovering offshoring is really about corporate growth, making better use of skilled U.S. staff, and even job creation in the U.S., not just cheap wages abroad. True, the labor savings from global sourcing can still be substantial. But it's peanuts compared to the enormous gains in efficiency, productivity, quality, and revenues that can be achieved by fully leveraging offshore talent.

Thus entrepreneurs such as Chapman see a chance to turn around dying businesses, speed up their pace of innovation, or fund development projects that otherwise would have been unaffordable. More aggressive outsourcers are aiming to create radical business models that can give them an edge and change the game in their industries. Old-line multinationals see offshoring as a catalyst for a broader plan to overhaul outdated office operations and prepare for new competitive battles. And while some want to downsize, others are keen to liberate expensive analysts, engineers, and salesmen from routine tasks so they can spend more time innovating and dealing with customers. "This isn't about labor cost," says Daniel Marovitz, technology managing director for Deutsche Bank's global businesses (DB). "The issue is that if you don't do it, you won't survive."

The new attitude is emerging in corporations across the U.S. and Europe in virtually every industry. Ask executives at Penske Truck Leasing why the company outsources dozens of business processes to Mexico and India, and they cite greater efficiency and customer service. Ask managers at U.S.-Dutch professional publishing giant Wolters Kluwer (**WTKWY**) why they're racing to shift software development and editorial work to India and the Philippines, and they will say it's about being able to pump out a greater variety of books, journals, and Web-based content more rapidly. Ask Wachovia Corp. (**WB**), the Charlotte (N.C.)-based bank, why it just inked a $1.1 billion deal with India's Genpact to outsource finance and accounting jobs and why it handed over administration of its human-resources programs to Lincolnshire (Ill.)-based Hewitt Associates (**HEW**). It's "what we need to do to become a great customer-relationship company," says Director of Corporate Development Peter J. Sidebottom. Wachovia aims to reinvest up to 40% of the $600 million to $1 billion it hopes to take out in costs over three years into branches, ATMs, and personnel to boost its core business.

Here's what such transformations typically entail: Genpact, Accenture (**ACN**), IBM Services, or another big outsourcing specialist dispatches teams to meticulously dissect the workflow of an entire human resources, finance, or info tech department. The team then helps build a new IT platform, redesigns all processes, and administers programs, acting as a virtual subsidiary. The contractor then disperses work among global networks of staff ranging from the U.S. to Asia to Eastern Europe.

In recent years, Procter & Gamble (**PG**), DuPont (**DD**), Cisco Systems (**CSCO**), ABN Amro (**ABN**), Unilever, Rockwell Collins (**COL**), and Marriott (**MAR**) were among those that signed such megadeals, worth billions.

In 2004, for example, drugmaker Wyeth Pharmaceuticals transferred its entire clinical-testing operation to Accenture Ltd. "Boards of directors of virtually every big company now are insisting on very articulated outsourcing strategies," says Peter Allen, global services managing director of TPI, a consulting firm that advised on 15 major outsourcing contracts last year worth $14 billion. "Many CEOs are saying, 'Don't tell me how much I can save. Show me how we can grow by 40% without increasing our capacity in the U.S.,'" says Atul Vashistha, CEO of outsourcing consultant neoIT and co-author of the book *The Offshore Nation.*

Some observers even believe Big Business is on the cusp of a new burst of productivity growth, ignited in part by offshore outsourcing as a catalyst. "Once this transformation is done," predicts Arthur H. Harper, former CEO of General Electric Co.'s equipment management businesses, "I think we will end up with companies that deliver products faster at lower costs, and are better able to compete against anyone in the world." As executives shed more operations, they also are spurring new debate about how the future corporation will look. Some management pundits theorize about the "totally disaggregated corporation," wherein every function not regarded as crucial is stripped away.

Processes, Now on Sale

In theory, it is becoming possible to buy, off the shelf, practically any function you need to run a company. Want to start a budget airline but don't want to invest in a huge back office? Accenture's Navitaire unit can manage reservations, plan routes, assign crew, and calculate optimal prices for each seat.

Have a cool new telecom or medical device but lack market researchers? For about $5,000, analytics outfits such as New Delhi-based Evalueserve Inc. will, within a day, assemble a team of Indian patent attorneys, engineers, and business analysts, start mining global databases, and call dozens of U.S. experts and wholesalers to provide an independent appraisal.

Want to market quickly a new mutual fund or insurance policy? IT services providers such as India's Tata Consultancy Services Ltd. are building software platforms that furnish every business process needed and secure all regulatory approvals. A sister company, Tata Technologies, boasts 2,000 Indian engineers and recently bought 700-employee Novi (Mich.) auto- and aerospace-engineering firm Incat International PLC. Tata Technologies can now handle everything from turning a conceptual design into detailed specs for interiors, chassis, and electrical systems to designing the tooling and factory-floor layout. "If you map out the entire vehicle-development process, we have the capability to supply every piece of it," says Chief Operating Officer Jeffrey D. Sage, an IBM and General Motors Corp. (**GM**) veteran. Tata is designing all doors for a future truck, for example, and the power train for a U.S. sedan. The company is hiring 100 experienced U.S. engineers at salaries of $100,000 and up.

Few big companies have tried all these options yet. But some, like Procter & Gamble, are showing that the ideas are not far-fetched. Over the past three years the $57 billion consumer-products company has outsourced everything from IT infrastructure and human resources to management of its offices from Cincinnati to Moscow. CEO Alan G. Lafley also has announced he wants half of all new P&G products to come from outside by 2010, vs. 20% now. In the near future, some analysts predict, Detroit and European carmakers will go the way of the PC industry, relying on outsiders to develop new models bearing their brand names. BMW has done just that with a sport-utility vehicle. And Big Pharma will bring blockbuster drugs to market at a fraction of the current $1 billion average cost by allying with partners in India, China, and Russia in molecular research and clinical testing.

Of course, corporations have been outsourcing management of IT systems to the likes of Electronic Data Systems (**EDS**), IBM (**IBM**), and Accenture for more than a decade, while Detroit has long given engineering jobs to outside design firms. Futurists have envisioned "hollow" and "virtual" corporations since the 1980s.

It hasn't happened yet. Reengineering a company may make sense on paper, but it's extremely expensive and entails big risks if executed poorly. Corporations can't simply be snapped apart and reconfigured like LEGO sets, after all. They are complex, living organisms that can be thrown into convulsions if a transplant operation is botched. Valued employees send out their résumés, customers are outraged at deteriorating service, a brand name can be damaged. In consultant surveys, what's more, many U.S. managers complain about the quality of offshored work and unexpected costs.

But as companies work out such kinks, the rise of the offshore option is dramatically changing the economics of reengineering. With millions of low-cost engineers, financial analysts, consumer marketers, and architects now readily available via the Web, CEOs can see a quicker payoff. "It used to be that companies struggled for a few years to show a 5% or 10% increase in productivity from outsourcing," says Pramod Bhasin, CEO of Genpact, the 19,000-employee back-office-processing unit spun off by GE last year. "But by offshoring work, they can see savings of 30% to 40% in the first year" in labor costs. Then the efficiency gains kick in. A $10 billion company might initially only shave a few million dollars in wages after transferring back-office procurement or bill collection overseas. But better management of these processes could free up hundreds of millions in cash flow annually.

Those savings, in turn, help underwrite far broader corporate restructuring that can be truly transformational. DuPont has long wanted to fix its unwieldy system for administering records, payroll, and benefits for its 60,000 employees in 70 nations, with data scattered among different software platforms and global business units. By awarding a long-term contract to Cincinnati-based Convergys Corp., the world's biggest call-center operator, to redesign and administer its human resources programs, it expects to cut costs 20% in the first year and 30% a year afterward. To get corporate backing for the move, "it certainly helps a lot to have savings from the outset," says DuPont Senior Human Resources Vice-President James C. Borel.

Creative new companies can exploit the possibilities of offshoring even faster than established players. Crimson Consulting Group is a good example. The Los Altos (Calif.) firm, which performs global market research on everything from routers to software for clients including Cisco, HP, and Microsoft (**MSFT**), has only 14 full-time employees. But it farms out research to India's Evalueserve and some 5,000 other independent experts from Silicon Valley to China, the Czech Republic, and South Africa. "This allows a small firm like us to compete with McKinsey and Bain on a very global basis with very low costs," says CEO Glenn Gow. Former GE exec Harper is on the same wavelength. Like Barry-Wehmiller, his new five-partner private-equity firm plans to buy struggling midsize manufacturers and use offshore outsourcing to help revitalize them. Harper's NexGen Capital Partners also plans to farm out most of its own office work. "The people who understand this will start from Day One and never build a back room," Harper says. "They will outsource everything they can."

Some aggressive outsourcers are using their low-cost, superefficient business models to challenge incumbents. Pasadena, (Calif.)-based IndyMac Bancorp Inc. (NDE), founded in 1985, illustrates the new breed of financial services company. In three years, IndyMac has risen from 22nd-largest U.S. mortgage issuer to No. 9, while its 18% return on equity in 2004 outpaced most rivals. The thrift's initial edge was its technology to process, price, and approve loan applications in less than a minute.

But IndyMac also credits its aggressive offshore outsourcing strategy, which Consumer Banking CEO Ashwin Adarkar says has helped make it "more productive, cost-efficient, and flexible than our competitors, with better customer service." IndyMac is using 250 mostly Indian staff from New York-based Cognizant Technology Solutions Corp. (**CTSH**) to help build a next-generation software platform and applications that, it expects, will boost efficiency at least 20% by 2008. IndyMac has also begun shifting tasks, ranging from bill collection to "welcome calls" that help U.S. borrowers make their first mortgage payments on time, to India's Exlservice Holdings Inc. and its 5,000-strong staff. In all, Exlservice and other Indian providers handle 33 back-office processes offshore. Yet rather than losing any American jobs, IndyMac has doubled its U.S. workforce to nearly 6,000 in four years—and is still hiring.

Superior Service

Smart use of offshoring can juice the performance of established players, too. Five years ago, Penske Truck Leasing, a joint venture between GE and Penske Corp., paid $768 million for trucker Rollins Truck Leasing Corp.—just in time for the recession. Customer service, spread among four U.S. call centers, was inconsistent. "I realized our business needed a transformation," says CFO Frank Cocuzza. He began by shifting a few dozen data-processing jobs to GE's huge Mexican and Indian call centers, now called Genpact. He then hired Genpact to help restructure most of his back office. That relationship now spans 30 processes involved in leasing 216,000 trucks and providing logistical services for customers.

Now, if a Penske truck is held up at a weigh station because it lacks a certain permit, for example, the driver calls an 800 number. Genpact staff in India obtains the document over the Web. The weigh station is notified electronically, and the truck is back on the road within 30 minutes. Before, Penske thought it did well if it accomplished that in two hours. And when a driver finishes his job, his entire log, including records of mileage, tolls, and fuel purchases, is shipped to Mexico, punched into computers, and processed in Hyderabad. In all, 60% of the 1,000 workers handling Penske back-office process are in India or Mexico, and Penske is still ramping up. Under a new program, when a manufacturer asks Penske to arrange for a delivery to a buyer, Indian staff helps with the scheduling, billing, and invoices. The $15 million in direct labor-cost savings are small compared with the gains in efficiency and customer service, Cocuzza says.

Big Pharma is pursuing huge boosts in efficiency as well. Eli Lilly & Co.'s (**LLY**) labs are more productive than most, having released eight major drugs in the past five years. But for each new drug, Lilly estimates it invests a hefty $1.1 billion. That could reach $1.5 billion in four years. "Those kinds of costs are fundamentally unsustainable," says Steven M. Paul, Lilly's science and tech executive vice-president. Outsourcing figures heavily in Lilly's strategy to lower that cost to $800 million. The drugmaker now does 20% of its chemistry work in China for one-quarter the U.S. cost and helped fund a startup lab, Shanghai's Chem-Explorer Co., with 230 chemists. Lilly now is trying to slash the costs of clinical trials on human patients, which range from $50 million to $300 million per drug, and is expanding such efforts in Brazil, Russia, China, and India.

Other manufacturers and tech companies are learning to capitalize on global talent pools to rush products to market sooner at lower costs. OnStor Inc., a Los Gatos (Calif.) developer of storage systems, says its tie-up with Bangalore engineering-services outfit HCL Technologies Ltd. enables it to get customized products to clients twice as fast as its major rivals. "If we want to recruit a great engineer in Silicon Valley, our lead time is three months," says CEO Bob Miller. "With HCL, we can pick up the phone and get somebody in two or three days."

Such strategies offer a glimpse into the productive uses of global outsourcing. But most experts remain cautious. The McKinsey Global Institute estimates $18.4 billion in global IT work and $11.4 billion in business-process services have been shifted abroad so far—just one-tenth of the potential offshore market. One reason is that executives still have a lot to learn about using offshore talent to boost productivity. Professor Mohanbir Sawhney of Northwestern University's Kellogg School of Management, a self-proclaimed "big believer in total disaggregation," says: "One of our tasks in business schools is to train people to manage the virtual, globally distributed corporation. How do you manage employees you can't even see?"

The management challenges will grow more urgent as rising global salaries dissipate the easy cost gains from offshore outsourcing. The winning companies of the future will be those most adept at leveraging global talent to transform themselves and their industries, creating better jobs for everyone.

Ephraim Schwartz

→ **NO**

Painful Lessons from IT Outsourcing Gone Bad

As companies look to economize in a weak economy worsened by rising energy costs, it may be more tempting than ever to consider outsourcing your IT—whether to a cloud-based provider, to a shop in your town, or to a provider in some far-off land. Certainly, outsourcing has worked well for many companies, but it can also lead to business-damaging nightmares, says Larry Harding, founder and president of High Street Partners, a global consultancy that advises company on how to expand overseas. After all, if outsourcers fail, you're left holding the bag without the resources to fix the problem.

In his consulting, Harding has seen many outsourcing horror stories, from corrupt general managers "with all sorts of conflicts of interest" (such as service providers getting kickbacks from landlords on the leased space) to projects torn apart by huge turnover rates. "You end up with project teams that are hugely inconsistent. You might have a good team in place, but a month later, three-quarters of the team has transitioned," Harding says.

"Only when executed well can it pull out hundreds of millions in cost and transform organizations," says Brian Keane, CEO of Dextrys, an outsourcing service provider that focuses mainly on China.

In the sometimes panicked desire to save money—especially with the powerful lure of "half-price" workers in places like India, China, and the Philippines—good execution flies out the window. And that's where the problems flock in. Outsourcing is not for the faint-hearted or the ill-prepared. It just doesn't "happen."

That's why understanding what can go wrong before you jump into outsourcing is a great way to reduce your risk because then you can approach outsourcing with eyes wide open, Harding notes. The companies who've lived through outsourcing horrors have two things in common: lack of preparedness going into a new relationship and lack of communication once the projects gets under way. Other factors can make these worse, of course.

Outsourcing's Biggest Horror Show

In the pantheon of outsourcing horror stories, the $4 billion deal between the U.S. Navy and global services provider EDS stands out as one of the most horrific. It started back in 2003 when the Plano, Texas, vendor beat out the likes of IBM and Accenture for the contract. The deal was to manage voice, video, networking, training, and desktops for 350,000 Navy and Marine Corps users. But just one year later, EDS was writing off close to $350 million due to its inability to come even close to fulfilling its obligations.

The reasons behind the failure are complex, but suffice it to say that one of the major causes behind the debacle was that EDS, perhaps anxious to win the prize, never realized that the Navy and Marine Corps had tens of thousands of legacy and custom applications for which it was expected to either integrate or rip and replace. An EDS spokesperson said at the time the company's goal was to get the number of legacy apps down to a mere 10,000 to 12,000.

While there was plenty of blame to go around at EDS, the Navy took its share of blame as well. One of the major issues with the Navy was that the buck stopped nowhere. There was no single person or entity that could help EDS determine what legacy applications were needed and what applications could be excised. EDS, for example, found 11 different label-making applications, but there was no one who could say which 10 to eliminate.

Most companies will never face outsourcing problems on the scale of the Navy and EDS. But many will face their own horrors on systems and projects just as critical. Consider these four modern examples and what lessons the companies painfully learned.

Horror No. 1: A Medical Firm's Configuration Management Surprise

When Fran Schmidt, now a configuration engineer with Orasi Consulting, was told at her previous job in the medical industry to head up a team to outsource the existing in-house development and quality assurance IT departments, she faced the usual problems.

"There was one Indian fellow no one could understand over the phone. It took us months to figure out what he was saying," Schmidt recalls with a smile.

That was expected. But what the medical firm didn't count on was that its existing configuration management tool, Microsoft Visual SourceSafe, which worked fine locally, would be a total bust when used collaboratively between two groups 8,000 miles apart. It took the remote teams in India an average of 13 hours to get updates on source code. And with a time difference of about 11 hours, the outsourcers were behind a full day's work.

"When we hit the [Send] button, there was no code done by the previous shift the entire time they were at work," recalls Schmidt. Not having immediate access to what was previously done the day before caused major problems for in-house developers. "All our progress schedules were behind. It's a domino effect with everyone playing catch-up." And the firm's customers paid the price: They were upset because they were not getting the same level of care that they expected.

The medical firm ultimately switched its configuration management tool to AccuRev, cutting the transoceanic updating from 13 hours to about an hour and a half. All told, it took around six months to recover from the disaster, Schmidt recalls.

The obvious lesson was the need to test your infrastructure before going live in an offshoring scenario. But the medical firm also learned another hard lesson: The desire to save big bucks so blinded the executives that they didn't realize they were replacing a group of people experienced with using a product to a group of people who were looking at it for the first time. "We underestimated the loss of knowledge that would take place during the transition," Schmidt says.

Horror No. 2: Manufacturing Efficiency Doesn't Extend to Marketing

Executives in charge of a small consumer product group at Hewlett-Packard were under the gun. They were told in no uncertain terms to cut all costs related to getting the product into the big-box stores such as Best Buy and Circuit City, recalls Margaret McDonald, then marketing manager for the HP department and now president of her own company, McDonald Wordsmith Communications. (McDonald would not name the product and would only say that it is sold today at places such as Best Buy.)

"We were trying to get as much work as possible over to the Taiwan manufacturer with the goal to get the cost for these products down as low as possible," McDonald recalls. The Taiwanese outsourcer had a great deal of experience in getting the bill-of-materials costs lower, and HP was seeing that benefit. So managers started pushing for more savings elsewhere, insisting that the entire project be handed over to Taiwan—everything from manufacture to writing the instruction manuals to all the marketing materials.

"These execs were being evaluated on cost, not on the quality of the brand," says McDonald. When she tried to tell her managers that what they wanted was unreasonable for an outsourced manufacturer to deliver, they accused her of just trying to hold on to her job.

As she predicted, the project turned out to be a disaster. Take this example of the Taiwan-produced marketing materials: "This glamour of new product will perfectly fit to your daily life from any of locations!" Of course, non-native English prose like that never saw the light of day, but it wasted six months until the higher-ups finally realized what was happening.

McDonald isn't sure her managers learned a lesson. She sees the failure not due to the offshore firm hired or even the miscommunication between the US and Taiwan firms. Instead, she sees the problems as a failure within HP, between its own internal organizations. "The main [HP] branding people had no idea was going on." And the local managers reacted to the extreme cost pressures in a vacuum, with no concern for protecting the brand, McDonald says. The fact that the job was outsourced simply created the right circumstances for these internal flaws to finally become evident.

Horror No. 3: Giant Telecom Stumbles in Transition to Offshore

Steve Martin, a consultant and partner at Pace Harmon, a company that is often called in to help fix outsourcing deals gone bad, recalls the giant telecommunications company headed for disaster: It never considered the fact that although its new offshore provider was good at coding, it did not understand the business side of telecommunications.

The outsourcing project was divided into two phases. In phase one, all the internally managed operations were moved to an outsourced service provider (in this case, based in the United States). The idea was to test and stabilize the outsourcing approach with a local provider first, before taking the riskier step of moving the application development offshore.

The first phase went fairly well, so the telecom initiated phase two, shifting the effort to India. That didn't proceed so smoothly. The Indian provider simply didn't understand the telecom business, so lost in the transition halfway across the globe was all the telecom's inherent knowledge of the business applications—what it is supposed to do and why. "All of that knowledge got left in the US," Martin recalls.

Because the Indian firm didn't understand what it was coding, it took much longer to develop the applications. And they didn't work well, resulting in even more time and effort to figure out where they went wrong and fix them. It got so bad that the telecom canceled the offshoring midway and brought the effort back home.

Of course, there were lingering problems to resolve, such as how to handle the disputes over tens of millions of dollars in service credits the telecom believed it was due from the Indian outsourcer, which argued that it delivered what it had been asked to do. "An amazingly large amount of costs had to be reconciled," Martin notes. The two companies eschewed a legal battle to avoid the bad publicity, ultimately settling the dispute privately.

What the telecom company learned the hard way was that there is more to a deal than signing the contract. In the original deal, pricing took precedence over every other consideration because the executives wanted to show that they saved millions of dollars. Shortchanged in the process were the details of the transition, the development processes, and the governance. Adequate thought was not given to the obligations of the people who were responsible for executing the transition.

"The contract was executed from a business perspective, where it looked great, but not enough thought was given to how to programmatically move to the new environment," Martin says.

Horror No. 4: Service Provider Blacks Out the Client

James Hills, president of marketing firm MarketingHelpNet, probably had one of the most terrifying offshore experiences of all. When a dispute between his new company and the Web site developers grew heated, he came into the office one day—only to discover the developers had shut his client's site down.

"I came in and checked e-mail. No e-mail, no Web site. They had simply turned it off. It was all gone," Hills recalls. While he was shocked to discover this, in some ways, he was not surprised. After all, the relationship with the offshore provider had been troubled from the start.

It started when Hills took on an assignment from a major client. Rather than trying to develop Web design skills needed to complete the client's project, Hills decided to farm that part of the job out to an offshore provider in the Philippines, at a savings of half of the cost of working with a local Web site designer, says Hills.

As soon as the offshore provider began sending back completed work, Hills knew there was trouble: "Functionality and community features didn't mesh properly, and the design wasn't what we were looking for." On top of that, the offshore provider continually missed deadlines.

Becoming increasingly frustrated, Hills didn't make the final payment. The result, of course, was a panicked wake-up call from his client telling him there was no e-mail and no Web site.

Looking back, Hills says that if had he to do it over, he would have been more diligent in checking references. He did only a perfunctory check of references, unfortunately taking it for granted that the offshore design firm actually created the Web sites they claimed.

Time differences also played a key role in the soured relationship. "We weren't able to communicate directly, only through IM," Hills says. And as a small startup at the time, he couldn't support multiple shifts at home to get overlap with India, nor ask his staff to work 20 hours a day to cover both time zones. And sending a manager to the Philippines was out of the question, Hills says.

Hills doubts he'll ever outsource again, but if he did, he would insist that the job be done with a US-based company that puts its offshore staff onto the company's payroll. "No contract workers," Hills says tersely.

POSTSCRIPT

Is Outsourcing a Wise Corporate Strategy?

The war on American outsourcing has moved beyond the talking stage. In March of 2004, the Senate passed an amendment that denies certain federal contracts from being awarded to organizations that outsource work overseas. This action has been echoed at the state level as well. Indiana, for example, cancelled a contract with an Indiana-based firm to upgrade the state's computer systems when it was discovered that the company employed workers in India. Instead, they spent $8 million more of taxpayers' money and awarded the contract to another firm. Examples such as this are becoming commonplace, which is not really surprising considering that a large majority of states had proposed or enacted anti-outsourcing legislation by the end of 2005.

More recently, in an apparent move to cash in on the popularity of Barack Obama, and only one day after his presidential inauguration, Rep. Sue Wilkins Myrick (Republican, North Carolina) introduced an anti-outsourcing amendment to the Troubled Assets Relief Program (TARP) legislation intended to help bail out the troubled financial industry. Myrick's amendment is directed at any firm that receives "assistance" from TARP and would prohibit any "assisted institution that became an assisted institution on or after October 3, 2008," from entering into "a new agreement, or expand a current agreement, with any foreign company for provision of customer service functions, including call-center services, while any of such assistance is outstanding." (William B. Bierce, "TARP relief law might discriminate against off-shore call centers," *Outsourcing-law.com*, January 24, 2009; http://blog.outsourcing-law.com/2009/01/increasing-accountability-under-us-tarp.html). Clearly, the outsourcing alarmist agenda is gaining traction, a fact reflected in the various federal and state legislative actions designed to penalize firms that choose to send work overseas.

Now, after having read both sides of this issue, do you believe this is a wise response to the current wave of corporate outsourcing? Given that you are more knowledgeable about this important management topic, which do you feel is more damaging to American business interests: allowing firms to outsource jobs overseas or passing legislation and empowering governments to punish corporate outsourcers?

Suggested Readings

William B. Bierce, "TARP Relief Law Might Discriminate Against Off-Shore Call Centers," Outsourcing-law.com (January 24, 2009). http://blog .outsourcing-law.com/2009/01/increasing-accountability-under-us-tarp.html

Daniel T. Griswold, "Outsource, Outsource, and Outsource Some More," Center for Trade Policy Studies, The Cato Institute (May 3, 2004). http://www.freetrade.org/pubs/articles/dg-05-03-04.html

Edwin A. Locke, "On May Day Celebrate Capitalism," The Ayn Rand Institute (April 24, 2003). http://www.aynrand.org/site/News2?page=NewsArticle&id=7449

Norm Alster, "Customer Disservice? Critics Say the Promised Savings from Offshoring Come at Too Steep a Price, While Companies Say Very Little at All," *CFO Magazine, CFO IT* (Fall 2005). http://www.cfo.com/article.cfm/4390954

Roderick Boyd, "Anti-Outsourcing Campaign Renewed by Lou Dobbs," *The New York Sun* (February 2, 2005). http://www.nysun.com/business/anti-outsourcing-campaign-renewed-by-lou-dobbs/8635/

Yahoo! News, "US Anti-Outsourcing Plans Won't Hit India: Lobby Group," *Yahoo! News Singapore* (May 6, 2009). http://sg.news.yahoo.com/afp/20090506/tbs-india-us-outsourcing-obama-politics-558302b.html

ISSUE 12

Does Expanding via Mergers and Acquisitions Make for Sound Corporate Strategy?

YES: Marc J. Epstein, from "The Determinants and Evaluation of Merger Success," *Business Horizons* (January–February 2005)

NO: Anand Sanwal, from "M&A's Losing Hand," *Business Finance*, (November 18, 2008). http://businessfinancemag.com/article/mas-losing -hand-1118

ISSUE SUMMARY

YES: Marc Epstein feels that the negative attention that M&As receive is largely due to faulty analysis of M&A activity. He contends that M&A transactions should be considered when a firm's strategic managers are looking for vehicles for growth. Success, however, is contingent upon several factors outlined by the author.

NO: In the "No" side selection, Anand Sanwal examines 33 large M&A transactions from Europe, Canada, and the United States. The evidence is that a great deal of these M&A transactions have actually destroyed value. He also contends of the transactions that did fare well, luck was often a large factor.

Banks, cars, pharmaceuticals, phones, and beer—what do all these have in common? If you said "abundant merger and acquisition (M&A) activity in their industries," you are absolutely correct. And these are by no means the only industries to experience M&A transactions. Indeed, mergers (two firms joining together to become one) and acquisitions (one firm buying another) are common means of expansion for many firms. They're also common means of expansion across industries, particularly when firms are looking to move into new business areas. Such firms undertake M&As for many, varied reasons. Among other things, the mergers and acquirers feel that they can increase revenues or cut costs through marketing activities such as cross-selling or bundling products together from the two firms. These companies may also believe that they can share various administrative duties, thus reducing costs further. Other firms undertake M&As as a means of obtaining valuable technology or critical skills that the target may possess. Still others try to diversify their business activities to help control their exposure to risk. Sometimes M&A activity is even triggered by other M&A activity, almost as if companies simply don't want to be left behind when an M&A wave is happening. Regardless of the varied reasons driving mergers and acquisitions, one thing seems evident: M&A transactions are not going away. Looking in current business periodicals, it doesn't take long to learn about the latest M&A transactions and deals. But this activity hides an important, seldom-asked question: In reality, do mergers and acquisitions actually generate the value that is expected?

Contrary to those advocates that view M&A activity as a good expansion vehicle, many people argue that past M&A activity has actually destroyed value—so much so, in fact, that it suggests that it may not be sound corporate strategy. Although actual failure rates for M&A transactions depend upon a variety of variables (timeframe examined, measures used, etc.), it is not uncommon to see estimates stating poor performance or failure for M&As in the range of one-half to two-thirds of all such activity (Ritza Vaughn, 2008, "Navigating a Successful Merger." *Risk Management*, 55(1), 36–38, 40–41.) Reasons for these failures can be numerous. They range from not being able to integrate opposing corporate cultures to failing to capture the synergies that were expected to emerge from the combined entities. Not surprisingly, given these risks, internally generated growth initiatives are often advocated over attempting M&As. Author John Cummings notes that this may be particularly salient given current market conditions: "With debt financing likely scarce for the foreseeable future, the only way forward for most growth-minded organizations is via internally generated profitable revenue expansion—the organic route." (John Cummings, 2008, "Why Organic Is Better." *Business Finance*, 14(12), 12–17).

Yet, in the "Yes" side selection, author Marc Epstein questions the assertion, "that mergers and acquisitions (M&A) are doomed to fail and that M&A success is somehow at odds with the reality of the business world" (p. 48). He believes that the negative attention that M&As receive is largely due to poor analyses and questionable success measures often used when studying this phenomena. As a means of supporting the M&A approach, Epstein proposes six factors required for successful mergers. Although he notes that some of these factors are easily controlled by the firm while others are more difficult to control due to external pressures, he suggests that an M&A strategy is workable when careful consideration of these factors is a high priority for management.

On the other hand, as seen in Anand Sanwal's article comprising the "no" selection for this debate, evidence suggests that a great deal of recent large M&A transactions have actually destroyed value. He also contends that many of the transactions that did fare well were often successful because of luck, rather than skill in managing the transaction. Although Sanwal discusses some factors that may increase the success of large M&As, he qualifies this by noting that ". . . all the research in the world won't change the fact that people like headlines and deals are going to happen." As you read through the selections, ask yourself if these M&A deals are the result of corporate executives chasing headlines or if they represent strategically sound corporate transactions.

YES ↵

Marc J. Epstein

The Determinants and Evaluation of Merger Success

1. Introduction

Many writers and business analysts have asserted that mergers and acquisitions (M&A) are doomed to fail and that M&A success is somehow at odds with the reality of the business world. They often point to a history of merger failures, concluding that bigger is not better and that mergers and acquisitions are failed strategies. While some studies have even indicated that 7 out of 10 mergers do not live up to their promises, the analysis of the causes of failure has often been shallow and the measures of success weak.

For decades, success and failure in M&A has been studied in terms of narrow and uninformative measures, such as short-term stock price, leading to the aforementioned claims that most mergers fail. Many have taken this finding at face value, moving on to the search for causes of failure, which include culture clash, lack of synergies, and flawed strategy. All things considered, the study of M&A desperately needs a new perspective and a new framework for analysis.

2. Mergers, Acquisitions, and Conglomerates

There is great need for clearer distinctions between three very different approaches to growth. Mergers, acquisitions, and conglomerates are often analyzed as if they were the same, but a clear distinction is necessary. Mergers of equals, such as JPMorganChase, involve two entities of relatively comparable stature coming together and taking the best of each company to form a completely new organization. Growth through acquisitions, such as Cisco's model, involves the much simpler process of fitting one smaller company into the existing structure of a larger organization. Conglomerates, such as Tyco, constitute a third type of entity in which large companies are brought together without any clear attempt to create synergies or meld strategies, keeping them separate to provide the advantages of decentralization and autonomy. To lump mergers, acquisitions, and conglomerates together prohibits a thorough understanding of either the determinants or the evaluation of success.

There are significant challenges in the integration of both the technical and human aspects of bringing another company into a large group, as occurs

From *Business Horizons*, vol. 48, January–February 2005, pp. 37–41, 45–46 (excerpts). Copyright © 2005 by Kelley School of Business. Reprinted by permission of Elsevier Inc. via Rightslink.

in acquisitions and conglomerates. However, these pale in comparison to the more common challenges faced when two similar-sized companies come together to create a new organization with significant competitive advantages. Whereas an acquisition conveys a clear sense of which company is in charge, a merger of equals often causes a power struggle as members of both companies seek control over the new organization. Every aspect of the company's business practices is subject to discussion, and the selection of best methods often takes a back seat to each company's desire to maintain their own status quo.

The lack of clarity regarding the elements of merger success and implementation, along with a plethora of measurement problems, has led to a never-ending debate as to whether mergers are generally desirable or of dubious value. Beyond that remains the issue of how to make them work. Studies of short-term stock prices have been contrasted with studies of long-range financial returns. Failure has been couched in terms as extreme as "resale" or "liquidation", or as conservative as "failing to reach certain projected growth or profit." Overpayment has been reported as the overwhelming culprit of merger failure, while less quantifiable causes, such as strategy and merger execution, have been downplayed. Without any focus or clarity, the discussion has inevitably descended into an exchange of uninformative case studies. A more complete discussion would acknowledge that mergers (rather than acquisitions) have often failed because of problems with the strategic vision of the merger, the appropriateness of the merger partner, or the deal structure. Mergers such as these faced almost certain failure even before any integration attempt had begun.

Although there have been numerous studies of the Cisco model of acquisitions integration and the G.E. model of integration of companies into a conglomerate, there is little literature and analysis of the drivers or evaluation of merger success. The research reported here focuses on what makes a merger successful and what is the appropriate manner of evaluating merger success. I have concluded that there are six determinants of merger success. It is these key success factors that should be relied upon in evaluating mergers and their long-term impact on profitability, rather than short-term indicators like current stock price as used to measure strategy and implementation success. Furthermore, my research shows that senior managers can significantly increase the likelihood of overall merger success through careful development and implementation of a merger strategy that considers these six factors. It also illustrates that commonly used narrow interpretations of merger success undervalue the contributions of mergers, and that a more comprehensive evaluation often leads to very different conclusions. . . .

3. The Six Determinants of Merger Success

Achieving merger success requires accomplishment in six factors. Failure of any one of the six can impede the achievement of merger goals. Some can be controlled easily through careful design and implementation, while others are more challenging due to numerous external forces. Mergers can provide superb opportunities for profitable growth, but companies need to take great care of their performance regarding these six determinants of merger success, with any evaluation of merger success including performance evaluation of each of these factors. The six determinants of a successful merger are:

3.1. Strategic Vision and Fit

The strategic vision should clearly articulate a merger rationale that is centered on the creation of long-term competitive advantage rather than just short-term improvements in operational efficiency. Prominent reasons for company mergers include attempts to increase scale, geographic scope, knowledge, and cross-industry extension. If the strategic vision focuses on scale, greater efficiency and cost cutting are high priorities, and the company tries to build advantages through size. In geographic scope mergers, two companies combine to expand geographic coverage. Talent-based mergers attempt to create advantage by improving company operations through matching people, skills, and knowledge to areas of need. Cross-industry mergers seek to combine complementary products and services and often redefine the business to better service customer needs. Whichever concepts are central to the vision, it is important that real growth is an expectation of the merger and that the entire rationale is not centered on cost cutting and elimination of redundancies. Clarity of the strategic vision is critical.

The Citibank–Travelers merger is often cited as one in which strategic vision helped overcome problems in postmerger integration (PMI) and other aspects of the deal. The strategic vision centered on the value of a diverse business platform, which included the benefits of "cross-selling" to both the company and its customers by attracting customers through assembling many products under one roof. Analysts greeted this concept with skepticism, arguing it had failed in the past, but CEO Sandy Weill insisted the vision was the "model financial institution of the future" and moved forward. Citigroup ultimately established leadership positions in nearly every product category and region, including some in which the prospects for cross-selling were questionable.

Whether the merger is designed for synergies in size, geography, assets, people, or competencies, companies must evaluate whether the entities are proper choices as merger partners and the right fit to fulfill the strategic vision. If the strategic vision focuses on scale, the companies must be confident that the cost savings and growth synergies associated with scale justify the merger costs. Participants in a geographic scope deal must be wary of too much overlap in markets and be certain that the two companies' combined areas of concentration will form significant synergies. Participants in talent-based mergers must be confident that the acquired skills, competencies, systems, and knowledge will be applicable in both lines of business or that the combined talents of the firms will create synergies. Finally, participants in a cross-industry deal must ensure that their particular combination of lines of business will be accretive and customers will not be confused by the combination.

Leadership from both companies must carefully analyze the strategic vision, how each company fits into that vision, and their compatibility in terms of culture, systems, and processes. The Daimler–Chrysler merger is an example of a merger whose strategic fit led to major problems. The merger was designed to provide increases in market share based on geographical fit and cost savings from sharing parts, research, and technical practices. However, the notion of sharing parts clashed with the corporate cultures and the prestige associated with the Mercedes brand. The original intent was to share research and practices, but differences in company policies and personnel made collaboration difficult. Daimler undermined this purpose even further by failing to retain Chrysler's senior design executive. Due to technical and cultural differences that were not adequately managed in the integration process, the merger has not yet delivered on its promises. It has led to internal strife and, ultimately, the denunciation of the "merger of equals" mantra.

3.2. Deal Structure

A successful merger requires careful attention to two aspects of the deal structure: price premium and financing type. Mergers often fail due to paying too high a purchase price and overburdening the new company with sky-high debt payments. The decision of whether to finance with cash, stock, or a combination depends on a number of factors, including accounting and tax implications. Stock deals have become more popular throughout the last decade as the stock market rose, but both companies must consider whether their own stock and the other company's stock may be overvalued or undervalued at the time of the deal.

Federated and Fingerhut is an example of a merger that had major problems due to deal structure. Most observers agree that Federated overpaid in the deal, hoping to land a partner with direct-marketing experience to pass on to its stores, such as Macy's. Fingerhut had just such experience from its catalog sales and nascent Internet business. The 30% premium price paid by Federated was especially high considering that Fingerhut's price had been bid up fairly recently before the merger. This, in part, led Federated to shut down Fingerhut and ultimately sell the operation for less than US$800 million in 2002, after originally purchasing the company in 1999 for US$1.7 billion.

3.3. Due Diligence

Merger partners must exercise care to ensure that the potential deal can succeed in implementing the proposed strategic vision. The due diligence team should comprise members from both companies across a number of different functional areas and include accountants, lawyers, technical specialists, and other experts.

Due diligence includes the formal financial review of assets, liabilities, revenues, and expenses and substantiation of the financial records. It also includes numerous nonfinancial elements, including the investigation and evaluation of organizational fit, ability to merge cultures, and the technological and human resources capabilities and fit. Other considerations include comparisons of accounting and budgeting practices and examination of employment contracts and labor union relations. The cultural aspect of due diligence must make certain that the differing cultures can be effectively integrated. This includes an examination of business philosophies, work practices, leadership styles, customs, expectations, and facilities. Companies need to devote effort to due diligence in order to ensure that there are no disruptive surprises in the integration process. Merger failures often result from a lack of careful evaluation of both the hard financial and soft personnel and organizational issues that are critical to organizational success.

The consequences of incomplete due diligence are demonstrated by the ongoing problems of Halliburton, which became embroiled in asbestos claims against Dresser, the company with which it merged in 1997. Although the extent of the due diligence process remains disputed, court documents allege that information on Dresser's situation, including a letter from a complainant, was available during the due diligence period and not uncovered by Halliburton. The cordial nature of the merger talks and friendship between the two company leaders is cited as a possible reason for this laxity. The cost to Halliburton for this liability is generally estimated at more than a half billion dollars.

3.4. Premerger Planning

The preparation during the period leading up to the merger announcement is vital to success since it is critical to present the merger to key constituencies with confidence. During this period, the integration process is formulated and key decisions are made in the areas of leadership, structure, and timeline for the process. It is important to establish clarity in roles and responsibilities for those involved in the integration process, versus those in operating businesses. Communication efforts must be coordinated, widespread, and quickly developed. Both speed in decisions and planning and overcommunication to all stakeholders is critical.

A new leadership team must be selected immediately and guidelines for lower levels of personnel decisions must be established. Selection of the new CEO and board can be particularly difficult in mergers of equals, creating hostilities and becoming extremely time-consuming. Shared responsibilities can be a solution, but power-sharing creates its own challenges, including a lack of clarity at the top of the organization. The source of final authority, direction, and responsibility must be clear. The new company's structure, as well as the structure of the integration management team, must also be planned before the announcement. In true mergers of equals, creating an entirely new organization is preferable to being constrained by either of the previous structures. The integration management team should be in place immediately and have fulltime contributions from at least one prominent member of senior management. Early dates should also be set for making key decisions and establishing metrics and targets. If the premerger planning process is not completed effectively, merger integration and success are typically unachievable.

3.5. Postmerger Integration

Companies often destroy mergers during the integration process. If the previous five keys have been executed properly, the company is positioned for a successful merger. The strategy of both the new company and the integration process must be clear and the new organizational structure must be well defined. During postmerger integration, processes including the management of human resources, technical operations, and customer relationships must be carefully blended and important decisions made.

The postmerger integration (PMI) process begins with proper premerger planning, but good planning does not guarantee good execution. After the announcement, a successful PMI can only be achieved if all parts of the organization have the knowledge, resources, and commitment to move forward at an often blistering pace without destroying value in the process. Key implementation decisions must be made rapidly. Early wins must be achieved to build momentum and attention must be paid to both cost reduction and revenue growth synergies. Measures and milestones for the PMI must be balanced both in terms of financial and nonfinancial indicators, and between leading and lagging measures.

Human resource management practices and candid communication focused on retaining the best people from the two companies must both be guided by meritocracy. Technical management must minimize risks associated with major integration events and focus on choosing the best and most compatible applications for the new organization. Customer management is vital to maintaining confidence and keeping customer attrition to a minimum during the merger. Postmerger integration is not business as usual. To avoid loss of business during the integration process, the company must continue to focus on customers since competitors often look to capitalize on any merger-generated lack of focus or confusion. The process should generate a culture where employees see the merger as enabling them to develop the business rather than inhibiting them from progress. Organizational leadership, structures, systems, and substantial, open communication are necessary to encourage this attitude.

3.6. External Factors

Not all factors that influence the success of mergers are under the control of the company itself. Changing economic conditions may introduce dynamics in employment and customer retention that could not have been anticipated. The company's industry or peer group may undergo drastic, unexpected change during the integration due to the success, failure, or actions of peer firms or economic conditions. In extreme cases, the company's business may be affected by the fortunes of a single client or partner. All of these factors can adversely affect an otherwise successful merger, and no amount of due diligence or risk mitigation may have foreseen or prevented such occurrences. In some cases, however, these conditions are entirely predictable, and companies that plan mergers while brazenly ignoring obvious warning signs of changes in the economy, interest rates, competitor actions, consumer purchases, and political climate are subject to harsher judgment of their merger planning.

In evaluating most mergers, however, the effects of external factors have to be considered more carefully, especially in the case of economic factors.

In a strong economy, a poor merger may appear to be more successful, while a strong merger may look weak under poor economic conditions. It is important, therefore, to distinguish between external factors that actually damage the value of the merger and those external factors that only damage perception of the merger. This distinction underlines the futility of measuring merger success with simple stock prices. In a down economy when stock prices are down throughout the market, a lower price for the merged company gives little or no information as to the real value created by the merger. . . .

4. Evaluating Merger Success

In this study, I have outlined six determinants of merger success that emphasize the importance of both strategy and process. Thus, our evaluation of merger success must be much broader than a simple change in stock price, which often tells us little about the merger and more about external factors. We must instead ask what the strategies were for the merger, and whether the goals were achieved. At the same time, we must ask whether the strategy and vision were well conceived and whether the merger's conception was superior to possible alternatives. Finally, we must be prepared to disaggregate the economic context from the results of the merger in order to ascertain which changes are truly attributable to the merger. Only then can we be less constrained by the notion of labeling every merger as a complete success or failure, which is characteristic of too many studies in this field. In this article, we cited major problems with the mergers at Federated, Daimler-Chrysler, and Halliburton. Yet the degree of failure associated with each of these mergers is highly variable. Federated has been forced to divest its interest in Fingerhut, DaimlerChrysler has abandoned much of its strategic vision, and Halliburton has accrued major losses. Branding each of these deals equally as failures is uninformative and not entirely accurate.

It is not that mergers cannot succeed. However, there are many barriers to merger success. Mergers can create significant value if companies successfully execute the six keys to merger success. Failure in any of the six can impede the achievement of merger goals. . . .

When a merger succeeds in each of the first six keys and short-term financial indicators represent its only criticism, one must ask whether it is the merger or the definition of success that is truly flawed.

Evaluating merger success based on short-term changes in stock price is ridiculous. Mergers should not be completed to impact these short-term changes and should not be evaluated on that basis. Successful mergers develop a clear strategic vision that leads to the creation of significantly higher long-term value. Mergers should, then, be evaluated on the same basis. Thus, we look at whether goals have been achieved and whether the new company is better positioned for long-term success. Short-term evaluations based on stock price or other narrow financial measures tell us little about the true value of a merger. Often, merger strategies require years of integration and synergies before the benefits are reflected in earnings and stock price.

Narrow definitions of merger success and failure must be replaced by broad and complete measures that take into consideration company goals and performance, as well as the economic and industry context. Both financial and non-financial measures should be considered. Leading indicators of performance that are predictors of future success must be evaluated in addition to historical results.

Inevitably, some mergers succeed and some fail. Those who automatically reject mergers and acquisitions as important vehicles for growth and profitability are relying on flawed evaluations and definitions of success. In fact, M&A is a perfectly viable business strategy if the blueprint above is followed, the design is well-conceived, and the postmerger integration is executed with strong leadership, communication, and alignment.

Anand Sanwal **NO**

M&A's Losing Hand

It's been an absolutely ugly October in global financial markets, and all indications point to continued uncertainty and volatility for the foreseeable future. Most CEOs and CFOs of public companies are looking dejectedly at company share prices that are a fraction of what they were just a year ago. For companies that are weathering the current storm, the question that progressive CEOs and CFOs will soon begin to consider, as they should, is where do we need to take our business in order to begin delivering shareholder value and returns once again?

Considering this question will require the crafting of a compelling narrative and strategy that these senior leaders can communicate to their employees, customers, and shareholders about what's next—i.e., where is the company's future profitable growth going to come from?

One of the often-used vehicles to achieve growth, in theory, has been mergers and acquisitions (M&A); however, current market conditions make M&A a dicey or even impractical option. The unavailability of credit and increasingly expensive short-term refinancing rates, coupled with the economic downturn and depressed equity prices, have all served to make M&A difficult to accomplish. This has resulted in a spate of dead deals in recent weeks.

According to Deal Logic, the first 13 days of October witnessed 49 deals valued at $57.6 billion pulled, after $62.8 billion worth of deals were pulled in September. Acquirers that were hit by M&A travails include the BG Group, Waste Management, Bristol-Myers Squibb, HSBC Holdings, Dubai World, Xstrata, and Walgreen, to name a few. From this list, it is obvious that the M&A downturn is hitting companies in a diverse array of sectors, industries, and geographies.

How should CEOs, CFOs, and shareholders react to the M&A malaise? Contrary to popular belief, and especially so for those considering a large M&A transaction, they should pop open a bottle of champagne and celebrate. Why? Because according to our research, "megadeals"—those in which the target's value exceeds $10 billion—more often than not destroy shareholder value.

This is the underlying conclusion of our study in which we evaluated all megadeals from 2002 to 2007. We examined 33 M&A megadeals from Europe, Canada, and the USA in which the acquirers were strategic buyers—not financial or private equity concerns. (Please note that because some data were unavailable, in some instances our results do not reflect all 33 deals; see the sidebar to get a list of the evaluated deals.)

In what was arguably one of the greatest bull markets we've ever seen, we observed that megadeals actually destroyed value over 60 percent of the time. On average, transactions resulted in negative cumulative excess beta returns (−4.03 percent) in the year after their announcement. (See the sidebar for insights into the research methodology.)

Even among the handful of deals that generated positive returns, we found that success was more often than not attributable to macroeconomic factors beyond the control of the acquirer. So it seems that it is often better to be "lucky than good" or "in the right place at the right time" when undertaking large M&A transactions. Furthermore, the data show that many of the deals, whether successful or not, increased the beta of the acquirer. Higher-risk profiles resulted in a higher cost of capital for the company post-acquisition, making such deals "costlier" in ways that can be very damaging to the larger entity over the longer term.

Following the quantitative analysis of all of the megadeals, we also sought to determine what lessons we could take away from the good, the bad, and the ugly so that future M&A megadeals can avoid past pitfalls and replicate elements of the few successful ones. However, before we do so, it is important to reiterate that our research showed few to no valid reasons to engage in megadeal M&A unless the desire is to redistribute shareholder money to needy investment bankers and lawyers. This being said, all the research in the world won't change the fact that people like headlines, and deals are going to happen. Armed with this level of pragmatism, we developed a set of dimensions that should be considered when engaging in megadeal M&A.

Peeling Back the Findings

Regarding measures that you can control, here are some observations about how you can increase a deal's chances of success:

- **It's important not to overpay.** This is straight from the "master of the obvious" file, but it's clear that disciplined buyers outperform loose spenders. Evidence suggested that premium and performance are inversely correlated, meaning that the greater the premium, the worse the performance. By way of example, Boston Scientific's acquisition of Guidant involved a bidding war with Johnson & Johnson that resulted in Boston Scientific paying a handsome $80 per share as opposed to their original offer of $72. In the case of the Sprint Nextel deal, Nextel took advantage of Sprint's insecurity regarding its ability to compete against other carriers and as a result secured an excellent exit price. Both of these deals resulted in miserable excess returns.

    In other cases such as Bank of New York's acquisition of Mellon Financial Corp., a very low premium was involved, as was the case in the CVS-Caremark and Manulife–John Hancock deals, which both did well. Price is not the only consideration, of course, but higher premiums generally make it more difficult for buyers to achieve high returns.

The challenge ultimately is that when an acquirer pays a high premium, its shareholders get diluted or it uses cash to prevent dilution. The only way ultimately for the firm to get that cash back is to reengineer expenses out of the combined company. The synergies needed to pay for premium and the excess premium make this impossible. Moreover, the need to significantly reduce expenses can mean cutting muscle, not just fat, resulting in weakened competency and poor morale.

- **Acquiring a faster-growth target is looked upon favorably.** When companies acquire targets with higher growth expectations than their own, it appears that the market supports the acquisition. In contrast, when companies acquire targets that are underperforming and whose growth expectations are lower than their own, acquisitions tend to fail. In cases where both companies underperform and a transaction occurs, postdeal performance tends to be quite lackluster, as such an M&A is used as a poor replacement for an inability to generate organic growth. Unfortunately, combining two cubic zirconias rarely results in a real diamond.
- **Mergers of Equals outperform outright acquisitions.** To determine the effect that the relative size of the buyer to the target has on M&A performance, we found that in general, acquisitions that fell in the Merger of Equals category performed better than those that fell into the outright Acquisitions category. Originally, this seemed slightly counterintuitive; however, a closer look at some of the best-in-class examples shows that in Mergers of Equals, both companies tend to have a fair amount of interest in deal success and thus are more collaborative. In Mergers of Equals, both companies often bring different strengths to the table and thus allow the whole to be greater than the sum of the parts. For example, when Manulife Financial Corporation acquired John Hancock Financial Services, the former provided strong brand recognition, while the latter offered strong access to capital markets, and both presented distinct distribution channels.

M&A Megadeal Success

Through research tied to individual transactions, we determined that high-performing deals considered the following dimensions and questions.

Practical Considerations

- **Macroeconomic and industry factors.** Am I appropriately considering macroeconomic factors on the upside and downside that could impact the industry and/or competitive landscape? Are my expectations for future growth of the target reasonable, and is the deal worthwhile even in a worst-case scenario?
- **Timing.** Are there internal concerns that should take managerial priority?
- **Price.** Am I being disciplined in my determination of the price?
- **Cost savings and revenue synergies.** Am I comfortable that the deal is attractive even if estimated cost savings or opportunities for revenue from the combined company are less than I expect?

A CLOSER LOOK: RESEARCH METHODOLOGY

For each of the megadeal transactions evaluated (all of which took place between 2002 and 2007), data were collected and analyzed as follows:

- **Data were collected from 60 business days prior to announcement until two years after close.**
- **Most of the analysis was conducted on data from 60 days prior to announcement until 265 days after announcement** (slightly over a year) in order to put all of the deals on the same time scale. This was a sufficient time span because on average the deals closed within 121 days and most companies' excess returns displayed discernible patterns by the end of this time period.
- **Excess beta return was used as the primary metric for financial success** because it measures how much the individual stock's excess return varies in comparison with the market as a whole. The cumulative excess beta return was calculated by zeroing out the returns at the day before announcement (day −1) and then aggregating the returns for each successive day while holding day −1 as the base.

M & A Megadeals Evaluated

Acquirer	Target
Capital One	North Fork Bank
Wachovia	South Trust
Regions Financial	AmSouth Bancorp
General Growth Properties	Rouse Company
Wachovia	Golden West Financial
Bank of America	MBNA
JPMorgan Chase	Bank One
Manulife Financial	John Hancock Financial Services
Bank of America	FleetBoston Financial Group
Travelers Companies	Travelers Property Casualty
National Grid	Lattice Group
Harrah's Entertainment	Caesar's Entertainment
Sears Holdings	Sears Roebuck
SUPERVALU	Albertsons
P&G	Gillette
Anadarko Petroleum	Kerr-McGee
ConocoPhillips	Burlington Resources
Chevron	Unocal
Duke Energy	Cinergy
AstraZeneca	Medimmune
CVS	Caremark Rx
J&J	Pfizer Consumer Healthcare
Thermo Fisher Scientific	Fisher Scientific International
Boston Scientific	Guidant
Pfizer	Pharmacia
Symantec	Veritas Software
Sprint Nextel	Nextel Communications
Freeport-McMoRan	Phelps Dodge
Barrick Gold	Placer Dome

- **Each acquirer's returns were also compared to the company's specific sector index,** in order to account for macroeconomic factors or market trends that may have affected individual segments.
- **Each deal was analyzed on an individual basis** using financial data, company reports and presentations, and media reports and news surrounding each deal.

About the Deals Analyzed

- **The deals spanned all nine of the S&P 500 sectors.**

Continued

- **The Financials sector was particularly well represented,** owing to the fact that several financial institutions were engaging in aggressive geographic and market expansion during the time span covered.
- **Deals were categorized as either a "Merger of Equals" or as an "Acquisition."** For the purposes of this study, a "Merger of Equals" was defined as a deal in which the market capitalization of the buyer was less than or equal to 1.5 times the market capitalization of the target at 60 days prior to announcement. All others were considered "Acquisitions."
- **The majority of the deals were from the United States and Canada** simply because of the greater amount of information that was available; however, a few European deals were also included.

Strategic Considerations:

- **Branding, distribution, and scale.** Does the deal provide the potential combined company with greater economies of scale, increased distribution channels, or stronger branding?
- **Organic growth.** Does the deal hamper the potential combined company's potential for organic growth?
- **Integration.** Have we properly accounted for managerial, technological, and cultural integration issues?
- **Geographic and product expansion.** Is there significant overlap between the potential combined companies' geographic and product markets, and will the deal provide an opportunity for expansion?

Our findings suggest in no uncertain terms that firms should be wary of undertaking M&A megadeals. If shareholders who are reeling from the last several months of performance can take solace in one fact, it is that the ability to do M&A may be hampered, at least in the short to medium term, by the economy and credit conditions.

However, these types of exogenous pressures on M&A will ultimately subside, and when this occurs, investment bankers and a host of others will come running back with suggestions for large M&A deals. They will also come equipped with facts and figures showing extensive strategic benefits and magnificent projections about cost and revenue synergies.

Oftentimes, they will paint a picture of market leadership, industry transformation, a bold new vision for the combined entity, and amazing shareholder returns. When this time comes, CEOs and CFOs must resist many elements of these "compelling" narratives, which we readily admit have a seemingly magnetic pull.

Instead, if—as stewards of shareholder money—they take a dispassionate view of the transaction in question, remember the abysmal historical track record of large M&A deals in the past, and also recognize the outsized role that luck plays in successful deals, the decision to say "no deal" should be quite easy.

POSTSCRIPT

Does Expanding via Mergers and Acquisitions Make for Sound Corporate Strategy?

When times are good, and market growth abounds, the results of strategic decisions may be confounded and hidden, and as long as the firms seems to be doing okay overall, individual decisions may not be highly scrutinized. On the other hand, in weakened economic conditions such as those we are experiencing currently, important strategic decisions are examined more closely than usual. Strategically based M&A activities are no exception. Indeed, the *Financial Times* online suggested that in the recent economic downturn, it has come light that ". . . management teams may have overpaid for acquisitions during boom times." (Lina Saigol, March 3, 2009. "Plunging markets expose goodwill gaps after M&A boom." *FT.com.*) Additionally, a sharp drop in the volume of merger and acquisition activity as compared to the same time period of the previous year has been reported. (Lina Saigol, Paul Davies, and Julie MacIntosh, March 29, 2009. "M&A volume starts year with 36% fall." *FT.com.*) Indeed, the current economic conditions make what Epstein calls the ". . . never-ending debate as to whether mergers are generally desirable or of dubious value" (p. 38) particularly salient. In the present economic environment, credit markets are tight, and investors are skittish; now, as much as ever, it is critical to understand whether mergers and acquisitions make for sound strategic policy.

A relatively large body of evidence exists to suggest that M&A transactions are highly risky and prone to underperformance or even failure. As you just learned in the "no" selection, scholars who study this topic such as Anand Sanwal have concluded that when M&As result in success, it is frequently due, in large part, to factors outside the firm's control. Countering this view is Marc Epstein, who asks us to question whether extant studies are really capturing the success of mergers and acquisitions. So, after having read the two sides of the debate, we hope that you have an appreciation for the complexities that surround the issue. If mergers and acquisitions are as bad as many indicate, why do highly successful, very prestigious, well-run firms undertake them?

Suggested Readings

Laurence Capron and Kevin Kaiser, "Does Your M&A Add Value?" *FT.com* (February 5, 2009).

John Cummings, "Why Organic Is Better," *Business Finance* (vol. 14, no. 12, pp. 12–17, December 2008).

Stuart E. Jackson, "Creating Value Through Acquisitions," *The Journal of Business Strategy* (vol. 28, no. 6, pp. 40–41, 2007).

Karen Kroll, "Deals in the Downturn," *Business Finance* (vol. 14, no. 5, pp. 20, 22, 24–25, May 2008).

Mark E Ruquet, "Cultural Fit Helps Drive Merger Success," *National Underwriter, P & C* (vol. 112, no. 33, pp. 19, 25–26, September 2008).

Joel Sinkin, Terrence Putney, "Keeping It Together," *Journal of Accountancy* (vol. 207, no. 4, pp. 24–28, 10, 2009).

Ritza Vaughn, "Navigating a Successful Merger," *Risk Management*, (vol. 55, no. 1, pp. 36–38, 40–41, 2008).

ISSUE 13

Is First-to-Market a Successful Strategy?

YES: William T. Robinson and Sungwook Min, from "Is the First to Market the First to Fail? Empirical Evidence for Industrial Goods Businesses," *Journal of Marketing Research* (February 2002)

NO: William Boulding and Markus Christen, from "Sustainable Pioneering Advantage? Profit Implications of Market Entry Order," *Marketing Science* (Summer 2003)

ISSUE SUMMARY

YES: Scholars William T. Robinson and Sungwook Min provide results of a study indicating that the advantages from being first outweigh the risks of implementing the strategy.

NO: William Boulding and Markus Christen take a contrary position and argue that first moving is not necessarily a wise strategy, presenting evidence from their own research that, in the long run, first-movers actually experience performance disadvantages.

$\mathbf{T}$he idea of being the first-to-market with a new product or service has strong intuitive appeal. Certainly it seems that being first would be an advantageous position for a firm to occupy. Two companies that are often cited as excellent examples of successful first movers are Amazon.com and eBay. These tremendously successful and well-known companies apparently owe much of their success to first-mover advantages. On the other hand, the dot-com bust represented a situation where numerous first movers struggled or failed miserably. That debacle left a bad taste in investor's mouths for the idea of first moving as a corporate strategy. In light of the first move, dot-com fiasco, one might reasonably ask whether Amazon.com and eBay really did secure advantages from being first or if they just got lucky. Or, perhaps, they were excellent firms that would have succeeded whether they were first, second, or ninety-eighth to market. The debate presented here specifically addresses the issue of market entry timing by asking, "Is first-to-market a successful strategy?"

Not surprisingly, persuasive arguments exist for both sides of this important question. Advocates of the first-to-market strategy often point to advantages that can be gained by first moving firms. In an important, time-tested paper management scholars Marvin Lieberman and David Montgomery discuss three advantages accruing to first movers: (1) the ability to influence consumers; (2) the ability to develop an advantage through the use of technology, and (3) securing important strategic assets before competitors do (*Strategic Management Journal*, 1988, vol. 9, 41–58). Consider the first advantage: first-to-market means that a company will be the first on the radar screen of consumers, thus increasing the likelihood it can influence its customers. It may, for instance, try to convince consumers that its product is not only unique, but also the best. Since consumers have nothing against which to compare this new product, they are likely to accept the view that the new product sets and defines the market for all subsequent products introduced by firms acting in a follower capacity. Concerning the second advantage, the first mover may have an advantage since following companies will need time to understand the technology, thus forcing them to play catch up in the marketplace. While followers work to produce a competitive product, the first mover is working to ingrain its product in the market. An example of the final type of advantage occurs when a first mover preempts inputs from its competitors. The first mover may contract with suppliers to lock-in supply of a component for their new product before competitors realize that the component is necessary. With limited access to this component the later movers will find it harder to respond, thus giving an advantage to the first mover.

Despite the potential advantages of being first-to-market, there are many examples of first-to-market firms that have failed. Clearly this suggests that first moves are very risky, and come with no guarantees of success. Not surprisingly, as compared to first movers, it is easy—perhaps easier—to name successful later movers. In fact, successful later movers have dominated many large, important markets. Two examples are Microsoft Windows and its graphical user interfaces and Apple's MP3 player, iPod. Given all the evidence against first moving, it is certainly reasonable to question whether this is a successful strategy or not.

The two readings that follow present different viewpoints of the viability of first moving as a business strategy. The article supporting the "yes" side is by management scholar William T. Robinson and marketing scholar Sungwook Min. They provide an analysis of the survival of first moving firms as compared to the survival of firms that enter later. Their results indicate the advantages from being first outweigh the risks of implementing the strategy. In the second article, also a scholarly research project, authors William Boulding and Markus Christen adopt a contrary position and argue that first moving is not necessarily a wise strategy. Indeed, they provide research evidence suggesting that, in the long-run at least, moving first leads to performance disadvantages! In any event, regardless of your perspective on this topic before you picked up this text, we are confident that your perspective will be affected by the persuasive points and arguments comprising this *Taking Sides* debate topic.

YES ↵

William T. Robinson and
Sungwook Min

Is the First to Market the First to Fail? Empirical Evidence for Industrial Goods Businesses

When entering a new market, the first entrant typically faces the greatest market and technological uncertainties. Memorable phrases reflect the associated survival risk, such as "the first to market is the first to fail" and "the pioneer is the one with the arrows in its back." Although research estimates the market pioneer's survival rate, the typical pioneer survival rate has not been compared with that of early followers. The authors' study compares survival rates for 167 first-entrant market pioneers versus 267 early followers. For these industrial goods businesses, 66% of the pioneers versus 48% of the early followers survived at least ten years. The main conclusion is that the pioneer's temporary monopoly over the early followers plus its first-mover advantages typically offset the survival risks associated with market and technological uncertainties. These results are consistent with previous research in the sense that first-mover advantages that increase a pioneer's market share also help protect the pioneer from outright failure.

Do market pioneers have unusually low survival rates? Unusually low survival rates can offset the pioneer's market share reward that often arises for surviving businesses (Robinson and Fornell 1985) and surviving brands (Urban et al. 1986). Unusually low survival rates can also deter investing in the costly and risky attempt to pioneer a new market.

In a recent *Management Science* article, Shepherd (1999, p. 623) says, "Common wisdom from the strategy literature suggests that . . . pioneers have higher returns if they are successful, . . . but [they] bear a higher risk of failure." Common or conventional wisdom in marketing seems to reach a similar conclusion. Research by both Lambkin and Day (1989, p. 15) and Golder and Tellis (1993) predicts a relatively high market pioneer attrition rate. Golder and Tellis (1993), for example, report a lifetime market pioneer survival rate of only 53%. Tellis and Golder (1996) provide many valid reasons why the first to market can be the first to fail.

Although conventional wisdom highlights survival risks, it does not highlight two key market pioneer benefits. Because a market pioneer is typically defined as the first entrant, a short-term benefit arises when the first entrant has a monopoly before the second entrant's arrival. If a market pioneer does

From *Journal of Marketing Research*, vol. 39, no. 1, February 2002, pp. 120–122, 126–128.

not face any competitors, its survival should be easier. After one or more competitors enter the market, a long-term benefit arises from first-mover advantages. Firstmover advantages include brand loyalty, switching costs, broad product lines that preempt competition, and scale economies (see Kerin, Varadarajan, and Peterson 1992; Lieberman and Montgomery 1998). Given these conflicting forces, the impact of order of market entry on survival is an empirical issue.

In Kalyanaram, Robinson, and Urban's (1995) survey, industry studies cover 7 cigarette markets (Whitten 1979), 18 Iowa newspaper markets (Glazer 1985), 39 chemical product markets (Lieberman 1989), 11 consumer non-durable markets (Sullivan 1992), and 5 medical diagnostic imaging subfields (Mitchell 1991). Because these industry studies yield mixed results, the authors conclude that order of market entry does not appear to be related to long-term survival rates (see Emerging Empirical Generalization #4).

More recent research by Agarwal and Gort (1996) and Agarwal (1996, 1997) uses *Thomas Register of American Manufacturers* data to examine survival rates in 33 markets. Long time-series data yield a negative relationship between entry by product life cycle stage and survival rates, which supports the importance of first-mover advantages.

In contrast to Agarwal's research, our study relates survival rates to order of market entry. Robinson and Fornell (1985), Robinson (1988), and Lambkin and Day (1989) classify an entrant as a market pioneer, an early follower, or a late entrant. Because Agarwal's research combines market pioneers and early followers in the product life cycle's introductory stage, it is silent in terms of their respective survival rates.

Our study compares survival rates for market pioneers versus early followers but does not examine late entrants. Agarwal's research indicates that late entrants have relatively lower survival rates than earlier life cycle stage entrants do. This may arise because late entrants tend to have a relatively low market share (Kalyanaram, Robinson, and Urban 1995), and low market share businesses appear to be more vulnerable to market exit (Caves 1998).[1]

We use the *Thomas Register of American Manufacturers* to develop a broad cross-section of 167 first-entrant market pioneers and 267 early followers. Our random sample covers new markets for manufactured industrial goods.

In contrast to previous research in marketing, our primary conclusion is that market pioneers have significantly higher survival rates than early followers do. This indicates that the pioneer's temporary monopoly and its first-mover advantages tend to offset the survival risks of market pioneering. Therefore, at least for industrial goods, the first to market does not appear to be the first to fail.

A second and less important research contribution examines the impact of pioneer lead time on survival. Brown and Lattin (1994) and Huff and Robinson (1994) show that first-mover advantages are also influenced by pioneer lead time. Consistent with prior research, increasing pioneer lead time tends to increase pioneer survival rates. A new result from our study is that a short delay tends to increase an early follower's survival chance. This can arise when a short delay helps resolve important market and technological uncertainties. However, any further delay tends to decrease early follower survival rates.

Hypotheses

The hypotheses compare market pioneers with early followers in the early years of a market's evolution. Because many forces influence survival, the hypotheses do not directly test a single theoretical mechanism. Instead, they compare the strength of the pioneer's first-mover advantages and pioneer lead time with the combined impact of market and technological uncertainty.

First-Mover Advantages and Survival

Market pioneers typically face the greatest market and technological uncertainties. Market uncertainty arises because it is unusually difficult to forecast sales for a pioneering product. In many cases, market entry is similar to "an archer shooting at a target shrouded by a veil of fog" (Hamel and Prahalad 1994, p. 238). Because an early follower has more time to learn about customer needs and wants, reduced uncertainty should increase its survival chance.

Yip (1982) describes how technological change provides a gateway for entry. Technological change is especially likely to arise during the market's early years. When an early follower has time to obsolete the pioneer's technology, a gateway for entry arises. Again, delayed entry reduces uncertainty, which enhances an early follower's chance of survival.

In summary, conventional discussions of market pioneer survival in the early years of a market's evolution typically emphasize market and technological uncertainties. Memorable phrases reflect the notion that pioneers face the greatest risk. The phrases include "the first to market is the first to fail" and "the market pioneer is the one with the arrows in its back." Because of market and technological uncertainties, conventional wisdom yields the following:

> H_1: When pioneer lead time is held constant, market pioneers have a lesser chance than early followers of surviving.

An alternative hypothesis is that first-mover advantages increase the pioneer's survival chance (see Kerin, Varadarajan, and Peterson 1992; Lieberman and Montgomery 1998). Although several first-mover advantages can arise, this literature is typically downplayed in discussions of market pioneer survival.

Some empirical evidence supports the importance of first-mover advantages. In Table 1, Agarwal's (1997) sample covers 33 categories of consumer, industrial, and military products. For entry into various stages of the product life cycle, her introductory stage entrants (Stage 1) have the highest 12-year survival rates. Introductory-stage entrants include both market pioneers and early followers. Assuming that late entry occurs after the early growth stage (Stage 2), late-entrant survival rates are relatively low. Shepherd's (1999) survey of Australian venture capitalists also supports relatively low late entrant survival rates. Therefore, if first-mover advantages more than offset market and technological uncertainties, we have the following:

> $H_{1\ alt}$: When pioneer lead time is held constant, market pioneers have a greater chance than early followers of surviving.

Table 1

12-Year Survival Rates by Product Life Cycle Stage for 33 Product Categories

Product life cycle stage and name	12-year survival rates (%)	Number of entrants
Stage 1: introduction	55.9	238
Stage 2: early growth	48.5	1911
Stage 3: growth	38.4	229
Stage 4: transition to maturity	37.5	431
Stage 5: maturity	45.3	626

Notes: The data are from Agarwal (1997, Table 1). The five life cycle stages are from Gort and Klepper's (1982) model. To link this material to the marketing literature, we have added product life cycle names, such as introduction, early growth, and so forth.

Pioneer Lead Time and Survival

Increasing pioneer lead time should increase the pioneer's chance of survival. A short-term benefit arises from the pioneer's monopoly before the second entrant's arrival. If the market pioneer does not face any competitors, its survival should be easier. A long-term benefit arises because increasing lead time tends to strengthen first-mover advantages (see Brown and Lattin 1994; Huff and Robinson 1994). By lengthening the pioneer's temporary monopoly and strengthening its first-mover advantages, we have the following:

H$_2$: Increasing pioneer lead time increases the market pioneer's chance of surviving.

Because increasing pioneer lead time makes the pioneer stronger, to the extent that the pioneer and early followers are competing for scarce resources, an early follower's chance of surviving should decrease. By strengthening the pioneer's first-mover advantages, even a short delay hurts an early follower. This yields the following:

H$_3$: Delayed market entry decreases an early follower's chance of surviving.

An alternative hypothesis for H$_3$ points to an inverted-U relationship. In the first year or two of the market's evolution, decreased market and technology uncertainties yield substantial benefits for an early follower. If so, a short delay can help an early follower's chance of survival. As time goes by, an early follower's learning yields diminishing marginal returns. With diminished learning and a pioneer that is developing stronger first-mover advantages, a long delay should hurt an early follower's survival chance. This yields the following:

H$_3$ alt: Delayed market entry initially increases an early follower's chance of survival. Any additional delay decreases an early follower's chance of surviving.

Data

The *Thomas Register of American Manufacturers* is a national buying guide that "is a comprehensive, detailed guide to the full range of products manufactured in the United States" (Lavin 1992, p. 129). The *Thomas Register* attempts to achieve comprehensive coverage by subscribing to a broad range of industry newsletters, searching for startup ventures in university incubators, and, last but not least, providing a free listing in each annual issue.[2]

The 1999 *Thomas Register* includes approximately 157,000 firms and roughly 63,700 product categories, so many products have numerous and highly specialized categories. The 1999 *Thomas Register*, for example, lists 128 different types of lights. They range from aircraft lights, airport lights, and aisle lights all the way down to water lights, waterproof lights, and work lights.

Market Boundaries

Thomas Register market boundaries are established by grouping together close product substitutes. The *Thomas Register's* professional staff does the grouping. Having a professional staff identify new markets helps an academic researcher avoid many subjective decisions—for example, when a new market starts and what competitors should be included in each market. A professional staff also helps gather a large and diverse group of new markets.

One potential danger with the *Thomas Register's* highly specialized product categories is that the first entrant in a highly specialized category is not a market pioneer. Instead, the first entrant is a late entrant in a broader market, such as lights. Even so, *Thomas Register* market boundaries attempt to reflect how industrial buyers shop for products. Industrial buyers do not just shop for a light, they shop for aircraft lights, airport lights, and aisle lights. Because specialized categories reflect specialized buyer demands, market boundaries are driven by industrial buyers' behavior. In contrast, in the *United States Census of Manufacturers* data, similar production processes often drive the Standard Industrial Classification (SIC) code market boundaries (Scherer and Ross 1990, p. 75).

Some new categories in the *Thomas Register* data are complementary products. Mechanical credit card imprinters, for example, were pioneered in 1962. With only three credit card manufacturers listed in 1960, the credit card market appears to have been in its infancy in the early 1960s. Other new categories represent a new technology, such as distance-measuring instruments, which are electronic devices that were pioneered in 1972. This is the same time period when other electronic devices were first introduced, such as the Bowmar pocket calculator (Schnaars 1994, p. 150).

A *Thomas Register* product category also needs to maintain meaningful product uniqueness over time. Animal access doors, for example, were first listed in 1972. In 1988, 14 firms were listed as manufacturing animal access doors. In 1989, this category was merged into the access doors category, which suggests that general purpose access doors had evolved to the point at which they could also be used for animal access.

Thomas Register Sample

As a national buying guide, the *Thomas Register* typically omits firms with exclusively local sales. (In the past five to ten years, local markets have received more coverage, especially in the *Thomas Regional* directories.) By excluding local markets, our sample emphasizes regional and national markets.

The *Thomas Register* includes international firms if they have a manufacturing facility, office, or distribution channel in the United States. Even so, because the *Thomas Register* highlights U.S. manufacturers, imported manufactured goods are often excluded. Therefore, our sample deletes product categories with a relatively high share of imports.[3]

Food and food-related products are covered in a separate issue, the *Thomas Food Industry Register*. By excluding food and food-related products, our random sample was too small to make accurate inferences about consumer goods. Therefore, our sample covers only industrial goods.

Overall, the *Thomas Register* provides detailed coverage of domestic manufacturing for nonfood products in regional and national markets. Given these strengths and the use of the *Thomas Register* in several survival studies in the economics literature (Agarwal 1996, 1997, 1998; Agarwal and Gort 1996; Gort and Klepper 1982), the data should provide meaningful insights into market pioneer versus early follower survival rates. . . .

Summary

Market pioneers typically face more market and technological uncertainty than early followers and late entrants do. Market uncertainty arises because it is difficult to forecast customer response to a pioneering innovation. Technological uncertainty arises because a pioneer's first-generation technology may not work very well. When an early follower learns from the pioneer's mistakes, its risks are reduced.

However, survival rates for market pioneers are typically enhanced by their temporary monopoly. After their monopoly disappears, market pioneers often benefit from first-mover advantages, such as retaining customer loyalty, setting the industry standard, having superior distribution, and having a broad product line. Although first-mover advantages are discussed in several contexts, conventional survival discussions typically emphasize market and technological uncertainties.

Because market and technological uncertainties are most prominent in the market's early years, survival rates are compared for 167 first entrant market pioneers versus 267 early followers. Across this sample of industrial goods businesses, market pioneers have significantly higher five- and ten-year survival rates than early followers do. Results from a logit regression analysis suggest that pioneers' first-mover advantages more than offset the market and technological uncertainties. Market pioneers' survival also tends to increase as their lead time over the first early follower increases. Increasing lead time gives the pioneers a longer temporary monopoly, which makes survival easier and should help strengthen their first-mover advantages.

In the early years of a market's evolution, an early follower's learning from a short delay can help its chance of survival. The data support this point in the sense that delayed entry initially increases but eventually decreases an early follower's chance of survival. This suggests that an early follower's learning from a short delay resolves a material amount of uncertainty. A longer delay, though, can hurt an early follower when additional learning is modest and the pioneer is getting stronger and stronger over time.

Limitations and Further Research

Because the *Thomas Register* has relatively narrow market boundaries, market and technological uncertainty should be lower than in broadly defined markets. This is because new markets with relatively narrow boundaries often extend existing knowledge on markets and technologies. Even so, first-mover advantages should also be weaker in markets with narrow boundaries. Therefore, research should examine the extent to which survival rates are influenced by market boundary breadth.

Our sample covers only industrial goods. Would similar results arise in markets for consumer goods? Services? High-technology products? Because market uncertainties, technological uncertainties, and first-mover advantages can vary dramatically across different types of markets, further research should examine the robustness of higher pioneer survival rates across various industry settings.

Risks of Market Pioneering

Absolute survival rates are strongly influenced by the scale of commercialization. A *Thomas Register* entrant only needs to sell its product in a regional market. In Golder and Tellis's (1993) study, a pioneer only needs to sell its product in a local market.[4] In Urban and colleagues' (1986) study, an entrant must sell its product nationally. By excluding small entrants that failed to achieve a national scope, Urban and colleagues' sample yields higher pioneer survival rates. This helps explain why Urban and colleagues (1986, p. 655) did not locate any market pioneer exits, whereas our study and Golder and Tellis's (1993) report market pioneer survival rates in the 53% to 87% range.

From this perspective, three key steps arise in the market entry process: (1) investing in the attempt to enter a new market, (2) entering the market on a local or regional scale, and (3) expanding to a national scale. Our results, along with those of Urban and colleagues (1986), suggest that when a regional or national scale of operations is achieved, survival rates tend to be higher for market pioneers than for early followers.

In the market entry process, empirical research has not yet linked order of market entry to the survival rate for firms that are attempting to pioneer a new market. We speculate that this is where the greatest risk arises for market pioneer hopefuls, because it is difficult to generate and commercialize an idea that will pioneer a new market.

To address these problems, Hamel and Prahalad (1994, Ch. 11) recommend experimenting with multiple options that are both fast and inexpensive. Although experimentation leads to many small failures, perhaps nine of every ten attempts, these small losses are easily offset by the large gains from pioneering new markets of the future. Thus, a market pioneering strategy has both high risks and high returns, and the greatest risk of failure arises before product launch.

Conclusion

Conventional wisdom on market pioneer survival highlights market and technological uncertainties. Although market pioneers face the greatest uncertainties, they also benefit from first-mover advantages and from the temporary monopoly that arises before they face the first early follower. For our sample of 167 industrial goods markets, market pioneer first-mover advantages plus their temporary monopoly more than offset these market and technological uncertainties. In showing that pioneers often survive past the early and turbulent years of a market's evolution, our results are consistent with Shepherd's (1999) recent survey of Australian venture capitalists. Both studies indicate that the first to market is typically not the first to fail.

Notes

1. Also, in the *Thomas Register* data, it is not always clear when an entrant shifts from being an early follower to being a late entrant, so it is often difficult to identify a late entrant objectively.

2. Many of the data insights are based on telephone conversations and e-mail communications with Glenn H. Moore, Associate Publisher/Editor of the *Thomas Register.*

3. To estimate the market share of imported goods, data from the *United States Census of Manufacturers* at the four-digit SIC code level estimate the ratio of imports divided by domestic shipments less exports plus imports. Because a natural break in our sample arises between 33% and 40%, our sample excludes the 13 import-oriented markets that exceed 33%.

4. Golder and Tellis's (1993) data include local markets, such as the Brooklyn, N.Y., market for Trommer's Red-Letter light beer. As mentioned previously, the *Thomas Register* excludes most but not all local markets.

References

Agarwal, Rajshree (1996), "Technological Activity and Survival of Firms," *Economics Letters,* 52 (July), 101–108.

———— (1997), "Survival of Firms over the Product Life Cycle," *Southern Economic Journal,* 63 (3), 571–84.

———— (1998), "Evolutionary Trends of Industry Variables," *International Journal of Industrial Organization,* 16 (July), 511–25.

———— and Michael Gort (1996), "The Evolution of Markets and Entry, Exit, and survival of Firms," *Review of Economics and Statistics,* 78 (November), 489–98.

Brown, Christina and James M. Lattin (1994), "Investigating the Relationship Between Time in Market and Pioneering Advantage," *Management Science,* 40 (October), 1361–69.

Caves, Richard E. (1998), "Industrial Organization and New Findings on the Turnover and Mobility of Firms," *Journal of Economic Literature,* 36 (December), 1947–82.

Dunne, Timothy, Mark J. Roberts, and Larry Samuelson (1989), "Patterns of Firm Entry and Exit in U.S. Manufacturing Industries," *RAND Journal of Economics,* 19 (Winter), 495–515.

Glazer, A. (1985), "The Advantages of Being First," *American Economic Review,* 75 (June), 473–80.

Golder, Peter N. and Gerard J. Tellis (1993), "Pioneer Advantage: Marketing Logic or Marketing Legend?" *Journal of Marketing Research,* 30 (May), 158–70.

Gort, Michael and Steven Klepper (1982), "Time Paths in the Diffusion of Product Innovations," *Economic Journal,* 92 (September), 630–53.

Griffin, Abbie (1997), "PDMA Research on New Product Development Practices: Updating Trends and Benchmarking Best Practices," *Journal of Product Innovation Management,* 6 (November), 429–58.

Hadlock, Paul, Daniel Hecker, and Joseph Gannon (1991), "High Technology Employment: Another View," *Monthly Labor Review,* 114 (July), 26–30.

Hamel, Gary and C.K. Prahalad (1994), *Competing for the Future.* Boston, MA: Harvard Business School Press.

Huff, Lenard C. and William T. Robinson (1994), "The Impact of Leadtime and Years of Competitive Rivalry on Pioneer Market Share Advantages," *Management Science,* 40 (October), 1370–77.

Kalyanaram, Gurumurthy, William T. Robinson, and Glen L. Urban (1995), "Order of Market Entry: Established Empirical Generalizations, Emerging Generalizations, and Future Research," *Marketing Science,* 14 (2), G212–G221.

—— and Glen L. Urban (1992), "Dynamic Effects of Order of Entry on Market Share, Trial Penetration, and Repeat Purchases for Frequently Purchased Goods," *Marketing Science,* 11 (Summer), 235–50.

Kerin, Roger A., P. Rajan Varadarajan, and Robert A. Peterson (1992), "First-Mover Advantage: A Synthesis, Conceptual Framework, and Research Propositions," *Journal of Marketing,* 56 (October), 33–52.

Lambkin, Mary and George S. Day (1989), "Evolutionary Processes in Competitive Markets: Beyond the Product Life Cycle," *Journal of Marketing,* 3 (July), 4–20.

Lavin, Michael R. (1992), *Business Information: How to Find It, How to Use It.* Phoenix: Oryx Press.

Lieberman, Marvin B. (1989), "The Learning Curve, Technological Barriers to Entry, and Competitive Survival in the Chemical Processing Industries," *Strategic Management Journal,* 9 (Summer), 431–47.

—— and David B. Montgomery (1998), "First-Mover (Dis)Advantages: Retrospective and Link with the Resource-Based View," *Strategic Management Journal,* 19 (December), 1111–25.

Mitchell. W. (1991), "Dual Clocks: Entry Order Influences on Incumbent and Newcomer Market Share and Survival When Specialized Assets Retain Their Value," *Strategic Management Journal,* 12 (January/February), 85–100.

Robinson, William T. (1988), "Sources of Market Pioneer Advantage: The Case of Industrial Goods Industries," *Journal of Marketing Research,* 25 (February), 87–94.

────── and Claes Fornell (1985), "Sources of Market Pioneer Advantage in Consumer Goods Industries," *Journal of Marketing Research,* 22 (August), 305–17.

Scherer, F. M. and David Ross (1990), *Industrial Market Structure and Economic Performance,* 3d ed. Boston: Houghton Mifflin.

Schmalensee, Richard (1982), "Product Differentiation Advantages of Pioneering Brands," *American Economic Review,* 27 (June), 349–65.

Schnaars, Steven P. (1994), *Managing Imitation Strategies.* New York: The Free Press.

Shepherd, Dean A. (1999), "Venture Capitalists' Assessment of New Venture Survival," *Management Science,* 45 (May), 621–32.

Sullivan, Mary W. (1992), "The Effect of Brand Extension and Other Entry Decisions on Survival Time," working paper, Graduate School of Business, University of Chicago (June).

Tellis, Gerard J. and Peter N. Golder (1996), "First to Market, First to Fail? Real Causes of Enduring Market Leadership," *Sloan Management Review,* 37 (Winter), 65–75.

Urban, Glen L., Theresa Carter, Steven Gaskin, and Zofia Mucha (1986), "Market Share Rewards to Pioneering Brands: An Empirical Analysis and Strategic Implications," *Management Science,* 32 (June), 645–59.

Whitten, Ira T. (1979), *Brand Performance in the Cigarette Industry and the Advantages of Early Entry, 1913–73.* Washington, DC: Federal Trade Commission.

Yip, George S. (1982), *Barriers to Entry: A Corporate-Strategy Perspective.* Lexington, MA: Lexington Books.

**William Boulding and
Markus Christen**

 **NO**

Sustainable Pioneering Advantage? Profit Implications of Market Entry Order

There is strong theoretical and empirical evidence supporting the idea that "first-to-market" leads to an enduring market share advantage. In sharp contrast to these findings, we find that at the business unit level being first-to-market leads, on average, to a long-term *profit disadvantage*. This result holds for a sample of consumer goods as well as a sample of industrial goods and leads to questions about the validity of first mover advantage, in and of itself, as a strategy to achieve superior performance. . . .

Introduction

"First mover advantage" is an oft-cited strategic principle for achieving superior performance. This principle is often high on managers' list of arguments to justify strategic moves such as, for example, the entry into emerging markets such as China, or the recent rush into e-business. Moreover, an impressive body of research in marketing, strategy and economics supports the validity of this principle. For example, at both the business unit level and the brand level, a strong inverse relationship between order of market entry and long-run market share has been found (e.g., Robinson and Fornell 1985, Urban et al. 1986). Empirical evidence is so extensive that this relationship exists as an "empirical generalization" in the marketing literature (Kalyanaram et al. 1995). At the consumer level, experiments have shown that the order of entry can have a significant impact on customer preferences, memory, learning, and judgment (Carpenter and Nakamoto 1989, Kardes and Kalyanaram 1992, Zhang and Markman 1998).

Surprisingly, there exists virtually no empirical research about the effect of entry order on business profit, even though reviews of the entry order literature have repeatedly pointed to profit implications as one of the key unanswered questions in this area of research (Lieberman and Montgomery 1988, 1998; Kerin et al. 1992; Robinson et al. 1994).[1] Whether a market share advantage is sufficient to support the existence of a sustainable profit advantage is questionable given the uncertainties in both the market share-profit relationship (e.g., Jacobson 1988, Boulding and Staelin 1993) and the entry order-cost relationship (Lieberman and Montgomery 1988).

From *Marketing Science*, vol. 22, no. 3, Summer 2003, pp. 371–386 (excerpts). Copyright © 2003 by Institute for Operations Research and the Management Sciences (INFORMS), 7240 Parkway Drive, Suite 300, Hanover, MD 21076 USA. Reprinted by permission.

The main objective of this paper is to address this gap in the literature and empirically examine the long-term profit implications of the order of market entry for a *business unit*. Consistent with the existing literature, we focus on the long-term consequences to identify whether profit differences persist even after competitive entry. A significant difference would suggest, for example, that part of today's profit difference in cola beverages between the Coca-Cola Company and PepsiCo could be attributed to the fact that the former created the cola market about 10 years before the latter entered. Our analysis, therefore, provides insights about the profit implications of entry order strategies.

To be precise, our interest is in looking at profit differences between pioneers and followers solely attributable to the timing of market entry, and not differences due to other characteristics (e.g., resources) of pioneers and followers. In all likelihood, these differences exist because, as first noted by Lieberman and Montgomery (1988), firms' resources and capabilities affect their choice of entry timing. That is, entry timing is an endogenous choice variable. For example, Sony generally tries to create new markets, while Matsushita pursues a strategy of following Sony into these markets. Therefore, Sony and Matsushita likely differ in ways that reflect the difference in their market entry strategies. More formally, the resource-based-view literature (e.g., Wernerfelt 1984, Barney 1986) suggests that an enduring competitive advantage must be due to differences in underlying resources. This literature is explicit in stating that there can be *no* pioneering advantage without heterogeneity in resources across firms (Barney 1991), and empirical research supports the presence of systematic firm differences associated with entry strategies (Robinson et al. 1992, Murthi et al. 1996). . . .

We start our analysis by determining the effect of entry order on profit for an average business unit. For two samples of business units derived from the PIMS database—a sample of consumer goods and a sample of industrial goods—we find a *long-term profit disadvantage of pioneering* for the average business unit. This result holds for both net income and ROI when used as measures of business unit profit. Given the strong evidence in the literature for the existence of a long-term demand-side advantage, this profit result implies that first-to-market must lead to a long-term average cost disadvantage. Thus, for both samples and with the same estimation methodology, we estimate the effect of entry order on demand and average cost, i.e., the economic components of profit, and find strong support for this conjecture. Pioneering leads to a long-term demand advantage and an even larger long-term cost disadvantage. We test the robustness of these results by varying the model specification and the instruments used to obtain consistent estimates. This sensitivity analysis strongly confirms the long-term profit disadvantage due to an average cost disadvantage.

We then examine conditions for which a pioneering profit advantage can exist. First, given the long-term profit disadvantage, it appears that pioneering a new market makes sense for the average business only if an early profit advantage exists (assuming rational decision making). We therefore examine the time path of profits for pioneers and find, for both samples and profit measures, an initial profit advantage, which decreases over time and turns into a disadvantage after 12 to 14 years. Second, we examine the moderating effect on the long-term profit difference for three factors: the likelihood of customer learning, the market share position of a business unit, and the presence of patent protection. Based on the existing literature, we hypothesize that these factors enable pioneering firms to avert the long-term profit disadvantage or even sustain a profit advantage.

In sum, this paper provides the first detailed empirical analysis of the profit implications of the order of market entry at the business unit level. . . .

Pioneering Advantages and Disadvantages

An extensive theoretical and empirical literature investigates the effects of the market entry order. This literature has been well summarized in various review articles (Lieberman and Montgomery 1988, Kerin et al. 1992, Robinson et al. 1994, Kalyanaram et al. 1995). Rather than repeat these findings, we very briefly point to two findings of relevance to the research herein.

First, as noted, there is an extensive list of theoretical arguments in favor of a pioneering demand advantage. These theoretical arguments are supported by strong empirical evidence, including findings based on experiments that are not subject to methodological problems raised in the literature (see Golder and Tellis 1993). Second, there is no unambiguous theoretical prediction about the effect of entry order on cost. The literature points to possible advantages due to patents, accumulation of experience, and preemption of scarce resources. At the same time, the literature also points to possible disadvantages due to followers' ability to free ride on information and market building efforts and incumbent inertia. Further, in contrast to the empirical generalization of a pioneering market share (demand) advantage (Kalyanaram et al. 1995), there is no systematic empirical evidence with respect to the effect of entry order on cost. Because of this ambiguity in the effects of entry order on cost, the effect of entry order on overall profit is also uncertain, and we next consider two possible profit scenarios.

Entry Order Profit Scenarios

We propose that two possible profit scenarios capture the current state of knowledge about pioneering effects, i.e., a demand advantage and an ambiguous cost effect.[2] Under the first scenario, we assume that motivation to enter first is driven by the likelihood of obtaining the "known" demand-side advantage, an advantage shown in both theoretical and empirical work. As argued in the strategy literature (e.g., Wensley 1982, Erickson and Jacobson 1992), if knowledge about a strategic relationship exists (e.g., first entrants are more profitable), then without what Wensley refers to as "isolating mechanisms," firms will compete away the returns implied by this relationship. Thus, knowledge about a demand-side pioneering advantage could lead to a race to entry that competes away this advantage through cost disadvantages. In sum, this scenario argues for a demand advantage, a cost disadvantage, and no significant long-term profit differences due to the order of market entry.

This same profit prediction emerges from the resource-based view of the firm. Given this view strategic actions, like the decision to create a new market, are contingent on business unit resources. Thus, there can be no sustainable advantage to the entry strategy, per se, unless firms have inimitable resources, because the entry strategy itself is perfectly imitable (Barney 1991). Consequently, after controlling for resource differences across firms (as we do in our empirical analysis), there should be no effect of entry order on profit. Importantly, if entry choices are driven by differences in firm resources, the market entry order must be an endogenous decision.

In addition to a sustainable demand advantage, the first entrant can also benefit from a period of monopoly profits that are eroded over time as later entrants make inroads. However, if in fact competition dissipates differences in lifetime profits due to entry order, this leads to an interesting prediction. Specifically, we should observe an initial profit advantage for the pioneering firm that is offset by a profit disadvantage in later years. While profit differences can exist at any given point in time, dissipation of economic rents should occur over time and there should be no lifetime profit differences due to entry order. . . .

Discussion

. . . Contrary to common expectations, our results show that, on average, *first-to-market leads to a long-term profit disadvantage relative to later entrants*. We replicate, in an economic framework, the well-established consumer-based *long-term demand advantage*, and show that first-to-market leads to an *even larger long-term average cost disadvantage*. These results hold for a sample of business units selling consumer goods as well as for a sample of business units selling industrial goods. . . .

In the extended analysis we provide evidence of two kinds of pioneering profit advantage. First, we show that for both data samples, pioneering leads to an *initial profit advantage that erodes over time*. The advantage lasts for about 12 to 14 years. Second, we show that the likelihood of customer learning, the market share position of a business, and patent protection—product patents for consumer goods and process patents for industrial goods—moderate the long-term profit effect of entry order. The moderating effects tend to be stronger for the consumer goods sample, where *limited customer learning, a strong market share position, or patent protection can eliminate the long-term profit disadvantage and even lead to a sustainable pioneering profit advantage*. Future research should focus on identifying other conditions and specific firm resources that moderate the effect of market entry order. . . .

What are the managerial implications of our findings? First, the presence of a long-term profit disadvantage does not mean that a pioneering strategy is strictly unprofitable. It means that in the long run, entering a market later is, on average, more profitable than pioneering. Thus, it would be incorrect to predicate an entry strategy on the sustainability of profits by being first to market. In this regard, it would be interesting to know what exactly managers expect when they pursue a strategy of being first-to-market.

Second, the worries of firms like Procter & Gamble that have not created new markets in a long time and instead rely on the profits from existing "pioneering" brands in well-established markets could be justified (Jarvis 2000). The initial profit advantage that appears to last a little over a decade suggests that firms may be better off pursuing a strategy that continuously creates new markets.

Third, pioneering firms may be able to benefit by paying closer attention to later entrants and in particular to their organization and processes, which yield lower average costs. In this regard, more theoretical and empirical work is needed to understand the relationship between entry order and costs beyond average cost. . . .

In sum then, while we believe our empirical findings provide new insights, many unanswered questions remain for future research. Still, we believe our empirical findings cast doubt on the basic strategic principle of "first mover advantage." When managers articulate and evaluate an entry timing strategy, we urge that consideration be given to precisely why and how the strategy will provide a sustainable advantage. . . .

Notes

1. Unpublished work (Boulding and Moore 1987, Srinivasan 1988) suggests that pioneering does not provide a profit advantage.

2. To be complete, one could posit a pioneering profit disadvantage, which could be explained by two different effects. First, an ex-ante overvaluation of the demand advantage could lead to overspending to obtain this advantage (i.e., the winner's curse). Second, loss aversion could lead to an ex-post overvaluation of the demand advantage and overspending to defend market share in the face of competitive entry. This could happen if the pioneer's initial market share provides the reference point and changes in market share after competitive entry fall in the loss domain.

References

Barney, Jay B. 1986. Strategic factor markets: Expectations, luck, and business strategy. *Management Sci.* 32, 1231–1241.

———. 1991. Firm resources and competitive advantage. *J. Management* **17** (1), 99–120.

Boulding, William. 1990. Unobservable effects and business performance: Do fixed effects matter? *Marketing Sci.* **9** (Winter) 88–91.

———, Michael J. Moore. 1987. Pioneering and profit: Structural estimates from a nonlinear simultaneous equations model with endogenous pioneering. Working paper, Fuqua School of Business, Duke University, Durham, NC.

———, Richard Staelin. 1993. A look on the cost side: Market share and the competitive environment. *Marketing Sci.* **12**(Spring) 144–166.

Carpenter, Gregory S., Kent Nakamoto. 1989. Consumer preference formation and pioneering advantage. *J. Marketing Res.* **26**(August) 285–298.

Erickson, Gary, Robert Jacobson. 1992. Gaining comparative advantage through discretionary expenditures: The returns to R&D and advertising. *Management Sci.* **38**(September) 1264–1279.

Golder, Peter N., Gerard J. Tellis. 1993. Pioneering advantage: Marketing logic or marketing legend? *J. Marketing Res.* **30**(May) 158–170.

Jacobson, Robert. 1988. Distinguishing among competing theories of the market share effect. *J. Marketing* **9**(October) 68–80.

Jarvis, Steve. 2000. P&G's challenge. *Marketing News.* August 28. **1** 13.

Kalyanaram, Gurumurthy, William T. Robinson, Glen L. Urban. 1995. Order of market entry: Established empirical generalizations, emerging empirical generalizations, and future research. *Marketing Sci.* **14**(2) G212–G221.

Kardes, Frank R., Gurumurthy Kalyanaram. 1992. Order-of-entry effects on consumer memory and judgment: An information integration perspective. *J. Marketing Res.* **29**(August) 343–357.

Kerin, Roger A., P. Rajan Varadarajan, Robert A. Peterson. 1992. First-mover advantage: A synthesis, conceptual framework, and research propositions. *J. Marketing* **56**(October) 33–52.

Lieberman, Marvin B., David B. Montgomery. 1988. First-mover advantages. *Strategic Management J.* **9**(Summer) 41–58.

Murthi, B. P. S., Kannan Srinivasan, Gurumurthy Kalyanaram. 1996. Controlling for observed and unobserved managerial skills in determining first-mover market share advantages. *J. Marketing Res.* **33**(August) 329–336.

Robinson, William T. 1988. Sources of market pioneer advantages: The case of industrial goods industries. *J. Marketing Res.* **25**(February) 87–94.

———, Claes Fornell. 1985. Sources of market pioneer advantages in consumer goods industries. *J. Marketing Res.* **22**(August) 305–317.

———, ———, Mary W. Sullivan. 1992. Are market pioneers intrinsically stronger than later entrants? *Strategic Management J.* **13**(November) 609–624.

———, Gurumurthy Kalyanaram, Glen L. Urban. 1994. First-mover advantages from pioneering new markets: A survey of empirical evidence. *Rev. Indust. Organ.* **9**(February) 1–23.

Srinivasan, Kannan. 1988. Pioneering versus early following in new product markets. Unpublished Ph.D. dissertation, University of California, Los Angeles, CA.

Urban, Glen L., Theresa Carter, Steven P. Gaskin, Zo.a Mucha. 1986. Market share rewards to pioneering brands: An empirical analysis and strategic implications. *Management Sci.* **32**(June) 645–659.

Wernerfelt, Birger. 1984. A resource-based view of the firm. *Strategic Management J.* **5** 171–180.

Wensley, Robin. 1982. PIMS and BCG: New horizons or false dawn. *Strategic Management J.* **3**(April–June) 147–158.

Zhang, Shi, Arthur B. Markman. 1998. Overcoming the early entrant advantage: The role of alignable and nonalignable differences. *J. Marketing Res.* **35**(November) 413–426.

POSTSCRIPT

Is First-to-Market a Successful Strategy?

Determining when to enter a market is a critical decision faced by virtually all corporations at some point in their existence. This is particularly true in today's fast-paced business environment where innovation and technological advancement are virtually mandatory. But when to enter? Should a firm strive to be first with a new product or service or should it avoid the accompanying risks and act as a follower? The two articles comprising the debate presented here offer opposing views on these questions.

In a study that supports the first-to-market strategy, William Robinson and Sunwook Min questioned whether there might too much focus on the risk of failure and not enough on the advantages that come from first moving. Their work examined the strategic moves of 167 companies that were first-to-market and 267 companies that were early-to-follow in industrial goods businesses. They concluded that advantages of being first-to-market are greater than the risks and uncertainties faced by the firm. Did you find their arguments and research findings persuasive enough to convince you that first-to-market is a successful strategy?

However, before you commit yourself, ponder the findings of the research discussed in the "No" side article by William Boulding and Markus Christen. There is no doubt that their findings cast serious doubt on the effectiveness of moving first in securing performance gains, at least in the long run. In a study of both consumer and industrial goods corporations, the two marketing researchers asked the question of whether or not the order of market entry affects firm performance. They provide evidence that being first actually results in "long-term profit disadvantage," a result that flies directly in the face of the conventional belief that first-moving is a wise and desirable corporate strategy.

Both articles presented here provided insightful analysis concerning the first-to-market strategy. So, given what you have just read, do you think that being first-to market is a successful strategy?

Suggested Readings

William T. Robinson and Jeongwen Chiang (2002), "Product Development Strategies for Established Market Pioneers, Early Followers, and Late Entrants," *Strategic Management Journal*, 23, 855–866.

Fernando Suarez and Gianvito Lanzolla (2005). The half-truth to first-mover advantage. *Harvard Business Review*, April 2005, p. 121.

Gary Hamel (2001). Inside the revolution: Smart mover, dumb mover. *Fortune,* September 3, 2001.

William Boulding and Markus Christen (2001). First-mover disadvantage. *Harvard Business Review,* October 2001, p. 20.

Marvin Lieberman and David Montgomery (1998). First-mover (dis)advantages: Retrospective and link with the resource-based view. *Strategic Management Journal,* 19, 1111–1125.

David Ketchen, Charles Snow, and Vera Street (2004). Improving firm performance by matching strategic decision-making processes to competitive dynamics. *Academy of Management Executive*, 18, 29–43.

ISSUE 14

Is Growth Always an Inherent Corporate Value?

YES: Clayton M. Christensen and Michael E. Raynor, from *The Innovator's Solution* (Harvard Business School Press, 2003)

NO: Jim Mackey and Liisa Välikangas, from "The Myth of Unbounded Growth," *MIT Sloan Management Review* (Winter 2004)

ISSUE SUMMARY

YES: Clayton M. Christensen and Michael E. Raynor argue that firms are subject to pressures to continually grow from sources both inside and outside of the organization.

NO: Business scholars Jim Mackey and Liisa Välikangas cite many interesting statistics to support the view that lasting growth is elusive and unrealistic and, thus, not necessary to define a firm as successful.

O pen any business periodical nowadays and you might expect to see headlines like these from recent editions of the *Wall Street Journal:*

> "Caterpillar Gets Bugs Out of Old Equipment; Growing Remanufacturing Division Is Central to Earnings-Stabilization Plan" (July 5, 2006, pg. A.16)
>
> "Changing the Light Bulb; No Joke: LED Technology Fuels Fast Growth in the Once-Staid Industry" (June 8, 2006, pg. B.1)
>
> "Churchill Downs Searches for Growth" (May 24, 2006, pg. B.3A)

What do these headlines have in common? If you noticed each assumes that corporate growth is a good and necessary strategy, kudos to you. Without a doubt growth can be beneficial for both corporations and society at large. Indeed, Caterpillar found that growth in remanufacturing was beneficial even when the economy was down, and the lighting industry is brightening up because of growth in the light-emitting diodes market.

On the other hand, it is also true that sustained growth is a difficult and elusive goal. For instance, consider these recent *Wall Street Journal* headlines:

> "Cadbury Schwepps PLC: Margin-Growth Target Stifled by Rising Energy Costs" (June 8, 2006, pg. n/a)

"Telenor's Messy Excursion in Russia Shows Pitfalls of Hunting for Growth" (July 7, 2006, pg. C.1)

Both of these articles detail problems resulting from strategic decisions driven by the need for growth. In fact, many business observers suggest that such predicaments seem to be the rule rather than the exception for companies attempting a growth strategy. This leaves us with the current debate where we ask—Must firms constantly grow to be considered successful?

Clayton M. Christensen and Michael E. Raynor argue that pressures to meet this "growth imperative" come from both inside and outside of the organization. Externally, the perpetuation of this imperative is largely fueled by shareholders who expect to see value created through growth. These expectations for growth are built in to the stock market's valuation of a company's stock. Indeed, if a firm fails to meet its expectations for growth—typically reflected in lower than anticipated earnings—the company will take a beating in the stock market. Moreover, if a company does meet its expectations for growth, it is often rewarded with even higher growth expectations for the future. And, although a company's main demand for growth may be from its shareholders, this is certainly not the only source of pressure the company needs to recognize. Typically, in a growing company, employees will expect that they will have opportunities to move up and gain better positions for themselves. In this manner, employees also demand growth. Thus, it is not surprising that most top-level executives consider growth as the dominant, underlying goal of the organization.

But what about the other side of the debate? Isn't it possible that the continuous, unbounded growth companies and investors hope for is really just a "myth" for most firms? This is the claim of the article by Jim Mackey and Liisa Välikangas. They cite many interesting statistics to support the view that lasting growth is elusive and unrealistic. Further, they argue, such growth is not only elusive, but can be very costly, particularly if the firm is currently not in a growth phase. To illustrate their point, Mackey and Välikangas state, "When stalled companies make massive investments in an attempt to return to double-digit growth, it seems analogous to spending life savings on a lottery ticket" (p. 90). Furthermore, although the company may experience resistance from investors and other stakeholders interested in corporate growth, there are other nongrowth options available that firms should consider as legitimate, realistic alternative business behaviors. Nevertheless, Mackey and Välikangas concede that the attitude in today's environment is toward propagating growth and warn investors, CEOs, and employees alike to be wary of potential pitfalls that may accompany a growth strategy. Their advice is wise, and we recommend it to you next time you pick up a business journal, read a headline about a company failing to meet its growth expectations, and conclude that the firm is failing.

YES ↵

Clayton M. Christensen and
Michael E. Raynor

The Growth Imperative

Growth is important because companies create shareholder value through profitable growth. Yet there is powerful evidence that once a company's core business has matured, the pursuit of new platforms for growth entails daunting risk. Roughly one company in ten is able to sustain the kind of growth that translates into an above-average increase in shareholder returns over more than a few years.[1] Too often the very attempt to grow causes the entire corporation to crash. Consequently, most executives are in a no-win situation: equity markets demand that they grow, but it's hard to know *how* to grow. Pursuing growth the wrong way can be worse than no growth at all.

Consider AT&T. In the wake of the government-mandated divestiture of its local telephony services in 1984, AT&T became primarily a long distance telecommunications services provider. The break-up agreement freed the company to invest in new businesses, so management almost immediately began seeking avenues for growth and the shareholder value that growth creates.

The first such attempt arose from a widely shared view that computer systems and telephone networks were going to converge. AT&T first tried to build its own computer division in order to position itself at that intersection, but was able to do no better than annual losses of $200 million. Rather than retreat from a business that had proved to be unassailable from the outside, the company decided in 1991 to bet bigger still, acquiring NCR, at the time the world's fifth-largest computer maker, for $7.4 billion. That proved only to be a down payment: AT&T lost another $2 billion trying to make the acquisition work. AT&T finally abandoned this growth vision in 1996, selling NCR for $3.4 billion, about a third of what it had invested in the opportunity.

But the company *had* to grow. So even as the NCR acquisition was failing, AT&T was seeking growth opportunities in technologies closer to its core. In light of the success of the wireless services that several of its spun-off local telephone companies had achieved, in 1994 the company bought McCaw Cellular, at the time the largest national wireless carrier in the United States, for $11.6 billion, eventually spending $15 billion in total on its own wireless business. When Wall Street analysts subsequently complained that they were unable to properly value the combined higher-growth wireless business within the lower-growth wireline company, AT&T decided to create a separately traded stock for the wireless business in 2000. This valued the business at $10.6 billion, about two-thirds of the investment AT&T had made in the venture.

But that move left the AT&T wireline stock right where it had started, and the company *had* to grow. So in 1998 it embarked upon a strategy to enter and reinvent the local telephony business with broadband technology. Acquiring TCI and MediaOne for a combined price of $112 billion made AT&T Broadband the largest cable operator in the United States. Then, more quickly than anyone could have foreseen, the difficulties in implementation and integration proved insurmountable. In 2000, AT&T agreed to sell its cable assets to Comcast for $72 billion.[2]

In the space of a little over ten years, AT&T had wasted about $50 billion and destroyed even more in shareholder value—all in the hope of *creating* shareholder value through growth.

The bad news is that AT&T is not a special case. Consider Cabot Corporation, the world's major producer of carbon black, a compound that imparts to products such as tires many of their most important properties. This business has long been very strong, but the markets haven't grown rapidly. To create the growth that builds shareholder value, Cabot's executives in the early 1980s launched several aggressive growth initiatives in advanced materials, acquiring a set of promising specialty metals and high-tech ceramics businesses. These constituted operating platforms into which the company would infuse new process and materials technology that was emerging from own research laboratories and work it had sponsored at MIT.

Wall Street greeted these investments to accelerate Cabot's growth trajectory with enthusiasm and drove the company's share price to triple the level at which it had languished prior to these initiatives. But as the losses created by Cabot's investments in these businesses began to drag the entire corporation's earnings down, Wall Street hammered the stock. While the overall market appreciated at a robust rate between 1988 and 1991, Cabot's shares dropped by more than half. In the early 1990s, feeling pressure to boost earnings, Cabot's board brought in new management whose mandate was to shut down the new businesses and refocus on the core. As Cabot's profitability rebounded, Wall Street enthusiastically doubled the company's share price. The problem, of course, was that this turnaround left the new management team no better off than their predecessors: desperately seeking growth opportunities for mature businesses with limited prospects.[3]

We could cite many cases of companies' similar attempts to create new-growth platforms after the core business had matured. They follow an all-too-similar pattern. When the core business approaches maturity and investors demand new growth, executives develop seemingly sensible strategies to generate it. Although they invest aggressively, their plans fail to create the needed growth fast enough; investors hammer the stock; management is sacked; and Wall Street rewards the new executive team for simply restoring the *status quo ante*: a profitable but low-growth core business.[4]

Even expanding firms face a variant of the growth imperative. No matter how fast the growth treadmill is going, it is not fast enough. The reason: Investors have a pesky tendency to discount into the *present* value of a company's stock price whatever rate of growth they *foresee* the company achieving. Thus, even if a company's core business is growing vigorously, the only way its managers can deliver a rate of return to shareholders in the future that exceeds the risk-adjusted market average is to grow *faster* than shareholders expect. Changes in stock prices are driven not by simply the *direction* of growth, but largely by *unexpected* changes in the *rate of change* in a company's earnings and cash flows. Hence, one company that is projected to grow at 5 percent and in fact keeps growing at 5 percent and another company that is projected to grow at 25 percent and delivers 25 percent growth will both produce for future investors a market-average risk-adjusted rate of return in the future.[5] A company must deliver the rate of growth that the market is projecting just to keep its stock price from falling. It must *exceed* the consensus forecast rate of growth in order to boost its share price. This is a heavy, omnipresent burden on every executive who is sensitive to enhancing shareholder value.[6]

It's actually even harder than this. That canny horde of investors not only discounts the expected rate of growth of a company's *existing* businesses into the present value of its stock price, but also discounts the growth from new, yet-to-be-established lines of business that they expect the management team to be able to create in the future. The magnitude of the market's bet on growth from unknown sources is, in general, based on the company's track record. If the market has been impressed with a company's historical ability to leverage its strengths to generate new lines of business, then the component of its stock price based on growth from unknown sources will be large. If a company's past efforts to create new-growth businesses have not borne fruit, then its market valuation will be dominated by the projected cash flow from known, established businesses.

Table 1-1 presents one consulting firm's analysis of the share prices of a select number of *Fortune 500* companies, showing the proportion of each firm's share price on August 21, 2002, that was attributable to cash generated by existing assets, versus cash that investors expected to be generated by new investments.[7] Of this sample, the company that was on the hook at that time to generate the largest percentage of its total growth from future investments was Dell Computer. Only 22 percent of its share price of $28.05 was justified by cash thrown off by the company's present assets, whereas 78 percent of Dell's valuation reflected investors' confidence that the company would be able to invest in new assets that would generate whopping amounts of cash. Sixty-six percent of Johnson & Johnson's market valuation and 37 percent of Home Depot's valuation were grounded in expectations of growth from yet-to-be-made investments. These companies were on the hook for *big* numbers. On the other hand, only 5 percent of General Motors's stock price on that date was predicated on future investments. Although that's a chilling reflection of the track record of GM's former management in creating new-growth businesses, it means that if the present management team does a better job, the company's share price could respond handsomely.

Probably the most daunting challenge in delivering growth is that if you fail once to deliver it, the odds that you ever will be able to deliver in the future are very low. This is the conclusion of a remarkable study, *Stall Points* that the Corporate Strategy Board published in 1998.[8] It examined the 172 companies that had spent time on *Fortune*'s list of the 50 largest

Table 1-1

Portion of Selected Firms' Market Value That Was Based on Expected Returns from New Investments on August 21, 2002

Fortune 500 rank	Company name	Share price	Percent of Valuation That Was Based on:	
			New investments	Existing assets
53	Dell Computer	$28.05	78%	22%
47	Johnson & Johnson	$56.20	66%	34%
35	Procter & Gamble	$90.76	62%	38%
6	Genaral Electric	$32.80	60%	40%
77	Lockheed Martin	$62.16	59%	41%
−1	Wal-Mart Stores	$53.88	50%	50%
65	Intel	$19.15	49%	51%
49	Pfizer	$34.92	48%	52%
9	IBM	$81.93	46%	54%
24	Merck	$53.80	44%	56%
92	Cisco Systems	$15.00	42%	58%
18	Home Depot	$33.86	37%	63%
16	Boeing	$28.36	30%	70%
11	Verizon	$31.80	21%	79%
22	Kroger	$22.20	13%	87%
32	Sears Roebuck	$36.94	8%	92%
37	AOL Time Warner	$35.00	8%	92%
3	General Motors	$49.40	5%	95%
81	Phillips Petroleum	$35.00	3%	97%

Source: CSFB/HOLT; Deloitte Consulting analysis.

companies between 1955 and 1995. Only 5 percent of these companies were able to sustain a real, inflation-adjusted growth rate of more than 6 percent across their entire tenure in this group. The other 95 percent reached a point at which their growth simply stalled, to rates at or below the rate of growth of the gross national product (GNP). Stalling is understandable, given our expectations that all growth markets become saturated and mature. What is scary is that of all these companies whose growth had stalled, only 4 percent were able to successfully reignite their growth even to a rate of 1 percent above GNP growth. Once growth had stalled, in other words, it proved nearly impossible to restart it.

The equity markets brutally punished those companies that allowed their growth to stall. Twenty-eight percent of them lost more than 75 percent of their market capitalization. Forty-one percent of the companies saw their market value drop by between 50 and 75 percent when they stalled, and 26 percent of the firms lost between 25 and 50 percent of their value. The remaining 5 percent lost less than 25 percent of their market capitalization. This, of course, increased pressure on management to regenerate growth, and to do so quickly—which made it all the more difficult to succeed. Managers cannot escape the mandate to grow.[9] Yet the odds of success, if history is any guide, are frighteningly low.

Is Innovation a Black Box?

Why is achieving and sustaining growth so hard? One popular answer is to blame managers for failing to generate new grow—implying that more capable and prescient people could have succeeded. The solve-the-problem-by-finding-a-better-manager approach might have credence if failures to restart growth were isolated events. Study after study, however, concludes that about 90 percent of all publicly traded companies have proved themselves unable to sustain for more than a few years a growth trajectory that creates above-average shareholder returns.[10] Unless we believe that the pool of management talent in established firms is like some perverse Lake Wobegon, where 90 percent of managers are below average, there has to be a more fundamental explanation for why the vast majority of good managers has not been able to crack the problem of sustaining growth.

A second common explanation for once-thriving companies' inability to sustain growth is that their managers become risk averse. But the facts refute this explanation, too. Corporate executives often bet the future of billion-dollar enterprises on an innovation. IBM bet its farm on the System 360 mainframe computer, and won. DuPont spent $400 million on a plant to make Kevlar tire cord, and lost. Corning put billions on the line to build its optical fiber business, and won big. More recently it sold off many of its other businesses in order to invest more in optical telecommunications, and has been bludgeoned. *Many* of the executives who have been unable to create sustained corporate growth have evidenced a strong stomach for risk.

There is a third, widely accepted explanation for why growth seems so hard to achieve repeatedly and well, which we also believe does not hold water: Creating new-growth businesses is simply unpredictable. Many believe that the odds of success are just that—odds—and that they are low. Many of the most insightful management thinkers have accepted the assumption that creating growth is risky and unpredictable, and have therefore used their talents to help executives manage this unpredictability. Recommendations about letting a thousand flowers bloom, bringing Silicon Valley inside, failing fast, and accelerating selection pressures are all ways to deal with the allegedly irreducible unpredictability of successful innovation.[11] The structure of the venture capital industry is in fact a testament to the pervasive belief that we cannot predict which new-growth businesses will succeed. The industry maxim says that for every ten investments—all made in the belief they would succeed—two will fail outright, six will survive as the walking wounded, and two will hit the home runs on which the success of the entire portfolio turns. Because of this belief that the process of business creation is unfathomable, few have sought to pry open the black box to study the *process* by which new-growth businesses are created.

We do not accept that most companies' growth stalls because the odds of success for the next growth business they launch are impossibly low. The historical results may indeed seem random, but we believe it is because the process for creating new-growth businesses has not yet been well understood. In this book we intend to pry open the black box and study the processes that lead to success or failure in new-growth businesses.

To illustrate why it is important to understand the processes that create those results, consider these strings of numbers:

1, 2, 3, 4, 5, 6

75, 28, 41, 26, 38, 64

Which of these would you say is random, and which is predictable? The first string looks predictable: The next two numbers should be 7 and 8. But what if we told you that it was actually the winning numbers for a lottery, drawn from a drum of tumbling balls, whereas the second is the sequence of state and county roads one would follow on a scenic tour of the northern rim of Michigan's Upper Peninsula on the way from Sault Ste. Marie, Ontario to Saxon, Wisconsin? Given the route implied by the first six roads, you can reliably predict the next two numbers—2 and 122—from a map. The lesson: You cannot say, just by looking at the result of the process, whether the process that created those results is capable of generating predictable output. You must understand the process itself. . . .

How to Manage the Dilemma of Investing for Growth

The dilemma of investing for growth is that the character of a firm's money is good for growth only when the firm is growing healthily. Core businesses that are still growing provide cover for new-growth businesses. Senior executives who are bolstered by a sense that the pipeline of new sustaining innovations in established businesses will meet or exceed investors' expectations can allow new businesses the time to follow emergent strategy processes while they compete against nonconsumption. It is when growth slows—when senior executives see that the sustaining-innovation pipeline is inadequate to meet investor expectations—that investing to grow becomes hard. The character of the firm's money changes when new things must get very big very fast, and it won't allow innovators to do what is needed to grow. When you're a corporate entrepreneur and you sense this shift in the corporate context occurring, you had better watch out.

This dilemma traps nearly every company and is the causal mechanism behind the findings in *Stall Points,* the Corporate Strategy Board's study that we cited (previously). This study showed that of the 172 companies that had spent time on *Fortune*'s list of the 50 largest companies between 1955 and 1995, 95 percent saw their growth stall to rates at or below the rate of GNP growth. Of the companies whose growth stalled, only 4 percent were able to successfully reignite their growth even to a rate of 1 percent above GNP growth. Once growth had stalled, the corporations' money turned impatient for growth, which rendered it impossible to do the things required to launch successful growth businesses.

In recent years, the dilemma has become even more complex. If companies whose growth has stalled somehow find a way to launch a successful new-growth business, Wall Street analysts often complain that they cannot value the new opportunity appropriately because it is buried within a larger, slower-growing corporation. In the name of shareholder value, they demand that the corporation spin off the new-growth business to shareholders so that the full value of its exciting growth potential can be reflected in its own share price. If executives respond and spin it off, they may indeed "unlock" shareholder value. But after it has been unlocked they are left locked again in a low-growth business, facing the mandate to increase shareholder value.

In the face of this sobering evidence, chief executives—whose task it is to create shareholder value—*must* preserve the ability of their capital to nourish growth businesses in the ways that they need to be nourished. When executives allow the growth of core businesses to sag to lackluster levels, new-growth ventures must shoulder the whole burden of changing the growth rate of the entire corporation's top and bottom lines. This forces the corporation to demand that the new businesses become very big very fast. Their capital as a consequence becomes poison for growth ventures. The only way to keep investment capital from. Spoiling is to use it when it is still good—to invest it from a context that is still healthy enough that the money can be patient for growth.

In many ways, companies whose shares are publicly held are in a self-reinforcing vise. Their dominant shareholders are pension funds. Corporations pressure the managers of their pension fund investments to deliver strong and consistent returns—because strong investment performance reduces the amount of profits that must be diverted to fund pension obligations. Investment managers therefore turn around and pressure the corporations whose shares they own to deliver consistent earnings growth that is unexpectedly accelerating. Privately held companies are not subject to many of these pressures. The expectations that accompany their capital therefore can often be more appropriate for the building of new-growth businesses.

Notes

1. Although we have not performed a true meta-analysis, there are four recently published studies that seem to converge on this estimate that roughly one company in ten succeeds at sustaining growth. Chris Zook and James Allen found in their 2001 study *Profit from the Core* (Boston: Harvard Business School Press) that only 13 percent of their sample of

1,854 companies were able to grow consistently over a ten-year period. Richard Foster and Sarah Kaplan published a study that same year, *Creative Destruction* (New York: Currency/Doubleday), in which they followed 1,008 companies from 1962 to 1998. They learned that only 160, or about 16 percent of these firms, were able merely to survive this time frame, and concluded that the perennially outperforming company is a chimera, something that has never existed at all. Jim Collins also published his *Good to Great* (New York: HarperBusiness) in 2001, in which he examined a universe of 1,435 companies over thirty years (1965–1995). Collins found only 126, or about 9 percent, that had managed to outperform equity market averages for a decade or more. The Corporate Strategy Board's findings in *Stall Points* (Washington, DC: Corporate Strategy Board, 1988), which are summarized in detail in the text, show that 5 percent of companies in the *Fortune 50* successfully maintained their growth, and another 4 percent were able to reignite some degree of growth after they had stalled. The studies all support our assertion that a 10 percent probability of succeeding in a quest for sustained growth is, if anything, a generous estimate.

2. Because all of these transactions included stock, "true" measures of the value of the different deals are ambiguous. Although when a deal actually closes, a definitive value can be fixed, the implied value of the transaction at the time a deal is announced can be useful: It signals what the relevant parties were willing to pay and accept at a point in time. Stock price changes subsequent to the deal's announcement are often a function of other, exogenous events having little to do with the deal itself. Where possible, we have used the value of the deals at announcement, rather than upon closing. Sources of data on these various transactions include the following:

NCR

"Fatal Attraction (AT&T's Failed Merger with NCR)," *The Economist*, 23 March 1996.

"NCR Spinoff Completes AT&T Restructure Plan," *Bloomberg Business News*, 1 January 1997.

McCaw and AT&T Wireless Sale

The Wall Street Journal, 21 September 1994.

"AT&T Splits Off AT&T Wireless," AT&T news release, 9 July 2001.

AT&I; TCI, and MediaOne

"AT&T Plans Mailing to Sell TCI Customers Phone, Web Services," *The Wall Street Journal*, 10 March 1999.

"The AT&T-Mediaone Deal: What the FCC Missed," *BusinessWeek*, 19 June 2000.

"AT&T Broadband to Merge with Comcast Corporation in $72 Billion Transaction," AT&T news release, 19 December 2001.

"Consumer Groups Still Questioning Comcast-AT&T Cable Merger," Associated Press Newswires, 21 October 2002.

3. Cabot's stock price outperformed the market between 1991 and 1995 as it refocused on its core business, for two reasons. On one side of the equation, demand for carbon black increased in Asia and North America

as car sales surged, thereby increasing the demand for tires. On the supply side, two other American-based producers of carbon black exited the industry because they were unwilling to make the requisite investment in environmental controls, thereby increasing Cabot's pricing power. Increased demand and reduced supply translated into a tremendous increase in the profitability of Cabot's traditional carbon black operations, which was reflected in the company's stock price. Between 1996 and 2000, however, its stock price deteriorated again, reflecting the dearth of growth prospects.

4. An important study of companies' tendency to make investments that fail to create growth was done by Professor Michael C. Jensen: "The Modern Industrial Revolution, Exit, and the Failure of Internal Control Systems," *Journal of Finance* (July 1993): 831–880. Professor Jensen also delivered this paper as his presidential address to the American Finance Association. Interestingly, many of the firms that Jensen cites as having productively reaped growth from their investments were disruptive innovators—a key concept in this book.

   Our unit of analysis in this book, as in Jensen's work, is the individual firm, not the larger system of growth creation made manifest in a free market, capitalist economy. Works such as Joseph Schumpeter's *Theory of Economic Development* (Cambridge, MA: Harvard University Press, 1934) and *Capitalism, Socialism, and Democracy* (New York: London, Harper & Brothers, 1942) are seminal, landmark works that address the environment in which firms function. Our assertion here is that whatever the track record of free market economies in generating growth at the macro level, the track record of individual firms is quite poor. It is the performance of firms within a competitive market to which we hope to contribute.

5. This simple story is complicated somewhat by the market's apparent incorporation of an expected "fade" in any company's growth rate. Empirical analysis suggests that the market does not expect any company to grow, or even survive, forever. It therefore seems to incorporate into current prices a foreseen decline in growth rates from current levels and the eventual dissolution of the firm. This is the reason for the importance of terminal values in most valuation models. This fade period is estimated using regression analysis, and estimates vary widely. So, strictly speaking, if a company is expected to grow at 5 percent with a fade period of forty years, and five years into that forty-year period it is still growing at 5 percent, the stock price would rise at rates that generated economic returns for shareholders, because the forty-year fade period would start over. However, because this qualification applies to companies growing at 5 percent as well as those growing at 25 percent, it does not change the point we wish to make; that is, that the market is a harsh taskmaster, and merely meeting expectations does not generate meaningful reward.

6. On average over their long histories, of course, faster-growing firms yield higher returns. However, the faster-growing firm will have produced higher returns than the slower-growing firm only for investors in the past. If markets discount efficiently, then the investors who reap above-average returns are those who were fortunate enough to have bought shares in the past when the future growth rate had not been fully discounted into the price of the stock. Those who bought when the future growth

potential already had been discounted into the share price would not receive an above-market return. An excellent reference for this argument can be found in Alfred Rappaport and Michael J. Mauboussin, *Expectations Investing: Reading Stock Prices for Better Returns* (Boston: Harvard Business School Press, 2001). Rappaport and Mauboussin guide investors in methods to detect when a market's expectations for a company's growth might be incorrect.

7. These were the closing market prices for these companies' common shares on August 21, 2002. There is no significance to that particular date: It is simply the time when the analysis was done. HOLT Associates, a unit of Credit Suisse First Boston (CSFB), performed these calculations using proprietary methodology applied to publicly available financial data. The percent future is a measure of how much a company's current stock price can be attributed to current cash flows and how much is due to investors' expectations of future growth and performance. As CSFB/HOLT defines it,

> *The percent future is the percentage of the total market value that the market assigns to the company's expected future investment. Percent future begins with the total market value (debt plus equity) less that portion attributed to the present value of existing assets and investments and divides this by the total market value of debt and equity.*

CSFB/Holt calculates the present value of existing assets as the present value of the cash flows associated with the assets' wind down and the release of the associated nondepreciating working capital. The HOLT CFROI valuation methodology includes a forty-year fade of returns equal to the total market's average returns.

> Percent Future = [Total Debt and Equity (market) − Present Value Existing Assets]/[Total Debt and Equity (market)]

The companies listed in table 1-1 are not a sequential ranking of *Fortune 500* companies, because some of the data required to perform these calculations were not available for some companies. The companies listed in this table were chosen only for illustrative purposes, and were not chosen in any way to suggest that any company's share price is likely to increase or decline. For more information on the methodology that HOLT used, see . . .

8. See *Stall Points* (Washington, DC: Corporate Strategy Board, 1998).

9. In the text we have focused only on the pressure that equity markets impose on companies to grow, but there are many other sources of intense pressure. We'll mention just a couple here. First, when a company is growing, there are increased opportunities for employees to be promoted into new management positions that are opening up above them. Hence, the potential for growth in managerial responsibility and capability is much greater in a growing firm than in a stagnant one. When growth slows, managers sense that their possibilities for advancement will be constrained not by their personal talent and performance, but rather by how many years must pass before the more senior managers above them will retire. When

this happens, many of the most capable employees tend to leave the company, affecting the company's abilities to regenerate growth.

Investment in new technologies also becomes difficult. When a growing firm runs out of capacity and must build a new plant or store, it is easy to employ the latest technology. When a company has stopped growing and has excess manufacturing capacity, proposals to invest in new technology typically do not fare well, since the full capital cost and the average manufacturing cost of producing with the new technology are compared against the marginal cost of producing in a fully depreciated plant. As a result, growing firms typically have a technology edge over slow-growth competitors. But that advantage is not rooted so much in the visionary wisdom of the managers as it is in the difference in the circumstances of growth versus no growth.

10. Detailed support for this estimate is provided in note 1.

11. For example; see James Brian Quinn, *Strategies for Change: Logical Incrementalism* (Homewood, IL: R.D. Irwin, 1980). Quinn suggests that the first step that corporate executives need to take in building new businesses is to "let a thousand flowers bloom," then tend the most promising and let the rest wither. In this view, the key to successful innovation lies in choosing the right flowers to tend—and that decision must rely on complex intuitive feelings, calibrated by experience.

More recent work by Tom Peters (*Thriving on Chaos: Handbook for a Management Revolution* [New York: Knopf/Random House, 1987]) urges innovating managers to "fail fast"—to pursue new business ideas on a small scale and in a way that generates quick feedback about whether an idea is viable. Advocates of this approach urge corporate executives not to punish failures because it is only through repeated attempts that successful new businesses will emerge.

Others draw on analogies with biological evolution, where mutations arise in what appear to be random ways. Evolutionary theory posits that whether a mutant organism thrives or dies depends on its fit with the "selection environment"—the conditions within which it must compete against other organisms for the resources required to thrive. Hence, believing that good and bad innovations pop up randomly, these researchers advise corporate executives to focus on creating a "selection environment" in which viable new business ideas are culled from the bad as quickly as possible. Gary Hamel, for example, advocates creating "Silicon Valley inside"—an environment in which existing structures are constantly dismantled, recombined in novel ways, and tested, in order to stumble over something that actually works. (See Gary Hamel, *Leading the Revolution* [Boston: Harvard Business School Press, 2001].)

We are not critical of these books. They can be very helpful, given the present state of understanding, because if the processes that create innovations were indeed random, then a context within which managers could accelerate the creation and testing of ideas would indeed help. But if the process is *not* intrinsically random, as we assert, then addressing only the context is treating the symptom, *not* the source of the problem.

To see why, consider the studies of 3M's celebrated ability to create a stream of growth-generating innovations. A persistent highlight of these studies is 3M's "15 percent rule": At 3M, many employees are given 15 percent of their time to devote to developing their own ideas for new-growth businesses. This "slack" in how people spend their time is supported by a broadly dispersed capital budget that employees can tap in order to fund. their would-be growth engines on a trial basis.

But what guidance does this policy give to a bench engineer at 3M? She is given 15 percent "slack" time to dedicate to creating new-growth businesses. She is also told that whatever she comes up with will be subject first to internal market selection pressures, then external market selection pressures. All this is helpful information. But none of it helps that engineer create a new idea, or decide which of the several ideas she might create are worth pursuing further. This plight generalizes to managers and executives at all levels in an organization. From bench engineer to middle manager to business unit head to CEO, it is not enough to occupy oneself only with creating a context for innovation that sorts the fruits of that context. Ultimately, every manager must create something of substance, and the success of that creation lies in the decisions managers must make.

All of these approaches create an "infinite regress." By bringing the market "inside," we have simply backed up the problem: How can managers decide which ideas will be developed to the point at which they can be subjected to the selection pressures of their internal market? Bringing the market still deeper inside simply creates the same conundrum. Ultimately, innovators must judge what they will work on and how they will do it— and what they should consider when making those decisions is what is in the black box. The acceptance of randomness in innovation, then, is not a stepping-stone on the way to greater understanding; it is a barrier.

Dr. Gary Hamel was one of the first scholars of this problem to raise with Professor Christensen the possibility that the management of innovation actually has the potential to yield predictable results. We express our thanks to him for his helpful thoughts.

Jim Mackey and
Liisa Välikangas

➜ **NO**

The Myth of Unbounded Growth

Growth is not perpetual and its continued pursuit can be a death knell, especially for large, mature companies.

Imagine the CEO of a growth company telling its shareholders, "Henceforth we will be pursuing no risky new research, acquisitions or new business ventures. We will concentrate on being stewards of our existing business and will simply pay all profits as dividends." This is an unlikely scenario, to say the least. The reality is that markets expect growth. There is a deeply held assumption that neither a company nor its management is viable unless it is able to grow. Growth gives investors a feeling that management is doing its job. Growth is typically perceived as a proactive (rather than a defensive) strategy. Or maybe, as the Red Queen says in Lewis Carroll's *Through the Looking Glass,* "Here it takes all the running you can do to keep in the same place. If you want to get somewhere else, you must run at least twice as fast as that!"

"The only way managers can deliver a return to shareholders that exceeds the market average," Clayton Christensen and Michael Raynor wrote in *The Innovator's Solution,* "is to grow *faster* than shareholders expect," however irrational that may be.[1] Indeed, a recent CSFB HOLT study found that 50% of the valuation of the 20 most valuable companies was based on expected cash flows from future investments.[2] Nevertheless, it has become almost a national sport to suggest that there is a set of visionary, great or otherwise noteworthy companies that can grow indefinitely—only to have those companies, almost invariably, fall from grace shortly thereafter. "The golden company that continually performs better than the markets has never existed. It is a myth," wrote Richard Foster and Sarah Kaplan in *Creative Destruction.*[3] Indeed, of the companies on the original *Forbes* 100 list in 1917, only 18 remained in the top 100 by 1987 and 61 had ceased to exist. Of these highly respected survivors, Foster and Kaplan point to only two companies—General Electric Co. and Eastman Kodak Co.—which outperformed the 7.5% average return on the S&P 500 during this 70-year period, and they beat the average by only 0.3%.

The truth is, companies are successful until they are not.[4] The consistent pattern of stalled or halted growth among the largest U.S. corporations over the last 50 years is eye-opening. Research by the Corporate Strategy Board (CSB) in 1998[5] suggested that there is a "cloud layer" at which growth starts to stall, beginning in the $30 billion range (CPI-adjusted 1996 dollars).[6] Of the 172 companies that have made it to the *Fortune* 50 from 1954 to 1995,[7] only 5% were able to sustain a growth rate above the GDP (and half of those have stalled since the study).[8] In addition, once stalled, no U.S. company larger than $15 billion has been able to restart growth that exceeded that of the GDP. In *How To Grow When the Markets Don't*,[9] Adrian Slywotzky, Richard Wise and Karl Weber call this "the Great Divide, moving from a past of strong growth . . . into a future of low or no growth." The authors say that many companies did so without fully recognizing the change, thereby exacerbating the problem, sometimes fatally. Companies often see a stall as a temporary blip, soon to be overcome with investment and execution of their growth strategy, but in their book *Permanently Failing Organizations*,[10] Marshall Meyer and Lynn Zucker write that many of these companies are merely lingering in a state of decay before they ultimately fail.

As companies increase in size, the variability in growth rate decreases (that is, growth slows down).[11] The classical model of growth—assuming a log-normal distribution of company sizes in a population of companies[12]—fails to explain this phenomenon.[13] Strictly from a numerical perspective, sustaining rapid growth is a massive challenge for a *Fortune* 50 company. For example, to sustain its current 17% growth rate, Merck & Co. Inc. (the 17th largest with revenue of $52 billion) must add $9 billion in revenue this year, $11 billion next year and so on. In five years, Merck's revenues would need to be $114 billion—more than double its current number.

The Cost of the Growth Chase

For a large company, not only are the odds of consistently achieving this kind of growth quite long, but the pursuit of that growth can also be very costly. To pursue billion dollar growth targets quickly, executives feel they must invest billions in the quest.[14] The result is falling profitability often accompanied by huge restructuring charges. Whereas the market cap decline may begin before or after the stall, the eventual fall is dramatic. The CSB study found that 28% of stalled firms lost over 75% of market cap relative to the Dow Jones Industrial Average (DJIA), and 69% lost at least 50%; the average valuation fell by 61%.[15] When this happens, a once great company begins to search for its lost formula, often until the very viability of the company is eventually questioned, as was the case for Sears, Roebuck and Co., IBM Corp., Digital Equipment Corp., Xerox Corp., Motorola Inc., Lucent Technologies and many others. Employees suffer as well. In 53% of the stalls, head count was reduced by over 20%, and morale declined noticeably.

Kodak, as noted, outperformed the S&P 500 for 70 years—from 1917 to 1987—but today it is the poster child for stalled companies. Its revenue stopped growing faster than the GDP in 1980 when it was No. 29 on the *Fortune* 50 list. Its recent *nominal* market cap is 41% below its 1980 level. When benchmarked against the 10-fold increase in the DJIA since 1980, Kodak's relative market cap has fallen a whopping 94%. Cutting more than 70% of its semiannual dividend, Kodak now seeks to migrate from film[16] and plans to invest $3 billion in digital photography, in which it has been investing since 1972. Kodak also recently announced its $250 million acquisition of Scitex Corp.'s Digital Printing to bolster its entry into the inkjet printer market. Yet film still accounts for about 50% of Kodak's profits.[17] Thus the odds that Kodak can reignite growth are not judged to be good. Kodak's long-term debt is rated triple-B-minus, one notch above speculative, by Standard & Poor's. In an unprecedented revolt, "investors have lost confidence" in Kodak's growth investments and now seek "radically different strategies to maximize shareholder value."[18]

Given the dismal track record that stalled growth companies have when attempting to return to double-digit internal growth, the massive (and often belated) investments they make in that regard seem analogous to spending the company's life savings on a lottery ticket. The reality for many shareholders is that unless the company is sold while still healthy, the promised payoff never comes, due to low valuation in the sale of nonperforming assets, restructuring charge write-offs, goodwill depreciation and pension- or product-related liabilities. The hard-earned equity evaporates, and assets are sold at near book value in fire sales or in bankruptcy to creditors. *Fortune* 50 bankruptcies are relatively rare,[19] but Enron, WorldCom, PG&E, United AirLines, Kmart, Bethlehem Steel and LTV are recent examples. Others like Lucent, Xerox, Fleming, AMR and Goodyear hover on the brink. Still others are sold for a fraction of their earlier value or at a slight premium to a long-stagnant stock price—for example, Digital, Compaq, Beatrice Foods, Firestone, Uniroyal, American Motors, Armour Food, Gulf Oil, RCA and Union Carbide.

What's a CEO To Do?

It is clear that many strong forces—ranging from natural limitations and managerial complexity to stakeholder harmony and antitrust concerns—make continuous growth very difficult for already-large companies. Rather than continue to seek growth at any cost, the solution is to seek alternatives to the dilemma—in a sense, to fool the natural limits to growth that large companies face. There are three logical alternatives: Break up the company, create a new corporate form, or make a graceful growth-to-value transition.

Breaking up the company   IBM spun off Lexmark, HP gave birth to Agilent, AT&T divested itself of Lucent, GM launched Delco, Sears separated from All-state, and 3M broke off Imation. Such spinoffs generally enhance stockholder value both at the time of the announcement and by about 20% in the subsequent 18 months.[20] J.P. Morgan discovered that smaller breakups performed better.[21] It is important, though, that the post-breakup units be small enough (less than $10 billion) to have significant room for growth. Although not all breakups create successful new companies, they do help bring focus to the parent company. J.P. Morgan also found that "the remaining, slimmer parent does materially better than the market following separation."[22]

Nevertheless there is significant resistance to divestiture because it seems "like a tacit admission of failure, evidence of poor management, or in some corporate cultures even . . . treason."[23] The myth of unbounded growth further perpetuates resistance to this seemingly reasonable solution. Indeed, "of the 50 largest divestitures . . . more than three-quarters were completed under pressure, most only after long delays when problems became so obvious that action was unavoidable."[24]

Experimenting with a new corporate form   Whereas attempts at internal independence, including tracking stocks and partial spinoffs, may prove not to offer lasting solutions, evolving new organizational forms and management practices over time can afford a company greater scale and scope.[25] Just as the divisional organization (supported by innovations including the telephone and railroads) extended the management capability beyond that of the functional organization in the early 1900s, perhaps an even more decentralized organization (supported by innovations including the Internet and e-commerce) will enable the next growth leap. Also, business models that foster competition between different parts of the organization (for example, GM's Chevrolet vs. Pontiac or HP's Inkjet vs. Laserjet) may offer growth advantages. In addition, internal markets for ideas and talent (such as Shell's GameChanger innovation program) that are open to anyone within the organization with a worthwhile contribution to make may provide new routes to growth.[26]

Take Visa, for example, with an estimated 2003 sales volume of $2.7 trillion. It is technically not a company nor does it appear in the *Fortune* rankings. Yet it has a powerful brand, a strategy for growth, and an integrated business system composed of hundreds of card-issuing financial institutions battling for customers.[27] Similarly, electronics firms today outsource manufacturing, integrate supplier design, engage in software alliances, participate in standards' bodies and contribute to and benefit from open-source movements.[28] They are integrated ecosystems that compete for ideas, innovation, people and investment. Here the corporation may no longer be the relevant unit of competitive analysis; the new corporate form is a boundaryless organization.

Making a transition from growth to value   Using reduced investment to grow earnings can help a company make a graceful transition from a high P/E growth stock to a moderate P/E value stock. Market cap may decline (relative to the DJIA), but this strategy can help avoid the dramatic poststall crash or near bankruptcy that can occur when former growth companies begin delivering neither growth nor profit and are assessed at breakup value. Specific tactics may include increasing earnings stability, balance-sheet strengthening, boosting dividend payout, cost and asset reduction, reductions in marketing and R&D, portfolio adjustments (especially divestitures and spinoffs), and stock repurchase (only if P/E is in single digits). Most companies that survive their growth stall eventually make this transition. It is often delayed, however, due to persistent attempts to recapture growth (for example, IBM in the mid-1980s and early 1990s), or forced after being acquired by a value-oriented firm (for example, Allied Signal's acquisition of Honeywell in 1999). GE, however, shifted focus from growth to profit in the 1950s and transitioned without a crisis. Microsoft's recent decision to begin paying dividends may imply an early recognition of the growth-to-value transition.

This strategy—which requires a shift in corporate culture and investor expectations—may be unpopular because it marks a radical departure from the past. It is thus difficult for any leader to achieve unless precipitated by a crisis. Even when there is a perceived crisis, preliminary case studies indicate that such a transition will take from five to eight years.[29] Denial and short-term incentives create additional barriers because management tends to want to believe they can win the lottery to recapture unbounded growth.

Facing the Liability of Corporate Size

In evaluating their options, the CEO and the board should consider where their company is in its life cycle—growth, stall or poststall. Growth stalls can be anticipated by assessing the natural limits of the company's dominant growth strategy and its pattern of financial performance. Senior managers and board members also have to realistically assess their company's capabilities in innovation and new business creation in order to decide whether their capital and talent would be better spent on core business development than on an increasingly fruitless pursuit of mega-growth. These are not easy decisions to make, especially given the almost unquestioned culture of growth that continues to exist in today's environment. The biggest challenge and first step toward making those decisions, however, is to overcome denial and acknowledge that unbounded growth is indeed a myth.

References

1. C.M. Christensen and M. Raynor, "The Innovator's Solution: Creating and Sustaining Successful Growth" (Boston: Harvard Business School Press, 2003).

2. M.J. Mauboussin and K. Bartholdson, "The Pyramid of Numbers," The Consilient Observer (Credit Suisse First Boston Newsletter) 2, no. 17 (Sept. 23, 2003): 5. See also Christensen and Raynor, "The Innovator's Solution," 22, note 7, regarding methodology.

3. S. Kaplan and R. Foster, "Creative Destruction: Why Companies That Are Built To Last Underperform the Market—and How To Successfully Transform Them" (New York: Doubleday/Currency, 2001).

4. G. Hamel and L. Välikangas, "The Quest for Resilience," Harvard Business Review 81 (September 2003): 52–63. See also Kaplan and Foster, "Creative Destruction," 11, 14. Kaplan and Foster note that the turnover rate among *Fortune* 500 companies has accelerated—reaching nearly 10% in 1998—implying that no more than one-third of today's major corporations will survive in an economically important way over the next 25 years. Further, according to unpublished research done by the Woodside Institute in 2003, the number of S&P 500 companies that have suffered a five-year earnings decline has more than doubled in the last 30 years, suggesting a severe lack of strategic resilience.

5. Corporate Strategy Board, "Stall Points: Barriers to Growth for the Large Corporate Enterprise" (Washington, D.C.: Corporate Executive Board, 1998).

6. The stall range had increased over time slightly faster than inflation (pp. 20–21).

7. This is also true for service companies of equivalent scale.

8. See Corporate Strategy Board, "Stall Points," 13. Wal-Mart, American International Group, Target, and United Parcel Service are still growing;

3M, Hewlett-Packard, PepsiCo and Procter & Gamble now appear to have stalled. In addition, this study by the Corporate Strategy Board cites six companies that stalled but then restarted growth to 1% over GDP. Of those, Chase, Coca-Cola, Fleming and Motorola appear to have stalled again. Only Johnson & Johnson and Merck are still growing. Thus only six out of 172 *Fortune* 50 (3.5%) are still growing relative to the economy.

9. A.J. Slywotzky, R. Wise and K. Weber, "How To Grow When the Markets Don't" (New York: Warner Books, 2003), 14–15.

10. M.W. Meyer and L.G. Zucker, "Permanently Failing Organizations" (Thousand Oaks, California: Sage Publications, 1989).

11. M.H.R. Stanley, L.A.N. Amaral, S.V. Buldyrev, S. Havlin, H. Leschhorn, P. Maass, M.A. Salinger and H.E. Stanley, "Scaling Behaviour in the Growth of Companies," *Nature* 379 (Feb. 29, 1996): 804–806.

12. R. Gibrat, "Les Inégalités Economiques" (Paris: Sirey, 1933).

13. G. Carroll and M. Hannan, "The Demography of Corporations and Industries" (Princeton, New Jersey: Princeton University Press, 1999). See also Mauboussin and Bartholdson, "The Pyramid of Numbers," which describes mathematical distributions called power laws and their abundance in nature and social systems.

14. Christensen and Raynor, "The Innovator's Solution," 236–243. In this passage, including the section titled "The Death Spiral From Inadequate Growth," the authors state that large targets and large investments paradoxically are "likely to condemn innovators to a death march" and that "capital becomes a poison for growth ventures."

15. Market cap changes are measured relative to the Dow Jones Industrial Average from peak to trough within 10 years of stall.

16. J. Bandler, "Kodak Cuts Dividend by 72% To Finance Digital Shift," Wall Street Journal Europe, Sept. 26, 2003, A4.

17. S. London, "Kodak Aims To Become a Model of Reinvention," Financial Times, Sept. 27, 2003, 8.

18. W.C. Symonds, "Commentary: The Kodak Revolt Is Short-Sighted," BusinessWeek, Nov. 3, 2003, 38.

19. Kaplan and Foster, "Creative Destruction," 3. However, of the 20 largest U.S. bankruptcies in the past two decades, 10 occurred in the last two years; see Hamel and Välikangas, "The Quest for Resilience."

20. D. Sadtler, A. Campbell and R. Koch, "Breakup! How Companies Use Spin-Offs To Gain Focus and Grow Strong" (New York: Free Press, 1997), 4, 27–31.

21. Ibid., p. 30.

22. J.P. Morgan, "J.P. Morgan's Spinoff Study" (New York: J.P. Morgan, June 6, 1995, updated August 20, 1997 and July 23, 1999); P.A. Gaughan, "Mergers, Acquisitions and Corporate Restructurings," 3rd ed. (New York: John Wiley & Sons, 1997), 414–417; G.L. Hite and J.E. Owers, "Security Price Reactions Around Corporate Spin-Off Announcements," *Journal of Financial Economics* 12, no. 4 (1983): 409–436; K. Schipper and A. Smith, "Effects of Recontracting on Shareholder Wealth: The Case of Voluntary Spin-Offs," *Journal of Financial Economics* 12, no. 4 (1983): 437–467; and J.A. Miles and J.D. Rosenfeld, "The Effect of Voluntary Spin-Off Announcements

on Shareholder Wealth," *Journal of Finance* 38, no. 5 (1983): 1597–1606. Each study documents a mean abnormal spin-off announcement return of approximately 3%.

23. L. Dranikoff, T. Koller and A. Schneider, "Divesting Proactively," McKinsey on Finance, summer 2002, 1, http://www.corporatefinance.mckinsey.com_downloads/knowledge/mof/2002_no4/divesting.pdf.

24. Ibid. Also see L. Dranikoff, T. Koller and A. Schneider, "Divestiture: Strategy's Missing Link," *Harvard Business Review* 80 (May 2002): 74–83; and D.J. Ravenscraft and F.M. Scherer, "Mergers, Sell-Offs and Economic Efficiency" (Washington, D.C.: Brookings Institution Press, 1987), 167.

25. A.D. Chandler, Jr., and T. Hikino, "Scale and Scope: The Dynamics of Industrial Capitalism" (Cambridge, Massachusetts: Belknap Press, 1990).

26. For a description of the GameChanger program, see G. Hamel, "Bringing Silicon Valley Inside," *Harvard Business Review* 77 (September-October 1999): 70–84.

27. M.M. Waldrop, "The Trillion Dollar Vision of Dee Hock," Fast Company, October 1996, 75; and D.W. Hock, "Birth of the Chaordic Age" (San Francisco: Berrett-Koehler, 2000).

28. G. von Krogh, "Open-Source Software Development," *MIT Sloan Management Review* 44, no. 3 (spring 2003): 14–18.

29. Refers to ongoing studies of *Fortune* 50 companies conducted by the Billion Dollar Growth Network. The work goes beyond the 50 growth-stall case studies developed jointly with the Corporate Strategy Board in 1997–1998, focusing instead on what happened after the stall—how the companies managed their transition to a lower growth value model. The studies generally examine companies over the past 20-year period, relying on annual reports, Compustat data, secondary sources and follow-up interviews.

POSTSCRIPT

Is Growth Always an Inherent Corporate Value?

Based the two previous selections, it would seem that there are clear reasons to both support and oppose the view that only growing firms are successful firms. Interestingly, the question of whether a firm needs to grow to be considered successful is often overlooked. The primary reason for this is the widespread assumption on the part of business scholars, executives, and other business observers that growth is good and that, therefore, not growing is bad. However, as the article supporting the "no" side points out, a growth strategy can be both costly and risky. It might, perhaps, prove fruitful if we take a moment and consider a hypothetical example and see if it can shed some light on the question at hand.

Consider a mom-and-pop diner of the type that might be around the corner from you. While enjoying "The Best Burger in the 'Burb!" you ponder the growth question, and ask Bob, the owner, why he doesn't build on his success by opening a new restaurant. Seems like a reasonable question, particularly if we associate success with growth. With pride, Bob replies that three generations of his family have led happy, full lives in the community supported by the income and profits generated by the diner. He has a loyal clientele including a lunch crowd that keeps the place buzzing and his profits steady. He sees no reason to expand and expose his successful business to the risks associated with growth. So, is Bob wrong? It's hard not to admit that his business is successful, at least in the sense Bob suggests. Indeed, it is this sort of response to the growth question that authors Mackey and Välikangas suggest corporations consider. That is, they argue corporations have options other than growth such spinning-off segments of the firm or focusing efforts primarily at becoming a value-driven firm.

Despite costs and risks as well as other options available to companies, growth is typically the focus of most corporate strategy in America. It is highly valued by investors and other stakeholders of the firm and, as Christensen and Raynor argue, can be viewed as an "imperative." Now that you have read both sides of the debate, what are your thoughts? Do you feel that it is "imperative" for firms to grow in order to be considered successful?

Suggested Readings

Clayton Christensen, *The Innovators Dilemma: When New Technologies Cause Great Firms to Fail.* Boston: Harvard Business School Press, 1997.

C.M. Christensen and M. Raynor, *The Innovators Solution: Creating and Sustaining Successful Growth*. Boston: Harvard Business School Press, 2003.

Jim Collins, *Good to Great*. New York: HarperBusiness, 2001.

G. Hamel and L. Välikangas, "The Quest for Resilience." *Harvard Business Review*, 2003, 81: 52–63.

S. Kaplan and R. Foster, *Creative Destruction: Why Companies that Are Built to Last Underperform the Market—and How to Successfully Transform Them*. New York: Doubleday/Currency, 2001.

Chris Zook and James Allen, *Profit from the Core*. Boston: Harvard Business School Press, 2001.

Internet References . . .

Committee For A Constructive Tomorrow (CFACT)

In 1985, the Committee For A Constructive Tomorrow (CFACT) was founded to promote a positive voice on environment and development issues. Its co-founders, David Rothbard and Craig Rucker, believed very strongly that the power of the market combined with the applications of safe technologies could offer humanity practical solutions to many of the world's pressing concerns. A number of leading scientists, academics, and policy leaders also agree with them and soon joined their effort, along with thousands of citizens from around the country.

http://www.cfact.org/site/about.asp

The American Immigration Law Foundation (AILF)

AILF was established in 1987 as a tax-exempt, not-for-profit educational, charitable organization. The foundation is dedicated to increasing public understanding of immigration law and policy and the value of immigration to American society; to promoting public service and excellence in the practice of immigration law; and to advancing fundamental fairness and due process under the law for immigrants.

http://www.ailf.org/

The Ayn Rand Institute

The ARI is a nonprofit educational organization whose goals are to spread the concepts and ideas contained in Ayn Rand's revolutionary philosophy, Objectivism. Their members appear frequently in the national media and have widespread influence in colleges and universities across America. In staunchly defending capitalism and limited government, ARI provides unique insight into numerous topics of interest to business, including globalization and the environmentalism movement.

http://www.aynrand.org

Globalization Guide

This site is the product of the Australian Apec Study Center and is designed to introduce students to the pros, cons, myths, and facts of globalization. Additional resources and access to other globalization links are also provided.

http://www.globalisationguide.org/

Environmental and International Management Issues

*A*s the worldwide recession intensifies, governments of many countries are enacting protectionist economic policies as a means of helping their domestic economies. According to many economists, however, both theory and practice strongly indicate that protectionist actions do more harm than good. Nevertheless, President Obama and the Democratic-controlled legislative branch appear to be receptive to protectionist suggestions, leading many intellectuals and social commentators to wonder if such policies might actually be beneficial to US business interests. Thus, here, in the final section of your Taking Sides text, we look at this newsworthy and important issue as well as three other interesting and controversial topics facing many managers and executives today.

- Should Corporations Adopt Environmentally Friendly Policies of CSR and Sustainable Development?

- Do Unskilled Immigrants Hurt the American Economy?

- Is Economic Globalization Good for Humankind?

- Are Protectionist Policies Beneficial to Business?

ISSUE 15

Should Corporations Adopt Environmentally Friendly Policies of CSR and Sustainable Development?

YES: Sierra Club, from "Sierra Club Purposes and Goals," (July 13, 2006). http://www.sierraclub.org/policy/

NO: Paul Driessen, from *Eco-Imperialism: Green Power, Black Death* (Free Enterprise Press, 2004)

ISSUE SUMMARY

YES: The Sierra Club is a leading environmentalist organization and has consistently advocated for the implementation of CSR policies in the workplace. The selection presented here provides insight into their philosophy and expectations as they relate to corporate behavior and its impact on the natural environment.

NO: Paul Driessen, trained in environmental science and a major advocate for the world's poor, writes a blistering attack on CSR and its constituent policies. He argues that these policies bring misery and death to the world's poor and act as camouflage for the environmentalist's anti-capitalism, pro-statism agenda.

$\mathbf{V}$irtually every introductory-level management textbook currently on the market includes a chapter examining the impact corporate business activities have on the earth's environment. Usually the discussion blames business for much of the damage done to the environment. A typical comment: "For years, businesses conducted their operations with little concern about environmental consequences. . . . [businesses were] responsible for consuming significant amounts of materials and energy and causing waste accumulation and resource degradation . . . Businesses would look the other way. . . . " (Archie B. Carroll & Ann K. Buchholtz, *Business and Society: Ethics and stakeholder management*, South-Western Cengage, 2009).

Generally, these texts proscribe the adoption of corporate social responsibility (CSR) initiatives to ensure greater acceptance of the needs of the natural environment. And beyond the ubiquitous advocacy of CSR, an increasing number of textbooks—reflecting not just the views of business academia but those of social commentators, environmental NGO activists, and government leaders across the globe—argue that corporations need to adopt policies of "sustainable development," a concept that emphasizes restricting economic growth to levels that won't outstrip the replenishment rate of our natural resources (Archie B. Carroll & Ann K. Buchholtz, *Business and Society: Ethics and stakeholder management*, South-Western Cengage, 2009).

Interestingly, both the concept of corporate social responsibility and the birth of the modern environmentalism movement were products of the 1960s. Actually, this is no coincidence; many scholars and social historians argue that the development of CSR was primarily due to the environmental activism of the 1960s successfully raising social awareness of the negative impact of corporate activity on the earth's environment (Chris Horner, *The Politically Incorrect Guide to Global Warming and Environmentalism*, Regnery Publishing: Washington D.C., 2007). Thus, it is not surprising that the strongest force advocating corporate social responsibility today is the environmentalism movement itself.

From an environmental perspective, the way to understand CSR is to view it as an umbrella concept under which a collection of related ideas fulfill specific roles in promoting responsible corporate behavior. *Stakeholder theory*, widely accepted in corporate America and the default approach for almost all business schools, argues that the traditional corporate concern for the creation of shareholder wealth first and foremost is misguided. A CSR/stakeholder approach suggests that all parties with a stake in a company's existence are entitled to input in determining the firm's activities, including the allocation of its revenues and profits. And currently, amid the political and social atmosphere, it is the environmental stakeholder that is receiving increased attention in the corporate boardroom. *Sustainable development* (SD) is another CSR-related, environmentally driven concept. SD came to prominence in the 1980s and has been very successful in raising awareness of the impact of corporate activity on the finite natural resources on our planet. As noted earlier, the key aspect of SD is concern for the natural resource needs of future generations. To this end, corporations should develop and implement business plans only after accounting for their potential long-term impact on the earth's natural resource base.

The *precautionary principle* (PP) is frequently invoked by environmentalists as a means of alerting the public about possible environmental harm, primarily from the implementation of new technology. As the name suggests, it represents a defensive, assume-the-worst-until-proven-otherwise posture. In a very real sense, it is a guide for regulation.

The last two decades have seen the emergence of *socially responsible investing* (SRI) around the world. The idea here is to promote social acceptance of the environmentalist agenda by encouraging investment in firms or financial products that specifically reinforce pro-environmental corporate conduct.

Taken together, the four concepts discussed here comprise the environmentalist's CSR agenda. But, as you will learn in a moment, there are those who are adamantly against these enviro-friendly CSR policies. Here then, is your chance to examine this issue from both sides, as we ask you to decide whether or not corporations should adopt enviro-friendly CSR policies.

YES ↙

From the Current Articles of Incorporation & Bylaws, June 20, 1981

The purposes of the Sierra Club are to explore, enjoy, and protect the wild places of the earth; to practice and promote the responsible use of the earth's ecosystems and resources; to educate and enlist humanity to protect and restore the quality of the natural and human environment; and to use all lawful means to carry out these objectives.

Beliefs about Environment and Society

Humans have evolved as an interdependent part of nature. Humankind has a powerful place in the environment, which may range from steward to destroyer. We must share the Earth's finite resources with other living things and respect all life-enabling processes. Thus, we must control human population numbers and seek a balance that serves all life forms.

Complex and diversified ecosystems provide stability for the Earth's life support processes. Development and other human activities can simplify ecosystems, undermine their dynamic stability, and threaten these processes. Wildness itself has a value serving all species, with too few remaining. We have more to fear from too little wildness than from too much.

Genetic diversity is the product of evolution acting on wildness, and is important because it is biological capital for future evolution. We must preserve genetic diversity in wild tracts and gene pools. No species should be hastened into extinction by human intervention.

The needs of all creatures must be respected, their destinies viewed as separate from human desires, their existence not simply for human benefit. All species have a right to perpetuation of the habitat necessary and required for survival. All creatures should have freedom from needless predation, persecution, and cruel or unduly confining captivity. We must seek moral restraints on human power to affect the well-being of so many species.

Humans must exercise stewardship of the Earth's resources to assure enough for other creatures and for the future. Thus, resources should be renewed indefinitely wherever possible, and resource depletion limited. Resources should be used as long as possible and shared, avoiding waste and needless consumption. We must act knowledgeably and take precautions to avoid initiating irreversible trends. Good stewardship implies a shared moral and social responsibility to take positive action on behalf of conservation.

The enjoyment of the natural environment and the Earth's wild places is a fundamental purpose of the Club, and an end in itself.

Ideal Goals (Summary)—for Environment and Society

To sustain natural life-support systems, avoid impairing them, and avoid irreversible damage to them.

To facilitate species survival; to maintain genetic diversity; to avoid hastened extinction of species; to protect prime natural habitat.

To establish and protect natural reserves, including representative natural areas, wilderness areas in each biome, displays of natural phenomena, and habitats for rare and endangered species.

To control human population growth and impacts; to limit human population numbers and habitat needs within Earth's carrying capacity; to avoid needless human consumption of resources; to plan and control land use, with environmental impact assessment and safeguards, and rehabilitation of damaged sites.

To learn more about the facts, interrelationships, and principles of the Earth's ecosystems, and the place and impact of humans in them; to understand the consequences of human activities within the biosphere.

To develop responsible and appropriate technology matched to end-uses; to introduce sophisticated technology gradually after careful assessment and with precautionary monitoring.

To control pollution of the biosphere; to minimize waste residuals with special care of hazardous materials; to use the best available control technology at sources; and to recycle wastes.

To manage resources soundly; to avoid waste with long-term plans; to sustain the yield of living resources and maintain their productivity and breeding stocks; to prolong availability of nonliving resources such as fossil fuels, minerals, and water.

To impart a sense of social responsibility among consumers, developers, and public authorities concerning environmental protection; to regulate threats to public health; to avoid private degradation of public resources; to minimize impacts on innocent parties and future generations.

Vision Statement for the Sierra Club's Second Century, Board of Directors, September 16–17, 1989
The Challenge

We are facing a global environmental crisis that grows more urgent every day. Threats that were once inconceivable—such as massive oil spill disasters, global climate change, and the poisoning of our air, land and water—are becoming common events. Species are being annihilated and wilderness is being destroyed at an alarming and accelerating rate.

We live each day knowing that in a few generations—unless humankind takes drastic steps to protect our planet—it is possible that the Earth will hurtle around the Sun devoid of life as we know it.

There is no priority more urgent than saving the Earth.

Our Vision

For nearly 100 years, Sierra Club members have shared a vision of humanity— living in harmony with the Earth.

We envision a world where wilderness areas and open spaces are pro- tected habitats sustaining all species . . . a world where oceans and streams are clean and the air is pure . . . a world where a healthy biosphere and a nontoxic environment are inalienable rights. In short, we envision a world saved from the threat of unalterable planetary disaster.

To save our planet, we must change the world –

Priorities must change: People must learn to live in ways that preserve and protect our precious resources.

Policies must change: Our institutions must abandon practices that reck- lessly endanger the environment.

Values must change: Progress must be measured by its long-term value to living systems and creatures rather than its short-term value to special interests or the economy.

To achieve this vision, people across the nation and around the world must speak out with a powerful voice that cannot be ignored. Aggressive grass- roots action on an unprecedented scale is essential to protect our environment and our species. There is no other choice. It will require leadership that is visionary, experienced, and strong.

Our Role

The Sierra Club is uniquely qualified to lead this grassroots action to save the Earth. We are America's largest and most effective grassroots environmental organization—an experienced, respected and committed fellowship of citizen activists. Within our ranks lie the expertise, wisdom, and vitality to find the new directions needed to meet the challenges of the future.

We offer proven ability to influence public policy and empower individu- als to confront local, national, and global problems. From town halls to our nation's capital to global institutions, Sierra Club activists are scoring enor- mous victories for the environment through personal action, education, litiga- tion, lobbying, and participation in the political process.

As the Sierra Club prepares for its second century, we offer to America and the world our vision of humanity living in harmony with nature. We dedicate ourselves to achieving this vision as we reaffirm our passionate com- mitment to explore, enjoy, and protect the Earth.

Statement of Purposes, Development by the Planning Committee in 1985; Amended by the Board of Directors, May 5–6, 1990

For purposes of planning, the Sierra Club's purpose, thus, is to preserve, protect, and enhance the natural environment.

The mission of the Sierra Club is to influence public, private and corporate policies and actions through Club programs at the local, state, national and international levels.

The strategy of the Sierra Club is to activate appropriate portions of a network of staff, members, and other concerned citizens, using legislative, administrative, electoral, and legal approaches, and to develop supporting public opinion.

Strategic Goals, Board of Directors, May 1–2, 1993

The following goals guide the Club's work:

I. Enhance public perception of "environment" (overcome the perception of limits):

   A. Develop pressure by consumers for green products.
   B. Educate public that strong environmental protection creates jobs.
   C. Reduce consumption levels in the U.S. through increasing efficiency, recycling, producing more durable goods, and by making waste and non-essential products and packaging socially unacceptable.

II. Build upon and develop new forms of political leverage:

   A. Mobilize market incentives to induce corporate environmental change.
   B. Develop hybrid or "coordinated campaigns," targeting multiple levels of decision making.
   C. Work to make existing institutions more responsive and accountable to community and environmental needs.
   D. Create new vehicles for responsive institutions of government.
   E. Develop unconventional alliances to overcome legislative obstacles.

III. Integrate concerns for environmental protection and social justice to strengthen the environmental movement:

   A. Develop more effective means for communicating through race, class, age, and cultural barriers.
   B. Re-position the Sierra Club as more visibly concerned about threats to community and workplace environments.
   C. Encourage more extensive coalition work between local Sierra Club entities and environmental justice groups.
   D. Develop a stronger capacity to influence state and local regulatory and land-use actions (particularly as these relate to pollution

threats to vulnerable groups in our society and land uses they find unacceptable).

IV. Enhance the Club's position of leadership within the environmental movement:

A. Continue to develop programs to cultivate and train new leaders.
B. Nurture a culture within the Club that encourages cooperation and collaboration, and that rewards innovative ideas and contributions.
C. Significantly enhance our ability for "quick responses" to issues and challenges.
D. Strengthen the Club's public affairs capacity for "telling our story."

Sierra Club "Premise" Poster, Presented to the Board November 13–14, 1999, by the Communication & Education GovCom

This is not about getting back to nature. It is about understanding we've never left.

We are deep in our nature every day. We're up to our ears in it. It is under our feet, it is in our lungs, it runs through our veins. We are not visitors here. We weren't set down to enjoy the view. We were born here and we're part of it—like any ant, fish, rock, or blade of grass.

This connection is as personal as it is fundamental. It can't be proved with theorems and diagrams. You either feel it our your don't.

Sierra Club members feel it.

Maybe it came to you on a mountain trail, or on a river bank, or at a windowsill watching a spider's unthinking intelligence unfold. Simply put, it's the sudden conviction that there is something out there, something wonderful. And it is much, much bigger than you.

A revelation like this could easily overwhelm a person. We choose to let it inspire us. Nature, vastly complex and infinitely subtle, is our perfect metaphor. Related to everythiing, signifying everything, it is the spring where we go to renew our spirit. And it, in turn, asks something of us. It compels us to take responsibility and then to take action.

Look, there is nothing inevitable about the future of our environment. A poisoned stream can get worse, stay the same, or get better. It depends largely on what we choose to do. That simple belief, backed by 100 years of effort and result, is what drives the Sierra Club.

So, forget the grim cliché of the selfless environmentalist. When you accept your connection to nature, suddenly you can't look at the world without seeing something very personal in it. You are part of it, and you work for the planet because it gives you joy to do so.

You work for the planet because you belong to it.

Clarification of Conservation Initiatives and their Emphases for 2006–2010, Board of Directors, March 4–5, 2006

The Sierra Club's 114-year history reflects a rich blend of activism and unifying campaigns. Over the last decades, periods of mobilization and focus have represented some of the Club's finest moments, and yielded some of our proudest victories: the Alaska Lands Act, Wild Forest campaign, the replacement of James Watt, the Superfund battle of 1986, California Desert Protection Campaign, the defeat of Newt Gingrich's Contract with America, and our 26-year long defense of the Arctic Refuge.

Now, we have the opportunity to distinguish ourselves again and to lead once more.

2006–2010 Conservation Initiatives

In November 2005, the Board of Directors adopted three long-term conservation initiatives for the Sierra Club—Smart Energy Solutions, America's Wild Legacy, and Safe and Healthy Communities.

Two of these three—America's Wild Legacy and Safe and Healthy Communities—have been part of the Sierra Club's priority conservation work for decades. In adopting them as Conservation Initiatives for 2006–2010, the Board declared its commitment to our continued leadership in these areas.

In contrast, the Sierra Club has not historically made broad energy policy a national priority campaign. Energy, historically, has been a less central and more episodic Club focus. But the times demand that we meet the challenge to move beyond a fossil fuel world and that the Club lead society through one of the largest transformational moments in American history.

The Club's leadership role in confronting global warming and transforming our energy economy advances not only the Club's Smart Energy vision, but our work for America's Wild Legacy and Safe and Healthy Communities as well. The Club must lead America in this moment; there is no other organization with the history, vision, and presence at the community level to play that role.

At the same time, the Club's highest priority for the next decade as an institution is to build its capacity and focus on Smart Energy Solutions. This is the Conservation Initiative where our existing capacities and abilities are least well developed. As a result, we want to identify those opportunities that address the threats from climate change and can contribute to effective solutions where our members live. In building support for this priority, we want to be promoting Smart Energy Solutions in our trainings, communications channels, fundraising, political work, activist outings, and other available opportunities. We ask and encourage all to participate in an early opportunity around Earth Day 2006. It will be our first opportunity to showcase, for example, our Cool Cities program around the country.

Paul Driessen

→ **NO**

Roots of Eco-Imperialism

Like a mad scientist's experiment gone terribly awry, corporate social responsibility has mutated into a creature radically different from what its original designers envisioned. It now threatens to cause a moral meltdown, to spawn a system in which the most farfetched worries of healthy, well-fed First World activists routinely dominate business, economic, technological, scientific and health debates—and override critical concerns of sick, malnourished people in poor Third World countries.

This mutant version of corporate social responsibility demands that businesses and nations conduct their affairs in accord with new "ethical" codes that derive from several intertwined doctrines of social and environmental radicalism.

- **Stakeholder participation** theory asserts that any group that has an interest in, or could arguably be affected by, a corporate decision or the outcome of a public policy debate has a right to pressure the decision makers until they accede to the activists' demands.
- **Sustainable development** (SD) says companies must minimize the extraction and use of natural resources, because corporate activities must "meet the needs and aspirations of the present without compromising the ability of future generations to meet their needs."
- **The precautionary principle** (PP) holds that companies should halt any activities that might threaten "human health or the environment," even if no clear cause-and-effect relationship has been established, and even if the potential threat is largely (or entirely) theoretical.
- **Socially responsible investing** (SRI) insists that pension funds and individual investors should purchase shares in companies that have pledged to conform their corporate policies and actions to sustainability, precautionary and responsibility ideologies.

There is a certain allure to these doctrines—reinforced by news stories and reports extolling the concepts and asserting their widespread acceptance. However, neither the terminology nor its constant repetition represents a groundswell of actual public support or obviates fundamental problems with these precepts. The language might sound clear at first blush. But it is highly elastic and can easily be stretched and molded to fit a wide variety of activist claims, causes and agendas.

As a consequence, the doctrines are the subject of deep concern and passionate debate, as thoughtful people struggle to assess the risks posed for corporations, investors, employees, creditors and customers—for scientific, economic and technological advancement—and for people whose hope for a better future depends on ensuring plentiful supplies of affordable electricity, conquering disease and malnutrition, and having unencumbered access to modern technology and greater economic opportunity. As the debate rages, it is becoming increasingly obvious that the doctrines solve few problems and, instead, create a vast multitude of new difficulties.

··❦··

At their root is the fact that these intertwined CSR doctrines primarily reflect the concerns, preferences and gloomy worldview of a small cadre of politicians, bureaucrats, academics, multinational NGOs and wealthy foundations in affluent developed countries. These self-appointed guardians of the public weal have little understanding of (and often harbor a deep distaste for) business, capitalism, market economies, technology, global trade, and the vital role of profits in generating innovation and progress.

Yet, it is they who proclaim and implement the criteria by which businesses are to be judged, decide which of society's goals are important, determine whether those goals are being met, and insist that countervailing needs, viewpoints and concerns be relegated to secondary or irrelevant status. In so doing, they seek to impose their worldview and change society in ways, and to degrees, that they have not been able to achieve through popular votes, legislation, treaty or even judicial decisions.

Inherent in the doctrines are several false, pessimistic premises that are at the core of ideological environmentalism. Eco activists erroneously believe, for example, that energy and mineral resources are finite, and are rapidly being exhausted. That activities conducted by corporations, especially large multinational companies, inevitably result in resource depletion, environmental degradation, impaired human and societal health, social harm and imminent planetary disaster. And that it is primarily profits, not societal or consumer needs and desires—and certainly not a desire to serve humanity—that drive corporate decision-making.

In a nutshell, CSR doctrines are rooted too much in animosity toward business and profits, too much in conjectural problems and theoretical needs of future generations—and too little in real, immediate, life-and-death needs of present generations, especially billions of poor rural people in developing countries. The mutant doctrines give radical activists unprecedented leverage to impose the loftiest of developed world standards on companies, communities and nations, while ignoring the needs, priorities and aspirations of people who struggle daily just to survive.

Actually implementing the doctrines requires significant centralized control of land and energy use, economic production and consumption, corporate innovation and initiative, markets, transportation, labor, trade, housing, policy making processes and people's daily lives. Under the activists' agenda, control would be monitored and enforced through United Nations, European Union, US and other government agencies. All this is the antithesis of the private property rights, capitalism, and freedom of nations, communities, companies and individuals to make their own decisions, in accord with their own cultural preferences and personal or societal needs—and thereby generate innovation, prosperity, human health and environmental quality.

The ideological version of corporate social responsibility thus stands in direct opposition to the systems that have generated the greatest wealth, opportunities, technological advancements, and health and environmental improvements in history. Its real effect is to cede decision-making to a few; reduce competition, innovation, trade, investment and economic vitality; and thereby impair future social, health and environmental improvements.

According to activist theology, adherence to CSR concepts generates a "triple bottom line" (economic, social and environmental) that companies should meet in judging "true" profitability and citizenship, David Henderson notes in *Misguided Virtue: False notions of corporate responsibility.* Only by measuring their costs, benefits and profits against all three standards can businesses meet "society's expectations," earn their "license to operate," and "give capitalism a human face," claim the activists.

But CSR's supposedly equal emphasis on all three components of the triple bottom line is typically skewed so that environmental considerations trump all others. This happens even where people's lives are put at risk, as in the case of strident activist opposition to pesticides despite widespread malaria, or to biotechnology despite rampant malnutrition and starvation.

Mutant CSR also enables countries to impose "legal" barriers to keep foreign goods out and protect domestic businesses and interests—typically through the use of malleable precautionary and sustainability rules that make it easy to cite far-fetched, unproven health or environmental risks, so as to justify heavy-handed actions.

❧❦❧

Stakeholder dialogue, according to the World Business Council for Sustainable Development, is "the essence of corporate social responsibility." However, many of the "stakeholders" who seek "dialogues" are actually well-funded activist groups that assert a "right" to participate in corporate and government decision-making, simply because they have a passionate devotion to their cause.

Some stakeholders are "shareholder activists," who own substantial shares in a company—or just enough to qualify them to introduce resolutions at annual meetings, demanding that a company adopt their positions and agendas on sustainable development, global warming, the precautionary principle or "human rights." Others may be politicians, bureaucrats and other elites in developing countries, whose personal careers and interests are advanced substantially by being aligned with these causes. That the lives of poor people in these countries might thereby be put at greater risk is often only a secondary consideration.

According to the *Boston Globe, Sacramento Bee,* Capital Research Center and others, the US environmental movement alone has annual revenues of some $4 billion, primarily as a result of contributions from foundations, corporations, unions, trial lawyers and taxpayer-funded government agencies. The international green movement's budget has been estimated to be well in excess of $8 billion a year.

As a result, well-organized, media-savvy pressure groups have unprecedented power to promote their agendas, define "society's expectations," and influence public perceptions, corporate decisions, and legislative and regulatory initiatives.

In the international arena, they frequently play a prominent role in negotiations, equal to or more dominant than many multinational companies and even some countries, especially Third World nations. Not surprisingly, the NGOs' agendas frequently conflict with and override the most pressing needs and concerns of people who are struggling to overcome widespread poverty and malnutrition, devastating epidemics, and a virtual absence of electricity and economic opportunity.

Corporate social responsibility, argues Gary Johns, can easily become "an assault on the interests and rights of 'real' stakeholders, those who have invested in or are creditors of corporations. It occurs when managers bow to pressure from interests that have no contract with the corporation, whether by way of employment, or supply of goods or services, or through ownership.

"CSR is also an assault on the interests of the electorate. It occurs by undermining the formal democratic consensus as to what constitutes reasonable business behavior. It also occurs when governments grant NGOs such status that it enables them to set themselves up as judges of corporate behavior," or of national decisions on critical health, economic and environmental concerns.

In many cases, the activist groups' cumulative membership might be less than 0.01 percent of a community's or country's population. No one elected them as stakeholders. No plebiscite was held to make their narrow definitions and agendas the arbiter of what is moral or in the broader public interest. No election, adjudication or even United Nations resolution gave them the authority to exclude other stakeholders from debates and decisionmaking processes—including entire nations and billions of destitute people, who are being denied the benefits of global trade, economic development, abundant affordable energy, and informed use of resources, pesticides and biotechnology.

And yet, the activists define what is responsible, sustainable or sufficiently cautious, often in a way that blocks any development which conflicts with their agendas. That other people might be adversely affected—or the world's most destitute citizens might remain mired in chronic hunger, poverty, disease and despair—enters only superficially into their calculations.

In asserting their demands, they downplay the complex needs and circumstances that confront companies, communities and nations. They ignore the science-based regulatory systems that already protect citizens from actual risks, and raise public fears of far-fetched risks to justify endless delays or outright bans.

Businesses, elected officials and citizens should take a leadership position on these issues, contest the demands of anti-business activists, challenge their motives and dispute their underlying premises. As Johns suggests, they need to "make the NGOs prove their bona fides." They need to "question the extent to which [the activists] represent anyone or anything; question the size of their membership; question the source of their funds; and question their expertise. In other words, question their standing and their legitimacy."

Instead, too many businesses, community leaders and citizens pursue a strategy of appeasement and accommodation, ceding moral authority to unelected NGOs, bureaucrats, "ethical" investor groups and other activists. Some have actually endorsed the activists' demands and collaborated closely with them, despite serious adverse impacts on the world's poor.

⋅❀⋅

As a result, says University of Houston economics professor Thomas DeGregori, developed country activists are often able to co-opt local movements, hijacking them to radical agendas, brushing aside legitimate local concerns, and leaving the indigenous people worse off than before.

When India's impoverished Chipko people initiated a movement to build a road and gain access to Himalayan forest resources, to create a small wood products industry, First World environmentalists took it over. The voices of real local stakeholders were all but silenced, says Australian professor Dr. Haripriya Ragan, and their struggle for resources and development were sacrificed to global environmental concerns. Leading the assault were radical anti-technology activist Vandana Shiva and groups that "tacitly support coercive conservation tactics that weaken local claims to resource access for sustaining livelihoods."

In other cases, "stakeholder involvement" becomes a form of extortion, in which "corporate greed" is replaced by "agenda greed." In 1995, Shell Oil was preparing to sink its Brent Spar offshore oil storage platform in the deep Atlantic, under a permit granted by the UK Environment Ministry. However, Greenpeace launched a vicious and sophisticated $2-million public relations assault that falsely accused the company of planning to dump tons of oil, toxic waste and radioactive material in the ocean. Shell's timid and unimaginative response to the ensuing media nightmare got the company nothing but a bigger black eye, and it was forced to spend a fortune dismantling the platform onshore.

A year later, Greenpeace issued a written apology, effectively admitting that the entire campaign had been a fraud. There had been no oil or wastes on the structure. Of course, the admission got buried in the business pages or obituaries. Flush from their victory, the Rainbow Warriors went on to shake down other companies and promote bogus claims about chemicals, wood products and genetically modified "Frankenfood."

Embarrassed by its stinging defeat, Shell tried to refurbish its reputation and learn from its mistakes. Apparently, the company's execs never actually graduated from the School of Hard Knocks. A few years later, when complaints alone failed to garner enough media attention to embarrass Shell over its alleged "failure to protect Nigeria's Ogoni people," Oxfam and Amnesty International hooked up with radical greens, to hammer the company for complicity in an "environmental catastrophe."

It turned out the catastrophe was caused by tribesmen sabotaging oil pipelines, says Dr. Roger Bate, a visiting fellow with the American Enterprise Insitute, to get gullible journalists to write stories that enabled Ogoni leaders to extort huge monetary settlements from the company. But Shell paid up anyway, in hopes that the problem would go away. Meanwhile, the rights groups and media ignored the racketeering, effectively aiding and abetting the tribal leaders, and setting the stage for future blackmail.

⌑

Sustainable development, as defined by environmental activists, focuses too little on fostering sustained economic development, and too much on *restricting* development—typically in the name of protecting the environment. It also reflects their erroneous doctrine that we are rapidly depleting our natural resources and destroying the planet. The putative welfare of "fragile ecosystems" again trumps even the most obvious welfare of people, frequently leading desperate people to wreak havoc on the very ecosystems the activists claim to be protecting.

Leon Louw, executive director of South Africa's Free Market Foundation, refers to sustainable development as "voodoo science." It never asks "sustainable for how long: 10, 200, 1000, a million years? For whom? Advanced people with unknowable future technology, needs and resources? For how long must we conserve so-called 'non-renewables'? Must our descendants, by the same twisted logic, do likewise? Forever?"

Not one person alive at the dawn of the twentieth century could have envisioned the amazing technological feats of that era, its changing raw material needs, or its increasing ability to control pollution. In 1900, coal and wood provided heat. Air pollution and diseases we no longer even hear about killed millions. Telephones, cars and electricity were novelties for the rich. Common folk and freight alike were hauled by horses, which left behind 900,000 tons of manure a year in New York City alone. The Wright brothers still made bicycles. Air conditioners, radios, televisions, plastics, antibiotics, organ transplants and computers could not even be imagined.

Today, the pace of change is exponentially faster than 100 or even 50 years ago. To define sustainability under these conditions is impossible. To suppose that anyone could predict what technologies will exist, what pollutants will be a problem, what fuels and minerals we will need—in what quantities—is to engage in sheer science fiction. Or in the most deceitful public policy scam.

In short, the fundamental problem with "sustainable development," says Oxford University economist Dr. Wilfred Beckerman, is its demand that radical prescriptions be followed to achieve narrowly defined ends, determine which trade-offs should be emphasized, and decide which trade-offs are to be ignored. Here the concept has nothing to add. "Indeed, it subtracts from the objective of maximizing human welfare, because the slogan of sustainable development seems to provide a blanket justification for almost any policy designed to promote almost any ingredient of human welfare, irrespective of its cost and hence irrespective of the other ingredients of welfare."

Precautionary theories likewise promote agendas set by eco-centric activists in developed countries. They ignore countervailing interests and needs of developing nations, such as: creating economic opportunity, ensuring adequate and reliable supplies of affordable energy, alleviating poverty, malnutrition and disease—and ultimately improving environmental quality and ensuring more sustainable practices. It gives CSR, SD and PP precepts credit for any potential public health and environmental risks they might reduce, public policy analyst Indur Goklany points out, but imposes no "discredit" for risks, injuries or deaths that they might generate.

Precautionary doctrines hold that, if anyone raises doubts about the safety of a technology, the technology should be severely restricted, if not banned outright, until it is proven to be absolutely safe. But improved safety resulting from introducing the new technology is typically ignored or given short shrift. The precautionary principle also holds that the more serious the theoretical damages, the more society should spend on precautionary measures, or be willing to sacrifice in opportunities foregone. Moreover, say its proponents, the inability to prove how much society might gain or lose from taking those measures should not stand in the way of extreme caution.

The net result is that the precautionary principle repeatedly stifles risk-taking, innovation, economic growth, scientific and technological progress, freedom of choice, and human betterment. Had it governed scientific and technological progress in past centuries, numerous historic achievements would have been limited or prevented, according to 40 internationally renowned scientists who were surveyed by the techno-whiz-kids at *Spiked,* in advance of its May 2003 London conference, "Panic Attack: Interrogating our obsession with risk."

The experts listed modern marvels from A to Z that the precautionary principle would have stopped dead in their tracks: airplanes, antibiotics, aspirin and automobiles; biotechnology, blood transfusions, CAT scans and the contraceptive pill; electricity, hybrid crops and the Green Revolution; microwaves, open heart surgery and organ transplants; pesticides, radar and refrigeration; telephones, televisions, water purification and x-rays—to name but a few.

Imagine what our lives would be without these technological miracles. As Adam Finn, professor of pediatrics at Bristol University's Institute of Child Health observed, "pretty much everything" would have been prevented or limited under this stifling principle, because "there is nothing we do that has no theoretical risk, and nearly everything carries some risk."

Had today's technophobic zealots been in charge in previous centuries, we would have to roll human progress back to the Middle Ages—and beyond, since even fire, the wheel and organic farming pose risks, and none would have passed the "absolute safety" test the zealots now demand. Putting them in charge now would mean an end to progress in the developed world, and perpetual deprivation and misery for inhabitants of developing nations.

Socially responsible investing (SRI) has become another major driving force behind today's CSR movement, courtesy of a growing coterie of activist pension funds and "ethical" investor advisory firms. They claim to represent people who "want to retire into a clean, civil and safe world." On this basis, pension fund directors pressure CEOs and shareholders to meet "acceptable standards" of precaution, sustainable development, social responsibility and societal expectations.

Now, prevailing notions of corporate social responsibility may bring about a cleaner, safer, more civil world for the activists and pensioners, at least in the short run. But what about for the poorest citizens of Africa, Asia and Latin America? Or even the poorest citizens of the United States, Europe, Canada, Australia and Japan?

As to "societal expectations"—don't African and Asian societies have a right to expect that they will be protected against malaria, malnutrition and dysentery? That they will not be told by rich First World foundations, government agencies and pressure groups how they may or may not respond to lethal threats, including those the developed countries have already eliminated?

To suggest that "socially responsible investors" should have free rein to ignore the conditions and needs of desperate people in the Third World is incomprehensible. But that is often the effect of CSR and SRI policies, as the following chapters demonstrate.

⋅⦿⋅

Corporate social responsibility may, as its advocates constantly assert, be based on a noble quest to improve society and safeguard humanity's and our Earth's future. This is a fundamental justification for modern ideological environmentalism. Of course, similar claims were made on behalf of other coercive, central-authority "isms" of the twentieth century.

However, debates over corporate social responsibility, stakeholder involvement, sustainable development, the precautionary principle and socially responsible investing have in far too many instances allowed science and logic to be replaced by pressure tactics, political expediency and a new form of tyranny. In the process, they have left many urgent questions unanswered.

- Are the asserted risks real? Do the benefits outweigh the risks? Will the radical policy proposals improve poor people's lives—or result in more poverty, misery, disease and death for those most severely and directly affected by the decisions?
- Why have other stakeholders—such as the rural poor in developing countries—had only a limited role or voice in this process? Why are *their* interests not reflected in CSR and precautionary definitions or applications?
- Why have some companies, foundations and nations collaborated so closely with NGO and government activists in promoting these mutant concepts?

- What is the source of the activists' supposed moral and legal authority for determining what is "ethical" or "socially responsible" or in accordance with "society's expectations"? Who elected them "stakeholders," to sit in judgment over what is or is not an "acceptable risk," or what costs, benefits and health or economic priorities must be considered (or ignored) in making this determination?

James Shikwati, director of Kenya's Inter-Regional Economic Network, raises additional questions that weigh heavily on the minds of people in his part of the world.

- "Why do Europe's developed countries impose their environmental ethics on poor countries that are simply trying to pass through a stage they themselves went through?
- "After taking numerous risks to reach their current economic and technological status, why do they tell poor countries to use no energy, and no agricultural or pest-control technologies that might pose some conceivable risk of environmental harm?
- "Why do they tell poor countries to follow sustainable development doctrines that really mean little or no energy or economic development?"

Most of these questions might be unanswerable. But they certainly merit careful reflection. For in its most insidious role, corporate social responsibility—as currently defined and applied—ignores the legitimate aspirations and needs of people who have not yet shared the dreams and successes of even lower and middle income people in the developed world. It should come as no surprise that the poor people in developing countries increasingly view CSR, not as a mechanism to improve their lives, but as a virulent kind of neo-colonialism that many call eco-imperialism.

As corporate executives are frequently reminded, nobody cares how much you know, until they know how much you care. It might be appropriate to suggest that ideological environmentalism should devote as much attention to Third World babies, as it does to adorable harp seal pups.

Television, email, websites, satellite transmissions and even old-fashioned newspapers have enabled well-financed activists to concoct, exaggerate and spread public anxiety over a seemingly endless parade of theoretical risks. Even for Americans—who live in the safest nation on earth and are unfazed by traffic and numerous other dangers that pose far greater risks than those trumpeted by precautionary propagandists—the constant drumbeat of doom is hard to ignore.

To suggest that the mutant version of corporate social responsibility doctrines represent progress, "environmental justice" or ethical behavior stretches the meaning of those terms beyond the breaking point. In the end, what is truly not sustainable are the human and ecological tolls exacted by the callous policies of radical environmentalism.

Perhaps nowhere is that more apparent than in the arenas of energy, malaria control, malnutrition and trade.

POSTSCRIPT

Should Corporations Adopt Environmentally Friendly Policies of CSR and Sustainable Development?

As you just read in Paul Driessen's pointed attack on environmentalism-driven corporate social responsibility, blind acceptance of ideas such as the precautionary principle can be just as damaging as the corporate actions the ideas are designed to restrain. The PP, for example, has dominated public discussion since its adoption by the environmentalists and has played a large role in the numerous laws and regulations that affect virtually every aspect of corporate behavior, not to mention our own personal lives. However, as Driessen and a rapidly growing number of critics have pointed out, in many instances, this view is much worse than a carelessly optimistic belief that there are no environmental problems at all.

Consider the case of the corporate average fuel economy ratings for automobiles (CAFÉ Standards). To address smog pollution and the widely accepted perception that worldwide oil supplies were running out, the federal government passed a law in 1975 establishing fuel-efficiency requirements for all cars. The problem is that, over time, these standards have forced automakers to make smaller, lighter, less safe cars. How unsafe? Two reputable studies (1989 by Harvard University and the Brookings Institution; 2001 by the National Academy of Sciences) concluded that the CAFÉ standards result in 1200–3900 additional deaths every year. (Robert James Bidinotto, "Death by Environmentalism, *The Navigator*, The Objectivist Center, March 2004, p. 4.) "In the trade-off between saving gasoline and saving lives, the government rules willingly sacrifice lives" (Bidinotto, p. 4). Given this, it is no surprise that large, safe SUVs are popular with the public; nor is it surprising that SUVs are viewed by environmentalists as major to the depletion of fossil fuels and to global warming.

The point of this example is that it is just as dangerous to err on the side of extreme pessimism about the environment as it is to be in a state of unfounded optimism. Further, business executives would be wise to refrain from engaging in unquestioned acceptance of CSR policies, particularly given the increasingly skeptical attitude of both the scientific community and the general public regarding the veracity of the man-made global warming position.

Suggested Readings

Steven Milloy, "Green Hell: How Environmentalist Plan to Control Your Life and What You Can Do to Stop Them," (Regnery Publishing, 2009).

Roy Spencer, *Climate Confusion: How Global Warming Hysteria Leads to Bad Science, Pandering Politicians and Misguided Policies That Hurt the Poor,* (Encounter Books, 2008).

New Scientist, "Why Our Economy Is Killing the Planet and What We Can Do About It," *New Scientist Special Report* (October 16, 2008). http://www.newscientist.com/article/mg20026786.000-special-report-how-our-economy-is-killing-the-earth.html

Jeff Wells, Susan Casey-Lefkowitz, & Gabriela Chavarria, "Danger in the Nursery: Impact of Tar Sands Oil Development in Canada's Boreal on Birds," Natural Resources Defense Council (November 2008). http://www.nrdc.org/wildlife/borealbirds.asp

Chris Horner, *The Politically Incorrect Guide to Global Warming and Environmentalism,* (Regnery Publishing, 2007).

ISSUE 16

Do Unskilled Immigrants Hurt the American Economy?

YES: **Steven Malanga**, from "How Unskilled Immigrants Hurt Our Economy," *City Journal* (Summer 2006)

NO: **Diana Furchtgott-Roth**, from "The Case for Immigration," *The New York Sun* (September 22, 2006)

ISSUE SUMMARY

YES: Columnist Steven Malanga believes the influx of unskilled immigrants results in job loss by native workers and lower investment in labor-saving technology. He also contends that illegal immigration taxes our already-strained welfare and social security systems.

NO: Diana Furchtgott-Roth, senior fellow at the Hudson Institute and a former chief economist at the US Department of Labor, points out that annual immigration represents a small portion of the US labor force, and, in any event, immigrant laborers complement, rather than replace, legal American citizens in the workplace.

In both the 2004 Presidential Election and the mid-term Congressional elections of 2006, the topic of illegal immigration and its allied issues were of paramount importance to the American electorate. Now, in the throes of a major recession threatening to descend into a depression, the immigration issue is overshadowed by economic concerns. Nevertheless, the issue is not going away, and we can expect it to re-emerge as a top concern of President Obama when economic conditions are more favorable. In the meantime, we consider a specific aspect of this issue by asking if unskilled immigrants threaten the US labor force and ultimately harm the American economy.

According to the Cato Institute, over the past 200 years, the United States has welcomed more than 60 million immigrants to its shores (http://www.freetrade.org/issues/immigration.html). Although the vast majority of those immigrants entered the country legally, in recent decades, the number of people entering the country illegally has grown tremendously. Estimates currently put the number of illegal immigrants in the US somewhere between 10 and 15 million. Regardless of the actual figure, there is no question that the continued growth of illegal aliens has important ramifications both politically and socially; indeed, one need only observe the behaviors of the two political parties to verify the truth of this statement. But of particular importance to this text is the impact of the growth of illegal aliens on the American workplace.

Those that believe the overall effect of these unskilled workers is generally beneficial to the US economy provide numerous points in support of their position. They point, for example, to research showing that immigrants and natives frequently do not compete for the same jobs. Interestingly, in areas where demand for labor is high relative to supply, hiring immigrants results in a complementary outcome rather than a competitive situation. Thus, supporters contend, the view that illegal aliens and other immigrants take jobs from native workers is simple minded. An often-overlooked fact is that many immigrants arrive in the United States with strong skill sets and a burning desire to make something of themselves. Indeed, many employers have found that there is a large degree of overlap between the characteristics of an individual willing to accept the risks and dangers of relocating to a foreign land to make a better life for himself and the characteristics of a loyal, dependable, and driven employee. Finally, supporters note that illegal aliens contribute mightily to our economy in ways beyond their physical labor: As a group, they contribute billions of dollars to social security through payroll taxes. However, owing to fears of being caught and deported, few actually collect payments, thus providing the social security program with a huge net gain. For example, *The Washington Post* estimated that during the period from 1990 to 1998, illegal aliens paid more than $20 billion in payroll taxes (Washingtonpost.com)

On the other side of the debate are those who are against corporations being allowed to hire illegal aliens because of the detrimental effects doing so has on the American labor force. Central to their position is the argument that illegal immigration disproportionately affects poor American natives because the immigrants are willing to work the unskilled jobs typically held by poor Americans and do so for much less pay. They further argue that from this perspective, firms that hire illegal aliens are anti-American because they are effectively displacing legitimate American employees. Another charge frequently leveled at supporters is the negative impact on the economy due to illegal immigration, particularly in the area of taxes. One the one hand, critics point out, states lose billions of dollars each year in the form of unpaid taxes. On the other, states are faced with growing demands for governmental services driven by the increase in their populations, much of which is the result of illegal immigration. The net result? States have to raise taxes to meet these needs; thus, the law-abiding American citizen foots the bill for the illegal immigrants. It's hard to see how this outcome can be viewed as anything but harmful to the US economy.

Thus, the question we pose here is whether the US economy suffers when American businesses hire unskilled illegal aliens. Answering in the affirmative is columnist Steven Malanga. He believes the influx of unskilled immigrants results in job loss by native workers and lower investment in labor-saving technology. Arguing the other side of the debate is Diana Furchtgott-Roth, senior fellow at the Hudson Institute and a former chief economist at the US Department of Labor. She points out that that annual immigration represents a small portion of the US labor force and, in any event, immigrant laborers complement, rather than replace, legal American citizens in the workplace.

YES ⬅

Steven Malanga

How Unskilled Immigrants Hurt Our Economy

The day after Librado Velasquez arrived on Staten Island after a long, surreptitious journey from his Chiapas, Mexico, home, he headed out to a street corner to wait with other illegal immigrants looking for work. Velasquez, who had supported his wife, seven kids, and his in-laws as a *campesino*, or peasant farmer, until a 1998 hurricane devastated his farm, eventually got work, off the books, loading trucks at a small New Jersey factory, which hired illegals for jobs that required few special skills. The arrangement suited both, until a work injury sent Velasquez to the local emergency room, where federal law required that he be treated, though he could not afford to pay for his care. After five operations, he is now permanently disabled and has remained in the United States to pursue compensation claims. . . .

Velasquez's story illustrates some of the fault lines in the nation's current, highly charged, debate on immigration. Since the mid-1960s, America has welcomed nearly 30 million legal immigrants and received perhaps another 15 million illegals, numbers unprecedented in our history. These immigrants have picked our fruit, cleaned our homes, cut our grass, worked in our factories, and washed our cars. But they have also crowded into our hospital emergency rooms, schools, and government-subsidized aid programs, sparking a fierce debate about their contributions to our society and the costs they impose on it.

Advocates of open immigration argue that welcoming the Librado Velasquezes of the world is essential for our American economy: our businesses need workers like him, because we have a shortage of people willing to do low-wage work. Moreover, the free movement of labor in a global economy pays off for the United States, because immigrants bring skills and capital that expand our economy and offset immigration's costs. Like tax cuts, supporters argue, immigration pays for itself.

But the tale of Librado Velasquez helps show why supporters are wrong about today's immigration, as many Americans sense and so much research has demonstrated. America does not have a vast labor shortage that requires waves of low-wage immigrants to alleviate; in fact, unemployment among unskilled workers is high—about 30 percent. Moreover, many of the unskilled, uneducated workers now journeying here labor, like Velasquez, in shrinking industries, where they force out native workers, and many others work in industries where the availability of cheap workers has led businesses to suspend investment in new technologies that would make them less labor-intensive.

Yet while these workers add little to our economy, they come at great cost, because they are not economic abstractions but human beings, with their own culture and ideas—often at odds with our own. Increasing numbers of them arrive with little education and none of the skills necessary to succeed in a modern economy. Many may wind up stuck on our lowest economic rungs, where they will rely on something that immigrants of other generations didn't have: a vast U.S. welfare and social-services apparatus that has enormously amplified the cost of immigration. Just as welfare reform and other policies are helping to shrink America's underclass by weaning people off such social pro-grams, we are importing a new, foreign-born underclass. As famed free-market economist Milton Friedman puts it: "It's just obvious that you can't have free immigration and a welfare state."

Immigration can only pay off again for America if we reshape our policy, organizing it around what's good for the economy by welcoming workers we truly need and excluding those who, because they have so little to offer, are likely to cost us more than they contribute, and who will struggle for years to find their place here.

Hampering today's immigration debate are our misconceptions about the so-called first great migration some 100 years ago, with which today's immigration is often compared. . . . If America could assimilate 24 million mostly desperate immigrants from that great migration—people one unsym-pathetic economist at the turn of the twentieth century described as "the unlucky, the thriftless, the worthless"—surely, so the story goes, today's much bigger and richer country can absorb the millions of Librado Velasquezes now venturing here.

But that argument distorts the realities of the first great migration. . . . Those waves of immigrants—many of them urban dwellers who crossed a con-tinent and an ocean to get here—helped supercharge the workforce at a time when the country was going through a transformative economic expansion that craved new workers, especially in its cities. A 1998 National Research Council report noted "that the newly arriving immigrant nonagricultural work force . . . was (slightly) more skilled than the resident American labor force": 27 percent of them were skilled laborers, compared with only 17 percent of that era's native-born workforce.

Many of these immigrants quickly found a place in our economy, partici-pating in the workforce at a higher rate even than the native population. Their success at finding work sent many of them quickly up the economic ladder: those who stayed in America for at least 15 years, for instance, were just as likely to own their own business as native-born workers of the same age, one study found. . . .

What the newcomers of the great migration did not find here was a vast social-services and welfare state. They had to rely on their own resources or those of friends, relatives, or private, often ethnic, charities if things did not go well. That's why about 70 percent of those who came were men in their prime. It's also why many of them left when the economy sputtered several times during the period. . . .

Today's immigration has turned out so differently in part because it emerged out of the 1960s civil rights and Great Society mentality. In 1965, a new immigration act eliminated the old system of national quotas, which critics saw as racist because it greatly favored European nations. Lawmakers created a set of broader immigration quotas for each hemisphere, and they added a new visa preference category for family members to join their relatives here. Senate immigration subcommittee chairman Edward Kennedy reassured the country that, "contrary to the charges in some quarters, [the bill] will not inundate America with immigrants," and "it will not cause American workers to lose their jobs."

But, in fact, the law had an immediate, dramatic effect, increasing immigration by 60 percent in its first ten years. Sojourners from poorer countries around the rest of the world arrived in ever-greater numbers, so that whereas half of immigrants in the 1950s had originated from Europe, 75 percent by the 1970s were from Asia and Latin America. And as the influx of immigrants grew, the special-preferences rule for family unification intensified it further, as the pool of eligible family members around the world also increased. Legal immigration to the U.S. soared from 2.5 million in the 1950s to 4.5 million in the 1970s to 7.3 million in the 1980s to about 10 million in the 1990s.

As the floodgates of legal immigration opened, the widening economic gap between the United States and many of its neighbors also pushed illegal immigration to levels that America had never seen. In particular, when Mexico's move to a more centralized, state-run economy in the 1970s produced hyperinflation, the disparity between its stagnant economy and U.S. prosperity yawned wide. Mexico's per-capita gross domestic product, 37 percent of the United States' in the early 1980s, was only 27 percent of it by the end of the decade—and is now just 25 percent of it. With Mexican farmworkers able to earn seven to ten times as much in the United States as at home, by the 1980s illegals were pouring across our border at the rate of about 225,000 a year, and U.S. sentiment rose for slowing the flow.

But an unusual coalition of business groups, unions, civil rights activists, and church leaders thwarted the call for restrictions with passage of the inaptly named 1986 Immigration Reform and Control Act, which legalized some 2.7 million unauthorized aliens already here, supposedly in exchange for tougher penalties and controls against employers who hired illegals. The law proved no deterrent, however, because supporters, in subsequent legislation and court cases argued on civil rights grounds, weakened the employer sanctions. Meanwhile, more illegals flooded here in the hope of future amnesties from Congress, while the newly legalized sneaked their wives and children into the country rather than have them wait for family-preference visas. The flow of illegals into the country rose to between 300,000 and 500,000 per year in the 1990s, so that a decade after the legislation that had supposedly solved the undocumented alien problem by reclassifying them as legal, the number of illegals living in the United States was back up to about 5 million, while today it's estimated at between 9 million and 13 million.

The flood of immigrants, both legal and illegal, from countries with poor, ill-educated populations, has yielded a mismatch between today's immigrants and the American economy and has left many workers poorly positioned to succeed for the long term. . . . Nearly two-thirds of Mexican immigrants, for instance, are high school dropouts, and most wind up doing either unskilled factory work or small-scale construction projects, or they work in service industries, where they compete for entry-level jobs against one another, against the adult children of other immigrants, and against native-born high school dropouts. Of the 15 industries employing the greatest percentage of foreign-born workers, half are low-wage service industries, including gardening, domestic household work, car washes, shoe repair, and janitorial work. . . .

Although open-borders advocates say that these workers are simply taking jobs Americans don't want, studies show that the immigrants drive down wages of native-born workers and squeeze them out of certain industries. Harvard economists George Borjas and Lawrence Katz, for instance, estimate that low-wage immigration cuts the wages for the average native-born high school dropout by some 8 percent, or more than $1,200 a year. . . .

Consequently, as the waves of immigration continue, the sheer number of those competing for low-skilled service jobs makes economic progress difficult. A study of the impact of immigration on New York City's restaurant business, for instance, found that 60 percent of immigrant workers do not receive regular raises, while 70 percent had never been promoted. . . .

Similarly, immigration is also pushing some native-born workers out of jobs, as Kenyon College economists showed in the California nail-salon workforce. Over a 16-year period starting in the late 1980s, some 35,600 mostly Vietnamese immigrant women flooded into the industry, a mass migration that equaled the total number of jobs in the industry before the immigrants arrived. Though the new workers created a labor surplus that led to lower prices, new services, and somewhat more demand, the economists estimate that as a result, 10,000 native-born workers either left the industry or never bothered entering it.

In many American industries, waves of low-wage workers have also retarded investments that might lead to modernization and efficiency. Farming, which employs a million immigrant laborers in California alone, is the prime case in point. Faced with a labor shortage in the early 1960s, when President Kennedy ended a 22-year-old guest-worker program that allowed 45,000 Mexican farmhands to cross over the border and harvest 2.2 million tons of California tomatoes for processed foods, farmers complained but swiftly automated, adopting a mechanical tomato-picking technology created more than a decade earlier. Today, just 5,000 better-paid workers—one-ninth the original workforce—harvest 12 million tons of tomatoes using the machines.

The savings prompted by low-wage migrants may even be minimal in crops not easily mechanized. Agricultural economists Wallace Huffman and Alan McCunn of Iowa State University have estimated that without illegal workers, the retail cost of fresh produce would increase only about 3 percent in the summer-fall season and less than 2 percent in the winter-spring season, because labor represents only a tiny percent of the retail price of produce and because without migrant workers, America would probably import more foreign fruits and vegetables. . . .

As foreign competition and mechanization shrink manufacturing and farmworker jobs, low-skilled immigrants are likely to wind up farther on the margins of our economy, where many already operate. For example, although only about 12 percent of construction workers are foreign-born, 100,000 to 300,000 illegal immigrants have carved a place for themselves as temporary workers on the fringes of the industry. In urban areas like New York and Los Angeles, these mostly male illegal immigrants gather on street corners, in empty lots, or in Home Depot parking lots to sell their labor by the hour or the day, for $7 to $11 an hour. . . .

Because so much of our legal and illegal immigrant labor is concentrated in such fringe, low-wage employment, its overall impact on our economy is extremely small. A 1997 National Academy of Sciences study estimated that immigration's net benefit to the American economy raises the average income of the native-born by only some $10 billion a year—about $120 per household. And that meager contribution is not the result of immigrants helping to build our essential industries or making us more competitive globally but instead merely delivering our pizzas and cutting our grass. Estimates by pro-immigration forces that foreign workers contribute much more to the economy, boosting annual gross domestic product by hundreds of billions of dollars, generally just tally what immigrants earn here, while ignoring the offsetting effect they have on the wages of native-born workers.

If the benefits of the current generation of migrants are small, the costs are large and growing because of America's vast range of social programs and the wide advocacy network that strives to hook low-earning legal and illegal immigrants into these programs. A 1998 National Academy of Sciences study found that more than 30 percent of California's foreign-born were on Medicaid—including 37 percent of all Hispanic households—compared with 14 percent of native-born households. The foreign-born were more than twice as likely as the native-born to be on welfare, and their children were nearly five times as likely to be in means-tested government lunch programs. Native-born households pay for much of this, the study found, because they earn more and pay higher taxes—and are more likely to comply with tax laws. Recent immigrants, by contrast, have much lower levels of income and tax compliance (another study estimated that only 56 percent of illegals in California have taxes deducted from their earnings, for instance). The study's conclusion: immigrant families cost each native-born household in California an additional $1,200 a year in taxes.

Immigration's bottom line has shifted so sharply that in a high-immigration state like California, native-born residents are paying up to ten times more in state and local taxes than immigrants generate in economic benefits. Moreover, the cost is only likely to grow as the foreign-born population—which has already mushroomed from about 9 percent of the U.S. population when the NAS studies were done in the late 1990s to about 12 percent today—keeps growing. . . . This sharp turnaround since the 1970s, when immigrants were less likely to be using the social programs of the Great

Society than the native-born population, says Harvard economist Borjas, suggests that welfare and other social programs are a magnet drawing certain types of immigrants—nonworking women, children, and the elderly—and keeping them here when they run into difficulty.

Not only have the formal and informal networks helping immigrants tap into our social spending grown, but they also get plenty of assistance from advocacy groups financed by tax dollars, working to ensure that immigrants get their share of social spending. Thus, the Newark-based New Jersey Immigration Policy Network receives several hundred thousand government dollars annually to help doctors and hospitals increase immigrant enrollment in Jersey's subsidized health-care programs. Casa Maryland, operating in the greater Washington area, gets funding from nearly 20 federal, state, and local government agencies to run programs that "empower" immigrants to demand benefits and care from government and to "refer clients to government and private social service programs for which they and their families may be eligible." . . .

Almost certainly, immigrants' participation in our social welfare programs will increase over time, because so many are destined to struggle in our workforce. Despite our cherished view of immigrants as rapidly climbing the economic ladder, more and more of the new arrivals and their children face a lifetime of economic disadvantage, because they arrive here with low levels of education and with few work skills—shortcomings not easily overcome. Mexican immigrants, who are up to six times more likely to be high school dropouts than native-born Americans, not only earn substantially less than the native-born median, but the wage gap persists for decades after they've arrived. A study of the 2000 census data, for instance, shows that the cohort of Mexican immigrants between 25 and 34 who entered the United States in the late 1970s were earning 40 to 50 percent less than similarly aged native-born Americans in 1980, but 20 years later they had fallen even further behind their native-born counterparts. Today's Mexican immigrants between 25 and 34 have an even larger wage gap relative to the native-born population. Adjusting for other socioeconomic factors, Harvard's Borjas and Katz estimate that virtually this entire wage gap is attributable to low levels of education. . . .

One reason some ethnic groups make up so little ground concerns the transmission of what economists call "ethnic capital," or what we might call the influence of culture. More than previous generations, immigrants today tend to live concentrated in ethnic enclaves, and their children find their role models among their own group. Thus the children of today's Mexican immigrants are likely to live in a neighborhood where about 60 percent of men dropped out of high school and now do low-wage work, and where less than half of the population speak English fluently, which might explain why high school dropout rates among Americans of Mexican ancestry are two and a half times higher than dropout rates for all other native-born Americans, and why first-generation Mexican Americans do not move up the economic ladder nearly as quickly as the children of other immigrant groups.

In sharp contrast is the cultural capital transmitted by Asian immigrants to children growing up in predominantly Asian-American neighborhoods. More than 75 percent of Chinese immigrants and 98 percent of South Asian immigrants to the U.S. speak English fluently, while a mid-1990s study of immigrant households in California found that 37 percent of Asian immigrants were college graduates, compared with only 3.4 percent of Mexican immigrants. Thus, even an Asian-American child whose parents are high school dropouts is more likely to grow up in an environment that encourages him to stay in school and learn to speak English well, attributes that will serve him well in the job market. Not surprisingly, several studies have shown that Asian immigrants and their children earn substantially more than Mexican immigrants and their children.

Given these realities, several of the major immigration reforms now under consideration simply don't make economic sense—especially the guest-worker program favored by President Bush and the U.S. Senate. Careful economic research tells us that there is no significant shortfall of workers in essential American industries, desperately needing supplement from a massive guest-worker program. Those few industries now relying on cheap labor must focus more quickly on mechanization where possible. Meanwhile, the cost of paying legal workers already here a bit more to entice them to do such low-wage work as is needed will have a minimal impact on our economy.

The potential woes of a guest-worker program, moreover, far overshadow any economic benefit, given what we know about the long, troubled history of temporary-worker programs in developed countries. They have never stemmed illegal immigration, and the guest workers inevitably become permanent residents, competing with the native-born and forcing down wages. Our last guest-worker program with Mexico, begun during World War II to boost wartime manpower, grew larger in the postwar era, because employers who liked the cheap labor lobbied hard to keep it. By the mid-1950s, the number of guest workers reached seven times the annual limit during the war itself, while illegal immigration doubled, as the availability of cheap labor prompted employers to search for ever more of it rather than invest in mechanization or other productivity gains.

The economic and cultural consequences of guest-worker programs have been devastating in Europe, and we risk similar problems. When post–World War II Germany permitted its manufacturers to import workers from Turkey to man the assembly lines, industry's investment in productivity declined relative to such countries as Japan, which lacked ready access to cheap labor. When Germany finally ended the guest-worker program once it became economically unviable, most of the guest workers stayed on, having attained permanent-resident status. Since then, the descendants of these workers have been chronically underemployed and now have a crime rate double that of German youth. . . .

"Importing labor is far more complicated than importing other factors of production, such as commodities," write University of California at Davis prof Philip Martin, an expert on guest-worker programs, and Michael Teitelbaum, a former member of the U.S. Commission on Immigration Reform. "Migration involves human beings, with their own beliefs, politics, cultures, languages, loves, hates, histories, and families."

If low-wage immigration doesn't pay off for the United States, legalizing illegals already here makes as little sense as importing new rounds of guest workers. The Senate and President Bush, however, aim to start two-thirds of the 11 million undocumented aliens already in the country on a path to legalization, on the grounds that only thus can America assimilate them, and only through assimilation can they hope for economic success in the United States. But such arguments ignore the already poor economic performance of increasingly large segments of the *legal* immigrant population in the United States. Merely granting illegal aliens legal status won't suddenly catapult them up our mobility ladder, because it won't give them the skills and education to compete. . . .

If we do not legalize them, what can we do with 11 million illegals? Ship them back home? Their presence here is a fait accompli, the argument goes, and only legalization can bring them above ground, where they can assimilate. But that argument assumes that we have only two choices: to decriminalize or deport. But what happened after the first great migration suggests a third way: to end the economic incentives that keep them here. We could prompt a great remigration home if, first off, state and local governments in jurisdictions like New York and California would stop using their vast resources to aid illegal immigrants. Second, the federal government can take the tougher approach that it failed to take after the 1986 act. It can require employers to verify Social Security numbers and immigration status before hiring, so that we bar illegals from many jobs. It can deport those caught here. And it can refuse to give those who remain the same benefits as U.S. citizens. Such tough measures do work: as a recent Center for Immigration Studies report points out, when the federal government began deporting illegal Muslims after 9/11, many more illegals who knew they were likely to face more scrutiny voluntarily returned home.

If America is ever to make immigration work for our economy again, it must reject policies shaped by advocacy groups trying to turn immigration into the next civil rights cause or by a tiny minority of businesses seeking cheap labor subsidized by the taxpayers. Instead, we must look to other developed nations that have focused on luring workers who have skills that are in demand and who have the best chance of assimilating. Australia, for instance, gives preferences to workers grouped into four skilled categories: managers, professionals, associates of professionals, and skilled laborers. Using a straightforward "points calculator" to determine who gets in, Australia favors immigrants between the ages of 18 and 45 who speak English, have a post–high school degree or training in a trade, and have at least six months' work experience as everything from laboratory technicians to architects and surveyors to information-technology workers. Such an immigration policy goes far beyond America's employment-based immigration categories, like the H1-B visas, which account for about 10 percent of our legal immigration and essentially serve the needs of a few Silicon Valley industries.

Immigration reform must also tackle our family-preference visa program, which today accounts for two-thirds of all legal immigration and has helped create a 40-year waiting list. Lawmakers should narrow the family-preference visa program down to spouses and minor children of U.S. citizens and should exclude adult siblings and parents.

America benefits even today from many of its immigrants, from the Asian entrepreneurs who have helped revive inner-city Los Angeles business districts to Haitians and Jamaicans who have stabilized neighborhoods in Queens and Brooklyn to Indian programmers who have spurred so much innovation in places like Silicon Valley and Boston's Route 128. But increasingly over the last 25 years, such immigration has become the exception. It needs once again to become the rule.

Diana Furchtgott-Roth → **NO**

The Case for Immigration

It was raining in Washington last week, and vendors selling $5 and $10 umbrellas appeared on the streets. They had Hispanic accents, and were undoubtedly some of the unskilled immigrants that Steven Malanga referred to in his recent *City Journal* article, "How Unskilled Immigrants Hurt Our Economy."

I already had an umbrella. But the many purchasers of the umbrellas did not seem to notice that the economy was being hurt. Rather, they were glad of the opportunity to stay dry before their important meetings.

The *City Journal* article is worth a look because it reflects an attitude becoming more common these days in the debate. The article speaks approvingly of immigrants from Portugal, Asia, China, India, Haiti, and Jamaica. But it also makes it clear that we have too many Mexicans, a "flood of immigrants" who cause high unemployment rates among the unskilled. They work in shrinking industries, drive down wages of native-born Americans, cost millions in welfare, and retard America's technology.

These are serious charges indeed. Similar charges, that immigrants have caused native-born Americans to quit the labor market, have been made by Steven Camarota of the Center for Immigration Studies. But are they true?

Annual immigration is a tiny fraction of our labor force. The Pew Hispanic Center Report shows that annual immigration from all countries as a percent of the labor force has been declining since its recent peak in 1999.

Annual immigration in 1999 equaled 1% of the labor force—by 2005 it had declined to 0.8%. Hispanics, including undocumented workers, peaked in 2000 as a percent of the labor force at 0.5%, and by 2004 accounted for only 0.4% (0.3% for Mexicans) of the labor force.

Looking at unskilled workers, Hispanic immigration as a percent of the American unskilled labor force (defined as those without a high school diploma) peaked in 2000 at 6%, and was 5% in 2004 (4% for Mexicans). Five percent is not "floods of immigrants."

Mr. Malanga writes that America does not have a vast labor shortage because "unemployment among unskilled workers is high—about 30%." It isn't. In 2005, according to Bureau of Labor Statistics data, the unemployment rate for adults without a high school diploma was 7.6%. Last month it stood at 6.9%.

Data from a recent study by senior economist Pia Orrenius of the Dallas Federal Reserve Bank show that foreign-born Americans are more likely to work than native-born Americans. Leaving their countries by choice, they are naturally more risk-taking and entrepreneurial.

In 2005 the unemployment rate for native-born Americans was 5.2%, but for foreign-born it was more than half a percentage point lower, at 4.6%. For unskilled workers, although the total unemployment rate was 7.6%, the native-born rate was 9.1% and the foreign-born was much lower, at 5.7%.

According to Mr. Malanga, unskilled immigrants "work in shrinking industries where they force out native workers." However, data show otherwise. Low-skilled immigrants are disproportionately represented in the expanding service and construction sectors, with occupations such as janitors, gardeners, tailors, plasterers, and stucco masons. Manufacturing, the declining sector, employs few immigrants.

One myth repeated often is that immigrants depress wages of native-born Americans. As Professor Giovanni Peri of the University of California at Davis describes in a new National Bureau of Economic Analysis paper last month, immigrants are complements, rather than substitutes, for native-born workers. As such, they are not competing with native-born workers, but providing our economy with different skills.

Education levels of working immigrants form a U-shaped curve, with unusually high representation among adult low- and high-skilled. In contrast, the skills of native-born Americans form a bellshaped curve, with many B.A.s and high school diplomas but relatively few adult high school drop-outs or Ph.D.s

Low-skill immigrants come to be janitors and housekeepers, jobs native-born Americans typically don't want, but they aren't found as crossing guards and funeral service workers, low-skill jobs preferred by Americans. Similarly, high-skilled immigrants also take jobs Americans don't want. They are research scientists, dentists, and computer hardware and software engineers, but not lawyers, judges, or education administrators.

Because immigrants are complements to native-born workers, rather than substitutes, they help reduce economic bottlenecks, resulting in income gains. Mr. Peri's new study shows that immigrants raised the wages of the 90% of native-born Americans with at least a high school degree by 1% to 3% between 1990 and 2004. Those without a high school diploma lost about 1%, an amount that could be compensated from the gains of the others.

If immigrants affect any wages, it's those of prior immigrants, who compete for the same jobs. But we don't see immigrants protesting in the streets to keep others out, as we see homeowners in scenic locations demonstrating against additional development. Rather, some of the biggest proponents of greater immigration are the established immigrants themselves, who see America's boundless opportunities as outweighing negative wage effects.

Mr. Malanga cites a 1998 National Academy of Sciences study to say, "The foreign-born were more than twice as likely as the native-born to be on welfare." Yet this study contains estimates from 1995, more than a decade ago, and mentions programs such as Aid to Families with Dependent Children that no longer exist. Even so, the NAS study says that foreign-born households "are not more likely to use AFDC, SSI, or housing benefits."

The NAS study concludes that, since the foreign-born have more children, the "difference in education benefits accounts for nearly all of the relative deficit . . . at the local government level." Mr. Malanga, writing about how unskilled immigrants hurt the economy, would likely be in favor of these immigrants trying to educate their children, especially since these children will be contributing to his Social Security benefits.

Mr. Malanga suggests that the availability of low-wage immigrants retards investments in American technology. He cites agriculture as an example where machines to pick produce could be invented if labor were not available. Or, Mr. Malanga says, we could import produce from abroad at little additional cost.

Although consumers don't care where their food comes from, farmers certainly do. Farms provide income to farmers as well as to other native-born Americans employed in the industry as well as in trucking and distribution, just as immigrants in the construction industry have helped fuel the boom that sent employment of native-born construction workers to record levels. It makes little sense to send a whole economic sector to other countries just to avoid employing immigrants.

If unskilled immigrants don't hurt our economy, do they hurt our culture? City Journal editor Myron Magnet writes that Hispanics have "a group culture that devalues education and assimilation." Similar concerns about assimilation were made about Jews, Italians, Irish, Germans, Poles, and even Norwegians when they first came to America. All eventually assimilated.

Moreover, for those who are concerned with Spanish-speaking enclaves, a September 2006 paper by a professor at Princeton, Douglas Massey, shows that within two generations Mexican immigrants in California stop speaking Spanish at home, and within three generations they cease to know the language altogether. He concludes, "Like taxes and biological death, linguistic death seems to be a sure thing in the United States, even for Mexicans living in Los Angeles, a city with one of the largest Spanish-speaking urban populations in the world."

Legalizing the status of the illegal immigrants in America by providing a guest-worker program with a path to citizenship would produce additional gains to our economy. This is not the same as temporary worker programs in Germany, which did not have a path to citizenship, and so resulted in a disenfranchised class of workers.

With legal status, workers could move from the informal to the formal sector, and would pay more taxes. It would be easier to keep track of illegal financial transactions, reducing the potential for helping terrorists.

For over 200 years, American intellectual thought has included a small but influential literature advocating reduced immigration. The literature has spawned political parties such as the Know-Nothing Party in the mid-19th century and periodically led to the enactment of anti-immigrant laws. Immigrants, so the story goes, are bad for our economy and for our culture.

The greatness of America is not merely that we stand for freedom and economic prosperity for ourselves, but that we have consistently overcome arguments that would deny these same benefits to others.

POSTSCRIPT

Do Unskilled Immigrants Hurt the American Economy?

In 1986, the Immigration Reform and Control Act passed into law with enforcement provided by the Immigration and Naturalization Service. The purpose of this law was, primarily, to discourage American employers from hiring illegal aliens as a source of cheap labor. According to the act, employers are required to collect and keep various types of documentation about their employees, including proof of their legality to work. Failing to do so can result in severe financial penalties for the organization. Although the intention of the act may be laudable to many, compliance with the law can be problematic for firms. University of Washington scholar Wendell French notes that "One of the most difficult aspects of the law is how an employer can actually comply with the law and at the same time avoid violating the Civil Rights Act." By way of example, consider the following case provided by French:

> They [business owners] say they're caught between the government's competing demands—fined if they inadvertently hire illegals bearing counterfeit documents, yet risking a Justice Dept. lawsuit if they question workers with suspicious papers too closely. This happened to Monfort, Inc., a beef packing company with headquarters in Greeley, Colorado. After the INS removed 300 illegals from a Nebraska plant, the company started its own immigration inspections at its other plants and was then fined $45,576 under the Civil rights Act for asking "overly intrusive" questions. (Wendell French, *Human Resource Management*. Houghton Mifflin Company: New York, 2003)

Certainly, dealing with the question of whether firms should be allowed to hire illegal aliens or not is complicated enough without organizations having to walk tip-toe on a fine line between stepping on the civil rights of legitimate employees and making sure they don't violate the IRCA of 1986!

Suggested Readings

Jeffery S. Passel, "Estimates of the Size and Characteristics of the Undocumented Population," Pew Hispanic Center, Washington D.C. (March 21, 2005).

Wall Street Journal Opinion, "American Brain Drain," *Wall Street Journal Review and Outlook* (November 30, 2007). http://online.wsj.com/article/SB119638963734709017.html?mod=opinion_main_review_and_outlooks

Open World Conference of Workers, "Amnesty for All Undocumented Immigrants and Full Labor Rights for All Workers!" OWC Continuations Committee. http://www.owcinfo.org/campaign/Amnesty.htm

Daniel Griswold, "Immigration Law Should Reflect Our Dynamic Labor Market," The Cato Institute (April 27, 2008). http://www.cato.org/pub_display.php?pub_id=9360

Tom Tancredo, "Illegal Aliens Taking American Jobs," House of Representatives, Capitol, Washington D.C. (November 17, 2005).

Investor's Business Daily Editorial, "The Real Cost of Immigration," *Investor's Business Daily* (April 4, 2008). http://www.ibdeditorials.com/IBDArticles.aspx?id=292204157102985

Harry Binswanger, "Immigration Quotas vs. Individual Rights: The Moral and Practical Case for Open Immigration," *Capitalism Magazine* (April 2, 2006). http://capmag.com/article.asp?ID=4620

ISSUE 17

Is Economic Globalization Good for Humankind?

YES: Paul A. Gigot, from "Foreword" and **Guy Sorman**, from "Globalization Is Making the World a Better Place," (2008). http://www.heritage.org/index/PDF/2008/Index2008_Foreword.pdf; http://www.heritage.org/index/PDF/2008/Index2008_Chap3.pdf

NO: Branco Milanovic, from "Why Globalization Is in Trouble—Parts 1 and 2," (August 31, 2006). http://yaleglobal.yale.edu/display.article?id=8073

ISSUE SUMMARY

YES: Arguing that globalization is good for humankind are Paul Gigot and Guy Sorman. They outline seven ways in which globalization has positively impacted life and what needs to be done to further its advancement.

NO: Branko Milanovic, an economist with both the Carnegie Endowment for International Peace and the World Bank, is against globalization. He addresses several reasons for his views while emphasizing the incompatibility of globalization with the ages-old ethnic and religious traditions and values that characterize much of the world.

$\mathbf{A}$ccording to a leading international business textbook, globalization is "the inexorable integration of markets, nation-states, and technologies . . . in a way that is enabling individuals, corporations, and nation-states to reach around the world farther, faster, deeper, and cheaper than ever before" (Ricky W. Griffin and Michael W. Pustay, *International Business*, 6th ed., Prentice Hall, 2010). Globalism is a phenomenon that has its roots in the rebuilding of Europe and Asia in the aftermath of World War II. As a measure of how powerful a phenomenon it has become, consider that the volume of international trade has increased over 3000 percent since 1960! Most of this tremendous growth has occurred in the TRIAD, a free-trade market consisting of three regional trading blocs: Western Europe in its current form as the European Union, North America, and Asia (including Australia). Increasingly, however, the developing nations of the world are contributing to the expansion in world trade. Foreign investment has grown at staggering rates as well: over three times faster than the world output of goods. In the early part of the twenty-first century, it is not a stretch to say that virtually all businesses in industrialized nations are impacted to some degree by globalization.

It seems pretty clear that globalization will continue to grow as a dominant force in international relations among countries, particularly as more Second and Third World countries open their borders to international trade and investment. What may be less clear, however, is whether or not this is a positive development. In other words, as we ask in this topic, is economic globalization good for humankind?

Like many of the topics in this book, globalization invokes strong arguments and strong emotions from supporters on each side. Those that believe globalization is a beneficial force for humans have a plethora of reasons for their view. From an economic perspective, the spread of free trade and free markets across the globe has liberated hundreds of millions from poverty over the past 40 years. Studies on economic freedom consistently show that countries that embrace globalization are more economically free and, as a direct result, enjoy higher per capita wealth than countries that are more isolated economically. Supporters also note that the growth in globalization has been accompanied by a growth in democracy as well. Along with these two benefits, globalization enhances the cultures of those countries that embrace it. Guy Sorman, one of the authors of the "yes" article in this debate, points out: "Through popular culture, people from different backgrounds and nations discover one another, and their 'otherness' suddenly disappears." Increases in cultural tolerance and openness to different worldviews is part-and-parcel of globalization. A tangentially related benefit involves the spread of respect for the rights of women and minorities around the globe. Discrimination is incompatible with freedom and democracy, and the spread of globalization brings pressure to bear on governments to recognize and protect the rights of all their citizens.

Detractors of globalization also raise several important points. Echoing anti-outsourcing advocates, they argue that globalization results in a loss of jobs due to competition with low-wage countries. Indeed, the major economic force driving the tremendous growth of the Indian and Chinese economies over the past 15 years is their competitive advantage in access to cheap labor. Many anti-globalization supporters argue that corporations are becoming too powerful politically and economically and believe that the search for overseas profits markets is the primary cause. Opponents also raise concerns over national safety and security issues. As the globe continues to shrink and the ease and speed of information exchange continues to increase, the likelihood of cyber-attacks and the theft of sensitive military, technological, and economic information is assumed to increase. The threat of terrorism has grown dramatically in the past 30 years due in large part, say the globalization critics, to the spread of globalization driven by the United States and other western, First-World civilizations. And, as the recent Swine Flu outbreak reminds us, the threat of a worldwide health pandemic grows larger the more integrated the world becomes.

YES ⬅

Paul A. Gigot
and Guy Sorman

Foreword

I don't know who first used the word "globalization," but he was probably no friend of capitalism. The word is bureaucratic and implies that the world economy is subject to the control of some vast, nefarious force beyond human influence. The reality is that the world economy is enjoying its strongest run of prosperity in 40 years thanks to the greater ability of billions of individuals to make free choices in their own self-interest. The *Index of Economic Freedom* has been encouraging this trend for 14 years, and at the end of 2007, we can happily say it continues.

The world economy extended its multiyear run of 5 percent or so annual GDP growth this year, notwithstanding an American slowdown due mainly to the housing correction. As I write this, the U.S. economy seems to have survived the August credit crunch related to the collapse of the sub-prime mortgage market. The summer squall showed once again how interrelated financial markets have become, with sub-prime losses popping up around the world and even causing an old-fashioned bank run at Northern Rock in the United Kingdom.

The episode is naturally leading to soul-searching about the stability of this brave new world of global finance—including the spread of asset securitization, the rise of hedge funds, and an explosion in derivatives. This introspection ought to be healthy. The sub-prime fiasco has, at the very least, exposed the need for more careful vetting by investors, but regulators and bankers are also sure to examine the rules for transparency and capital requirements to prevent the spread of problems throughout the financial system. The event also shows the need for more careful driving by America's Federal Reserve, whose easy-money policy in the first half of this decade was the root cause of the housing boom and bust. The good news is that, at least so far, there hasn't been a regulatory overreaction that could stymie growth.

The irony of the year has been the shifting economic policy trends in America and France, of all places. The U.S. political debate is moving in a negative direction as "fairness" and income redistribution replace growth as the policy lodestar and proposals for tax increases proliferate. The Bush tax cuts of 2003 were crucial to kicking the economy out of its post-9/11, post-dot.com

From *Index of Economic Freedom*, 2008, pp. ix–x, 35–38. Copyright © 2008 by Heritage Foundation. Reprinted by permission.

doldrums. But they expire after 2010 and are in serious jeopardy. The free-trade agenda has also stalled as bilateral pacts with Latin America and South Korea face heavy going on Capitol Hill. The 2008 election will be as much a referendum on economic policy as on foreign policy.

Perhaps the rest of the world will have to teach America a policy lesson or two. As the *Index* shows, Europe overall has moved in a freer direction this decade. This is due in large part to reform in the former Eastern Europe, as well as to the policy competition caused by the success of the euro. With capital and people free to move and governments no longer able to inflate their way out of fiscal difficulty, the trend has been toward lower tax rates and labor market liberalization.

Miracle of miracles, even France has been mugged by this reality. Nicolas Sarkozy made the revival of the French economy a main theme of his successful campaign for president, and he has followed with proposals for what he called "a new social contract founded on work, merit and equal opportunity." We should all hope he succeeds—not merely to compensate for any slowdown in America, but for its own sake to help Europe break away from its self-imposed sense of diminished expectations. In any event, this policy churning in Europe shows how the ability to move capital freely across borders imposes a price on bad government decisions.

The larger point is that if we step back from the daily turmoil, we can see that we live in a remarkable era of prosperity and spreading freedom. Hundreds of millions of people are being lifted out of poverty around the world as global trade and investment expand and countries like India and China liberalize parts of their economies. The International Monetary Fund reported in early 2007 that every country in the world, save for a couple of small dictatorships, was growing. This prosperity can itself create discontent due to the rapidity of change, and it certainly poses a challenge to political leaders who are obliged to explain and manage its consequences. The *Index of Economic Freedom* exists to help in that explanation, and we hope readers continue to find it a source of comparative policy wisdom.

Globalization Is Making the World a Better Place

What we call "globalization," one of the most powerful and positive forces ever to have arisen in the history of mankind, is redefining civilization as we know it. This is one of my hypotheses. To be more specific, I will try to describe what globalization is, its impact on world peace, and the freedom it brings from want, fear, and misery.

Globalization has six major characteristics: economic development, democracy, cultural enrichment, political and cultural norms, information, and internationalization of the rule of law.

Economic Development

Usually, globalization is described in terms of intensified commercial and trade exchanges, but it is about more than just trade, stock exchanges, and currencies. It is about people. What is significant today is that through globalization many nations are converging toward enhanced welfare.

This convergence is exemplified by the 800 million people who, in the past 30 years, have left poverty and misery behind. They have greater access to health care, schooling, and information. They have more choices, and their children will have even more choices. The absolutely remarkable part is that it happened not by accident but through a combination of good economic policy, technology, and management.

Of course, not all nations are following this path, but since the fall of the Berlin Wall, more and more are coming closer. Only Africa's nations have yet to join, but who would have hoped and predicted 30 years ago that China and India, with such rapidity and efficiency, would pull their people out of misery? There is no reason why Africa, when its turn comes, will not do the same. Convergence should be a source of hope for us all.

Democracy

In general, since 1989, the best system to improve the welfare of all people—not only economically, but also in terms of access to equality and freedom—appears to be democracy, the new international norm. As more and more countries turn democratic or converge toward democratic norms, respect for other cultures increases.

Democracy has guaranteed welfare far better than any dictatorship ever could. Even enlightened despots cannot bring the kind of safety democracy is bringing. Sometimes a trade-off between economic allotment and democracy occurs. Sometimes the economy grows more slowly because of democracy. Let it be that way. Democracy brings values that are as important for the welfare of the human being as [the] economy is.

After all, as history shows, the chance of international war diminishes step by step any time a country moves from tyranny to democracy, as democracies do not war against one other. That more and more nations are turning democratic improves everyone's way of life.

Cultural Enrichment

Critics of globalization frequently charge that it results in an "Americanization of culture" and concomitant loss of identity and local cultural values. I would propose a more optimistic view, and that is that globalization leads to never-ending exchange of ideas, especially through popular culture, since it affects the greatest number of people.

Through popular culture, people from different backgrounds and nations discover one another, and their "otherness" suddenly disappears. For example, a popular Korean television sitcom now popular in Japan has shown its Japanese viewers that, like them, Koreans fall in love, feel despair, and harbor the same hopes and fears for themselves and for their children. This sitcom has transformed the image Japanese have of the Korean nation more profoundly than any number of diplomatic efforts and demonstrates that globalization can erode prejudices that have existed between neighboring countries for centuries.

Furthermore, this process of better understanding allows us to keep our identity and add new identities. The Koreans absorb a bit of the American culture, a bit of the French, a bit of other European societies. Perhaps they have become a different sort of Korean, but they remain Korean nonetheless. It is quite the illusion to think you can lose your identity. And it goes both ways. When you look at the success of cultural exports out of Korea—this so-called new wave through music, television, movies, and art—Korea becomes part of the identity of other people.

Now, as a Frenchman, I am a bit Korean myself. This is how globalization works. We do not lose our identity. We enter into the world that I call the world of multi-identity, and that is progress, not loss.

Political and Cultural Norms

One of the most significant transformations in terms of welfare for the people in the globalized world is the increased respect given to the rights of women and minorities. In many nations, to be a woman or to belong to a minority has not been easy. In the past 30 years, however, women and minorities everywhere have become better informed and have learned that the repression they suffered until very recently is not typical in a modern democracy.

Let us consider India, where a strong caste system historically has subjugated women and untouchables. Thanks to the globalization of democratic norms, these minorities are better protected; through various affirmative action policies, they can access the better jobs that traditionally were forbidden to them. This transformation has positive consequences for them, of course, and also creates better outcomes for their children's welfare and education. We are entering into a better world because of their improved status, thanks to the cultural and democratic exchanges generated by globalization.

Information

Through legacy media and, more and more, through the Internet and cellular phones, everyone today, even in authoritarian countries, is better informed. For one year, I lived in the poorest part of China, and I remember well how a farmer, in the most remote village, knew exactly what was happening not only in the next village, but also in Beijing and New York because of the Internet and his cellular phone. No government can stop information now. People know today that, as they say, "knowledge is power."

Now let us imagine if the genocide in Darfur had happened 20 or 30 years ago. The Darfur population would have been annihilated by the Sudanese government, and no one would have known. Today we all know about the genocide. The reason why the international community has been forced to intervene is because of the flood of information. Knowledge is proving to be the best protection for oppressed minorities and, thus, one of the most vital aspects of globalization.

Internationalization of the Rule of Law

Internationalization of rule of law, of course, has limitations. The institutions in charge of this emerging rule of law, whether the United Nations or the World Trade Organization, are criticized. They are not completely legitimate. They are certainly not perfectly democratic, but you cannot build a democratic organization with non-democratic governments. It becomes a trade-off.

In spite of all the weaknesses of international organizations, the emergence of a real international rule of law replaces the pure barbarism that existed before, which had consisted of the most powerful against the weak. Even though globalization cannot suppress war, it is remarkably efficient at containing war. If you examine the kinds of wars we have today, compared to the history of mankind, the number of victims and number of nations involved are very few. We are all safer because of both this emerging rule of law and the flow of information provided by globalization.

Invented by Entrepreneurs

We also need to remember that globalization is not some historical accident but has been devised and built by those who wanted it. Diplomats did not invent it. Entrepreneurs did.

Let us look at Europe. After World War II, the Europeans discovered that they had been their own worst enemies. For 1,000 years, we were fighting each other. Why? We do not remember very well. Every 30 years, we went to war. The French killed the Germans. The Germans killed the French. When you try to explain this history to your children, they cannot understand. Diplomats and politicians from the 18th century onward unsuccessfully made plans to avoid this kind of civil war within Europe.

Then, in the 1940s, a businessman came along named Jean Monnet. His business was to sell cognac in the United States, and he was very good at it. The idea Jean Monnet had was that perhaps the unification process of Europe should not be started by diplomats. Maybe it should be started by business people. He proceeded to build the European Union on a foundation of commerce. He started with coal and steel in 1950, and it was through the liberation of that trade that he conceived the unification of Europe, which has played a crucial role in the globalization process.

Monnet's guiding principle was that commercial and financial ties would lead to political unification. The true basis of European solidarity has come through trade. Through this method, all of the benefits of globalization have been made possible, because free trade has been at the root level. An attack on free trade is an attack on both globalization and the welfare of the peoples of the world, so we must be very cautious when we discuss trade, as it is the essential key allowing the rest to happen.

None of this is to imply that trade is easy. In the case of Europe, it was made easier because all of the governments were democratic. It is much more complicated to build free trade with non-democratic governments, but because globalization starts with the construction of this materialistic solidarity, ideals must come afterwards.

Two Threats to Globalization

Perhaps what I have presented so far is too optimistic a picture of globalization, but I believe we have good reason to be upbeat. However, there are two threats to globalization that may be taken too lightly today.

Global epidemics.   In terms of health care, we are more and more able to cope with the current illnesses of the world. Though Africa still poses a problem, through global efforts it will be possible in the years to come to reduce the major epidemics there: AIDS and malaria.

But new epidemics are threatening the world. If we remember what happened in China some years ago with the SARS epidemic, which was very short, and then the avian flu threat in 2005, you understand that there are new threats somewhere out there and that the modern world is not really prepared. One of the consequences of globalization is that people travel more, which means that viruses travel more and adapt.

Therefore, I think globalization should require the international community to develop ever more sophisticated systems to detect and cure the new epidemics that have been a negative consequence of globalization.

Terrorism.   Although wars these days are more limited, new forms of warfare have emerged, which we call terrorism. Terrorism today can seem like a distant menace somewhere between the United States and the Middle East. Because of the global progress of the rule of law, however, violent groups know that it is no longer possible to wage war in the traditional way; therefore, people driven by ideological passions are increasingly tempted by terrorist methods as a way of implementing their agenda.

Those are the true negative aspects of globalization: epidemics and terrorism. Regretfully, we are too focused on the traditional problems like free trade. We are not focused enough on the future threats.

I wish globalization were more popular, but it is our fault if it is not. Perhaps we should use different words. "Globalization" is ugly. We should find a better word, and we should try to explain to the media and students that we are entering into a new civilization of welfare, progress, and happiness, because if they do not understand the beauty of globalization, they will not stand up for it when it is threatened.

Branko Milanovic   ➔ **NO**

Why Globalization
Is in Trouble – Parts 1 and 2

Part I

Washington: Historically, the dominant power tends to support globalization as a way to increase the ambit of its influence, expand trade and gain economic advantage, co-opt new citizens and possibly show the advantages of its own pax. This was the case with the Roman, British and now American-led globalizations. But recently, the rich West—which saw globalization as a prelude to "the end of history"—is having second thoughts.

Two fears drive this unease with globalization: The first is a fear of job loss due to competition from low-wage countries. The second is the fear of ethnic and cultural dilution due to increased immigration.

The cause of the first fear is a fast reemergence on the world stage of China and India. For students of history, the rise of China and India is not a surprise. The two countries are just recapturing the ground lost during the 19th and most of the 20th century. Before the Industrial Revolution, China's and India's combined output accounted for one half of the world's total. Now, after a quarter-century of China's spectacular growth, and more than a decade of India's growth acceleration, the two countries contribute less than a fifth of total world output. Although their share is, in the long-term historical sense, still below what it used to be, it has nevertheless increased dramatically compared to where it was 30 years ago. The rise of the two Asian giants, reflected in their dynamic trade, large Chinese export surpluses and India's role as an outsourcing center and a potential leader in information technology, has made the West wonder whether it can compete with such hardworking, cheap, plentiful and yet relatively skilled labor.

While the fear of job loss is driven by fast economic growth of the two giants, the fear of immigration is, ironically, caused by the slow economic growth of the rest of the developing world. The people who try to reach the shores of Europe or cross from Mexico into the US come from the countries that have disastrously fallen behind Western Europe and the US during the last quarter century. In 1980, Mexico's real per-capita income, adjusted for the differential price level between Mexico and the US, was a third of that in the US. Today, the ratio is almost 4.5 to 1. The poor Africans who land daily on beaches of the Spanish Canary Islands come from the countries that have seen no economic growth in 50 years. Take Ghana, a country often touted as an African success case: Around its independence, in 1957, its income was one half of Spain's; today, it is one tenth.

Immigration puts a similar pressure on low- or medium-skilled jobs in the West as do cheap imports from China and outsourcing to India. And indeed, wages of low- and medium-skilled workers in the rich countries have failed to keep pace with incomes of educated workers at the top of the pyramid. While the median US real wage has not risen in real terms over the last 25 years, real wages of the top 1 percent have more than doubled. The richest 1 percent of Americans today controls almost 20 percent of total US income, a proportion higher than at any time since the Roaring Twenties. The U-turn of inequality—a sharp increase that started during the Thatcher-Reagan era, after a long decline—has affected, to a varying extent, all Western countries.

But at stake is something more profound than a threat to jobs and stagnant wages in a few "exposed" sectors. After all, the West is no stranger to structural change. Ricardo in his "Principles" written in 1815 discusses labor dislocation "occasioned" by the introduction of machinery. The Western countries handled the decline of powerful industries like coal, textile and steel. Economists have never been sympathetic to the protection arguments of sunset industries: In an expanding economy, structural change is necessary and inevitable; jobs lost in one industry will reappear as new jobs in another industry.

The difference now is that the twin challenge undermines the consensus upon which the West's welfare state was built since World War II. To understand why, recall that the Western welfare states rest on two building blocks: those of ethnic and social solidarity. The first building block implies that one is willing to be taxed if certain that aid will flow to somebody who is ethnically or culturally similar. But once large stocks of immigrants with different, and not easily adaptable, social norms, arrive, that certainly is no longer. More immigrants will strain the already-tattered solidarity among citizens of rich European countries.

The second building block of the welfare state is class solidarity. For it to exist, there must be relatively similar economic conditions between classes so that one can reasonably expect that for social transfers paid out of his pocket today, he may be compensated—if the need arose—by a similar benefit in the future. If, for example, unemployment rates are relatively equal across skill levels, then the highly skilled will pay for unemployment benefits; but if unemployment rates are different, the highly skilled may opt out. As the income divide widens in the West between the rich and the highly educated who have done well, and the middle classes and the unskilled who are merely scraping by, the second building block on which welfare capitalism was built crumbles. Economic inequality also translates into a cultural divide. "Ethnic" migrants who fill the rungs of low-paid workers are not the only ones economically and culturally different from today's Western elites; the elites are also growing more different from their own poorer ethnic brethren.

So far reaching, these developments require an entirely new social contract, a redefinition of capitalism no less. Such fundamental changes are not easy to come by when the threat is subtle, continuous, incremental and far from dramatic in a daily sense. Difficult decisions can be postponed, and neither politicians nor the electorate have an appetite for change. A battle of attrition regarding who would bear the costs of adjustment ensues, and this is at the heart of Europe's present immobilism.

Why is the development of "new capitalism" and rethinking of the old social contract so much more difficult for Europe than for the US? First, for an obvious reason, because Europe's welfare state is much more extensive, more embedded in ordinary life, and its dismantlement is more socially disruptive. Second, because a low population growth—or in many countries, a decline—necessitates continuing large immigration. But, and this is the crux of the matter, Europe struggles more in absorbing immigrants than the US. Historically, of course, Europe was not a society of immigrants. Europeans were happy to receive foreign workers as long as they would do low-paying jobs and stay out of the way. This quasi-apartheid solution preserved immigrants' culture, which then, most famously in the Netherlands, was found to clash with some European values. Immigrants, more so their daughters and sons, were not happy to remain in subaltern jobs. And while Europe was good about welcoming them to its soccer and basketball teams, it was more stingy when it came allowing them to direct operating rooms or boardrooms.

The bottom line is that Europe needs no less than a social revolution: replacement of its welfare state, and acceptance that Germans, French or Italians of tomorrow will be much darker in their skin color, composed of individuals of various religions, and in many respects indeed a different people. As fusion of Frankish ethnicity and Latin culture created France, a similar Christiano-Islamic and Afro-European fusion may create new European nations, perhaps with a different outlook on life and social norms. No society can accomplish such epochal transformation quickly and painlessly.

Part II

Washington: In the rich world globalization had driven the wedge between social classes, while in the poor world, the main divide is between countries: those that adjusted to globalization and, in many areas, prospered and those that adjusted badly and, in many cases, collapsed.

Indeed the Third World was never a bloc the way that that the first and second worlds were. But it was united by its opposition to colonialism and dislike for being used as a battlefield of the two then-dominant ideologies. As the Second World collapsed and globalization took off, the latter rationale evaporated, and a few countries, most notably India and China, accelerated their growth rates significantly, enjoying the fruits of freer trade and larger capital flows. And although these two countries adapted well to globalization, there is little doubt that their newfound relative prosperity opened many new fissure lines. Inequality between coastal and inland provinces, as well as between urban and rural areas, skyrocketed in China. So did, and perhaps by even more, inequality between Southern Indian states, where the hub cities of Mumbai, Chennai and Bangalore are located, and the slow-growing Northeast. For China, which still may face political transition to democracy, widening inequality between different parts of the country, could have disastrous consequences.

But another large group of Third World countries, from Latin America to Africa to former Communist countries, experienced a quarter century of decline or stagnation punctuated by civil wars, international conflicts and the plight of AIDS. While between 1980 and 2002, the rich countries grew, on average, by almost 2 percent per capita annually, the poorest 40 countries in the world had a combined growth rate of zero. For large swaths of Africa where about 200 million people live, the income level today is less than it was during the US presidency of John F. Kennedy.

For these countries the promised benefits of globalization never arrived. The vaunted Washington consensus policies brought no improvement for the masses, but rather a deterioration in the living conditions as key social services became privatized and more costly as was the case, for example, with water privatizations in Cochabamba, Bolivia, and Trinidad, electricity privatization in Argentina and Chad. They were often taken over by foreigners, and to add insult to injury, Western pundits arrived by jets, stayed in luxury hotels and hailed obvious worsening of economic and social conditions as a step toward better lives and international integration. For many people in Latin America and Africa, globalization appeared as new, more attractive label put on the old imperialism, or worse as a form of re-colonization. The left-wing reaction sweeping Latin America, from Mexico to Argentina, is a direct consequence of the fault lines opened by policies that were often designed to benefit Wall Street, not the people in the streets of Lima or Caracas.

Other Third World states—particularly those at the frontline of the battle between communism and capitalism, with ethnic animosities encouraged during the Cold War, efforts by Washington and Moscow to get the upper hand in the conflict—exploded in civil wars and social anomies. That part of the world associates globalization with disappointment (because Washington consensus never delivered), resentment (because others got ahead) and poverty, disease and war. In several sub-Saharan African countries, life expectancy at the turn of the 21st century is not only where it was in Europe almost two centuries ago but is getting worse. In Zimbabwe, between 1995 and 2003, life expectancy declined by 11 years to reach only 39 years.

Ideologies which proposed some economic betterment and offered self-respect to many people in Africa (from Kwame Nkrumah's African socialism to Julius Nyerere's "cooperative economy") and parts of the former Communist bloc (Tito's "labor management") all collapsed and have given way to self-serving oligarchies that justified their policies, not by calling on their own citizens, but by publishing excerpts from reports written by the World Bank and the International Monetary Fund.

In the Third World as a whole, globalization, at best, produced what Tocqueville, with a touch of aristocratic disdain, called a government of the commercially-minded middle classes, "a government without virtue and without greatness"; at worst, it produced governments of plutocrats or elites unconcerned about their own populations. Globalization thus appeared in the poorest and weakest countries at its roughest.

Perhaps the greatest casualty of the money-grubbing global capitalism was loss of self-respect among those who have failed economically—and they are preponderantly located in the poorest countries. The desperate African masses who want to flee their own countries leave not only because incomes are low and prospects bleak, but also because of a lack of confidence that either they or their governments, no matter who is in power, can change life for the better. This despondency and loss of self-respect is indeed a product of globalization. In the past one could feel slighted by fortune for having been born in a poor country, yet have as compensation a belief that other qualities mattered, that one's country offered the world something valuable, a different ideology, a different way of life. But none of that survives today.

The problem was, strangely, noticed by Friedrich Hayek. Market outcomes, Hayek argued, must not be presented as ethically just or unjust because the market is ethically neutral. But to buttress the case for global capitalism, its proponents insist in an almost Calvinist fashion that economic success is not only good in a purely material sense, but reveals some moral superiority. Thus winners are made to feel not only richer but morally superior, and the converse: The losers feel poor and are supposed to be ashamed of their failure. Many people do, but understandably not all take gladly to such judgment.

An interesting coincidence of interests emerges between the desperate masses and the rich in advanced countries. The latter, educated and with considerable property "interests," are, economically, often in favor of greater Third World competitiveness and migration since, either as investors abroad or as consumers of cheap labor services at home, they benefit from low-wage labor. This unlikely coincidence of interest lends some superficial justification to the claims of George Bush and Tony Blair that the opponents of free-trade pacts work against the interests of the poor. The problem that the president and the prime minister fail to acknowledge, or perhaps even to realize, is that many of the policies urged by their governments on poor countries in the last two decades have indeed brought people to their current point of desperation.

Sandwiched between this unlikely "coalition" of the global top and the global bottom, are globalization's losers: the lower and middle classes in the West, and those in the "failed" states, not yet sufficiently desperate to board the boats to Europe or cross the US border at night. They too lost in terms of their national sovereignty and personal income. They may not gladly accept, though, that they are morally inferior. At first sight, they do not seem likely to derail globalization because their power is limited. Yet in a more interdependent world with an easy access to deadly weapons, politics of global resentment may find many followers.

POSTSCRIPT

Is Economic Globalization Good for Humankind?

According to Freedom House, a non-partisan think tank that monitors the progress of freedom and democracy around the world, the rise in globalization and free trade over the past 35 years has been accompanied by an increase in the percentage of countries whose population enjoys civil and political freedom. Since 1972, the share of those countries where these rights are denied has dropped from 47% to 34%, whereas the share of those countries enjoying these rights has increased from 34% to 46%. Freedom House also reports that the most economically open—that is, receptive to the idea of globalization—are three times more likely to enjoy full civil and political liberties than are economically closed countries. Further, numerous studies indicate that nations that are receptive to free trade grow faster and have higher levels of per capita income than nations that resist economic openness.

Facts such as these seem to provide considerable support for the pro-globalization stance. But keep in mind that an integral aspect of Branko Milanovic's argument is that a country's national and cultural identity will be swept away in the wake of rapid economic growth. And in case you think his fears are unfounded, consider the existence of the European Union. There is strength in size, and joining a unified collection of European nations allows each country to better compete in the global marketplace. However, membership in the EU has come at a price: Member countries have to agree to dissolve their currency and adopt a new, single currency, the euro. Across Europe, the history and cultural identity of many countries is intimately tied to its currency, and the decision to disband it for economic reasons was the source of much social unrest. Many critics of the EU fear that this is merely an early example of the destructive effects globalization—in the form of the EU—has on the national sovereignty of those countries that embrace it.

Suggested Readings

Arch Puddington, "Findings of *Freedom in the World 2008*—Freedom in Retreat: Is the Tide Turning?" Freedom House.org (2008). http://www.freedomhouse.org/template.cfm?page=130&year=2008

Investor's Business Daily, "The Backlash Against Globalization," *Investor's Business Daily Editorial* (July 23, 2007). http://www.ibdeditorials.com/IBDArticles.aspx?id=270083115591444

Gennady Stoylarov, "Globalization: Extending the Market and Human Well-Being," *The Freeman* (vol. 59, no. 3, April 2009).

Christine Elsaeßer, "Strength in Numbers for Globalization's Critics," *Deutch Welle* (September 5, 2007). http://www.dw-world.de/dw/article/0,2144,2473215,00.html

Andrew Nikiforuk, *Pandemonium: How Globalization and Trade Are Putting the World at Risk*, (University of Queensland Press, 2007).

Martin Wolf, "Remarks at a National Center for Policy Analysis Conference in London," National Center for Policy Analysis (May 2006). http://www.ncpa.org/sub/dpd/index.php?Article_ID=3386

ISSUE 18

Are Protectionist Policies Beneficial to Business?

YES: Ha-Joon Chang, from "Protecting the Global Poor," *Prospect Magazine* (July 2007)

NO: Robert Krol, from "Trade, Protectionism, and the US Economy: Examining the Evidence" in *Trade Briefing Paper No. 28*, The Cato Institute (September 16, 2008)

ISSUE SUMMARY

YES: In support of the idea that protectionist policies help business, Ha-Joon Chang focuses attention on developing industries in poor countries. Further, he describes and advocates historical protectionist policies from around the world.

NO: In the "No" selection, Robert Krol describes the findings of various economic studies of international trade. The areas that he surveys include the effect of trade on employment and wages as well of the costs of trade restrictions. He concludes that overall the benefits from protectionist policies are overshadowed by their negative effects.

It is understandable that a country would want to take care of its own citizens first. To this end, many countries adopt policies that prop up domestic industries and limit foreign organizations from engaging in business in their country. Generally speaking, such policies are typically labeled "protectionism." A formal definition of protectionism is the "National economic policies designed to restrict free trade and protect domestic industries from foreign competition" (S. Tamer Cavusgil, Gary Knight, and John R. Riesenberger, *International Business*. 2008. Pearson, p. 620). Protectionist policies include governmental actions such as tariffs (taxes on imported goods), quotas (limits on the amount of goods that can be imported), subsidies (government support of certain domestic businesses or industries), and other policies like the "Buy American" requirements in the United States.

Let's take a look at a couple of broad examples. When foreign competitors in a particular industry operate with a lower cost basis, home governments will frequently provide funds (subsidies) to that industry in their own country to help the domestic companies compete against foreign competitors. The ultimate goals of such policies are many: keeping specific domestic industries competitive, keeping the country's workers employed, and keeping them employed at higher wages than would be the case without subsidies. Another protectionist strategy is using tariffs assessed on foreign goods. This causes foreign competitors to charge higher prices than they would otherwise be able to in order to remain profitable.

For a more concrete example, we can look at the US steel industry. To address increasing fears that foreign steelmakers will increase market share in the United States, politicians and US steel industry advocates want to implement economic stimulus legislation requiring that infrastructure projects in the United States use domestic steel (Quentin Hardy and Taylor Buley, 2009. "The Greening of Trade Wars" Forbes, 183(8), 26). Further, there is concern that market share increases from foreign competitors will hurt not only the steel industry but also have negative effects on the environment. Consider the following comments from a union leader in the US steel industry: "In congressional testimony in March [2009], United Steelworkers boss Leo Gerard explained how unfettered trade in steel would both ship jobs abroad and make the world's pollution worse. Ton for ton, he said, Chinese steel leaves a carbon footprint three times as large as American steel."(Quentin Hardy and Taylor Buley, April 2009. "The Greening of Trade Wars" Forbes, 183(8), 26. Retrieved May 10, 2009, Forbes.com.)

Although many believe that protectionism may indeed afford some advantages for domestic business, opponents of protectionism argue that due to the interdependence of global trade and financial systems, these advantages are offset by many negative consequences (William A. Kerr. (2009). "Recession, International Trade and the Fallacies of Composition." *The Estey Centre Journal of International Law and Trade Policy: Special Section on Geographical Indicators*, 10(1), 1–11). For instance, an unintended—and unavoidable—consequence of subsidies and tariffs is higher prices for products available to consumers. Protectionist policies also tend to lower the overall quality of goods available and ultimately increase the tax burden on the general public.

Writing in the "No" selection for this debate topic, Professor of Economics at California State University Robert Krol describes the findings of various economic studies of international trade. He looks at the effect of trade on employment and wages as well as examining the costs of trade restrictions. From his research, he concludes that "Although international trade forces significant adjustments in an economy, as the evidence shows, the costs of international trade restrictions on the economy outweigh the limited benefits these restrictions bring to import-competing industries." (p. 10)

The opposing view, taken from *Prospect Magazine*, is provided by Ha-Joon Chang, who focuses attention on the benefits of protectionism for infant, or developing, industries in poor countries. Chang describes and advocates historical protectionist policies from all around the world. Interestingly, the article contains many examples taken from the histories of today's wealthiest countries. The point behind this approach is that history shows that in order for today's poorer nations to succeed, they need to be allowed to adopt regulations that protect their fledgling key industries.

YES ↵

Ha-Joon Chang

Protecting the Global Poor

Once upon a time, the leading car-maker of a developing country exported its first passenger cars to the US. Until then, the company had only made poor copies of cars made by richer countries. The car was just a cheap subcompact ("four wheels and an ashtray") but it was a big moment for the country and its exporters felt proud.

Unfortunately, the car failed. Most people thought it looked lousy, and were reluctant to spend serious money on a family car that came from a place where only second-rate products were made. The car had to be withdrawn from the US. This disaster led to a major debate among the country's citizens. Many argued that the company should have stuck to its original business of making simple textile machinery. After all, the country's biggest export item was silk. If the company could not make decent cars after 25 years of trying, there was no future for it. The government had given the car-maker every chance. It had ensured high profits for it through high tariffs and tough controls on foreign investment. Less than ten years earlier, it had even given public money to save the company from bankruptcy. So, the critics argued, foreign cars should now be let in freely and foreign car-makers, who had been kicked out 20 years before, allowed back again. Others disagreed. They argued that no country had ever got anywhere without developing "serious" industries like car production. They just needed more time.

The year was 1958 and the country was Japan. The company was Toyota, and the car was called the Toyopet. Toyota started out as a manufacturer of textile machinery and moved into car production in 1933. The Japanese government kicked out General Motors and Ford in 1939, and bailed out Toyota with money from the central bank in 1949. Today, Japanese cars are considered as "natural" as Scottish salmon or French wine, but less than 50 years ago, most people, including many Japanese, thought the Japanese car industry simply should not exist.

Half a century after the Toyopet debacle, Toyota's luxury brand Lexus has become an icon of globalisation, thanks to the American journalist Thomas Friedman's book *The Lexus and the Olive Tree*. The book owes its title to an epiphany that Friedman had in Japan in 1992. He had paid a visit to a Lexus factory, which deeply impressed him. On the bullet train back to Tokyo, he read yet another newspaper article about the troubles in the middle east, where he had been a correspondent. Then it hit him. He realised that "half the world seemed to be . . . intent on building a better Lexus, dedicated to modernising, streamlining and privatising their economies in order to thrive in the system of globalisation. And half of the world—sometimes half the same country, sometimes half the same person—was still caught up in the fight over who owns which olive tree."

According to Friedman, countries in the olive-tree world will not be able to join the Lexus world unless they fit themselves into a particular set of economic policies he calls "the golden straitjacket." In describing the golden straitjacket, Friedman pretty much sums up today's neoliberal orthodoxy: countries should privatise state-owned enterprises, maintain low inflation, reduce the size of government, balance the budget, liberalise trade, deregulate foreign investment and capital markets, make the currency convertible, reduce corruption and privatise pensions. The golden straitjacket, Friedman argues, is the only clothing suitable for the harsh but exhilarating game of globalisation.

However, had the Japanese government followed the free-trade economists back in the early 1960s, there would have been no Lexus. Toyota today would at best be a junior partner to a western car manufacturer and Japan would have remained the third-rate industrial power it was in the 1960s—on the same level as Chile, Argentina and South Africa.

Had it just been Japan that became rich through the heretical policies of protection, subsidies and the restriction of foreign investment, the free-market champions might be able to dismiss it as the exception that proves the rule. But Japan is no exception. Practically all of today's developed countries, including Britain and the US, the supposed homes of the free market and free trade, have become rich on the basis of policy recipes that contradict today's orthodoxy.

In 1721, Robert Walpole, the first British prime minister, launched an industrial programme that protected and nurtured British manufacturers against superior competitors in the Low Countries, then the centre of European manufacturing. Walpole declared that "nothing so much contributes to promote the public wellbeing as the exportation of manufactured goods and the importation of foreign raw material." Between Walpole's time and the 1840s, when Britain started to reduce its tariffs (although it did not move to free trade until the 1860s), Britain's average industrial tariff rate was in the region of 40–50 percent, compared with 20 percent and 10 percent in France and Germany, respectively.

The US followed the British example. In fact, the first systematic argument that new industries in relatively backward economies need protection before they can compete with their foreign rivals—known as the "infant industry" argument—was developed by the first US treasury secretary, Alexander Hamilton. In 1789, Hamilton proposed a series of measures to achieve the industrialisation of his country, including protective tariffs, subsidies, import liberalisation of industrial inputs (so it wasn't blanket protection for everything), patents for inventions and the development of the banking system.

Hamilton was perfectly aware of the potential pitfalls of infant industry protection, and cautioned against taking these policies too far. He knew that just as some parents are overprotective, governments can cosset infant industries too much. And in the way that some children manipulate their parents into supporting them beyond childhood, there are industries that prolong government protection through clever lobbying. But the existence of dysfunctional families is hardly an argument against parenting itself. Likewise, the examples of bad protectionism merely tell us that the policy needs to be used wisely.

In recommending an infant industry programme for his young country, Hamilton, an impudent 35-year-old finance minister with only a liberal arts degree from a then second-rate college (King's College of New York, now Columbia University) was openly ignoring the advice of the world's most famous economist, Adam Smith. Like most European economists at the time, Smith advised the Americans not to develop manufacturing. He argued that any attempt to "stop the importation of European manufactures" would "obstruct . . . the progress of their country towards real wealth and greatness."

Many Americans—notably Thomas Jefferson, secretary of state at the time and Hamilton's arch-enemy—disagreed with Hamilton. They argued that it was better to import high-quality manufactured products from Europe with the proceeds that the country earned from agricultural exports than to try to produce second-rate manufactured goods. As a result, Congress only half-heartedly accepted Hamilton's recommendations—raising the average tariff rate from 5 percent to 12.5 percent.

In 1804, Hamilton was killed in a duel by the then vice-president Aaron Burr. Had he lived for another decade or so, he would have seen his programme adopted in full. Following the Anglo-American war in 1812, the US started shifting to a protectionist policy; by the 1820s, its average industrial tariff had risen to 40 percent. By the 1830s, America's average industrial tariff rate was the highest in the world and, except for a few brief periods, remained so until the second world war, at which point its manufacturing supremacy was absolute.

Britain and the US were not the only practitioners of infant industry protection. Virtually all of today's rich countries used policy measures to protect and nurture their infant industries. Even when the overall level of protection was relatively low, some strategic sectors could get very high protection. For example, in the late 19th and early 20th centuries, Germany, while maintaining a relatively moderate average industrial tariff rate (5–15 percent), accorded strong protection to industries like iron and steel. During the same period, Sweden provided high protection to its emerging engineering industries, although its average tariff rate was 15–20 percent. In the first half of the 20th century, Belgium maintained moderate levels of overall protection but heavily protected key textile sectors and the iron industry.

Tariffs were not the only tool of trade policy used by rich countries. When deemed necessary for the protection of infant industries, they banned imports or imposed import quotas. They also gave export subsidies—sometimes to all exports (Japan and Korea) but often to specific items (in the 18th century, Britain gave export subsidies to gunpowder, sailcloth, refined sugar and silk). Some of them also gave a rebate on the tariffs paid on the imported industrial inputs used for manufacturing export goods, in order to encourage such exports. Many believe that this measure was invented in Japan in the 1950s, but it was in fact invented in Britain in the 17th century.

It is not just in the realm of trade that the historical records of today's rich countries burst the bindings of Friedman's golden straitjacket. The history of controls on foreign investment tells a similar story. In the 19th century, the US placed restrictions on foreign investment in banking, shipping, mining and logging. The restrictions were particularly severe in banking; throughout the 19th century, non-resident shareholders could not even vote in a shareholders' meeting and only American citizens could become directors in a national (as opposed to state) bank.

Some countries went further than the US. Japan closed off most industries to foreign investment and imposed 49 percent ownership ceilings on the others until the 1970s. Korea basically followed this model until it was forced to liberalise after the 1997 financial crisis. Between the 1930s and the 1980s, Finland officially classified all firms with more than 20 percent foreign ownership as "dangerous enterprises." It was not that these countries were against foreign companies per se—after all, Korea actively courted foreign investment in export processing zones. They restricted foreign investors because they believed—rightly in my view—that there is nothing like learning how to do something yourself, even if it takes more time and effort.

The wealthy nations of today may support the privatisation of state-owned enterprises in developing countries, but many of them built their industries through state ownership. At the beginning of their industrialisation, Germany and Japan set up state-owned enterprises in key industries—textiles, steel and shipbuilding. In France, the reader may be surprised to learn that many household names—like Renault (cars), Alcatel (telecoms equipment), Thomson (electronics) and Elf Aquitaine (oil and gas)—have been state-owned enterprises. Finland, Austria and Norway also developed their industries through extensive state ownership after the second world war. Taiwan has achieved its economic "miracle" with a state sector more than one-and-a-half times the size of the international average, while Singapore's state sector is one of the largest in the world, and includes world-class companies like Singapore Airlines.

Of course, there were exceptions. The Netherlands and pre-first world war Switzerland did not adopt many tariffs or subsidies. But they did deviate from today's free-market orthodoxy in another, very important way—they refused to protect patents. Switzerland did not have patents until 1888 and did not protect chemical inventions until 1907. The Netherlands abolished its 1817 patent law in 1869, on the grounds that patents created artificial monopolies that went against the principle of free competition. It did not reintroduce a patent law until 1912, by which time Philips was firmly established as a leading producer of lightbulbs, whose production technology it "borrowed" from Thomas Edison.

Even countries that did have patent laws were lax about protecting intellectual property (IP) rights—especially those of foreigners. In most countries, including Britain, Austria, France and the US, patenting of imported inventions was explicitly allowed in the 19th century.

Despite this history of protection, subsidy and state ownership, the rich countries have been recommending to, or even forcing upon, developing countries policies that go directly against their own historical experience. For the past 25 years, rich countries have imposed trade liberalisation on many developing countries through IMF and World Bank loan conditions, as well as the conditions attached to their direct aid. The World Trade Organisation (WTO) does allow some tariff protection, especially for the poorest developing countries, but most developing countries have had to significantly reduce tariffs and other trade restrictions. Most subsidies have been banned by the WTO—except, of course, the ones that rich countries still use, such as on agriculture, and research and development. And while, of course, no poor country is obliged to accept foreign inward investment (and most receive none or very little), the IMF and the World Bank are always lobbying for more liberal foreign investment rules. The WTO has also tightened IP laws, asking all but the poorest developing countries to comply with US standards—which even many Americans consider excessive.

Why are they doing this? In 1841, Friedrich List, a German economist, criticised Britain for preaching free trade to other countries when she had achieved her economic supremacy through tariffs and subsidies. He accused the British of "kicking away the ladder" that they had climbed to reach the world's top economic position. Today, there are certainly some people in rich countries who preach free trade to poor countries in order to capture larger shares of the latter's markets and to pre-empt the emergence of possible competitors. They are saying, "Do as we say, not as we did," and act as bad samaritans, taking advantage of others in trouble. But what is more worrying is that many of today's free traders do not realise that they are hurting the developing countries with their policies. History is written by the victors, and it is human nature to reinterpret the past from the point of view of the present. As a result, the rich countries have gradually, if often sub-consciously, rewritten their own histories to make them more consistent with how they see themselves today, rather than as they really were.

But the truth is that free traders make the lives of those whom they are trying to help more difficult. The evidence for this is everywhere. Despite adopting supposedly "good" policies, like liberal foreign trade and investment and strong patent protection, many developing countries have actually been performing rather badly over the last two and a half decades. The annual per capita growth rate of the developing world has halved in this period, compared to the "bad old days" of protectionism and government intervention in the 1960s and the 1970s. Even this modest rate has been achieved only because the average includes China and India—two fast-growing giants, which have gradually liberalised their economies but have resolutely refused to put on Thomas Friedman's golden straitjacket.

Growth failure has been particularly noticeable in Latin America and Africa, where orthodox neoliberal programmes were implemented more thoroughly than in Asia. In the 1960s and the 1970s, per capita income in Latin America grew at 3.1 percent a year, slightly faster than the developing-country average. Brazil especially was growing almost as fast as the east Asian "miracle" economies.

Since the 1980s, however, when the continent embraced neoliberalism, Latin America has been growing at less than a third of this rate. Even if we discount the 1980s as a decade of adjustment and look at the 1990s, we find that per capita income in the region grew at around half the rate of the "bad old days" (3.1 percent vs 1.7 percent). Between 2000 and 2005, the region has done even worse; it virtually stood still, with per capita income growing at only 0.6 percent a year. As for Africa, its per capita income grew relatively slowly even in the 1960s and the 1970s (1–2 percent a year). But since the 1980s, the region has seen a fall in living standards. There are, of course, many reasons for this failure, but it is nonetheless a damning indictment of the neoliberal orthodoxy, because most of the African economies have been practically run by the IMF and the World Bank over the past quarter of a century.

In pushing for free-market policies that make life more difficult for poor countries, the bad samaritans frequently deploy the rhetoric of the "level playing field." They argue that developing countries should not be allowed to use extra policy tools for protection, subsidies and regulation, as these constitute unfair competition. Who can disagree?

Well, we all should, if we want to build an international system that promotes economic development. A level playing field leads to unfair competition when the players are unequal. Most sports have strict separation by age and gender, while boxing, wrestling and weightlifting have weight classes, which are often divided very finely. How is it that we think a bout between people with more than a couple of kilos' weight difference is unfair, and yet we accept that the US and Honduras should compete economically on equal terms?

Global economic competition is a game of unequal players. It pits against each other countries that range from Switzerland to Swaziland. Consequently, it is only fair that we "tilt the playing field" in favour of the weaker countries. In practice, this means allowing them to protect and subsidise their producers more vigorously, and to put stricter regulations on foreign investment. These countries should also be allowed to protect IP rights less stringently, so that they can "borrow" ideas from richer countries. This will have the added benefit of making economic growth in poor countries more compatible with the need to fight global warming, as rich-country technologies tend to be far more energy-efficient.

I am not against markets, international trade or globalisation. And I acknowledge that WTO agreements contain "special and differential treatment" provisions which give poor country members certain rights, and which permit rich countries to treat developing countries more favourably than other rich WTO members. But these provisions are limited and generally just give poor countries longer time periods to liberalise their economic rules. The default position remains blind faith in indiscriminate free trade.

The best way to illustrate my general point is to look at my own native Korea—or, rather, to contrast the two bits that used to be one country until 1948. It is hard to believe today, but northern Korea used to be richer than the south. Japan developed the north industrially when it ruled the country from 1910–45. Even after the Japanese left, North Korea's industrial legacy enabled it to maintain its economic lead over South Korea well into the 1960s.

Today, South Korea is one of the world's industrial powerhouses while North Korea languishes in poverty. Much of this is thanks to the fact that South Korea aggressively traded with the outside world and actively absorbed foreign technologies while North Korea pursued its doctrine of self-sufficiency. Through trade, South Korea learned about the existence of better technologies and earned the foreign currency to buy them. In its own way, North Korea has managed some technological feats. For example, it figured out a way to mass-produce vinalon, a synthetic fibre made out of limestone and anthracite, which has allowed it to be self-sufficient in clothing. But, overall, North Korea is technologically stuck in the past, with 1940s Japanese and 1950s Soviet technologies, while South Korea is one of the most technologically dynamic economies in the world.

In the end, economic development is about mastering advanced technologies. In theory, a country can develop such technologies on its own, but technological self-sufficiency quickly hits the wall, as seen in the North Korean case. This is why all successful cases of economic development have involved serious attempts to get hold of advanced foreign technologies. But in order to be able to import technologies from developed countries, developing nations need foreign currency to pay for them. Some of this foreign currency may be provided through foreign aid, but most has to be earned through exports. Without trade, therefore, there will be little technological progress and thus little economic development.

But there is a huge difference between saying that trade is essential for economic development and saying that free trade is best. It is this sleight of hand that free-trade economists have so effectively deployed against their opponents—if you are against free trade, they imply, you must be against trade itself, and so against economic progress.

As South Korea—together with Britain, the US, Japan, Taiwan and many others—shows, active participation in international trade does not require free trade. In the early stages of their development, these countries typically had tariff rates in the region of 30–50 percent. Likewise, the Korean experience shows that actively absorbing foreign technologies does not require a liberal foreign investment policy.

Indeed, had South Korea donned Friedman's golden straitjacket in the 1960s, it would still be exporting raw materials like tungsten ore and seaweed. The secret of its success lay in a mix of protection and open trade, of government regulation and free(ish) market, of active courting of foreign investment and draconian regulation of it, and of private enterprise and state control— with the areas of protection constantly changing as new infant industries were developed and old ones became internationally competitive. This is how almost all of today's rich countries became rich, and it is at the root of almost all recent success stories in the developing world.

Therefore, if they are genuinely to help developing countries develop through trade, wealthy countries need to accept asymmetric protectionism, as they used to between the 1950s and the 1970s. The global economic system should support the efforts of developing countries by allowing them to use more freely the tools of infant industry promotion—such as tariff protection, subsidies, foreign investment regulation and weak IP rights.

There are huge benefits from global integration if it is done in the right way, at the right speed. But if poor countries open up prematurely, the result will be negative. Globalisation is too important to be left to free-trade economists, whose policy advice has so ill served the developing world in the past 25 years.

Robert Krol   ⇨ **NO**

Trade, Protectionism, and the U.S. Economy: Examining the Evidence

Introduction

America's trade with the rest of the world expanded significantly after World War II. U.S. goods (exports plus imports) increased from 9.2 percent of gross domestic product in 1960 to 28.6 percent in 2007. This expansion of international trade has benefited the United States and its trading partners considerably. The benefits include a higher standard of living, lower prices for consumers, improved efficiency in production, and a greater variety of goods.

The expansion of international trade raises concerns about the impact on domestic firms. In particular, many people fear that international trade reduces job opportunities for workers and depresses wages. These fears create political support for protectionist policies. However, international trade restrictions are costly to consumers as well as producers.

A recent survey found that 59 percent of Americans have a favorable view of international trade, although survey trends also indicate that a growing number of Americans now view international trade less favorably. When asked about their attitudes concerning the expansion of U.S. trade relations with the rest of the world, 36 percent thought it was "somewhat bad" or "very bad" in 2007 compared with 18 percent in 2002.

In this presidential election year, interest in the international trade views of the likely Democratic and Republican nominees is high. A meaningful way to determine the candidates' thinking on international trade is to look at their legislative voting records.

According to the Cato Institute's Center for Trade Policy Studies, Republican Sen. John McCain (R-AZ) voted against trade restrictions 88 percent of the time over his career. He is classified as a free trader based on his voting record. Sen. Barack Obama (D-IL) voted against trade barriers only 36 percent of the time. Clearly, the outcome of the November election could significantly affect future U.S. trade policy. Whether the United States continues to promote free trade will depend in part on who is elected president.

Opinion surveys and congressional voting records suggest Americans disagree strongly about the costs and benefits of international trade. This paper reviews empirical studies that examine the evidence on how international trade affects the economy. The goal of this paper is to discuss the evidence with respect to four important areas of international trade: the causes of expanded

From *Trade Briefing Paper*, No. 28, September 16, 2008, pp. 2–10 (notes omitted). Copyright © 2008 by Cato Institute/Center for Trade Policy Studies. Reprinted by permission.

international trade, the benefits of trade, the impact of trade on employment and wages, and the cost of international trade restrictions.

The following points summarize the evidence from a survey of major research in the field:

- Comparative advantage remains the major driver of global trade flows.
- Income growth accounts for two-thirds of the growth in global trade in recent decades, trade liberalization accounts for one-quarter, and lower transportation costs make up the remainder.
- Trade expansion has fueled faster growth and raised incomes in countries that have liberalized. A 1-percentage-point gain in trade as a share of the economy raises per capita income by 1 percent. Global elimination of all barriers to trade in goods and services would raise global income by $2 trillion and U.S. income by almost $500 billion.
- Competition from trade delivers lower prices and more product variety to consumers. Americans are $300 billion better off today than they would be otherwise because of the greater product variety from imports.
- International trade directly affects only 15 percent of the U.S. workforce. Most job displacement occurs in sectors that are not engaged in global competition.
- While trade has probably caused a net loss of manufacturing jobs since 1979, those losses have been more than offset by employment gains in other sectors of the economy. Net payroll employment in the United States has grown by 36 million in the past two decades, along with a dramatic increase in imports of goods and services.
- Growing levels of trade do not explain most of the growing gap between wages earned by skilled and unskilled workers. The relative decline in unskilled wages is mainly caused by technological changes that reward greater skills. Demand for unskilled workers has been in relative decline in all sectors of the economy, not just those exposed to trade.
- Trade barriers impose large, net costs on the U.S. economy. The cost to the economy per job saved in protected industries far exceeds the wages paid to workers in those jobs.
- Protectionism persists because small, homogeneous, and concentrated interests are better able to lobby the government than the large, heterogeneous, and dispersed mass of consumers.

Why Countries Trade

Comparative advantage remains the basis of international trade. Differences in production costs within countries determine much of the flow of goods and services across international borders. Economists use the term "comparative advantage" to indicate that a country has a cost advantage in producing certain goods relative to other goods that could be produced within that same country. In other words, what spurs trade and specialization is not the absolute cost advantage that one country's producers have over their competitors in another country, but the relative advantage they have compared to other sectors within their own country.

Consider the example of a more-developed Country A and a less-developed Country B. Country A may be able to produce t-shirts twice as efficiently as Country B; but if it can produce computers 10 times more efficiently, it will make economic sense for Country A to specialize in producing and exporting computers while importing t-shirts from Country B. Trade allows both countries to direct their internal resources—principally labor and capital—to those sectors where they are relatively more productive compared to other sectors in the domestic economy.

Comparative advantage can spring from multiple sources. A country can have a cost advantage in the production of a particular good because of superior production technology. This superiority can include better ways to organize the production process or a climate that allows the country to grow certain crops, such as bananas and mangos, more cheaply. It can also include greater investments in skilled labor and equipment that can result in a comparative advantage in such areas as computer software.

The United States has proportionately more skilled labor than unskilled labor compared with most countries. This makes the United States the low-cost producer for goods that rely on skilled labor and sophisticated machinery. Therefore, the United States exports high-tech manufactured goods that can be produced using relatively more skilled labor and imports shoes and apparel that are produced using a large amount of unskilled labor.

However, sometimes trade involves similar goods. For example, the United States both exports and imports golf clubs. This type of trade occurs in markets where businesses differentiate their products and experience declining average costs as production expands. In this setting, opening an economy to international trade increases the size of the market. Average costs fall, resulting in lower prices and a wider array of products being sold in each of the trading countries. Consumers can select from products produced by domestic as well as foreign firms. Lower prices and greater variety increase consumer welfare.

Global trade has expanded significantly since World War II for a number of reasons, including lower transportation and information costs, higher per capita income, and changes in government policies. The containerization of shipping has reduced loading times, improving efficiency, just as less expensive air transportation has increased international trade in perishable items. Improvements in information technology have made it less costly for consumers to determine the characteristics of products produced abroad. Information technology has also made it easier for producers to assess consumer preferences, allowing better customization of products and services for buyers in foreign markets. Income growth in developed countries and even in some less-developed countries has increased the demand for goods and services produced domestically as well as from abroad. Finally, trade restrictions have decreased significantly since World War II.

Evidence is now available that quantifies the relative contribution of these different factors to the growth of world trade. Scott Baier and Jeffrey

Bergstrand attribute 67 percent of the increase in international trade to income growth, another 25 percent to tariff reductions, and the remaining 8 percent to falling transportation costs. Critics of trade blame trade agreements for spurring global competition, when in fact most trade growth simply stems from rising global incomes. A reversion to protectionism would not necessarily stop the growth of global trade, but it would sacrifice the considerable economic benefits of more open competition.

Benefits from International Trade

Since World War II, multilateral and unilateral tariff negotiations have reduced barriers to international trade. Several attempts have been made to quantify the resulting welfare gains to consumers and producers. In brief, trade leads to specialization based on comparative advantage, which lowers production costs, allowing for greater levels of output and, therefore, consumption. Individuals are able to purchase products at lower prices, resulting in higher real incomes and a higher standard of living. In addition, trade allows countries to import products that embody new technologies which are not produced at home.

One way to assess the gains from international trade is to compare the level of welfare (measured imperfectly by real per capita GDP) before and after trade restrictions are dropped. A dramatic example of this type of trade reform occurred in Japan during the early 1850s. For 200 years up until then, Japan had almost no economic or cultural contact with other countries. Then the Japanese government signed a treaty with the United States that was designed to shift the country from a no-trade to a free-trade regime in seven years. Daniel Bernhofen and John Brown estimate that, with the increase in international trade, Japan's real GDP was 8 percent higher by the end of the seven-year period than if the economy had remained closed. Furthermore, by opening its economy to the rest of the world, Japan was able to import capital goods, new technologies, and new production methods that promoted faster economic growth and even higher living standards over time.

In another historical episode, the United States closed its borders to international trade in 1807 when President Thomas Jefferson imposed a trade embargo to avoid conflicts with the warring British and French navies. Dartmouth economist Douglas Irwin estimates the embargo reduced U.S. GDP by about 5 percent in one year. Jefferson quickly ended the embargo because of the high economic cost it imposed on the country.

Research economists have used computer models of the economy to capture the industry adjustments and aggregate GDP gains from trade liberalization. Work by Drusilla Brown, Alan Deardorff, and Robert Stern represents this type of study. They estimate that a one-third reduction in agricultural, manufacturing, and service-sector trade restrictions worldwide would increase world GDP by $686 billion (measured in 1995 dollars) over a prereduction baseline. In the United States, GDP would rise 1.8 percent. If all trade barriers were eliminated, world GDP would increase by more than $2 trillion and U.S. GDP would be $497 billion, or 4.8 percent, higher than before liberalization.

Although the association between free trade and prosperity has been well documented, the correlation between international trade and increased per capita income has been difficult to illustrate—perhaps because countries with higher per capita income choose to trade more. In a well-known study, Jeffrey Frankel and David Romer examined the relationship between international trade and per capita income using 1985 data for a large cross-section of countries. To deal with the causality issue, Frankel and Romer used geographic variables correlated with international trade but not per capita income. This approach isolates the portion of international trade not caused by growth in per capita income. They found that, as the share of exports-plus-imports to GDP rises by 1 percentage point, per capita income increases by 2 percentage points.

However, Frankel and Romer's work has been criticized because the geographic variables they used may be correlated with other geographic factors that influence GDP. For example, distance from the equator correlates with per capita income, possibly invalidating the results. Marta Noguer and Marc Siscart used an improved specification to reestimate the relationship. Controlling for distance from the equator, they found that a 1-percentage-point increase in trade share raises per capita income by 1 percentage point. Noguer and Siscart concluded that trade does indeed raise a country's standard of living.

More recently, Romain Wacziarg and Karen Horn Welch examined the relationship between trade and economic growth for 133 countries over most of the post–World War II period. Using country case studies and trade policy indicators, they identified the year countries in the study liberalized their trade policies. They found that, on average, countries grew 1.5 percentage points faster per year following trade liberalization during the period 1950 to 1998. Focusing on a subgroup of countries that had at least eight years of data before and after liberalization, they found 54 percent of these countries grew faster. Of the remaining countries examined, 21 percent did not experience faster growth while 25 percent of the countries grew more slowly.

Wacziarg and Welch found that the countries that experienced faster economic growth maintained their liberalization polices while the others did not. Also, some of the countries that did not grow faster following trade liberalization experienced political instability and restrictive macroeconomic policies that hindered growth in the post-trade-liberalization period. Obviously, trade liberalization alone is not always enough to overcome other factors inhibiting growth.

Economists have also turned to individual factory-level data to better understand the connection between international trade and a country's standard of living. Looking at U.S. manufacturing data from 1987 to 1997, Andrew Bernard, J. Bradford Jensen, and Peter Schott found that a one-standard-deviation decrease in tariffs and transportation costs increased productivity growth by 0.2 percentage points per year, primarily as a result of a shift in production from low- to high-productivity plants. Many low-productivity plants closed. At the same time, however, exports from plants already exporting increased, and high-productivity plants that previously produced only for the domestic market entered the export market.

Daniel Trefler found productivity gains of 1.9 percent per year in Canadian manufacturing following the implementation of the 1989 free trade agreement with the United States. Average manufacturing employment fell by 5 percent in the seven years following the agreement. Those job losses were disproportionally in manufacturing plants that received the greatest tariff protection prior to the trade agreement. However, employment growth in more efficient manufacturing plants helped to reemploy displaced workers over time. These studies show that the short-run adjustment costs and job displacement associated with the closing of inefficient plants can be offset by greater productivity and higher standards of living in the longer-run.

These estimates of the gains from international trade probably underestimate the improvement in well-being that increased trade brings. Moving to freer international trade also increases the variety of goods and services individuals can choose from. If consumers value variety, then welfare improves in an open economy. This welfare gain may not show up in income data, but it does make people better off. In addition, greater variety in intermediate capital goods benefits producers. Better intermediate goods improve efficiency and speed productivity growth, resulting in a higher standard of living for workers.

Christian Broda and David Weinstein examined the benefits of greater import variety in the United States over the period 1972 to 2001. They estimated that the variety of international goods imported into the United States tripled over the period. One traditional measure of the welfare gain from international trade is the decline in prices as measured by an import price index. However, Broda and Weinstein point out that the United States' import price index is not adjusted for changes in variety. If greater variety increases a consumer's satisfaction and standard of living without raising prices, then consumers should be able to achieve the same level of welfare while spending less. When Broda and Weinstein adjusted the U.S. import price index for changes in variety, they estimated the U.S. welfare gain from a greater variety of imports to be approximately 2.8 percent of GDP, or $300 billion per year.

These empirical studies provide evidence that international trade raises income and productivity. They also show that the greater product variety brought about by expanding international trade improves welfare.

Trade's Effect on Employment

People concerned about trade worry that gains in productivity and product variety come at the expense of domestic employment. Yet, the evidence shows little relationship between greater imports and any change in aggregate employment. Over the past 20 years, U.S. *aggregate* net employment has increased from 102 million jobs to nearly 138 million jobs, while imports of goods and services have gone from a little over $500 billion to $2.35 trillion. As shown in Figure 1, employment tends to rise along with imports. Demographic trends, worker education and skill levels, labor-market regulations, and business-cycle developments—not trade—are the dominant factors influencing the overall level of employment and the unemployment rate in the U.S. economy.

Figure 1

Growth of Employment and Imports, 1987–2007

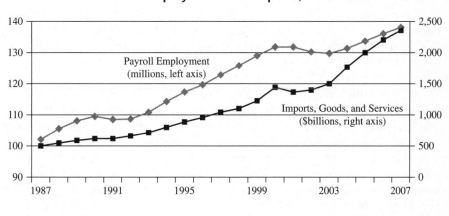

Sources: Economic Report of the President, 2008; Bureau of Labor Statistics, and U.S. Department of Commerce.

International trade does have distributive effects. Although the country as a whole is better off, individual groups of workers or industries may be worse off. This occurs because, once a country opens itself up to international trade, import prices fall because of greater competition and export prices rise because producers can sell to a larger global market. Domestic production of import-competing goods contracts while production in export industries expands, changing the real earnings of inputs employed in these sectors.

What are the implications for the United States? As noted earlier, the United States exports goods that use relatively more skilled labor and imports goods that use relatively more unskilled labor. As the economy adjusts to changing trade patterns, the demand for skilled labor increases and the demand for unskilled labor decreases. Thus, as the United States opens its economy to greater international trade, real wages of skilled labor rise relative to the real wages of unskilled labor. Making matters more difficult for unskilled laborors, displaced workers may also experience a period of unemployment before they find a new job.

Researchers who investigate the impact of international trade on employment and wages find that, despite public rhetoric, international trade has a relatively small impact on wages and employment in the United States. Growth in wage inequality over the last 25 years has apparently been driven more by technological change than international trade.

Two facts shed some light on this general conclusion. First, international trade directly affects only 15 percent of the U.S. workforce. This suggests that international competition is an issue for only a minority of workers. Second, high rates of job loss occur in sectors of the economy that are not engaged in international trade, indicating that factors other than international trade play an important role in labor-market disruptions.

In addition, the decline in employment in the manufacturing sector has been driven primarily by greater labor productivity rather than by growth in international trade. The net employment impact of international trade on manufacturing is small because the United States is both an importer and exporter of manufactured goods.

In a series of studies, Lori Kletzer examined the impact of increased imports on gross U.S. industry employment. For industries most affected by imports, she estimated 7.45 million *gross* manufacturing jobs were lost between 1979 and 2001, or 28,219 per month. This represents a loss of 15 percent of all manufacturing jobs during the 22-year period.

Kletzer points out that data limitations make it difficult to determine if displaced workers have lost their jobs because of imports or for some other reason. Other factors, such as changes in technology or consumer tastes, can also result in job loss. For example, high labor-productivity growth has resulted in a long-run decline in manufacturing jobs—independent of foreign competition. These studies also ignore the jobs created from exporting or from the lower business costs that result from imports, which can expand employment in other sectors.

The more important finding is the *net* effect of imports and exports on employment. Economists at the Federal Reserve Bank of New York have estimated the number of workers needed to produce U.S. goods—imports and exports—with the difference representing the net number of jobs gained or lost in the goods sector because of international trade. Because imports are greater than exports, the calculation shows a net loss in jobs from trade. For the period 1997–2003, they found that net job loss from trade averaged 40,000 per month, or 2.4 percent of total employment. However, the study does not capture employment gains in other sectors, like services, which result from access to lower cost inputs and new technology embedded in imports. It is important to recognize that total net employment in the United States increased by 7.2 million jobs over this period, which indicates that job creation in nonmanufacturing sectors more than offset job losses in manufacturing.

Trade's Impact on Wages

A more contentious labor-market issue concerns the increase in wages of skilled workers relative to unskilled workers. Is this trend the result of changes in information technology, or is international trade to blame? Most studies conclude that international trade has played only a modest role in rising wage inequality. The empirical evidence suggests that skill-biased technological change has had a bigger impact.

First, the demand for skilled labor has increased relative to the demand for unskilled labor in most industries, even those not heavily engaged in international trade. If international trade were driving this trend, we would not observe high relative demand for skilled labor in all sectors, or in sectors that do not engage in significant international trade.

If international trade was driving the growing wage inequality between skilled and unskilled workers, then import prices of unskilled-labor-intensive goods should be declining over time and export prices of skilled-labor-intensive goods should be rising over time as trade expands. That is, import prices should decline as we replace higher-cost, domestically produced products with similar products produced at lower cost from countries that have a comparative advantage in those items. Similarly, export prices should be higher in foreign markets because those markets tend to be high-cost producers of the products we export due to our comparative advantage. Using aggregate export and import price indices, Robert Lawrence and Matthew Slaughter found this not to be the case over the 1979 to 1991 period. Their result is consistent with many (though not all) studies that take this approach. A few studies did find a shift in relative international prices in the 1970s, but they still concluded that the relative wage change was driven primarily by technological change rather than shifting international prices.

More recently, using a similar approach for the period 1981 to 2006, Robert Lawrence found a 12 percentage-point decline in the ratio of blue- to white-collar compensation which he attributed to greater international trade. Most of the decline occurred during the 1980s, a period of fairly stable import-to-export price ratios. The evidence from the 1980s is inconsistent with the theory that international trade is the primary driver of greater wage inequality.

Robert Feenstra and Gary Hanson argue that the outsourcing of less-skilled jobs does reduce demand for unskilled workers in the United States (lowering relative wages), but it is not the primary cause. They examined the impact of this type of outsourcing for 435 U.S. manufacturing industries from 1972 to 1990. For the 1972–1979 period, they found that changes in wage inequality were not related to outsourcing. For the 1979–1990 period, outsourcing appeared to explain about 15 percent of the increased wage inequality, while the introduction of computers explained 35 percent.

Expanding international trade can influence employment patterns and relative wages in an economy. The evidence reviewed in this paper indicates that trade is not the primary source of U.S. job displacement or wage inequality. Technological change and faster productivity growth play the dominant role in these developments.

Cost of Protectionism

Countries can influence international trade by using tariffs and quotas. The purpose of an import tariff is to reduce imports and expand domestic production in the protected industry. With higher output, industry profits and employment expand. However, that expansion comes at a cost. Domestic consumers pay more for products, and domestic resources are used less efficiently. Downstream industries that would use imported products as an input face higher costs, lowering output and employment in those industries.

Gary Hufbauer and Kimberly Elliott examined the welfare gains from the elimination of tariffs and other quantitative restrictions in 21 major sectors of the U.S. economy in the 1980s. Perhaps the most interesting and striking result they reported is their calculation of the consumer gains per job lost if the United States were to eliminate tariffs on an industry. They estimated the dollar cost savings for consumers relative to the total number of jobs lost due to the elimination of an international trade restriction. The average for all 21 sectors was $168,520 per job annually—far higher than the annual earnings of an individual worker. The dollar cost savings ranged from a high of more than $1 million per job in the ball bearings industry to a low of $96,532 per job in costume jewelry. For the sugar sector, the figure was $600,177 per job. For each job "saved," consumers paid three times the average wage in manufacturing. In other words, trade restrictions impose costs on consumers three times the gain to protected workers.

Why do these costly international trade restrictions remain in place? The simple explanation is that the benefits from these types of policies are concentrated in the affected labor force while the costs are spread out over the entire population of consumers.

Producers tend to be a small, relatively homogeneous group. Often they are geographically concentrated. As a result, the costs per person associated with organizing and lobbying for protection from imports are low. Because they form a small group, the benefits per person (higher profits and wages) from import protection are high. The benefit-cost ratio or payoff associated with lobbying government officials is high. Producers and workers find it worthwhile to organize in order to place political pressure on governments for protection from imports. Since elected officials are interested in reelection, they respond by providing protection in exchange for political support.

For consumers, the benefit-cost ratio per person is low. Consumers are a large, geographically diverse, heterogeneous group. As a result, the costs of organizing to lobby against international trade restrictions are high. Furthermore, although the total cost to consumers of these restrictions is high, the cost is typically low on a per-person basis. The benefit-cost ratio or payoff associated with lobbying elected officials is low. Consumers are less likely to expend the resources needed to generate political action in their favor. For example, in the sugar industry the benefits per producer for import restrictions are more than $500,000 per year. For sugar consumers, although the total costs are high, the per-person cost comes to only $5 per year. Not surprisingly, sugar producers actively lobby for import protection and sugar consumers take few steps to oppose it, despite the high total cost to consumers.

Conclusion

International trade has expanded dramatically since World War II. Recent polls and political rhetoric suggest support for continued trade liberalization may be waning—and that is of concern. A movement away from the relatively open global trading system that is currently in place would impose significant economic costs on the United States and the rest of the world.

This paper has provided a comprehensive review of the important empirical studies that quantify the impact of trade on the economy. The evidence is clear: International trade raises a country's standard of living. Lower prices on imported products and greater product variety enhance consumer well-being. Specialization based on comparative advantage and increased competition from foreign businesses improves production efficiency, raising GDP. Firms also get access to foreign capital goods that often contain new technologies, further improving productivity.

Concerns over international trade often center on the effect on jobs and wages. The evidence shows trade can result in the displacement of workers in industries that must compete with imports. However, the impact is modest relative to overall employment growth. Although displaced workers do face adjustment costs, overall the United States has experienced robust total employment growth in the presence of expanded trade. Furthermore, studies show that international trade has a relatively small affect on wages. Greater wage inequality has been driven more by skill-biased technological change than by international trade.

Although international trade forces significant adjustments in an economy, as the evidence shows, the costs of international trade restrictions on the economy outweigh the limited benefits these restrictions bring to import-competing industries.

POSTSCRIPT

Are Protectionist Policies Beneficial for Business?

Business leaders around the globe are well aware that there is no guarantee that those things that have worked in the past will work in the future. This is not to say, however, that history can't teach us valuable lessons. As Ha-Joon Chang points out in the "yes" side selection, there is a long record of protectionist activity in the history of today's most economically successful nations. Referring to the recent economic rise of South Korea, Chang claims that "The secret of its success lay in a mix of protection and open trade, of government regulation and free(ish) market, or active courting of foreign investment and draconian regulation of it, and of private enterprise and state control."

However, others point to very different conclusions from history. Daniella Markheim, Senior Analyst at the Heritage Foundation's Center for International Trade and Economics, compares regulations instituted in the United States around the time of the Great Depression to what has happened in the United States with the recent economic downturn. "Large majorities of economists and historians now say that Smoot-Hawley played a significant role in worsening the Great Depression . . . While not the same, the expansion of the Buy American program represents a step toward the same type of destructive protectionism instituted by Smoot-Hawley." (Daniella Markheim. [2009, January 30]. Buy American Hurts America. Web Memo. The Heritage Foundation.)

Today, many countries participate in organizations like the World Trade Organization (WTO) or take part in various regional trade agreements as a means of reducing trade barriers around the world. Nevertheless, many countries, reacting to the current global recession and tough economic times, have increasingly implemented protectionist policies as safeguards against foreign competition. And it is very probable that the longer the economic downturn, the more attractive protectionist policies are likely to be to policymakers.

Ultimately, the protectionism debate can be viewed by asking which is really more beneficial for business: a) protecting and supporting industries that may otherwise struggle against foreign competition and possibly even go out of business, or b) facilitating international trade and investment that may allow for country-wide efficiencies and learning, even if certain business are hurt in the end?

Suggested Readings

Tula Connell, "Buy American Is About Building Jobs, Not Protectionism," *AFL-CIO NOW* (February 20, 2009). http://blog.aflcio.org/2009/02/20/buy-american-is-about-building-jobs-not-protectionism/

Ian Johnson, "World News: Foreign Businesses Say China Is Growing More Protectionist," *Wall Street Journal* (Eastern Edition) (p. A.8, April 28, 2009).

"United States: Low Expectations Exceeded; Obama and Trade," *The Economist* (vol. 391, no. 8629, p. 28, May 2009).

William A. Kerr, "Recession, International Trade and the Fallacies of Composition," *The Estey Centre Journal of International Law and Trade Policy:* Special Section on Geographical Indicators (vol. 10, no. 1, pp. 1–11, 2009).

Contributors to This Volume

EDITORS

DR. MARC. D STREET is currently an Assistant Professor of Management at Salisbury University in Salisbury, Maryland. He received his BA (Economics) from the University of Maryland, College Park (1983); his MBA from the University of Baltimore (1993); and his Ph.D. (Organizational Behavior) from Florida State University (1998). His primary research interests include business ethics and entrepreneurship. Dr. Street's research has appeared in journals such as *Organizational Behavior and Human Decision Processes, Journal of Business Ethics, Journal of World Business,* and *Small Group Research,* among others. He is also the recipient of numerous research and teaching, and service awards. Prior to entering academia, Dr. Street spent 10 years in the private sector, the last four as a financial consultant for Merrill Lynch in Baltimore, Maryland.

DR. VERA L. STREET is currently an Assistant Professor of Management at Salisbury University in Salisbury, Maryland. She received her BA (Chemistry) from Denison University, her MBA from Rollins College, and her Ph.D. from Florida State University (Strategic Management). Her research interests include competitive dynamics, the resource-based view, decision-making, and entrepreneurial strategies. Her research has been published in journals such as *Journal of Management, Journal of Business Venturing,* and *Academy of Management Executive.*

AUTHORS

SARAH ANDERSON, IPS Fellow, has current work that includes conducting research and writing on the impact of the international financial institutions.

RUSS BELVILLE has been a journalist and radio show host. He currently lives outside of Portland.

AARON BERNSTEIN, in Washington, is a writer for *BusinessWeek*.

WILLIAM BOULDING, a graduate of the Wharton School of Business, is a professor of marketing in the Fuqua School of Business at Duke University. His research interests include marketing strategy, customer relationship metrics, and marketing decision making.

JOHN CAVANAGH has been director of the Institute for Policy Studies since 1998. In this capacity, he oversees programs, outreach, and organizational development.

HA-JOON CHANG teaches economics at Cambridge University. His book, *Bad Samaritans—Rich Nations, Poor Policies and the Threat to the Developing World*, is published by Random House.

MARKUS CHRISTEN is an associate professor of marketing at INSEAD in Fontainebleu, France. His research interest focuses on the development of profitable marketing strategies.

CLAYTON M. CHRISTENSEN is the Robert and Jane Cizik Professor of Business Administration at the Harvard Business School, with a joint appointment in the Technology & Operations Management and General Management faculty groups. His research and teaching interests center on the management issues related to the development and commercialization of technological and business model innovation.

CARL COHEN is a philosophy professor.

CHUCK COLLINS is a senior scholar at the Institute for Policy (IPS) and directs IPS's Program on Inequality and the Common Good.

AMY CROWE is a legal scholar.

ELAINE DAVIS is a professor at St. Cloud University and the author of more than 40 journal publications on human resource topics.

PAUL DRIESSEN is trained in environmental science and a major advocate for the world's poor.

ROSS EISENBREY is a lawyer and former commissioner of the U.S. Occupational Safety and Health Review Commission. Prior to joining EPI in 2002, he worked for many years as a staff attorney in the House of Representatives.

PETE ENGARDIO, in Washington, is a writer for *BusinessWeek*.

MARC J. EPSTEIN studies mergers and acquisitions at the Jones Graduate School of Management, Rice University, and at the Harvard Business School.

MILTON FRIEDMAN, winner of the 1974 Nobel Prize for Economics, was one of the most important economists of the twentieth century. He was the author of numerous academic publications as well as several highly influential books written primarily from a free-market, pro-capitalism perspective.

DIANA FURCHTGOTT-ROTH is senior fellow at the Hudson Institute and a former chief economist at the US Department of Labor.

PAUL GIGOT is the editorial page editor and vice president of The Wall Street Journal, a position he has held since 2001. He is responsible for the newspaper's editorials, op-ed articles and Leisure & Arts criticism and directs the editorial pages of the Journal's Asian and European editions and the OpinionJournal.com Web site. He is also the host of the weekly half-hour newsprogram, the Journal Editorial Report, on the Fox News Channel.

EDNA GILLIGAN works in the insurance industry and is working toward her master's degree at East Stroudsburg University.

EDMUND R. GRAY is professor and chair of the department of management at Loyola Marymount University. He has authored or coauthored five books and over 70 articles and other scholarly publications.

DANIEL GRISWOLD is Director of the Center for Trade Policy Studies at the Cato Institute in Washington, DC. Since joining Cato in 1997, Mr. Griswold has authored or co-authored major studies on globalization, trade, and immigration.

HEIDI I. HARTMANN is a scholar at the Institute for Women's Policy Research.

ROBERT D. HAY is a professor of management at the University of Arkansas. He retired in 1990 after 41 years of teaching, research, and service. He is the author of 11 books as well as numerous articles and cases.

STACIE HUELLER is an accounting instructor and a C.P.A.

STANLEY HOLMES, in Seattle, is a writer for *BusinessWeek*.

XIANG JI, in Beijing, is a writer for *BusinessWeek*.

IRA T. KAY is the practice director in charge of Watson Wyatt Worldwide's compensation practice. He has written and spoken widely on executive compensation issues. He is also the author of several books on the subject.

BRIAN H. KLEINER is a professor of management at California State University, Fullerton. Dr. Kleiner has published over 500 articles and publications and has served as an expert witness in numerous court cases.

ROBERT KROL is a professor of economics at California State University, Northridge.

DAVE KUSNET is an occasional contributor to the Economic Policy Institute.

MIKE LAPHAM is an associate fellow at the Institute for Policy Studies.

KENNETH LEVITT, Ph.D. is currently an associate professor of management at East Stroudsburg University.

JIM MACKEY is the managing director at the Billion Dollar Growth Network, a research consortium focused on large-company growth and innovation.

STEVEN MALANGA is a columnist.

GARTH MASSEY is Professor of Sociology and Director of the International Studies Program at the University of Wyoming. His major writings include studies in nationalism and ethnic conflict in the Balkans, social inequality and mobility in socialist societies, and comparative rural change.

K.C. MCALPIN is Executive Director of ProEnglish. He is also a C.P.A. with an international business degree from the University of Texas at Austin and a master's degree in international management from the Thunderbird School of Global Management.

IAN D. MEKLINSKY and **ANNE CIESLA BANCROFT** are partners in the labor and employment law department at Fox Rothschild, LLP, in the firm's Princeton, New Jersey, office.

BRANKO MILANOVIC is an economist with the Carnegie Endowment for International Peace and the World Bank. His most recent book is *Worlds Apart: Measuring International and Global Inequality.*

SUNGWOOK MIN studies the effects of first moving on firm performance. Min is currently an assistant professor of management in the College of Business, California State University, Long Beach.

SAM PIZZIGATI is an associate fellow at the Institute for Policy Studies.

MICHAEL E. RAYNOR (D.B.A., Harvard University) is a director in Deloitte Research, the thought leadership arm of Deloitte, the global professional services firm. His client work, research, writing, and speaking focus on the fields of corporate and competitive strategy.

DEXTER ROBERTS, in Washington, is a writer for *BusinessWeek.*

WILLIAM T. ROBINSON is a management scholar.

STEPHEN J. ROSE, is a scholar at the Institute for Women's Policy Research, formerly a senior economist at the Educational Testing Service, is now with ORC Macro.

ANAND SANWAL is a managing director at Brilliont, a firm specializing in corporate portfolio management, innovation, and reengineering. He is the former vice-president, corporate portfolio management and strategic business analysis, at American Express.

EPHRAIM SCHWARTZ is an editor-at-large at InfoWorld.com. He also writes the Reality Check blog at http://www.infoworld.com/blogs/ephraim-schwartz.

ANDREW SIMONE is a senior financial analyst at Young's Market Company in Orange, California.

GUY SORMAN is a leading French public intellectual and the author of twenty books on contemporary affairs, covering the five continents. He is a regular columnist for Le Figaro in France, the Wall Street Journal and City Journal in the United States, and other publications around the world. Mr. Sorman taught economics at the Paris Institute of Political Sciences from 1970 to 2000. He has held several public offices, including advisor to the prime minister of France (1995–1997) and deputy mayor of Boulonge, near Paris.

LIISA VÄLIKANGAS is the managing director at the Woodside Institute, a research laboratory that develops new management practice for corporate resilience.

F. VINCENT VERNUCCIO, an attorney, is a former Special Assistant to the Assistant Secretary for Administration and Management in the Department of Labor under President George W. Bush. He is editor of http://efcaupdate .com.

TERRY WILSON, Ph.D., currently teaches marketing courses at East Strouds-burg University. Dr. Wilson has published more than 50 articles and is the author of 7 books.

FRANK ZEPEZAUER received a MA in English from the University of Chicago and is the author of more than 50 articles in both academic and commercial publications. He is also a prominent influence in the men's rights movement.